PRESSING
THE FIGHT

Studies in Print Culture and the History of the Book

Editorial Advisory Board

Roger Chartier
Robert A. Gross
Joan Shelley Rubin
Michael Winship

PRESSING
THE FIGHT

Print, Propaganda,
and the Cold War

Edited by **Greg Barnhisel**
and **Catherine Turner**

University of Massachusetts Press   Amherst and Boston

LC 2009045926
ISBN 978-1-55849-736-8

Designed by Dennis Anderson
Set in Minion Pro and Univers by Westchester Book Composition
Printed and bound by Thomson-Shore, Inc.

Library of Congress Cataloging-in-Publication Data

Pressing the fight : print, propaganda, and the Cold War / edited by Greg Barnhisel and Catherine
Turner.
    p. m. — (Studies in print culture and the history of the book)
Includes bibliographical references and index.
ISBN 978-1-55849-736-8 (cloth : alk. paper)
1. Book industries and trade—Political aspects.   2. Press and propaganda—History—20th century.
3. Cold War—Political aspects.   4. Cold War—Social aspects.   5. Publishers and
publishing—Political aspects.   6. Book industries and trade—History—20th century.
7. Popular culture and literature—History—20th century.   8. Politics and literature.
9. Propaganda, International.   10. Propaganda, Anti-communist.
I. Barnhisel, Greg, 1969–   II. Turner, Catherine, 1968–
    Z278.P68 2009
    302.23'209045—dc22

                                    2009045926

British Library Cataloguing in Publication data are available.

Contents

Introduction
GREG BARNHISEL AND CATHERINE TURNER   1

Part I. Printing from Left to Right

1   The Medium, the Message, the Movement: Print Culture
    and New Left Politics
    KRISTIN MATHEWS   31

2   The Education of a Cold War Conservative:
    Anti-Communist Literature of the 1950s and 1960s
    LAURA JANE GIFFORD   50

Part II. Establishing a Beachhead

3   Literature and Reeducation in Occupied Germany,
    1945–1949
    CHRISTIAN KANIG   71

4   Democratic Bookshelf: American Libraries in Occupied Japan
    HIROMI OCHI   89

5   The British Information Research Department and
    Cold War Propaganda Publishing
    JAMES B. SMITH   112

6   Books for the World: American Book Programs in
    the Developing World, 1948–1968
    AMANDA LAUGESEN   126

7   Impact of Propaganda Materials in Free World Countries
    MARTIN MANNING   145

Part III. Print as a Tool to Shape Domestic Attitudes

8   "How Can I Tell My Grandchildren What I Did in the Cold
War?": Militarizing the Funny Pages and Milton Caniff's
Steve Canyon
    EDWARD BRUNNER   169

9   Pineapple Glaze and Backyard Luaus: Cold War Cookbooks
and the Fiftieth State
    AMY REDDINGER   193

10 Mediating Revolution: Travel Literature and the
Vietnam War
    SCOTT LADERMAN   209

Part IV. The Cultural Cold War in the United States and Abroad

11 Promoting Literature in the Most Dangerous Area in
the World: The Cold War, the Boom, and *Mundo Nuevo*
    RUSSELL COBB   231

12 "Truth, Freedom, Perfection": Alfred Barr's *What Is
Modern Painting?* as Cold War Rhetoric
    PATRICIA HILLS   251

    About the Contributors   277

    Index   281

PRESSING THE FIGHT

Introduction

GREG BARNHISEL AND CATHERINE TURNER

THE ESSAYS in this volume represent just a small sampling of the work that scholars of the Cold War have been producing over the last ten years. With the end of the Soviet Union and the opening of that nation's archives to historians, a small explosion of scholarship has been in progress for the last decade (epitomized, perhaps, by the evidence emerging from the KGB archive that the Rosenbergs were more guilty than their most stalwart defenders ever allowed). The now-available archives of the former Soviet bloc, the declassification of U.S. documents, and the "Interagency Security Classification Appeals Panel" initiative of President Clinton (later limited and in some cases reversed by Bush administration directives and executive orders) have resulted in a "New Cold War History" movement, one that seeks to reinterpret the events of that prolonged conflict beyond the dominant narratives once used to explain the Cold War as it happened.

A key component of this New Cold War History has been an intensified attention to how culture was used in the Cold War and how particular metaphors—images of containment, of bridging, and, of course, of curtains, iron and otherwise—have determined our understanding of the ways that the Cold War shaped culture. There has been no shortage of attention to the ways the Cold War and its attendant narratives had shaped American culture; this can be seen in works from Richard Hofstadter's 1964 *The Paranoid Style in American Politics* to Stephen Whitfield's *Culture of the Cold War* (1991) to Paul Boyer's *By the Bomb's Early Light* (1994) to Alan Nadel's *Containment Culture* (1995) to Bruce McConachie's *American Theatre in the Culture of the Cold War* (2003). The idea of "containment"—originally proposed by George Kennan—has been a powerful lens through which to look at the period. While containment has long dominated discussion of foreign relations, revisionists have seen how it applied to a number of different domestic and cultural issues as well. Elaine Tyler May's groundbreaking *Homeward*

Bound (1988) argues that "domestic containment" (by which she means the renewal of traditional gender roles alongside increasing focus on domestic life as a means of personal fulfillment) and the Kennan-inspired crusade against Communism were "two sides of the same coin." May shows that men and women hoped to create a secure "psychological fortress" in the apolitical, affluent, middle-class home which could contain "potentially dangerous social forces" such as women's sexuality, homosexuality, labor unions, and civil rights activism, all of which threatened to disrupt American domestic security.[1]

The logic of containment was devastating both for global politics, as each side demonized the other and aggressive posturing came replace diplomacy, and for diversity of thought within many nations. As Nadel has noted, in the United States the cultural narrative of containment led to "the general acceptance during the Cold War of a relatively small set of narratives by a relatively large portion of the population," and the resulting drive toward conformity served to "unify, codify, and contain—perhaps intimidate is the best word—personal narratives of [the United States'] population."[2] These scholars have provided us with important lenses through which to view the events of the Cold War, but, more important, they have identified the ways in which that tumultuous, fraught period thought, wrote about, and represented *itself.*

As powerful a metaphor as containment is, recent work such as Christina Klein's *Cold War Orientalism* points to other metaphors that operated alongside containment. Klein suggests that a more liberal metaphor of integration, which "imagined the world in terms of open doors that superseded barriers and created pathways between nations," allowed progressive Americans to continue to see foreign and domestic policy in ways more closely related to the agenda of the New Deal era without seeming suspiciously communistic.[3] Print could serve as an ideal medium for many of these metaphors. While print could be easily contained through any number of means, printed materials were easy to transport, easy to copy, and, as Cold War pressures drove increased access to literacy, easy to share. As a result, print could also serve to integrate and connect—to "bridge" the gaps between—people in different countries and with different ideologies. Print had long been assigned the power to give readers access to worlds outside of their experience, and both sides in the Cold War marshaled print to bridge the space between readers' small local spheres and the outside world. Governments struggled to control what both domestic and foreign readers found out about their own countries and about other countries but, as the essays in this book show, they also hoped that print could forge new ties, shore up support for foreign-policy commitments, and disseminate a powerful positive message about their ideological positions. The essays by Martin Manning and Christian Kanig highlight the ways that Communist governments and groups used printed materials to bridge national differences and to better integrate separate national parties. And in her essay on the "New Left" in the United States and its use of print, Kristin Mathews shows how Students for a Democratic Society relied upon inexpensive technologies of reproduction such as the mimeograph and photocopy machine to unify a disparate and shaggy national "Movement."

The present collection, though, is less about the ways that the Cold War shaped culture and cultural products than about the material means through which cultural products were used as weapons in the Cold War. In this, we look back to Christopher Lasch's history of the Congress for Cultural Freedom, written soon after the spectacular 1966 revelations of the CCF's secret CIA funding, and to Max Kozloff's 1973 *Artforum* article "American Painting in the Cold War" as touchstones for the type of scholarship included here. Kozloff's work was one of the first pieces to deal extensively with the use of the visual arts—particularly Abstract Expressionism—in Cold War propaganda efforts, and he was followed in this by Eva Cockroft, Jane de Hart Mathews, and Serge Guilbaut, among others. Other scholars, such as Reinhold Wagnleitner, have looked not at governmental efforts to promote American values through "highbrow" art but at American *popular* culture's seemingly irresistible invasion of Europe—what some have called "Coca-colonization."[4]

While scholars' attention in the 1970s and 1980s focused primarily on how the visual arts and popular culture were used in the Cold War, in the last ten years a number of books have appeared looking not at a particular art form but at the agencies and groups that used art and culture as Cold War propaganda: Peter Coleman (*The Liberal Conspiracy*), Frances Stonor Saunders (*The Cultural Cold War: The CIA and the World of Arts and Letters*), and Giles Scott-Smith (*The Politics of Apolitical Culture*) all examined the Congress for Cultural Freedom, while Volker Berghahn's *America and the Intellectual Cold Wars in Europe* examined one person—Shepard Stone—and his role as a cultural Cold Warrior for the government and for the Ford Foundation. Penny Von Eschen's *Satchmo Blows Up the World* describes the State Department/USIA–sponsored jazz tours of Europe, while Yale Richmond's *Cultural Exchange and the Cold War* describes how the cultural exchange programs that brought over 50,000 Soviet intellectuals and artists to the United States ended up transforming the Soviet Union. And finally, David Caute's *The Dancer Defects* attempts a comprehensive survey of the cultural Cold War in all of its manifestations and from both sides—in various art forms and through the myriad overt and covert programs intended to make use of culture for propagandistic purposes. Clearly, the last fifteen years have brought forth a wealth of studies on the cultural Cold War, and on the culture *of* the Cold War. We hope that this collection makes a small contribution to our understanding of how print itself—magazines, journals, books—was used to carry ideological messages.[5]

Why print, in particular? In *The Culture of the Cold War*, historian Steven Whitfield juxtaposes two events to illustrate how censorship worked on each side of the ideological battle of the Cold War. In Russia, after Stalin's death in 1953 Lavrentii Beria, former head of the Soviet Secret Service and member of Stalin's inner circle, appeared poised to take Stalin's place. Instead, Nikita Khrushchev and his allies engineered Beria's trial and execution. Still, the ghostly presence of Beria represented such a threat to the new members of the Politburo that subscribers to the *Great Soviet Encyclopedia* were instructed to replace his entry with an extended entry on the "Bering Sea" using a "small knife or razor blade." As Beria's biographer Amy Knight notes, outside of the haunting memory of Beria as the embodiment of evil ("Stalin's Himmler"), "no Soviet history, no textbook, no officially sanctioned memoirs mentioned Beria's name, except for the occasional reference to him as a criminal."[6]

Whitfield is quick to note that the Soviets were not the only country where such excisions played an important role in creating public narratives about the nation and power. As he created the children's book *Famous American Negroes* for Dodd, Mead, in the same year that Beria was cut from the *Encyclopedia*, Langston Hughes gave in to his publishers' demands that he cut incidents of racially motivated violence from entries on Charles Spaulding, George Washington Carver, A. Philip Randolph, and Ralph Bunche. Hughes also had to cut the entry on Walter White, because White did not look sufficiently black and thus an image of him suggested miscegenation. Most tellingly, Hughes was asked to leave out any reference to W. E. B Du Bois: of course, there was no entry on Du Bois himself, but even Hughes's entry on Booker T. Washington had to be cleansed of any reference to the debate between Washington and Du Bois.[7]

While Whitfield provocatively uses these two events to suggest that ideological censorship occurred even in the United States (notwithstanding its trumpeting of its own intellectual freedom), these two examples also demonstrate that for both superpowers, *print* provided a critical medium for defining state power, creating narratives about the nation, and controlling the meaning of history. They also show, quite literally, that print was a weapon in the Cold War and played a role not just in the containment of figures who were inconvenient for the state but in defining those figures' existence.

Such power was not entirely new. The Office of War Information told Americans in the 1940s that "Books are Weapons in the War of Ideas" and used the chilling image of German crowds burning books at mass rallies in 1933 to provide an enduring propaganda trope. The Council on Books in Wartime, the Office of War Information, and other governmental and private groups used this idea to differentiate American openness from Nazi totalitarianism for audiences at home and abroad. The Nazis burned books; the U.S. government promoted them. Inspired by a proposal of Treasury Secretary Henry Morgenthau, a group of American writers formed the partly government-funded "Writers' War Board" in 1942 to produce pro-U.S. novels, plays, songs, and poems aimed at a domestic audience. On the tenth anniversary of the German book burnings, the actor Ralph Bellamy staged Stephen Vincent Benét's radio play *They Burned the Books* for an audience at the New York Public Library.[8] Books represented the United States overseas, as well. The first of what would eventually become over 200 American reading rooms was established in Mexico City in 1942, and Overseas Editions, best known for producing millions of cheap books for U.S. soldiers, also translated American books for distribution to Italian, French, and German populations at the end of the war.[9]

In a 1945 article in *The English Journal*, Jean Hatfield Barclay summarized the way the war had changed the market for books and attitudes toward reading in the United States: "More Americans are reading now than ever before. There is an unprecedented book-buying boom; book-club memberships have reached a peak; rentals are up; and library circulation is beginning to rise." While she notes an immediate slump in book sales after Pearl Harbor, overall the war led to a boom in the market for all types of print. Throughout the nation Barclay saw a "new book-reading public" led by soldiers who began reading "when there [was] nothing else to do." She added a long list of why Americans had begun buying books in record numbers: the increase in the number of Americans getting an education, the decrease in book prices, the lack of other merchandise to buy, increased time spent at home because of gas rationing, the need to read up on new jobs, and "the unusual importance given certain types of books by the war itself."[10] The war ended some two months after the article appeared, but the trends that Barclay cited persisted. Despite the scorn heaped on "eggheads" during the era, print continued to be an important business in America, a critical way for American ideology to circulate, and a leisure activity that addressed the personal, professional, and national demands of the Cold War.

Much has been made of power of the Council on Books in Wartime to encourage reading among servicemen and to improve soldiers' access to better books through Armed Services Editions, which published some 1,180 different titles by authors from Willa Cather to Laurence Sterne, from Zane Grey to William Faulkner. The list was heavily dominated by fiction although it did include a number of nonfiction titles, including Alfred Kazin's *On Native Grounds*, an important re-evaluation of the American literary tradition. According to the official history of the Council on Books in Wartime, these "little paper books" were called "more popular than pin-up girls" by the *New York Times Book Review*.[11] More recent scholars have credited Armed Services Editions with making paperback books reputable and conditioning returning soldiers to read paperbacks.[12]

Libraries too played a new role both during the war and after. As the library historian Wayne Wiegand has noted, during the 1930s and 1940s librarians in the United States embraced a "Library Bill of Rights" asserting that libraries played a central role in protecting intellectual freedom and fighting censorship. At war's end, this stance held political advantages for librarians, who argued for libraries' importance as civic institutions and eventually gained federal funding through the 1956 Library Services Act. However, this importance became a liability when libraries came under attack by Wisconsin Senator Joseph McCarthy and, as a result, removed controversial materials from their shelves. Despite many librarians' commitment to the Library Bill of Rights, a study of librarians in California found that as many as one-fifth "habitually avoided buying any material which is known to be controversial or which they believe might be controversial." In practice, the rights that librarians most often championed were the rights to popular reading, so patrons increasingly found books on the shelves that librarians in the past might have deemed "unfit" or unworthy.[13]

Whatever role Armed Services Editions and libraries played in changing Americans' tastes, paperback books had a profound impact on the market for books throughout the world. Europeans had been buying books with paper covers for over a hundred years before World War II, and Pocket Books had already had some success with the model in 1939. Barclay's article on wartime reading identified the "prime phenomenon of the boom" in 1945 as paperback books, priced at twenty-five cents, from firms like Pocket, Avon, Dell, and Penguin.[14] That boom in paperbacks remained a central factor in print culture throughout the Cold War and, while there was some hope that once wartime paper rationing and other shortages were over business would improve, as the publishing historian John Tebbel noted, "few . . . could have believed what lay ahead." The Cold War was awash in the "mightiest outpouring of mass market books of every kind."[15] Changing tastes might have had something to do with it, but more likely it was the fact that paperback publishers found new retail outlets. Key to the paperback's power was the fact that it was both cheap and *available*. In the 1930s, American publishers relied on around 500 major bookstores to distribute the majority of their hardback books. Paperback books were sold by drug stores and newspaper dealers and were available at 100,000 outlets where consumers shopped for other goods.[16]

In addition, America in the 1950s experienced a boom in consumer goods as groups such as the National Association of Manufacturers began a public-relations campaign equating consumer spending with patriotism. Liz Cohen points to the way that *Bride* magazine made this message explicit in its handbook for newlyweds, stressing that buying new things created "greater security" for industry and helped to ensure "our whole American way of living."[17] The freedom Americans had to consume became a keystone of American Cold War ideology, and the free thought encouraged by books connected to freedom so central to Cold War rhetoric. While they faced competition from other forms of entertainment, especially television, books had long been valued as meaningful indicators of an individual's taste and filled a need many Americans felt to assert their individuality through goods in the face of the growing anonymity of American life.[18] The Modern Library attempted to tie its long associations with culture to this new consumer culture with promotions such as "Let Marcel Proust Put You in the Driver's Seat!" Consumers who could match caricatures of famous authors with their names could win a fiberglass replica of a 1931 Model A Ford, a prize which, according to the advertisement, offered the same sense of classic style that books held coupled with the promise of the open road central to American consumer culture.[19]

Such an ad emblematizes the increasing commercialization of books during the Cold War. Kenneth Davis uses Dr. Benjamin Spock's *Baby and Child Care* to show how paperback publishing reworked the usual economics of publishing as its titles also revised issues central to American culture. Spock, whose training in pediatrics and psychology made him fairly unique among doctors, was persuaded to write the book when Donald Porter Geddes of Pocket Books told him, "It doesn't have to be a very good book because at twenty-five cents a copy, we'll be able to sell a hundred thousand a year." Spock's book sales topped even those estimates and outsold previous bestsellers. The first printing of *The Pocket Book of Baby and Child Care* in 1946 was 248,000; available in Rexall drugstores and Woolworth's, the edition sold out in five months. Quickly, two additional printings of 50,000 were issued. The fourth printing was 400,000 and the next a mere 250,000. Significantly, Spock and Pocket arranged for paperback publication before they worried about the hardback edition. Spock arranged for his college friend Charles Duell to bring the book out through his new company Duell, Sloan, & Pierce, but publication in hardback was simply a formality, necessary to get reviews but unimportant in terms of sales.[20] For purposes of comparison, we might look to Richard Tregaskis's 1943 hardcover *Guadalcanal Diary*, a book both topical and heavily promoted by Random House. Random House sold the film rights to Twentieth Century Fox, and it was selected by the Book-of-the-Month Club. With all these advantages, the book was considered wildly successful for its time, selling over 100,000 copies.[21]

The power of paperback books fueled intense competition for markets and for authors, and that competition, in turn, made the Cold War a time of mergers and globalization for publishers and of the integration of publishing firms within larger, multi-industry conglomerates. Even before the end of World War II, the department-store chain Marshall Field's bought Simon & Schuster and Pocket Books in 1944 and appeared to be preparing to buy Grosset & Dunlap. Fearful that this firm would dominate publishing, Random House's Bennett Cerf created a cartel of buyers (including Book-of-the-Month Club; Harpers; Little, Brown; and Charles Scribner) that successfully countered Field's offer and eventually created Bantam Books. Cerf recognized how combination with firms that shared his firm's interests could strengthen his own market position. At the end of the 1950s, the company went public with its stock and began a series of acquisitions, starting with Alfred A. Knopf in 1960. These acquisitions in turn made Random House attractive to entertainment media companies, and Cerf's firm would be bought out by RCA in 1965. In 1980, RCA sold Random House to the Newhouse newspaper organization; Random House, still the largest U.S. trade publisher, is now part of the multinational Bertelsmann organization.[22] Many houses followed a similar process—mergers, public stock offerings, and acquisition by national or international conglomerates.

While many scholars who write about this era mourn the loss of creativity that results from political repression and consumer culture, in many ways the Cold War was a good time for authors. Publishers offered unheard-of sums for the reprint rights to books by high- and lowbrow authors. Benjamin Spock made comparatively little money from *Baby and Child Care* in 1946 (about $5,000).[23] As the possibilities for paperback sales became clear, in 1949 William Faulkner received $3,000 for the paperback rights to *Intruder in the Dust*. By 1950 Kathleen Winsor, author of the racy bestseller *Forever Amber*, was offered $30,000, and in 1949 Norman Mailer got $35,000 for *The Naked and the Dead*. Thereafter, the auctions began to take off. James Jones got $100,000 for *From Here to Eternity*, as did Vladimir Nabokov for *Lolita*. By 1965, James Michener got $700,000 for *The Source* and later the first million-dollar advance for *The Drifters*. In 1975, Bantam paid E. L. Doctorow $2 million for the paperback rights to *Ragtime*.[24] While the 1950s might have begun with a series of high-profile authors losing their position because of former (or imagined) ties to the Communist Party, in the United States the Cold War was initially a bonanza for those who were free from political taint, and, by the end, politics no longer mattered. Of course, Soviet authors like Boris Pasternak who were able to find a market in the West benefited as well—or at least their foreign publishers and trustees did. In the Soviet Union, restrictions on print made access to popular, classic works extremely valuable so that such books became increasingly costly. As Stephen Lovell has noted, the commodification of books in the USSR "tended to underwrite the[ir] value" and at times better the status of authors and publishers.[25]

Demographic developments also drove the changes in the book market. The post-1946 baby boom led to a boom in the number of American children in school, and post-Sputnik fears drove increased per-student spending. The historian Maris A. Vinovskis estimates that between 1940 and 1965 the number of students in grades K–8 increased from 20.3 to 35.5 million; during those same years the number of students in high school increased from 7.1 to 16.5 million. College enrollments grew even more quickly, from 1.5 in 1940 to 5.9 million in 1965, in part due to the G.I. Bill. Obviously, overall public spending on schools increased but, in addition, during the Cold War years spending per capita on students also increased. Using constant 1997 dollars, Vinovskis estimates that Americans spent $1,020 in 1939–40 but $4,733 in 1979–80.[26] As Laura Miller, a historian of the book trade, has observed, the increase in school-age children and Americans attending college led many in the book trade to believe that there would be "a vast new market of institutional and individual book buyers."[27]

Institutional purchases of paperback classics did increase, but individual purchases grew very little. Instead as Americans moved to the suburbs, bookstores had to change to address their shopping habits. The first Waldenbooks store to open in a suburban mall did so in 1962, setting off a wave of changes in the bookselling business. Later, beginning in the 1980s, larger stores with more inventory came to dominate the market and replace traditional, downtown stores. These stores also drove improvements in distribution and inventory control, providing greater access to a greater selection of books. While such developments made book buying easier, alongside the conglomeration of the publishing industry these "big-box" bookstores drove fears that American culture was becoming too commercial; good literature or books that held unpopular opinions might be sacrificed to the financial interests of these corporate media empires.[28]

As the economic models of authorship, publishing, and bookselling changed in the United States, so did issues of control over what was said. The 1950s are notorious as an era in which authors were routinely attacked for their political associations. The House Committee on Un-American Activities required that authors who had been politically active in the 1930s testify about their membership in the Communist Party and more problematically demanded that they name others who attended meetings or signed petitions with them. But in the West, official censorship on ideological grounds—as opposed to censorship on grounds of obscenity—was relatively rare, and de facto censorship somewhat more easily circumvented than in the East, as the state did not control access to printing technology as effectively. (As the example of Hughes shows, though, the "free market" does exert its own kind of ideological censorship.) Blacklisted author Howard Fast published *Spartacus* (1951) on his own, selling thousands of copies even before the Hollywood movie in 1960.[29] In perhaps the most important evasion of official censorship in the United States during the Cold War, access to Xerox machines allowed Daniel Ellsberg in 1971 to leak the "Pentagon Papers" to the *New York Times* and the U.S. Senate, widening the "credibility gap" between the White House and the American people. Because print produced enduring physical objects, even those authors subject to de facto censorship "lived on" and were read: Julia Willett points to Jackie Long of Birmingham, Alabama, an African-American hairdresser, who installed an "unexpected library that housed an extensive collection of African-American history books and other 'treasures,'" allowing Du Bois (and Hughes, as he too was written out of history and literature throughout the mid-1960s) to continue to circulate through communities desperate for ties to their political, intellectual, and activist past.[30] Even though American culture may have become, as Ellen Schrecker says, "banal" and deeply apolitical, print was the prime medium of dissent on all sides of the Cold War. Schrecker shows how economics and a desire for a wide national audience made censorship (formal and informal) in the television and film industries highly effective, while, unlike performers such as Paul Robeson, Schrecker observed, "writers could still write, even if they could not reach a large audience."[31]

A large audience, though, was certainly the target of Western and Soviet propaganda and "cultural diplomacy" agencies as the Cold War began. After the war, the U.S. Department of State retained much of the same structure it had used to generate and distribute printed propaganda and literature abroad, even as it shifted the nature of its propaganda from anti-Nazism to anti-Communism and frequently worked jointly with the British government in these efforts. In occupied Germany, in contested Greece and Italy, and even in England and France, the United States and Great Britain quickly moved to create, promote, or even secretly fund publishing, printing, and library projects intended to disseminate a pro-Western message. The Office of Military Government for Germany (U.S.), known as OMGUS, sponsored and directed several publications with a dual mission: denazification, and the more delicate task of explaining the U.S. perspective on the balance of power in Europe without attacking America's erstwhile ally on the other side of the East-West divide. *Die Neue Zeitung* was the American daily newspaper of the occupied zone, while *Der Monat*, founded in 1947 by the future Congress for Cultural Freedom stalwart Melvin Lasky, became a model for the CCF's long-running journal, *Encounter*.

In these efforts the Americans and the British often worked jointly along covert and overt lines. Great Britain created the Information Research Department in February 1948 specifically to, as Frances Stonor Saunders puts it, "set about dismantling the untruths [about former ally Joseph Stalin that the British government] had systematically constructed or defended in the previous years."[32] The IRD produced what they called "unattributable propaganda." Saunders shows that the "unattributability" allowed the IRD to disseminate its propaganda through key figures who would have objected to being used by His Majesty's government. Similarly, George Kennan created the Office of Policy Coordination in July 1948 to direct covert anti-Soviet psychological operations outside of the United States. (The OPC was folded into the CIA in 1951.) The IRD and the OPC/CIA collaborated on such secret projects as the creation and funding of the Congress for Cultural Freedom, which sponsored symposia, published magazines, and created national subsidiary groups around the world while avoiding, at least until 1966, the stigma of being seen as a puppet of the U.S. or British government.[33]

The U.S. government's *official* cultural mouthpiece, on the other hand, was of course the Department of State, specifically its International Information Agency (IIA). Given the responsibilities of the Office of War Information, for several years the IIA took charge of creating, cultivating, and disseminating a positive image of the United States across the world. With the passage of the Smith-Mundt Act in 1948, books became a central part of that effort. Among other provisions, Smith-Mundt created an "Informational Media Guaranty Program" intended to allow American publishers (and other media producers) to sell their titles in nations, such as Poland and Yugoslavia, whose currencies were not convertible into dollars. Titles covered under the IMG, though, had to "reflect the best elements in American life and shall not be such as to bring discredit upon this Nation in the eyes of other nations." (In 1961, these criteria were tightened further; titles covered had to explicitly support U.S. policy objectives.)[34]

In 1953, the United States Information Agency (USIA) was created to replace the IIA—everything from the Voice of America to our focus here, the dissemination of print materials, came under USIA's mandate. As Richard Arndt and Frank Ninkovich, among others, have shown, USIA defined "cultural diplomacy" to be the unidirectional provision of politically inflected information about the United States to foreign audiences. In this, USIA rejected the more open, exchange-based model of cultural diplomacy favored by World War II–era Assistant Secretary of State for Cultural and Public Affairs Archibald MacLeish.[35] USIA also took charge of the rapidly expanding library and reading-room program; by 1955 it had 197 libraries and reading rooms in 65 nations. The program weathered a domestic political storm in 1953 when Joseph McCarthy sent Roy Cohn and David Schine to Europe to ferret out subversive titles in the reading rooms; in response, the American Library Association and the American Book Publishers Council took a public stand against McCarthy as a "book-burner" (calling to mind the durable image of the Nazi rallies) and even President Eisenhower spoke out against censorship.[36]

The Department of State and, later, USIA also sought to place sympathetic books and magazines in foreign markets. With State Department assistance, the *Reader's Digest* was translated into Spanish in 1940, and the Office of War Information produced Portuguese/Brazilian and Swedish editions in 1942 and an Arabic edition in 1943. Thereafter, the *Digest* followed the path of the hot spots of the Cold War closely; it was translated into Japanese in 1946, into Italian in 1948, and finally into a Chinese-language edition which circulated throughout East Asia in 1964. At one point *Reader's Digest*'s "roving editor" David Reed said of the magazine that "the three great international institutions are the Catholic Church, the Communist Party and the *Reader's Digest*." Reed's comment may have been somewhat self-serving, but it also suggests the power that the Department of State saw in the magazine.[37]

Foreign markets also needed books in local languages, and both State and USIA undertook programs to provide them. USIA officers carefully selected titles intended to shed light on American history and political philosophy (Learned Hand's *Spirit of Liberty*, for instance, and Benjamin Thomas's biography of Abraham Lincoln), to give audiences portraits of American life and culture (the novels of Willa Cather, for instance, were translated for almost every one of USIA's target markets), or to coordinate with special initiatives such as the "Atoms for Peace" program (books linked with this initiative included Gordon Dean's *Report on the Atom* and John Lewellen's children's book *The Mighty Atom*). USIA bought foreign rights to these titles, arranged to have them translated, and then subsidized local publication by such means as purchasing a third of the print run at retail. It also arranged to translate and distribute textbooks abroad as well as "Ladder Editions," books and collections translated specifically for English language learners. Sol Schindler, a former USIA officer, describes how he had 5,000 copies of Bradley, Beatty, and Long's workhorse textbook *The American Tradition in Literature* printed up in Belgrade and made available to any USIA post that wanted to distribute it to local populations.[38] In the early 1950s, USIA largely targeted European nations—Spain, Portugal, Italy, Yugoslavia, and Poland—with these programs, but by the later part of the decade the focus shifted to non-aligned India, Pakistan, Indonesia, Egypt, and Turkey, and the nations of Latin America. The number of books published under these programs is considerable: just in 1956 they published 2 million books in India in six different languages, and 865,000 in Japan that same year. In all, USIA Books-in-Translation and textbook programs produced 60 million books between 1951 and 1960.[39]

Sometimes, as well, the target populations spoke back, as in Nigeria. While English and literacy were uncommon outside large commercial centers before World War II, the discovery of oil and the postwar boom increased opportunities for schooling throughout the country. Such opportunities increased both the quality of authors, nurturing highbrow Nigerian fiction writers such as Chinua Achebe and Amos Tutuola, and the number of readers demanding access to popular fiction. Particularly in the market town of Onitsha, the combination of Western-style modernization, which demanded both self-help manuals and warnings against the dangers of urban life, and newly trained English language readers drove an exciting market for new, cheap literature. For about the price of a beer, Nigerian English readers could find small (about 5 inches by 8 inches), poorly printed chapbooks written in nonstandard English sold alongside car parts and records. These books included titles such as *Love at First, Hate at Last*; *How to Avoid Corner Corner Love and Win Good Love From Girls*; and *Money Hard to Get but Easy to Spend*.[40] While these titles might suggest the type of moralism once found in missionary tracts, the relationship between these books and standard Cold War messages toward African nations is far more complex. For example the book *The Life Story and Death of John Kennedy* described the "final words" of John F. Kennedy at Parkland Hospital in Dallas. The anonymous Nigerian author imagines Kennedy dictating a long speech before he died, forgiving his killer and expressing sorrow for his own family, but also asserting his solidarity with African Americans, saying "blessed be the American Negroes whom I am sacrificing my blood for their own safety." While most of the text uses this statement to present Kennedy as an ally of black-skinned people throughout the world, a short addendum to the text includes a warning from Nigerian President Nnamdi Azikiwe to other African states, encouraging leaders to hesitate before placing their trust in American democracy because Americans do not "respect human dignity nor regard the black race as human beings."[41]

If some of these USIA programs at times blurred the line between overt and covert propaganda—as the extent or existence of an American subsidy was downplayed or hidden—other undertakings concealed their governmental origins completely. Franklin Publications (later Franklin Book Programs) was among these projects. Founded in 1952 by five American commercial publishers and secretly funded by the IIA/USIA, Franklin Books aimed to make available in the Middle East, in local languages, books on American culture, politics, and history, but also books by local authors and of local interest, all with the aim of countering Soviet influence in this unstable part of the world. Franklin's devotion to including local voices was crucial to the program's success: according to Louise Robbins, Franklin's edition of *This I Believe*, with many essays by Arabic authors, "sold 30,000 copies in six months' time."[42] Kenneth Osgood points out that "although Franklin Publications' identification with the government was not a classified secret . . . few consumers would have known that Franklin books were essentially USIA products," Some of these projects operated domestically: the commercial publisher Frederick A. Praeger told the *New York Times* in 1967 that he had published books "at the behest of the CIA," the Pentagon, or USIA.[43] In the present volume, Amanda Laugesen provides an extensive discussion of the creation and activities of Franklin and other similar "public-private partnerships."

In the West, and especially in the United States, nonprofit foundations also took part in the circulation of printed materials as a front in the Cold War. The Ford Foundation, which in the late 1940s became by far the richest U.S. foundation, aggressively sought to disseminate literature and other materials that explained and endorsed American political, cultural, and economic values through such undertakings as Intercultural Publications (1952–56) and the Congress for Cultural Freedom. From the later 1950s through the 1980s, the Ford Foundation took a particular interest in supporting such projects in India, Southeast Asia, and Latin America. In the 1950s and 1960s the Carnegie Endowment for International Peace—on whose board John Foster Dulles served—published studies aimed at intellectuals and policymakers in the West, intended to strengthen the UN and the international legal system. Other nonprofits, such as the liberal Fund for the Republic (incorporated in 1952 and founded with money from the Ford Foundation), the conservative John M. Olin foundation (created in 1953), and the John Birch Society (founded in 1958), underwrote the publication of printed materials intended to influence internal political debates in the United States. Covert funding also came through foundations, such as the dummy "Farfield Foundation," created to channel money from the CIA to the CCF.[44]

In addition to these projects, which we might call "official" or "directed" propaganda, came a type of material that might better be termed "unofficial" or even "inadvertent" propaganda—messages, often commercial in nature, that nonetheless advanced the geopolitical priorities and stances of the West and of the United States. Alan Nadel, Elaine May, and many others have insightfully elucidated how the cultural products of the times were implicated in general pushes for "domesticity" or "containment," but one does not have to look on a theoretical level to spot such "propaganda." Just in this volume we see three explicit discussions of this phenomenon. Laura Gifford describes a number of for-profit publishing firms specializing in anti-Communist books, while Amy Reddinger provocatively links the "Hawaii fad" of the 1960s to a deeper cultural anxiety about whether, and how, to assimilate Hawaii, and the Asian/Pacific culture it represented, into the idea of America. Finally, in his discussion of travel books about Vietnam, Scott Laderman shows how the interests of the U.S. and Vietnamese governments and the travel industry converged in their desire to frame South Vietnam as an attractive destination for tourism.

WHILE THE United States undertook a wide variety of official and unofficial programs to get printed materials to target populations in hostile (Poland, Yugoslavia), friendly (Italy, France), and nonaligned (India, Egypt, Indonesia) nations, the Soviet Union was equally busy with its own propaganda projects. By the mid-1950s, the Soviet Union had produced and distributed over forty million pro-Soviet books abroad, and through the Communist Information Bureau (Cominform), founded in 1947 and dissolved in 1956, produced a great deal of printed propaganda. The Cominform's official weekly, *For a Lasting Peace, For a People's Democracy*, claimed massive circulation numbers—520,000 in China in 1949, for instance—but was aimed primarily at Party members around the world, not at the public at large. Under a 1956 cultural exchange agreement that came about as a result of de-Stalinization, the United States and the Soviet Union agreed to distribute in the opposite nation a cultural magazine—the U.S. created *Amerika*, and the USSR *Soviet Life*—intended to present a positive image of life in each nation. Both magazines were glossy, photo-rich publications available primarily in official institutions such as government reading rooms, libraries, and embassies, and each was limited to a circulation of 30,000. The Soviet Communist Party newspaper *Pravda* and the official Soviet government newspaper *Izvestiya* were also widely read and their contents disseminated, if not easily available, outside of the Soviet Union.

Central planning and control, unsurprisingly, characterized the internal Soviet publishing industry. "Soviet publishing, printing, and book distribution, with a combined personnel of over 300,000," Gregory Walker explained in 1978, "are administered in many respects as a single undertaking."[45] This was because of a "general acceptance in the USSR that publishing, like the other mass media, is in some sense a cultural, and more specifically an ideological activity."[46] Mark Hooker, for example, has described the "made-to-order" Socialist Realist fiction produced by the Main Political Directorate of the Red Army and Navy specifically for Soviet soldiers and sailors to read.[47] The Party exercised control over publishing firms at many junctures, beginning with biweekly "Instructional Meetings" for those involved in the media industry and devolving down through local government oversight of and presence of Party members in publishing firms. According to Walker, the State Committee for Publishing, Printing, and the Book Trade, in conjunction with the Secretariat's wonderfully named Department of Agitation and Propaganda, set policy for most of the aspects of the publishing industry: what kinds of books would be published, the size of print runs, the cost and allocation of paper, the extent of distribution, the cost of the books, and the range of fees paid to authors. Author fees were based on the kind of work, number of copies printed, and number of "sheets" (equivalent to 16 pages of copy) delivered. Individual publishers—in 1974, Walker notes, there were 198—could propose particular titles to be published as well as publication dates, although publishers were required to submit annual approval plans to the State Committee for Publishing, summarizing each proposed title in great detail. Although book prices were set centrally, publishers were encouraged to publish titles that would be popular, and the publishers could keep some of the profit, although the tax on profits was quite high—over 75 percent.[48] Interestingly, however, although publishing for profit was met with high taxes, a certain degree of competition was not only allowed but encouraged. Publishers could respond to local demand for material—the State Committee subsidized many publishers whose mission was to make available unprofitable books in minority languages, for instance—but they could also seek out books they predicted would be popular and compete with other houses for authors (by offering slightly higher author fees).

In addition, in the Eastern bloc printed material served as an underground voice of dissent *within* Communist nations. Print may emblematize the erasure of Beria, but it also circulated dissent, through *samizdat*, clandestine works created and circulated by underground groups and dissidents throughout Eastern Europe and the USSR. Books such as Solzhenitsyn's *Gulag Archipelago* and the bulletin *Chronicle of Current Events* circulated privately. In many cases, these texts appeared as regularly as official media. For example, despite constant harassment, the *Chronicle* managed to publish twice a month from 1968 to 1972. Nonetheless, there were significant differences between official and unofficial publication; according to historian Ann Komaromi, *samizdat* circulated largely in typescript because access to technology like mimeograph machines was controlled by the state. Hence private typewriters—which themselves had to be registered with the security services (a central plot point in the 2006 German film *The Lives of Others*)—churned out carbon copies that were "characteristically wretched and regularly featured mistakes and corrections as well as blurred or pale type." Copies became even less reliable and more dog-eared as they were passed from hand to hand. Yet these error-filled texts, ironically, chronicled the truth in opposition to official press, and their worn and tattered appearance made them all the more authoritative. Komaromi notes that when a Russian-English version of the *Chronicle* began publishing in New York in 1973, the cover deliberately attempted to replicate the cheap typewritten page as a way of appropriating the sincerity of the original.[49] The editors regret that we were not able to find a suitable article on *samizdat* for this collection.

Of course, not all national Communist publishing industries operated like the Soviet Union's. In his book *The Uses of Literature: Life in the Socialist Chinese Literary System*, Perry Link argues that despite superficial similarities, censorship and the publication of dissent were notable areas of difference. While Link points to a number of underlying factors, including the traditional role of writers in China, he also explains that the system of censorship worked differently. Unlike in the Soviet system, where the Chief Administration for the Preservation of State Secrets in the Press (known as Glavlit) gave its 70,000 employees official handbooks that outlined what would and would not be permitted, Chinese writers, editors, and publishers often had to rely on their sense of "the weather," a shifting and contingent sense of what officials might allow, developed by informal state contacts and personal networks. Changes in "the weather" might be predicted by political developments or signaled by material factors—paper quotas and the controlled price of books, for instance. Those who could read the shifting winds accurately reaped enormous benefits; however, missing important but ambiguous signals could result in enormous losses as officials might destroy an entire run of a novel or journal because it displeased the Party. As a result, while Soviet authors (and publishers) could get a sense of what they could or could not write before they started, Chinese authors could not be sure. The vague and seemingly arbitrary nature of the system meant that self-censorship was stricter than bureaucratic censorship.[50]

The radically increased production quotas demanded during the Great Leap Forward (1958–61) also applied to literature. Link speculates that more poetry may have been written and published then than at any other time in Chinese history. However, this writing was created "under strict guidelines, sometimes even to set formulae." During the Cultural Revolution (1966–78) even this sort of publication ceased. Writers were not paid for their work, and by the late 1960s Mao's works were nearly the only publications available.[51] By 1979 writers were again being paid, but, as in the Soviet Union, in China the State Publications Administration (SPA) controlled each publishing house's allotment of paper. A publishing house with too many risky works in its catalog might get almost no paper or might be allocated only the most expensive types (which differed little in quality from the cheaper stock). In addition, the state dictated the price of printed works. The cheapest material was primary school textbooks and mass political propaganda, which cost around .055 yuan per page. Traditional literature might cost .075 yuan per page or slightly less if the state deemed a particular work worth recommending. As Chinese officials insisted that publishers become self-sufficient, these price differentials shaped publishers' catalogs and readers' access to materials as much as official censorship.[52]

There were efforts among literary elites and politically engaged readers to circulate works that might seem to parallel Soviet *samizdat*, but often people in China took the risk of stealing paper so that they could create, copy, and privately circulate fiction focused less on political dissent than on romantic love, daring heroes, and the conflict of good and evil. Perhaps the best known of these hand-written documents is Zhang Yang's *The Second Handshake*, a melodramatic potboiler featuring a love triangle and a hero who is both a brainy young scientist and a martial-arts expert. Zhang began this work in 1964 under the title *Sea Spray* or the *Vagabond Beauty*, lengthening and expanding the book seven times during the Cultural Revolution. Though it was hardly a work of political dissent (the rejected woman remains single and focuses on her patriotic duty to create an atomic bomb for China), the "Gang of Four" attacked the book because it propagated the "concept of bourgeois love." Anyone caught with a copy could be jailed. In fact, despite his efforts to remain anonymous, Zhang was sent to jail in 1975 where he nearly died before he was released in 1979. At that point, the book was revised by the China

Youth Publishing Company and published, selling 3.3 million copies even with much of the sex sanitized.[53]

THIS COLLECTION is intended to reflect the power and complexity of print culture during this turbulent and exciting era. We begin antipodally, with studies of opposite poles of political opinion in the United States and how they used print to shape domestic attitudes about the Cold War, the threat of Communism, and the Vietnam War. Both authors point to ways in which structural and technological changes in printing expanded print's power to convey both far right and far left discourse. Kristin Matthews's "The Medium, the Message, the Movement: Print Culture and New Left Politics" describes how Students for a Democratic Society deployed new reproduction technologies to generate reams of printed material intended both to inform Americans and to change their consciousness. She points to the distribution of the *Port Huron Statement* to indicate how the student movement hoped to use print to redemocratize American life and shift the power that centralizing access to information had given the U.S. government. The faith that SDSers had in print was absolute; they saw reading as a transformative action. Once a person had read the truth, that person would naturally become an active democratic citizen with the power to resist the injustice and intolerance of life in the United States.

While Laura Gifford describes a movement with sharply different political leanings, her account of the way right-wing publishers and authors used the inexpensive paperback to promote their own brand of political discourse shows how thoroughly Americans all along the political spectrum believed in print as the primary medium of personal and political development. Gifford's "The Education of a Cold War Conservative: Anti-Communist Literature of the 1950s and 1960s" indicates that regarding the power of print, right and left shared the faith. Gifford shows how the paperback revolution of the 1950s allowed small, politically oriented publishing firms to promote anti-Communist literature and to connect readers with other texts and other like-minded readers. While they may have existed in what Gifford calls an "alternative publishing reality," the books and series that they promoted gave voice to a political movement that was just as committed to the transformative and democratic power of print as SDS. In addition, Gifford uses these printed works to show that conservative anti-Communism was hardly a monolithic movement best represented by pundits and politicians, but instead embraced a range of thinkers who encouraged and enabled their readers to become activists and writers themselves.

The book's next section looks at print outside of the United States, particularly in Europe and East Asia. Christian Kanig's essay "Literature and Reeducation in Occupied Germany, 1945–1949" describes how the Soviets took over East German publishing and bookselling in the late 1940s. As the United States and the Soviet Union competed for German allegiance, the Soviets created their own army-controlled publishing house, ISVA. Taking over the devastated German publishing industry in the name of reeducation, ISVA aggressively printed and distributed works such as the Central Committee's *Short Course of the History of the VKP(b),* a summary of the thirteen volumes of Stalin's works, in editions as large as 6.2 million. These efforts profoundly changed the publishing industry in East Germany, modernizing the divided country's printing capabilities and homogenizing its cultural output to bring it into line with Soviet Communist priorities. Kanig describes how printed materials became increasingly important in the U.S.-USSR conflicts over Germany's future. While ISVA closed up shop when the Soviets left in 1949, Kanig demonstrates that it effectively handed the new East German Communist Party a centralized print industry that was easily censored and controlled.

On the other hand, Hiromi Ochi's "Democratic Bookshelf: American Libraries in Occupied Japan" shows how the United States used libraries to shape pro-democratic and pro-Western attitudes in Japan. Like Kanig, she demonstrates that the selection of books for Civil Information and Education (CIE) Libraries intended to root out what the occupiers deemed to be the racist and militaristic attitudes of the Japanese people. However, Ochi finds that the political messages projected through the selection processes reflected powerful divisions within the American government, as New Deal liberalism gave way to Cold War conservatism. Yet for Japanese library patrons the most important message that these libraries conveyed was the prosperity and affluence that capitalist democracy promised. Additionally, the versions of equality and diversity that the United States presented to the Japanese people were filtered and mitigated by the CIE library's reliance on glossy magazines that suggested that the "equality" of American democracy would not overturn traditional gender roles. Hence these American libraries propagated what Ochi calls a "self-colonizing hegemony" within the Japanese people.

While no longer called "reeducation," efforts to shape political attitudes continued once the occupation of the defeated Axis nations ended. James Smith, in his essay "The British Information Research Department and Cold War Propaganda Publishing," describes the activities of the propaganda wing of the British government, the Information Research Department (IRD). Initially founded to promote British social democracy as an alternative both to Soviet Communism and American free-market capitalism, the IRD became

increasingly anti-Communist as the ideological conflict of the Cold War demanded absolute loyalty. Smith reveals how the British IRD sponsored several
commercial publishing ventures as a way to covertly distribute anti-
Communist literature around the world. The most significant of the efforts—
the publication of the Background Books—involved a number of well-known
authors, including Bertrand Russell. While Smith acknowledges that governmental interference was not heavy-handed, he does indicate that the government's involvement with postwar publishing was "uncomfortable" but also
quite successful in shaping domestic attitudes.

Amanda Laugesen tells a similar story in connecting the U.S. government
to various book and library programs around the world. Laugesen begins by
describing the USIA reading rooms and translation programs and then looks
at the book programs of Freedom House Books USA, a private program, and
Franklin Books, a "quasi-governmental" government/private program. She
argues that while these programs might have appeared to be simply an instance of distributing pro-capitalist propaganda messages to developing countries where Americans had commercial and strategic interests, such assumptions oversimplify the situation. The government bureaucrats, librarians,
publishers, and entrepreneurs who ran these programs had deeply mixed feeling about American aims in the countries where they operated. They believed
both that books could help contain Communism and that books could help to
establish a worldwide community of book lovers that might, as Laugesen suggests, counter some of the "darker aspects of American foreign policy."

In the last essay of this section, Martin Manning describes the State Department's propaganda collection. Unlike many of the printed materials treated in
the present volume, these were *prevented* from circulating—confiscated by U.S.
customs and postal officials. As Manning explains, after the war, the State Department shifted its focus from Nazi propaganda to Soviet propaganda and
eventually Communist propaganda of all kinds, including that produced in
the United States. His essay details both the ways in which Communist materials were controlled as they entered the United States and how they were
collected and catalogued. He provides a glimpse of how Communist propaganda entered the United States and how propaganda agencies distributed it.
He argues that as print came to be less and less important to waging the Cold
War, the collection was abandoned for lack of staffing and money. Underused
today, this collection suggests a number of different directions for future
scholars to follow.

A sense of fluidity between author and audience informs the opening essay of the next section, Edward Brunner's "'How Can I Tell My Grandchildren What I Did in the Cold War?': Militarizing the Funny Pages and Milton

Caniff's *Steve Canyon*." This section focuses on print that circulated within the United States and considers both how print represented the Cold War and how Cold War pressures shaped the contents and form of print. Brunner begins by showing how Milton Caniff's success as a comic-strip artist stemmed from his close connection to the U.S. military and to his readers. Throughout the strip's history, Caniff carefully responded to readers' concerns and enlisted their support for this war that was often fought outside the public eye in covert operations or secret diplomatic efforts. As a result, he was able to naturalize the military posturing of the United States for readers who might have been skeptical of further military intervention, while showing readers how they—and popular culture—had a role to play in this conflict.

Amy Reddinger's essay focuses on a type of print perhaps even more mundane and domestic than the Sunday comics: mass-produced and mass-marketed cookbooks. The very domesticity of these objects allowed them to introduce and help American housewives integrate Hawaiian food on their tables, even as the United States hoped to integrate the strange but strategically important territory of Hawai'i into the nation. Reddinger argues that these cookbooks served to promote a number of different Cold War agendas. First, they presented foods that were "foreign" or "ethnic" as safe and normal, helping Americans adjust to a global policy that viewed the world outside as manageable. Second, these cookbooks presented Hawai'i as a quaint set of customs (rather than an exploited colony) that helped make the territory appear to be a natural part of the United States.

Like Hawai'i, Vietnam seemed extremely strange and remote to American readers. Scott Laderman's essay "Mediating Revolution: Travel Literature and the Vietnam War" shows how the U.S. State Department and the government of the pro-Western Republic of Vietnam sponsored, created, and distributed travel literature that encouraged Western readers to visit Vietnam. Throughout the 1950s and 1960s, this literature served not so much to generate tourists as to mediate the revolution in Vietnam for Western audiences, structuring and defining the meaning of the Vietnamese conflict. In particular, these texts and magazine articles allowed the Saigon government to legitimate itself and engage in the project of nation-building. Although by the late 1960s most guidebooks discouraged tourists, as late as 1967 the Saigon government continued to distribute guides that hardly mentioned the war. Laderman suggests that using tourism guides to promote a geopolitical agenda had mixed results but, nonetheless, was central to setting that agenda.

The final section of this collection examines the role "highbrow" art played in fighting the Cold War. While "great art" is traditionally seen as distinct from day-to-day political conflicts, these essays reveal how classic modernists from Gabriel García Márquez to Jackson Pollock were implicated in Cold War conflicts. In the first of these essays, Russell Cobb demonstrates how discussions over the value of the arts in the English-speaking world spilled over into the Latin American journal *Mundo Nuevo*. Competing with the Cuban-sponsored *Casa de las Américas*, *Mundo Nuevo*, which like *Encounter* was CIA-sponsored, had to tread carefully to both appear to be an apolitical supporter of the arts and address the interests of its readers and contributors, many of whom found U.S. Cold War policies distasteful (at best). Cobb traces the changing politics of the journal and argues that its political position was more complicated than its funding source might indicate. Because the journal did not follow U.S. ideological dictates, it was able to focus on assessing Latin American literary output and placing that output within the ideological discourse of freedom and independence that was so important to figures like García Márquez. In turn, the journal was able to transform the reputation of Latin American art, replacing "revolutionary politics with revolutionary art." Cobb's essay shows the contradictions implicit in American foreign and cultural policy and ties together many of the explicit contradictions that these essays discuss. Finally, in "'Truth, Freedom, Perfection': Alfred Barr's *What Is Modern Painting?* as Cold War Rhetoric," Patricia Hills shows how Alfred Barr revised his classic catalog *What Is Modern Art?* in ways that presented modern art as a key anti-Communist front. Created and distributed in ways that encouraged its use in American high school classes, this catalog played a key role both in promoting the Museum of Modern Art and in setting the terms through which Americans could understand modern art. In particular, as the ideological discourse of the Cold War heated up, Barr carefully connected modernism to key Cold War terms, especially "freedom," and used that connection to establish American superiority in the arts.

Looking at this collection as a whole gives rise to several questions and issues. The first, addressed by many of the essays here, is "What are the differences between official cultural propaganda, such as the USIA or the Cominform produced, and unofficial propaganda?" What are the differences not only in the *content* of the propaganda, but also in its production and distribution and consumption? The printed representations of Lenin, Stalin, and Mao, omnipresent and oppressive to their intended local audiences and sinister to the West, are now kitschy and ironic, appropriated and reinscribed by postmodern capitalism. Did Soviet audiences ever share this ironic response? And in the West, the "winning side" of the Cold War, will our rhetoric of freedom ever acquire such an ironic tinge? Synthesizing the concerns of Amanda Laugesen's, Scott Laderman's, and Amy Reddinger's essays, we are also forced to ask questions about how the "superpowers" packaged other cultures, and the ultimate effects of that packaging. The essays included here deal with how the United States used Vietnam, indigenous Hawai'i, and the Middle East, but we could also ask how official Soviet propaganda used signifiers of cultures such as those of the Ukraine, the Central Asian nations, the Baltic nations, and Cuba.

Patricia Hills and Russell Cobb force us to look at the ways that high culture—literature and the visual arts—served either as propaganda or as a site for ideological conflict. These essays, along with books such as Caute's, Nadel's, and Guilbaut's, force us to realize that the fine arts were central to the cultural Cold War. How, then, was this conflict seen in the Soviet Union? In nations such as Vietnam or Cuba, where the understanding of what constituted "high culture" was different? And what has been the power of famed defectors such as Mikhail Baryshnikov to reinforce Western notions about the essential connection between art, individual freedom, and Western capitalist democracy?

As always in any discussion of print culture, the question of technologies of reproduction and distribution are key. In the present collection, we see this question addressed by authors such as Kristin Matthews, Christian Kanig, and Laura Jane Gifford. Gifford and Matthews bookend each other nicely: the home-made publications of the SDS, produced on mimeograph machines in massive numbers and circulated among students and activists, are here opposed to the insurgent conservative publications of firms like Liberty Bell Press, Praeger, and Palo Duro Press. Both eschewed, or were blocked from, the world of New York–based mainstream trade publishing, and both produced books that were consumed in the millions, but for the most part the materials on the *left* were circulated and those on the *right* were sold. (Later in the 1960s, certainly, books by movement figures on both the left and the right—such as Jerry Rubin and Barry Goldwater—did appear from mainstream trade publishers.) This raises the question, though, of how oppositional literature came into print behind the "Iron Curtain." The question of how oppositional materials were produced and distributed calls forth many other issues that could profitably be explored by historians of print—how did the Viet Cong guerrillas produce and distribute propaganda? Do Cuban dissident works see print in Cuba? How did exile networks contribute to the printing and distribution (back into the home country) of oppositional materials? Again here we might think of the Cuban community in Miami. How did guerrilla movements in places like El Salvador, Nicaragua, Angola, and Indonesia access print technologies and how were their materials circulated?

Finally, one might see the major question of this collection—one unasked in the essays, but omnipresent in its absence—to be that of the putative *demise* of print. Is the Age of Print over? Are today's great ideological conflicts (the "War on Terror," the struggles over neoliberalism and globalization) bound to be fought exclusively in the electronic and broadcast media, or is print still relevant? Did print "win" the cultural Cold War, or was its importance secondary to that of performance, individual contact, and the broadcast media? Should, and how could, the American government more effectively use print to counteract rampant anti-Americanism throughout the world? How would the Cold War be waged today, in the age of electronic communication, of reproducibility not limited by physical factors like paper and ink, of the erosion of stable concepts of ownership and intellectual property? How would SDS spread its message today? (We can perhaps see that question answered in real time, as a revived SDS now has appeared.) Could a repressive regime such as the Soviet Union clamp down on the circulation of dissent as effectively today as it did in the 1950s and 1960s? To some extent, we see this in China, where an authoritarian "Communist" regime is working quite effectively *with* some of the emblematic companies of the "information revolution" (Yahoo!, Google) to suppress the flow of information. What, in the end, differentiates print from electronic impulses and binary code in terms of how it is generated, circulated, used, owned, suppressed, destroyed, altered, marked up?

We hope that the impressive, important scholarship by the contributors to this volume will answer some of your questions, but, more important, that it will raise further questions and spark even more investigation of how print was used in the Cold War and how print is being used in ideological conflicts today. We would like to express our gratitude to our contributors, who come from four continents, and to the editors at the University of Massachusetts Press for making this book a reality.

Notes

1. Elaine Tyler May, *Homeward Bound: American Families in the Cold War Era* (New York: Basic Books, 1988), 3–15.

2. Alan Nadel, *Containment Culture: American Narrative, Postmodernism, and the Atomic Age* (Durham, N.C.: Duke University Press, 1995), 4. For a sense of the extent to which the American left was silenced by this "containment" see Richard Lingeman, "Domestic Containment: The Downfall of Postwar Idealism and Left Dissent, 1945–1950," in Mark C. Carnes, ed., *The Columbia History of Post–World War II America* (New York: Columbia University Press), 201–25.

3. Christina Klein, *Cold War Orientalism: Asia in the Middlebrow Imagination, 1945–1961* (Berkeley: University of California Press, 2003), 41–44.

4. Christopher Lasch, "The Cultural Cold War: A Short History of the Congress for Cultural Freedom," in Barton J. Bernstein, ed., *Towards a New Past: Dissenting Essays in American History* (New York: Vintage, 1969); Max Kozloff, "American Painting during the Cold War," *Artforum* (May 1973); Eva Cockcroft, "Abstract Expressionism: Weapon of the Cold War," *Artforum* (June 1974); Jane de Hart Matthews, "Art and Politics in Cold War America," *American Historical Review* 81 (October 1976); Serge Guilbaut, *How New York Stole the Idea of Modern Art,* trans. Arthur Goldhammer (Chicago: University of Chicago Press, 1983); Reinhold Wagnleitner, *Coca-Colonization and the Cold War: The United States in Austria after the Second World War* (Chapel Hill: University of North Carolina Press, 2007).

5. Peter Coleman, *The Liberal Conspiracy* (New York: Free Press, 1989); Frances Stonor Saunders, *The Cultural Cold War: The CIA and the World of Arts and Letters* (New York: New Press, 1999); Giles Scott-Smith, *The Politics of Apolitical Culture* (London: Routledge, 2001); Volker Berghahn, *America and the Intellectual Cold Wars in Europe* (Princeton: Princeton University Press, 2001); Penny Von Eschen, *Satchmo Blows Up the World* (Cambridge: Harvard University Press, 2004); Yale Richmond, *Cultural Exchange and the Cold War* (University Park, Pa.: Penn State University Press, 2003); David Caute, *The Dancer Defects* (Oxford: Oxford University Press, 2003).

6. Amy Knight, *Beria: Stalin's First Lieutenant* (Princeton: Princeton University Press, 1993), 3.

7. Stephen J. Whitfield, *The Culture of the Cold War* (Baltimore: Johns Hopkins University Press, 1991), 15–16. Whitfield is quick to point out, as most historians of the Cold War, that the type of repression represented here operated on a different scale in the USSR from that in the United States. In the Soviet Union, "the penalties for dissidence were lethal"; in the United States "the penalties for political dissidence were capricious . . . generally economic and social rather than legal." Historian Ellen Schrecker, far more critical of American repression than Whitfield, explains in an aggravated note, "of course Joseph Stalin was far more repressive than Joseph McCarthy and J. Edgar Hoover . . . while what happened in the Soviet Union was much worse than anything in this country, within the American context McCarthyism was a disgrace." *Many Are the Crimes* (Princeton: Princeton University Press, 1998), xx. Hughes's experience with Dodd Mead is further described in Arnold Rampersad, *The Life of Langston Hughes* (Oxford: Oxford University Press, 2002), 229–30.

8. *A History of the Council on Books in Wartime, 1942–1946* (New York: The Country Life Press, 1946), 1–16.

9. Ibid., 81–92.

10. Jean Hatfield Barclay, "Reading: Our Wartime Discovery," *The English Journal* 34:6 (June 1945): 295–303.

11. *A History of the Council on Books in Wartime, 1942–1946*, 81.

12. Kenneth C. Davis, *Two-Bit Culture: The Paperbacking of America* (New York: Houghton Mifflin, 1984), 79.

13. Wayne Wiegand, "Tunnel Vision and Blind Spots: What the Past Tells Us about the Present: Reflections on the Twentieth-Century History of American Librarianship," *The Library Quarterly* 69:1 (January 1999): 11–17.

14. Barclay, "Reading," 300.

15. John Tebbel, *A History of Book Publishing in the United States*, vol. 5 (New York: R. R. Bowker Company, 1981), 98, 347.

16. Davis, *Two-Bit Culture*, 6, 16.

17. Liz Cohen, *A Consumers' Republic: The Politics of Mass Consumption in Postwar America* (New York: Vintage Books, 2004), 119.

18. George Cotkin, "The Commerce of Culture and Criticism," in Carnes, *The Columbia History of Post-World War II America,* 182–84.

19. As Jay Satterfield notes, the fact that the car was a replica is in itself a sign of the way the new market for paperbacks had made the Modern Library increasingly less relevant in the Cold War: *'The World's Best Books': Taste, Culture, and the Modern Library* (Amherst: University of Massachusetts Press, 2002), 168.

20. Davis, *Two-Bit Culture,* 5.

21. Bennett Cerf, *At Random* (New York: Random House, 1977), 162–63, Tebbel, *History of Book Publishing,* vol. 5, 20.

22. Tebbel, *History of Book Publishing,* vol. 5, 181–94. Cerf, *At Random,* 276–92. For a more complete (and less sanguine) history of the wave of mergers and globalization of the American publishing industry see Thomas Whiteside, *The Blockbuster Complex: Conglomerates, Show Business, and Book Publishing* (Middletown, Conn.: Wesleyan University Press, 1997).

23. Davis, *Two-Bit Culture,* 6.

24. Ibid., 148, Tebbel, *History of Book Publishing,* vol. 5, 349–50.

25. Stephen Lovell, "Publishing and the Book Trade in the Post-Stalin Era: A Case-Study of the Commodification of Culture," *Europe-Asia Studies* 50:4 (June 1998): 698.

26. Maris A. Vinovskis, "Federal Education Policy and Politics," in Carnes, *The Columbia History of Post-World War II America,* 457–59.

27. Laura Miller, *Reluctant Capitalists: Bookselling and the Culture of Consumption* (Chicago: University of Chicago Press, 2006), 23–54.

28. Ibid., 1–6.

29. Howard Fast, *Being Red* (Boston: Houghton Mifflin, 1990), 286–95.

30. Julia Willett, "Beauty Shops and Bouffants: The Political Uses of Beauty, Style and Domestic Space," in *Containing America: Cultural Production and Consumption in Fifties America,* ed. Nathan Abrams and Julie Hughes (Birmingham, UK: University of Birmingham Press, 2000), 58.

31. Schrecker, *Many Are the Crimes,* 395–96, 1; Daniel Ellsberg, *Secrets: A Memoir of Vietnam and the Pentagon Papers* (New York: Viking, 2002) 331, 371. See also Tom Wells, *Wildman: The Life and Times of Daniel Ellsberg* (New York: Palgrave, 2001). For more on the ways that easily reproduced print both contained and disseminated state secrets, see Jonathan Auerbach and Lisa Gitelman, "Microfilm, Containment, and the Cold War," *American Literary History* 19:3 (Fall 2007): 745–68.

32. Saunders, *The Cultural Cold War,* 58.

33. Ibid.

34. USIA, letter to Alfred A. Knopf, 11 October 1961. AAK Archive, Harry Ransom Humanities Research Center, University of Texas at Austin.

35. Richard J. Arndt, *The First Resort of Kings: American Cultural Diplomacy in the Twentieth Century* (Dulles, Va.: Potomac Books, 2005); Frank Ninkovich, *U.S. Information Policy and Cultural Diplomacy* (Foreign Policy Association Headline Series #308, Fall 1996).

36. Louise Robbins, "The Overseas Libraries Controversy and the Freedom to Read: U.S. Libraries and Publishers Confront Joseph McCarthy," *Libraries and Culture* 36:1 (2001): 27–39.

37. Samuel Schreiner, Jr., *The Condensed World of the Reader's Digest* (New York: Stein and Day, 1977), 11; Christina Klein, *Cold War Orientalism: Asia in the Middlebrow Imagination, 1945–1961* (Berkeley: University of California Press, 2003), 70.

38. Sol Schindler, personal interview with Greg Barnhisel, October 4, 2008.

39. Kenneth Osgood,. *Total Cold War: Eisenhower's Secret Propaganda Battle at Home and Abroad* (Lawrence: University Press of Kansas, 2006), 300; Curtis G. Benjamin, *U.S. Books Abroad: Neglected Ambassadors* (Washington, D.C.: Library of Congress, 1984), 91.

40. Kurt Thometz, "High Life, Useful Advice, and Mad English," in Thometz, ed., *Life Turns Man Up and Down: African Market Literature* (New York: Pantheon Books, 2001), xiii–xliv. For more on the development both of popular and highbrow media in Africa, see Bernth Lindfors, *Loaded Vehicles: Studies in African Literary Media* (Trenton, N.J.: Africa World Press, 1996), which discusses Nigeria, South Africa, and Malawi.

41. *The Life Story and Death of John Kennedy*, in Thometz, *Life Turns Man Up and Down*, 309–12.

42. Louise Robbins, "Publishing American Values: The Franklin Book Programs as Cold War Cultural Diplomacy," *Library Trends* 55:3 (2007): 638.

43. Osgood, *Total Cold War,* 297.

44. See Saunders for a detailed description of the funding of the CCF.

45. Gregory Walker, *Soviet Book Publishing Policy* (Cambridge: Cambridge University Press, 1978), 1.

46. Ibid., 6.

47. Mark Hooker, *The Military Uses of Literature: Fiction and the Armed Forces in the Soviet Union* (Westport, Conn: Praeger), 1996.

48. Ibid., 12.

49. Ann Komaromi, "The Material Existence of Soviet Samizdat," *Slavic Review* 63:3 (Autumn 2004): 599–603. Traditionally the authors and disseminators of *samizdat* have been seen as heroic champions of Western-democratic values in the face of repression, even though many have pointed out that these authors were as anti-Western as their censors. For the vision of *samizdat* as "the domain of free thought in the Soviet experience," see Hyumg-Min Joo, "Voices of Freedom: Samizdat," *Europe-Asia Studies* 56:4 (June 2004): 571–94; F. I. M Feldbrugge, *Samizdat and Political Dissent in the Soviet Union* (Leyden: A. W. Sithoff, 1975); and George Saunders, *Samizdat: Voices of the Soviet Opposition* (New York: Monad, 1974). For a more complicated view see Serguei Alex Oushakine, "The Terrifying Mimicry of Samizdat," *Public Culture* 13:2 (Fall 2001): 191–214.

50. Perry Link, *The Uses of Literature: Life in the Socialist Chinese Literary System* (Princeton: Princeton University Press, 2000), 101–2.

51. Ibid., 113–14, 130–31.

52. Ibid., 95, 171.

53. W. J. F. Jenner, "1979: A New Start for Literature in China?" *The China Quarterly* 86 (June 1981): 283n, 290–91; Emily Honig, "Socialist Sex: The Cultural Revolution Revisited," *Modern China* 29:2 (April 2003): 147. Link, *Uses of Literature,* 194–95, 227.

PRINTING FROM LEFT TO RIGHT

1 The Medium, the Message, the Movement

Print Culture and New Left Politics

KRISTIN MATHEWS

MANY SCHOLARS of post–World War II American culture have recognized speech's function in energizing the New Left, yet none have examined reading's essential role in the evolution of New Left politics. This oversight has produced a significant blind spot when it comes to understanding the motivation, medium, and message for student radicals of the 1960s. Limiting radical politics to the spoken word has indirectly located power in the hands of the recognizably vocal few and thereby has constructed a hierarchical structure of political participation with spokesmen at the top—a structure akin to those the New Left was striving to dismantle as it worked for civil and human rights. Furthermore, such stratification has reinforced the "spokesperson" or "celebrity" narrative of the New Left employed by the mainstream media and political establishment that sought to diminish the movement's reach and power by reducing it to the "ranting" of a few leaders such as Tom Hayden, Mario Savio, and Mark Rudd. While many scholars have acknowledged the volumes of print material produced and disseminated by the New Left, they have done so in passing, focusing primarily on content or the material's corollary "event," thereby failing to examine that medium itself in its ideological and historical context.

Because the New Left was comprised of many loosely affiliated groups that at times worked together and at other times did not, mapping out a comprehensive and coordinated schema of New Left print culture is not possible. Accordingly, here I focus primarily on the writings of the radical student movement, particularly those of Students for a Democratic Society (SDS) for whom print culture was alpha and omega. If one surveys the bulk of print matter disseminated in the 1960s, one sees that SDS produced the majority of it while working independently and in larger coalitions for human and civil rights. In fact, "SDS became known, among other things, as the *'writingest'* organization around."[1] Founded in 1962, SDS drove New Left print production, adapting and extending radical print traditions such that print was both a means and an end, and simultaneously recruiting, teaching, organizing, and radicalizing large portions of America's dispossessed with its ever-present and ever-abundant materials. SDS's means of populist education thematized its message, for its use of inexpensively copied or mimeographed pamphlets, flyers, leaflets, posters, manuals, and open letters worked to construct a democratic community in which each individual's participation was equally sought and valued. While only part of the larger radical whole, SDS was recognized as "the organized expression of that Movement, its intellectual mentor and the source of much of its energy," as well as "the organization that most obviously represented" the "grass-roots, often spontaneous, political expression of discontent, opposition, and desire for change."[2]

SDS's radical print culture transformed the politics of media and the medium of politics in the 1960s. The group's ubiquitous print outlined an ideology whose endgame—unseating the paternalistic power at the heart of poverty, racism, and imperialistic militarism—was rooted in literacy, both literal and social. This literature called people to read, learn, know, and do, thereby asserting a causal connection between the act of reading and the civic participation embodied in its ultimate goal of "participatory democracy." As the movement evolved, it equated reading with action, such that the production or consumption of print was a revolutionary act in itself—a belief prompting the proposition "that, through the counter-institution of young people's media, we take over the media in order to take over the government."[3] Informing this conflation of reading and political action was the belief that only a lack of information prevented America's downtrodden from participating—that "the key to understanding the oppressive class structures now developing in American society is found less in the maldistribution of the nation's property than in the maldistribution of its knowledge."[4] Thus, SDS strove to help people "find their way out of the restricted perspectives imposed by their condition," claiming that "only then will they be able to make fulfilling use of new programs and institutions. The alternative is the perpetuation—indeed, the technological strengthening—of minority rule and mass powerlessness."[5] The masthead of *New Left Notes* said, "let the people decide," and the flood of print disseminated by SDS seemingly offered the people many choices.

However, close-reading SDS's print matter provides only part of the story, and it is when one recognizes that "the medium is the message" that one best understands the revolutionary role of "the word" in student activism.[6] SDS's print was a product of its Cold War context, wielding a message and method counter to the government's postwar modus operandi, which demanded secrecy and a centralization of knowledge to wage its war of words against Communism. Indeed, many of SDS's projects used print to provide information to populations traditionally denied such, whether they be poor urban dwellers without access to education, job training, or public representation; students subject to paternalistic university policies; or an American populace from whom news of the "actual" events taking place in Vietnam was withheld. Student radicals employed print's matter and mechanisms to strike a blow at Cold War America's dominant narratives, questioning the authority by which those narratives wrote "America" for millions of individuals denied that creative opportunity, and proposing an alternative mode of meaning-making that was decentralized, collaborative, and transformative. SDS's perpetually producing presses strove to liberate print from the confines of a centralized author and authority, democratizing production, reproduction, and distribution of print matter to help "the people" articulate, replicate, and circulate their own ideas, and thereby define themselves as subjects and citizens. Grounding this project was a faith in print's power to transform individuals through reading, changing the literal and epistemological world in which they lived and thereby transforming reader-citizens into sites of revolutionary activity. At the same time, SDS print culture's decentralized production and distribution complicated the movement's operations as the volume and variety of print hastened fragmentation, problematized coalition, and prevented the movement from outlining a singular political strategy. Thus, examining SDS's print culture provides a way of reading the power and contradictions endemic to the New Left as it participated in a significant front of America's domestic Cold War—the battle of and over information— and in so doing, brings us to a better understanding of the politics of constituting America in the postwar period.

The Prodigal Writers

Characterizing the New Left is a challenge. While Van Gosse and others have demonstrated that the New Left was comprised of many groups, some like historian Jennifer Frost have indicated that even "the white New Left was not monolithic and that not all participants experienced it in the same way."[7] Although *The Port Huron Statement* (1962) self-identified members of the radical student Left as "people of this generation, bred in at least modest comfort, housed now in universities, looking uncomfortably to the world we inherit," elsewhere members of the New Left had a hard time articulating a succinct definition of membership and program, admitting, "It's difficult to say really who we are."[8] Even Georgetown's radical student handbook, "NOT WITH MY LIFE YOU DON'T!!!" (1968), admits "THE MOVEMENT" is "a difficult and complex thing to describe: it is as much a form of on-going experience as an organization. In a sense, sds undergoes a perpetual identity crisis. Because of its strong anti-elitist and decentralist strains, sds is as diverse as its 300 college chapters and its 40,000 members."[9] That decentralized diversity was mirrored by the movement's print culture, the fluidity of which resisted a singular narrative.

In many ways, the New Left's obscurantism signaled its resistance to what participants saw as American liberalism's faith in prescriptive or bound ideologies. The "crazy-quilt pattern" of membership and activity was "an essentially anti-organizational politics" typified by "the attempt to embody personal and anti-hierarchical values in politics" as student radicals worked toward a "living" activism that would grow and change with each new member.[10] The New Left embraced a bottom-up "organizational" structure in order to encourage complexity and a populist diversity. In so doing, they broke with their Old Left predecessors who they believed were wedded to Marxist dogma and hierarchy, and turned on postwar intellectuals whom they criticized for clinging to a "vital" political center delimited by rabid anti-Communism. Proclaiming "we have no sure formulas, no closed theories," student radicals argued that "the search for orienting theories and the creation of human values is complex but worthwhile," and in many ways what initially distinguished the New Left from its radical predecessors was its search for, rather than application of, theory.[11]

Nevertheless, the student-based New Left did not appear ex nihilo, but rather emerged from a tradition of radical print culture rooted in a revolutionary humanism. Many members of the New Left first encountered and later joined the movement through radical literature. Some were "red diaper babies," whose parents were involved in the Old Left and exposed their children to the power of print. Others who joined SDS inherited the print tradition of its "parent" student organization, the Student League for Industrial Democracy (SLID), which had become a "social-democratic clearinghouse for liberal and left-liberal . . . ideas and causes," focused on "educating younger generations through pamphlets, newsletters, and an occasional conference."[12] Still others came to the New Left through their involvement in the civil rights movement, particularly after working with the Student Non-Violent Coordinating Committee (SNCC), which strove to educate "the people" in the south's poor black communities on how they could register to vote and participate in local and national politics. Many students were recruited to these efforts through flyers, inheriting both a legacy of radically populist American thought and provisional models for radical political change. Kevin Mattson's *Intellectuals in Action* (2002) recounts how the New Left's political "heroes," including C. Wright Mills, Paul Goodman, William Appleman Williams, and Arnold Kaufman, actively wrote and published radical materials as leaflets and pamphlets—forms readily available to and affordable for a student audience. Goodman, whose *Growing Up Absurd* (1960) provided radical youth with a legitimized vocabulary of dissent, was ever willing to write pamphlets, leaflets, and speeches for the radical cause.[13] Meanwhile, works like Williams's pamphlet "The Cold War Revisionists" and Mills's *Listen, Yankee*, his pro-Cuban Revolution "paperback pamphlet that sold four hundred thousand copies," modeled a radical ideology for the nascent New Left and revealed the potential power in cheaply printed and distributed words.[14]

However, the New Left broke from previous radical generations that saw print merely as a vehicle for ideas, instead valuing radical print for communicating a populist politic with a form that could be created, reproduced, and disseminated by and for any person. Technologies—the mimeograph and the recently invented Xerox machine, in particular—allowed this radical generation to print materials in large numbers for little cost. At SDS's national office, "the phones were occupied at all hours, the ancient typewriters clacked incessantly, [and] the new $300 multilith machine, the organization's proudest symbol of becomingness, churned out broadsheets and announcements far into the night."[15] Locating SDS's "becomingness" within its multilith's reproductive capability signals how the organization's birth and intellectual offspring were one and the same. Student radicalism was part of an old tradition being "born again" through the Left's access to and means of reproducing information. The labor involved in "churn[ing] out broadsheets and announcements far into the night" facilitated the "birth" of new recruits into the movement and the coordination of diverse peoples into an organization.[16] Thus, one could argue that print culture helped deliver the "new" of the New Left.

SDS in particular exhibited a fervent faith in the power of print, or "the word," to help people become born again into a consciousness of their "self" and their part in the democratic process. *The Port Huron Statement* reveals much about the organization's hoped-for place in and transformation of America's radical print heritage. On the one hand, the framers of the statement announced it was "an effort rooted in the ancient, still unfulfilled conception of man attaining determining influence over his circumstances of life,"[17] claiming a radical heritage in the strict sense of getting at the root or origin of an idea—in this case, self-determination. On the other hand, the "Introductory Note" declared that *The Port Huron Statement* was "a living document open to change with our times and experiences," recognizing that "since its adoption there have been changes in the American and world scenes, and changes in SDS as well. And although few of its original writers would agree today with all of its conclusions, it remains an essential source of SDS direction, a continual stimulus to thinking on campuses and in the movement, and one of the earliest embodiments of the feelings of the new movement of young people which began in the sixties."[18] "Ancient," yet "living," "rooted," yet "open to change," focused on the "individual," yet "movement"-based, *The Port Huron Statement* embodied complexity as it tackled the evils facing that generation—ills including poverty, racism, the H-bomb, and American military imperialism—and proposed a solution: "participatory democracy."

The manifesto defined "participatory democracy" as a method of civic engagement "governed by two central aims: that the individual share in those social decisions determining the quality and direction of his life; and that society be organized to encourage independence in men and provide the media for their common participation."[19] Participatory democracy was both an end goal—a societal organization predicated on common participation by enlightened individuals—and a means of achieving such—a mode of organizing disparate individuals into a movement through encouraging individual engagement and activity. Whether utopian, idealistic, or radical, at the heart of the emerging New Left was the belief that informed individuals with access to information could help bring about a second democratic revolution in America. Conceived as a document always already changing form, *The Port Huron Statement* thematized participatory democracy as it offered readers both a mode of civic action and "the media for common participation"—media generic yet specific enough to fit particular moments, movements, and members.

The Port Huron Statement's communal production and distribution further illustrated the power that access to knowledge and freedom to express one's informed opinion could provide in a participatory democracy. SDS's 1962 Port Huron meeting was largely a drafting session.[20] Prior to the meeting, Tom Hayden sent approximately 100 draft copies of the manifesto to fellow attendees. Once there, all participants were involved in hammering out ideas and language—men, women, students, and community members.[21] After much wrangling and revision, the writers finished an initial version of the statement that they mimeographed and distributed by hand and mail to new SDS chapters across the country.[22] The demand was great and "often the National Office's slowness in reproducing copies meant that one tattered document passed through the hands of a dozen students," who were thereby practicing a democracy both individual and communal.[23] Within five months, the National Office was out of copies and "in the next two years no fewer than twenty thousand mimeographed copies (sixty-six single-spaced pages) were sent out." The 35-cent pamphlet version too sold out its 20,000 copies in both its 1964 and 1966 printings.[24] New Left chronicler Massimo Teodori estimates that over 100,000 copies of the pamphlet were circulated within the first five years of its conception.[25] At the beginning, SDS's print culture was collectively authored, reproduced, and distributed to the many; furthermore, it was action-oriented, as campus and neighborhood canvassing magnified the civic action performed in and by the text.

Port Huron's form also worked to capture the eye and mind of potential activists and thereby trigger a revolutionary democratic movement. The pamphlet's cover displayed participatory democracy's dual aims in a large, italicized font to attract people's attention and draw them inside the pamphlet and the movement. The statement was cheap and portable, reinforcing its primary focus of returning democracy to the people. Its second printing as a pocket-sized pamphlet made it easier to keep it on and make it part of one's person. Because the pamphlet could be perpetually on hand, its chances of being shared were greatly increased; thus its portability was bound to its community-building power. This pocket-sized manifesto's form created and filled a revolutionary need, getting print to the people in efforts to make knowledge "accessible" and help cultivate humankind's potential to live "with dignity and creativeness."[26]

As a result of this informational blitz, New Left groups swelled in numbers and could then turn their print efforts toward the larger community.[27] Participation in SNCC's voter registration drives increased, SDS branches opened in universities across the country, and student involvement in the Committee for a Sane Nuclear Policy (SANE) broadened and culminated in the 1965 anti-war march in Washington, D.C. Formation of groups like SDS's Economic Research and Action Project (ERAP), a multi-city program in which student volunteers moved into poor, white, urban neighborhoods to help organize and mobilize communities for causes like tenants' rights, hiring equity, and fair housing practices, reinforced the link between radical print distribution and activism as organizers measured a program's efficacy "largely in terms of *how successfully they give away their own power.*"[28] Because the New Left equated information with power, giving information away to "the people" in the literal form of print matter was, in fact, giving "power to the people." During this period of governmental secrecy and information control, the New Left saw words as weapons, such that action and education were "completely united.... A leaflet or dorm-canvassing is no less radical activity than seizing a building."[29] Accordingly, student radicals believed and saw that the better they distributed "the word," the more powerful the movement would and did become.

The Information War

The sheer volume of radical student print is staggering, and even a brief sampling cannot capture its extent since pamphlets, flyers, and leaflets were produced on individual, local, regional, and national levels. The medium's beauty—anybody can use it—also makes a strict accounting impossible. Nevertheless, records do show that over 100,000 copies of *The Port Huron Statement* were distributed in its first five years; that by 1964, SDS's *Bulletin* was read by at least 2,000; that by mid-1964 SDS had published over 92 papers and pamphlets; that at least 400,000 pieces of literature were distributed during the anti-war teach-ins that dotted the country in 1965; that approximately one thousand SDSers handed out over 500,000 copies of the four-page "National Vietnam Examination" to those taking the Selective Service exam in efforts to reveal Vietnam's untold story; that over 250,000 leaflets were dispersed in Chicago in 1970 by SDS members organizing a demonstration against unemployment; and that "hundreds of thousands of copies" of the call to the first anti–Vietnam War march in Washington were "distributed on campuses since SDS had decided to organize the March that previous December."[30] In addition, the circulation numbers of underground newspapers used or "endorsed" by the New Left numbered in the millions in the late 1960s with approximately 5 million in circulation in 1970.[31] One word that could describe the New Left was "prolific," and SDS in particular kept the presses afire with formal position papers and informal "calls to arms" distributed on local and national levels alike.[32]

That SDS was able to generate so much print is a testament to the members' tenacity and industriousness as participants in this information war. The organization's National Office had its own mimeograph, multilith, and (eventually) Xerox machines—hardware featured by CBS in its 1965 piece on SDS, which "showed SDS office staff mimeographing and printing pamphlets."[33] Yet, keeping those machines running took most, if not all, of the dues members theoretically paid, as well as funds donated by sympathetic patrons. In spring 1963, the National Office received $67.59 in dues, but paid out $48.05 for postage and $167.25 for mimeo paper and ink, therein working SDS into the red as it labored to keep the information flowing.[34] SDS historian Alan Adelson noted, "Raising enough money to pay the phone bills and keep printing literature is a chronic problem in SDS";[35] yet, SDSers somehow found means to reproduce their materials, even in times of conflict. During the 1968 Columbia takeover, for instance, SDS "liberated" President Grayson Kirk's Xerox 3000, using it to copy scores of documents[36] and to leave him a note: "Stopped by to visit you, but you weren't in. Sorry to have missed you. —SDS."[37] Putting the note in the Xerox both reinforced print's primacy in SDS's struggle and signaled the group's dedication to keep information accessible at all costs.

More significantly, SDS's strategically placed note symbolized student radicals' declaration of war on America's message makers and secret keepers. For the military-industrial complex and the New Left had been engaged in a battle for the minds of Cold War Americans—a battle based on the premise that whoever controlled the dominant narratives of nation, self, and other would control the idea of "America." Both the right and left recognized the national narrative's instability at this time—that "after the Fifties . . . the idea of America the indivisible was unraveling."[38] The materials produced by both camps expressed a particular "Americanness" that the authors hoped would construct a more perfect union of sorts. Although each organization's short-term aim was to "disrupt" the other with print, their long-term goals differed significantly, for groups like SDS used disruption to trigger a radical reconstitution of America such that it more closely adhered to the democratic principles of equality and self-determination it purported to hold, whereas the FBI's counter-intelligence program (COINTELPRO) employed disruption to maintain a status quo predicated on sociopolitical and economic stratification.[39] To put it another way, whereas the New Left strove to create an open or "living" narrative of individual and nation, the FBI attempted to author a closed narrative of citizen and country. Governmental agencies cited radical student print culture as evidence of illegal, dangerous, and un-American activity, referencing petitions, flyers, pamphlets, and posters to substantiate claims of subversion and justify surveillance in a manner hauntingly similar to earlier efforts to "expose" and eradicate Communism in the 1940s and 1950s. Documents, not individuals, stood "on trial," collapsing the distinction between the medium, the message, and the members of the New Left. According to a 1968 FBI memo outlining its plan to discredit and destroy the New Left, print matter would be the Bureau's most effective weapon as it mimicked the mode and form of radical print culture in its efforts to dismantle it.[40] COINTELPRO distributed scores of fraudulent "New Left" pamphlets, letters, and press releases, thinking it could divide New Left groups and create disenchantment within the movement. The FBI constructed a profane "type" of radical student and publication, reducing the New Left into an overtly simplistic enemy upon whom all of America's social ills could be blamed. This postwar struggle to author a particular imagined community through print suggests that the medium really was the message—that *how* one constructed what constituted "America" also determined the face of the *who* reading it.

SDS print's diverse subject matter, target audience, and distribution methods make it difficult to collect and map out a comprehensive reader response; however, if one takes into consideration both SDS's membership numbers and its attendance figures for major actions (marches, teach-ins, etc.), one can provisionally assert radical print's power for postwar readers. Furthermore, personal narratives of student activists repeatedly profess print's potency: "I got [recruited] to the demonstration by being handed a leaflet on the Berkeley campus"; "a woman in SDS gave me some literature to read. . . . Back at my dorm I talked to all my friends about SDS and the war"; "back at the apartment I read a mimeographed paper by Tony Papert called *The Mass Strike*. . . . it hit me kind of hard. Like it dispelled my dominant illusion"; "I got to Berkeley . . . and went up to a woman who was giving out leaflets at Sproul Plaza. I asked if she knew anywhere where I could meet with political people . . . I wound up in a house with the people who formed SLATE, the student political party."[41] In these accounts and others, individuals locate their recruitment, activism, and consciousness-raising in radical print, suggesting that these materials indeed had the intended affect on some real readers.

Although SDS print's ultimate goal was participatory democracy, its first use in this battle was necessarily recruitment, as illustrated by the ubiquitous "Join us!" found on pamphlets, flyers, and posters. Adelson's SDS history claims, "about one hundred reams of paper were stashed in the SDS office at the beginning of the first semester"—reams that were used "in a month."[42] As the movement wore on, word of mouth and press coverage often did the recruiting for SDS; however, in its early stages, SDS waged an aggressive recruitment campaign through community canvassing and blanket leafleting. Bold headlines, provocative photos, and "the truth" were splashed across these materials in hopes of starting conversations.[43] For instance, the writers of Georgetown SDS's "alternative" handbook invited discussion and debate by saying, "If you have questions, or if you have reservations about our position, feel free at any time to contact us: we look forward to seeing you. If you find yourself in substantial agreement, *JOIN US*."[44] Door-to-door leafleting campaigns like those called for in *Don't Mourn: Organize!* (1968) were *de rigueur*, most notably during "Vietnam Summer" of 1967 in which tens of thousands of volunteers went knocking on doors to "provide clear factual information to ordinary citizens," "spread the antiwar message,"[45] and recruit additional support. Time and time again, radical literature worked to "somehow reach the unconvinced with arguments and analyses that speak to their day-to-day oppression in America."[46] Getting the word out was meant to get the people in to meetings and the movement.

Implicit in SDS print culture's recruitment effort was its educative aim: organizers believed that as people learned the "facts," their consciousness would be raised and they would join the movement. Yet SDS never articulated explicitly *how* print itself could change consciousness, stimulate action, or form community; rather, it seemingly assumed that its materials would affect a readerly transformation that was immediate and unmediated—that once people "knew" they would automatically "resist."[47] Few movement print materials entertained the notion that their ideas would not be accepted, or accepted but not acted upon; instead, they naïvely took for granted that access to information was all that was limiting change—"the truth shall set you free." Howard Zinn's "How Democratic Is America?" (1971) illustrates this in his definition of "democratic" that rooted participation in people's access to information.[48] Zinn and other New Left writers assumed that "information" would be transmitted seamlessly from writers to readers, who then would be moved to immediate action. Sometimes this assumption played out, as was seen in the first and well-attended anti-war march on Washington in 1965;[49] other times, however, the assumption that all who read would be moved to act was disproved, as with SDS's "National Vietnam Examination," which failed to incite a mass refusal to sit for the Selective Service exam.

Nevertheless, SDS believed that teaching people to read print matter, social problems, and ultimately, their selves was central to the revelation of "new potentialities" and "levers for change."[50] SDS printed position papers on a range of issues, consciously resisting becoming a single-issue movement in hopes of reaching a broader audience representative of America's "living" multiplicity. The decentralization of radical print meant that a campus or neighborhood could be leafleted by multiple groups on issues like poverty, civil rights, draft resistance, or American imperialism at any one point in time. *Don't Mourn—Organize!* argued that such "multi-issue organizing" allowed one to "reach more people in a community, for it is more in line with the reality of a community."[51] In addition, multi-issue organizing allowed for individuals and specific communities to learn about and work for issues that moved them, therein allowing them to participate in the governance of their lives as they would choose. Ideally, the "truths" of their democracy would be localized and fitted to their particular lived experience.

At the same time, SDS's scattershot focus also gave the impression that the group was trying to do "too many things,"[52] suggesting perhaps that its faith in print's power overstepped its ability to make them happen. SDS's educational print efforts subordinated focus and reliable access—a pattern compounded by the medium itself, for leaflets, pamphlets, and posters are temporary by nature, something to be glanced at and thrown away. The medium's ephemerality also suggested impermanence. Some within the movement recognized and criticized this perceived disposability, arguing that "deep understanding" of oppression and resistance did not come from having "ten students descending on a community, passing out leaflets about urban renewal or the draft," but from learning as well as teaching as permanent members of a community.[53] ERAPers stressed that the temporary nature of the initial print contact must be followed up with a more sustained educative project—that activists must put down geographic and epistemological roots in order to form a radical community.

These ERAPers' criticism points to a larger problem: while print materials were produced for mass distribution to "the people," the distinction between "writer" and "audience" set up an us/them division that troubled SDS's aim of decentralized politics. Many pamphlets were written to mobilize and ultimately liberate oppressed peoples; yet, oppressed peoples were either spoken of and not to, or talked down to by the materials' authors. For instance, both "Getting Ready for the Firing Line" (1968) and "We've Got to Reach Our Own People" (1967) repeatedly referred to the working poor as "these people" and members of "these communities," thereby signaling that the "you" of the pamphlet was a student audience. This division was echoed in Richard Flacks's "Chicago: Organizing the Unemployed" (1964) which argued that "an extensive supply of literature on economic and social issues, suitable for working class readers needs to be created immediately."[54] The rhetoric in and dissemination of this print matter created two categories of print and community: one for the educated organizer and one for the "ignorant" organized. "Take a Step Into America" identified this well-intentioned elitism and argued that "legitimacy won't come from 4–6 or 8 years of college, superior knowledge, conceptualization or awareness" because these reinforce the very hierarchies that the movement was trying to dismantle.[55] These criticisms cut to the quick of SDS's methods: print materials went into communities, but were rarely produced by or sent out from the communities themselves on a national scale.

Another perceived limit on participatory democracy's power was illustrated by the prescriptive print produced by the National Office teaching individuals "how to" be a radical. Although SDS disdained prescription on local and individual levels, it recognized that a degree of organization and prescription was necessary in order to mobilize a large-scale movement.

National events like the 1964 anti-war march or the 1968 Democratic National Convention (DNC) demonstration required another level of coordination to bring together a mass of individuals who were either unaffiliated or attached to activist groups that did not necessarily coalesce. For instance, prior to the 1968 DNC, both national and local SDS chapters distributed literature on anticipated practical considerations involved in the upcoming civil disobedience. Various leaflets documented "Suggestions For Legal Self-Defense In Chicago," like informing protestors of "Your 'Rights' Under the Law," what to do "If You Are Arrested," where to find "Medical Help in Chicago," and "Things To Know And Do."[56] Student activists coming to Chicago were counseled to "bring this instruction sheet, a supply of dimes (for phone calls), a supply of cigarettes, and reading material."[57] These materials seemingly trouble the self-determination and individual "creativity" promised by participatory democracy; however, "how to" missives like these were necessary to prepare participants to navigate various possible outcomes of their civil disobedience and to transform this motley crew of protestors and activists into a national "who" of some force. As such, SDS's print helped create an organizational structure predicated on prescribed "knowledge" and anticipated resistance to their demonstration.

Furthermore, these "how to" materials recognized that readers did not live in a vacuum, but rather in a space marked by competing epistemological demands. SDS trusted neither the mainstream press to report the whole story nor Cold War readers dulled by "closed" discourses to see gaps in official narratives; hence, it used print to revive readers' ability to receive "living" ideas. And, if words are actions as Rudd and other SDSers claimed, then these materials could be considered acts of resistance. SDS print violated the ideological hold the mainstream press had on events themselves and, by extension, on participants in and observers of events. Calling for a redefinition of "free speech" to include acts of civil disobedience and protest further blurred the line between "text" and "action," reaffirming that writing, reading, and doing were one and the same. In this light, the reader herself was a medium for the message—one whose ontology and epistemology knit together to affect ideology—rendering activism a text and texts a site of activism in a manner not unlike that proposed by Roland Barthes in "From Work to Text" (1971). Barthes argues that the Text "asks of the reader a practical collaboration" in which she helps "produce" the Text and with it "participates in its own way in a social utopia," or "that space where no language has a hold over any other."[58] Both SDS and Barthes saw readers and texts as mutually constitutive, and recognized that it was through the process of producing each other that reader-texts participated in a democratic space. This process of exchange not only rendered the reader a medium for the radical message, but also transformed her into a revolutionary site—one that could not help but reject official narratives that disallowed her part in their creation.

Reading the Left Anew

Rereading SDS through its print culture complicates simplistic representations of the New Left found in conventional histories and cultural memory. The volume and variety of genres, issues, and authors in SDS's archive resist reductive narratives that either demonize or deify the movement and its participants, instead revealing an organization of many contradictory parts which catalyzed significant social change even as its flawed membership and methods seemingly thwarted its endgame of creating a participatory democracy in America. SDS print demonstrates that many participated in authoring their selves and the movement, challenging the narrative that SDS consisted of three or four dominant personalities, and replacing it with a story of popular difference. Contrastingly, the continuity of print modes and aims among different factions of the New Left too suggests greater cohesion to this loose coalition than scholars have recognized heretofore. The belief that print's production, replication, and transmission was power, action, and revolution bridged widely varying factional territory, including the two camps into which SDS split in 1969, the "action faction" and the "praxis axis." Most scholarship marks this split as the end of the movement. Although the "action faction" demanded aggressive confrontation, as opposed to the continued educative grassroots organizing of the "praxis axis," SDS's print problematizes this division since readers, like Weathermen, were considered revolutionary sites that could not help but be actively engaged in the radical cause. SDS's theories of revolutionary literacy collapse "action" and "praxis" into one behavior—reading—therein demonstrating that the movement's various "factions" were united even when "divided." Student radical print culture provides a new occasion for and means of examining the structure, ideology, and practices of the New Left, as well as the dominant narratives describing the rise and fall of student activism in the postwar period.

Studying SDS's print culture too offers a more nuanced understanding of "participatory democracy" as a political mode, highlighting both its limitations and successes as necessarily authored by its print. While radical student print did awaken many individuals to political self-determination, the potentiality of "living documents" to effect perpetual change in each individual also contributed to the movement's struggles. Early documents called for self-determination and individual choice, but the multiplicity of choices also facilitated political transience. Indeed, the many radical causes with their individual members, programs, aims, and presses institutionalized fragmentation of the New Left into Yippies, Diggers, Weathermen, Young Lords, Black Panthers, PLPers, RYMers, and women's libbers. Even within particular organizations, multi-issue organizing split the focus among many issues all readily printed for anticipated readers' consumption. It was easy to move from one cause to another and subsequently forestall organizational structures from taking hold. Despite these limitations, however, participatory democracy had its successes, as evidenced both by increased activism and grassroots civic participation that persist even now in the face of the Iraq War, and by the "rebirth" of SDS in 2006.[59] In fact, even SDS's fragmentation, which many scholars have deemed an unqualified "failure," is evidence of a movement toward participatory democracy. If one end of the New Left's struggle was helping informed individuals work toward and share in the "decisions determining the quality and direction" of their lives, then the many groups emerging from the radical student Left can be seen as both vehicles and evidence of this concerted, individualized civic engagement. The members of these groups chose to participate in their specific organization because it spoke to their particular lived condition and needs. Thus, on a micro-level, they were independently determining the social structure of their lives, and they did so through adapting the radical print culture they engaged with as part of the larger movement.

Finally, examining the radically collaborative readership conjured by New Left print reveals the movement's place in the larger postwar epistemological revolution that sought to liberate knowledge for all reader-subjects. It is no coincidence that SDS emerged as a significant movement in the 1960s that also marked the arrival of poststructuralism, reader-response, and metafiction, all which invoked a radical revision of reading and challenged the dominance of singular, paternalistic "truths." Julie Rivkin and Michael Ryan have identified this link between medium and message, arguing "post-structuralism would be self-consciously radical, a putting into question or play of the methods rational thought traditionally used to describe the world."[60] Categories like "author," "reader," and "work" became increasingly complicated in this sociocultural climate which unflinchingly interrogated the power dynamics implicit in these seemingly static positions. Thus, revisiting the New Left via its print culture helps illuminate the complex relationship between readership and citizenship in Cold War America, and provides another way of understanding the processes involved in narrating nation.

Notes

1. Kirkpatrick Sale, *SDS* (New York: Random House, 1973), 125.

2. Ibid., 7; and Wini Breines, *Community and Organization in the New Left: 1962–1968* (New York: Praeger, 1982), 67.

3. "Dialogue or Revolution?" in *The Politics and Anti-Politics of the Young*, ed. Michael Brown (Beverly Hills: Glencoe Press, 1969), 127.

4. John McDermott, "Knowledge Is Power," in *The Movement toward a New America*, ed. Mitchell Goodman (New York: Alfred A. Knopf, 1970), 343.

5. Todd Gitlin, "The Battlefields and the War," in *The New Student Left*, ed. Mitchell Cohen and Dennis Hale (Boston: Beacon Press, 1967), 133.

6. This reference and the chapter's title allude to Marshall McLuhan's books *Understanding Media* (New York: Signet Books, 1964) and *The Medium Is the Massage* (New York: Bantam Books, 1967), which influenced student radicals' understanding of the mass media, the military-industrial complex, and print culture's political potential.

7. Jennifer Frost, *"An Interracial Movement of the Poor": Community Organizing and the New Left in the 1960s* (New York: New York University Press, 2001), 3; Van Gosse. *Rethinking the New Left* (New York: Palgrave, 2005).

8. Students for a Democratic Society, *The Port Huron Statement* (New York: SDS, 1964), 3; and James Simon Kunen, *The Strawberry Statement: Notes of a College Revolutionary* (New York: Avon Books, 1970), 11.

9. Students for a Democratic Society, "NOT WITH MY LIFE YOU DON'T!!!," in *Vandals in the Bomb Factory*, ed. G. Louis Heath (Metuchen, N.J.: The Scarecrow Press, 1976), 302–3.

10. James Miller, *"Democracy Is in the Streets": From Port Huron to the Siege of Chicago* (New York: Simon and Schuster, 1987), 166; and Breines, *Community*, 6.

11. SDS, *Port Huron*, 6.

12. Sale, *SDS*, 30.

13. Kevin Mattson, *Intellectuals in Action: The Origins of the New Left and Radical Liberalism, 1945–1970* (University Park: Penn State University Press, 2002), 129.

14. Ibid., 81.

15. Sale, *SDS*, 73.

16. New Left materials are rife with images of birth and rebirth, suggesting the new life to which the radical is born. William L. O'Neill's *Coming Apart* discusses this rhetoric of rebirth, noting "Tom Hayden said that to become a radical was like giving birth to yourself" (New York: Quadrangle Books, 1971), 279.

17. SDS, *Port Huron*, 5.

18. Ibid., 2.

19. Ibid., 7.

20. Sale, *SDS*, 49.

21. Although SDS was not particularly successful at gender parity, Sara Evans notes that women were important participants in the Port Huron convention. Evans, *Personal Politics* (New York: Alfred A. Knopf, 1979), 113.

22. Sale's *SDS* referred to the titular group as "the prodigal writers" (89).

23. Ibid., 69.

24. Ibid.

25. Massimo Teodori, ed., *The New Left: A Documentary History* (Indianapolis, IN: Bobbs-Merrill, 1969), 163.

26. SDS, *Port Huron*, 61, 50.

27. This membership groundswell also owed much to the New England Free Press (NEFP), which reprinted many of SDS's pamphlets for wider circulation. Founded as a collective in South Boston, the NEFP was responsible for many of the radical publications in America from 1967 on, including the groundbreaking feminist text *Our Bodies, Ourselves* (1970).

28. Richard Rothstein qtd. in Breines, *Community*, 136–37.

29. Mark Rudd, "Columbia: Notes on the Spring Rebellion," in *The New Left Reader*, ed. Carl Oglesby (New York: Grove Press, 1969), 294.

30. Sale, *SDS*, 125; Louis Menashe and Ronald Radosh, *Teach-ins: U.S.A.* (New York: Frederick A. Praeger, 1967), 343; Sale, *SDS*, 255; Alan Adelson, *SDS* (New York: Scribner's, 1972), 177; and Todd Gitlin, *The Whole World Is Watching* (Berkeley: University of California Press, 1980), 53.

31. Robert J. Glessing, *The Underground Press in America* (Bloomington: Indiana University Press, 1970), 10. Postwar America's underground press began with *The Village Voice* (1955) and *The Realist* (1958). These papers and subsequent others increasingly targeted the young, articulated radical politics, and challenged the status quo. Two radical press syndicates emerged in the 1960s in response to the anti-Left bias in the mass media. The Underground Press Syndicate and the Liberation News Service both sought to "serve their community" and report the stories that were not making it into mainstream news sources: Roger Lewis, *Outlaws of America* (London: Heinrich Hanau, 1972), 24. While the UPS and LNS disseminated articles nationally, local underground papers focused on what was "goin' down" in their backyard, with hundreds of papers like Berkeley's *Barb*, Chicago's *Seed*, and Milwaukee's *Kaleidoscope* springing up in the 1960s. These papers and others covered topics from the Black Power, Women's, and anti–Vietnam War movements to sex, drugs, and rock 'n' roll. Unlike mainstream news sources, many underground papers had open submission policies. Some published first name by-lines only, reinforcing the "everyman" quality to authorship, readership, and community. For examples of such, see *The Movement toward A New America: The Beginnings of a Long Revolution: A Collage of What?* that was "assembled by Mitchell Goodman A Charter Member of the Great Conspiracy, in behalf of The Movement" (New York: Alfred A. Knopf, 1970), title page; *Fire!: reports from the underground press* which was "put together by Paul, Jon & Charlotte" and which illustrates the creative, collage-like format of underground print that resisted the "straight line" format and ideology of the mainstream mass media (New York: E. P. Dutton, 1970); or Raymond Mungo's autobiography, *Famous Long Ago: My Life and Hard Times with Liberation News Service* (Boston: Beacon Press, 1970). Glessing, Lewis, and Mungo discuss the underground press, oftentimes performing the form and content of the media they are examining. An early work that resists such is James Danky's *Undergrounds* (Madison: The State Historical Society of Wisconsin, 1974), and a more recent example is Ellen Gruber Garvey's "Out of the Mainstream and into the Streets" in *Perspectives on American Book History*, ed. Scott E. Casper, Joanne D. Chaison, and Jeffrey D. Groves (Amherst: University of Massachusetts Press, 2002), 367–402.

32. The power of SDS's print can be seen in Xerox's branding. Originally called "Scientific Data Systems," or "SDS," the Xerox Company changed its name to discourage

confusion or perception of collusion with Students for a Democratic Society. Sale, *SDS*, 612.

33. Gitlin, *Whole World*, 62–63.

34. Sale, *SDS*, 77.

35. Adelson, *SDS*, 168, 169.

36. Kunen, *Strawberry*, 36–37.

37. Jerry L. Avorn, Andrew Cane, Mark Jaffe, et al., *Up Against the Ivy Wall: A History of the Columbia Crisis* (New York: Atheneum, 1969), 122.

38. Todd Gitlin, "From Universality to Difference: Notes on the Fragmentation of the Idea of the Left," *Contention* 2, 2 (1993), 34.

39. For further discussion of COINTELPRO's activities, see Cathy Perkus, *COINTEL-PRO: The FBI's Secret War on Political Freedom* (New York: Monad Press, 1975); Athan Theoharis, *Spying on Americans* (Philadelphia: Temple University Press, 1978); Ward Churchill and Jim Vander Wall, *The COINTELPRO Papers* (Cambridge: South End Press, 2002); and James Kirkpatrick Davis, *Spying on America* (New York: Praeger, 1992).

40. Seven of twelve points recommended the use of print culture to "confuse and disrupt New Left activities," including leafleting campuses and neighborhoods; sending anonymous letters to parents, employers, and presses; looking to thwart activities through "misinformation"; and ridiculing the New Left with "cartoons, photographs, and anonymous letters." Churchill and Vander Wall, *COINTELPRO*, 184–85.

41. Mario Savio, "Thirty Years Later," *The Free Speech Movement*, ed. Robert Cohen and Reginald E. Zelnik (Berkeley: University of California Press, 2002), 63; Sandy Lillydahl, "Adventures in Participatory Democracy," *Students for a Democratic Society: A Graphic History*, ed. Paul Buhle (New York: Hill and Wang, 2008), 197; Kunen, *Strawberry*, 101; Tom Hayden qtd. in Miller, *"Democracy Is in the Streets,"* 45.

42. Adelson, *SDS*, 177.

43. Ibid., 175, 177, 180.

44. SDS, "NOT WITH MY LIFE," 305.

45. Van Gosse, *Rethinking the New Left* (New York: Palgrave, 2005), 94; and Maurice Isserman and Michael Kazin, *America Divided: The Civil War of the 1960s*, 2nd ed. (Oxford: Oxford University Press, 2004), 188.

46. William Slate, ed., *Power to the People!* (New York: Tower Publications, 1970), preface.

47. Students for a Democratic Society, *Don't Mourn—Organize!* (San Francisco: THE MOVEMENT PRESS, 1968), 5.

48. Howard Zinn, "How Democratic Is America?" *How Democratic Is America? Responses to the New Left Challenge*, ed. Howard Zinn (Chicago: Rand McNally, 1971), 49.

49. Gitlin, *Whole World*, 53.

50. SDS, *Port Huron*, 61.

51. SDS, *Don't Mourn*, 14.

52. Miller, *"Democracy,"* 323.

53. Students for a Democratic Society, "Take a Step Into America," in *Don't Mourn—Organize!*, 16.

54. Richard Flacks, "Chicago: Organizing the Unemployed" (New York: SDS/ERAP, 1964), 6.

55. SDS, "Take a Step," 11. Mitchell Cohen and Dennis Hale write in the preface to their anthology *The New Student Left* that a central tension of SDS (and SNCC) was the

"indigenism" versus "elitism" debate. The authors note "indigenism refers to the theory that the exploited know best how to solve their problems, but are lacking organizational and administrative skills which it is the role of the student organizer to provide. This is a commonly accepted theory within SDS, and the debate is usually couched in terms of helping the poor to discover their 'real' needs." Cohen and Hale, *The New Student Left* (Boston: Beacon Press, 1967), xxv. This was not unrecognized by SDS. A key question on SDS's "ERAP summer institute agenda" was "Should we—have we the right to—impose our values and our vision on the community?" Miller, "Democracy," 194.

56. Heath, ed., *Vandals in the Bomb Factory*, 247–53, 256–57, 270–72.

57. Students for a Democratic Society, "Suggestions for Legal Self-Defense in Chicago," in ibid., 249.

58. Roland Barthes, *Image-Music-Text* (New York: Hill and Wang, 1977), 163, 164.

59. SDS's rebirth is chronicled in the recent book *Students for a Democratic Society: A Graphic History*. Significantly, the book's form—with its collection of accounts from multiple authors in varied visual layouts—mirrors that of earlier radical print, as does its cover reading "written (mostly) by Harvey Pekar; Art (mostly) by Gary Dumm, Edited by Paul Buhle." The text depicts the "rebirth" of SDS as an evolution that modifies old concepts in light of new ideologies and media (like the Internet). Former SDSer Maurice Isserman's article "How Old Is the New SDS?" (*Chronicle of Higher Education*, March 2, 2007) points out some similarities between the new and old New Left, but notes that the media differences (paper versus virtual) make for very different organizations.

60. Julie Rivkin and Michael Ryan, *Literary Theory: An Anthology* (London: Blackwell, 1998), 334.

2 The Education of a Cold War Conservative

Anti-Communist Literature of the
1950s and 1960s

LAURA JANE GIFFORD

CONSERVATIVE COLD Warriors of the 1950s and 1960s used books, and especially paperback books, as a primary means of mobilizing support for conservative anti-Communist causes. Conservative scholars such as James Burnham, Friedrich Hayek, and Russell Kirk saw their volumes become bestsellers. Government activists and public intellectuals including J. Edgar Hoover and William F. Buckley, Jr., wrote widely read anti-Communist polemics. Former Communists like Whittaker Chambers published memoirs of their days on the dark side. By the 1960s, with conservatives ascending to a dominant position in the Republican Party, programmatic statements such as Barry Goldwater's *Conscience of a Conservative* (1960) shared space on conservative Cold Warriors' bookshelves with conspiracy-oriented works like John A. Stormer's *None Dare Call It Treason* (1964).

Anti-Communist publications reached heights of popularity difficult for twenty-first-century Americans to comprehend, steeped as we are today in the political culture of the Internet and cable television news. Goldwater's *Conscience* went through twenty printings in its first four years, eventually selling 3.5 million copies.[1] Stormer's volume, first published in February 1964 by the vanity publisher Liberty Bell Press, went through twelve printings and sold 1.8 million copies within six months of its release.[2] Anti-Communist conservative writers and their supporters, however, saw their texts not just as stand-alone works, but also as a part of an alternative library aimed at creating networks of educated readers.

First, to create this network, small publishers like Liberty Bell Press offered quantity discounts, urging readers to buy in bulk to "do your part in this vital educational job." For example, one copy of Stormer's book cost 75 cents, but 25 copies were available for $10 and 100 for $30—and for the wealthy and optimistic, orders of 1000 or more copies wholesaled for 20 cents apiece.[3] The Constitution and Free Enterprise Foundation offered purchasers of their reprint of Roger Lea MacBride's *Treaties versus the Constitution* (1955) the opportunity to obtain up to a 50 percent discount on quantity orders.[4] Other publishers made similar offers.

Second, reading groups, educational organizations, and periodicals ranging from current-events magazines to mail-order catalogs provided guidance and encouragement for readers. Interested citizens could choose to attend well-subscribed courses like the "History of Communistic Aggression," an adult education offering at Santa Ana Junior College in Orange County, California, or utilize the "Freedom Study Clubs Guide" provided by the California Free Enterprise Association, a group funded by berry magnate Walter Knott.[5] Even organizations like the Texas-based Life Line Foundation, established in 1958 by H. L. Hunt and famous for its radio programs, distributed a thrice-weekly newsletter and book club information.[6] Citizens took advantage of these guides; the historian Lisa McGirr tells of one southern California doctor who was reputed to have organized 44 study groups. Letters written by conservatives to the editor of the Orange County (California) *Register* in the early 1960s "urged their fellow citizens to read, read, and read some more."[7] College students could join the Intercollegiate Society of Individualists, an organization founded by the libertarian journalist and editor Frank Chodorov in 1952 that mailed conservative literature, free of charge, to students on its mailing list and organized intellectual gatherings for young people.

Conservative periodicals ranging from *National Review*, the "switchboard" of the conservative movement, to single-author publications like *The Dan Smoot Report* maintained a symbiotic relationship with authors, advocating specific volumes while authors recommended their publications.[8] The Bookmailer, a mail-order distribution company, offered a substantial selection of general-interest volumes on subjects as diverse as the Abominable Snowman and Dr. Spock's childcare advice. The company used its catalogs to guide readers and chose to publish only right-thinking texts. The Bookmailer may have carried Herbert L. Matthews's apologetic biography of Cuban dictator Fidel Castro, *The Cuban Story*, but the October 15, 1961, edition of "The Bookmailer News" shaped readers' attitudes by explaining, "The author expands his tortured logic which still justifies admiration for the ideals, talents and personality of Castro." On the other hand, company president Lyle H. Munson promoted the in-house publication of *HUAC AND FBI: Targets for*

Abolition, as a "stirring indictment of those who seek to destroy these two investigative bodies."[9]

Third, leading conservative authors provided comprehensive reading lists. Convinced though they were of their own books' importance, these writers understood that cultivating a citizenry enlightened to the dangers of both Communism and the slippery slope called liberalism required more extensive education. Some authors, like Hoover, encouraged their readers to explore the works of the Communist canon to respond effectively to left-wing arguments.[10] Others, like Stormer, provided more comprehensive lists that would educate readers on Communist tactics, the threat of liberalism, and the conservative options available to them.

History has buttressed these authors' belief in print culture's importance. Several recent scholars have described the significance of the written word in forging conservative networks. Sara Diamond has gone so far as to state that the anti-Communist movement survived the demise of Senator Joseph McCarthy partly "because it was the beneficiary of a corporate-sponsored flood of anticommunist print and broadcast propaganda, directed at the U.S. public."[11] The difference between "corporate" and "establishment" is, as we shall see, significant; oil tycoons like Hunt and J. Howard Pew donated millions toward conservative educational causes, but anti-Communist literary activism continued to operate largely outside traditional publishing networks. Chip Berlet, Diamond, and others have explored how right-wing publishing networks supported preferred ideological positions and shifted movement causes into the political mainstream, and scholars including John Andrew, Mary Brennan, McGirr, Gregory Schneider, and Jonathan Schoenwald have traced the conservative movement's progression from ideology to activism.[12]

Careful reading reveals many perspectives regarding the details of the Communist menace, but one consistent theme: a fundamental optimism regarding the capability of the United States to successfully repel the Soviet threat *if* Americans were educated in the tools their Founding Fathers had provided for them. To speak of optimism among citizens dedicated to "anti" activity might appear contradictory, but all of these authors believed the United States was an exceptional nation, set apart—at least in the beginning—by a unique set of republican and classical liberal economic principles. These principles provided the best opportunity in history for humans to live free lives and develop to their fullest potential. The authors' optimism, however, was tempered with anxiety that socialist ideas could hoodwink Americans, leading them to abandon their unique and exceptional heritage. Without exception, these writers believed they were undertaking a vital mission. Their knowledge of America's promise and the dangers to it had to be disseminated, studied, discussed and acted upon immediately for the survival of the free world.

In addition to existing in an alternate political reality, many of these volumes constitute an alternate *publishing* reality. For example, of the 26 books on Stormer's list, only eight were published in the general-market press. Of these, two came from the relatively small Idaho press Caxton Printers, Ltd. Two major publishers of primarily conservative material, Henry Regnery Co. and Devin-Adair, Inc., published six additional volumes. Interest groups and vanity presses including the Foundation for Economic Education, the Church League of America and the Heritage Foundation published the remaining twelve volumes, plus Stormer's own work. Even Goldwater's *Conscience of a Conservative* began its print run as a product of Victor Publishing Company, a dummy imprint set up by supporter Clarence Manion and licensed as a nonprofit based in Shepherdsville, Kentucky.[13]

Newspaper editor and author M. Stanton Evans explained the ramifications of this pattern in a 1964 review of *None Dare Call It Treason* and two other vanity-press publications of the same year, Phyllis Schlafly's *A Choice Not an Echo* (Pere Marquette Press) and J. Evetts Haley's *A Texan Looks at Lyndon* (The Palo Duro Press). Because each of these books, like several others on Stormer's list, was published "privately, outside recognized channels of communication," "none is to be found on any certified best-seller list." Indeed, only *Conscience* and J. Edgar Hoover's *Masters of Deceit* made the all-time combined bestseller list of volumes selling over two million copies between 1895 and 1975. More significant, despite its powerful sales, Stormer's book did not make the top ten list of books sold in 1964.[14]

Evans acknowledged that many "one-man" publications were put out by "crackpots who produce outside the going circuits of communication and rail at the community which denies them facilities and an audience." He placed authors like Stormer squarely in a different milieu—that of the "private pamphleteer," like Tom Paine, "who tilts his pen at the machinery of established discourse." For Stormer and others, "dissent is their vocation," and this vocation led them to "[fill] the gap between what the Establishment thinks people ought to read and what they in fact want to read." With a communications industry "in thrall to the ideologues of the Left," the Liberty Bell Presses of the world delivered an essential product. Evans noted that the hunger for this sort of publication was visible in the volume of requests for conservative books in stores and the stacks of them available in drugstore and airport bookstalls. Stormer and his cohort were patriots, enlightening the populace to the dangers at hand.[15]

Recent scholars have noted that while alerting Americans to the danger Communists posed to American freedom, these "patriots" often supported some less enlightened notions of freedom—most notably, unfounded concerns about Communist infiltration of the civil rights movement, and fear of the non-white world's rising power in organizations like the United Nations. Indeed, as McGirr notes, Stormer sputtered that "nearly one-third of the new nations of the world have no traditional concepts of law. Some have not completely rejected cannibalism."[16] Racial extremism was not limited to vanity presses. A commercial press, Devin-Adair, published Rosalie Gordon's *Nine Men Against America*. In this book she excoriated the Supreme Court's *Brown v. Board of Education* decision as a "revolution of totalitarian proportions."[17] Sara Diamond has observed that Fred Schwarz at Prentice-Hall and Edgar Bundy of The Church League of America maintained limited contacts with anti-Semitic and racist organizations, while J. Edgar Hoover's concerns about Communist influence upon civil rights leaders like Martin Luther King, Jr., were published by Henry Holt and Co.[18]

While the Liberty Bell Presses and Victor Publishing Companies of the publishing sphere tilted their pens at the establishment, larger conservative publishers like Henry Regnery Co. were also "born in opposition," to borrow the words of the company's founder.[19] Henry Regnery's disillusionment with the New Deal began in graduate school, and while working for the Resettlement Administration in 1937 he was horrified by what he termed a "bureaucratic nightmare."[20] Regnery became associated with the journal *Human Events* shortly after its inception in 1944. The *Human Events* group began publishing pamphlets, leading to the development of the Henry Regnery Co. imprint, which released its first books in 1947.[21] Over time, the Regnery catalog came to include many standards of the conservative canon, including the Budenz and McCarthy/Bozell volumes on Stormer's list and Russell Kirk's paradigmatic *The Conservative Mind* (1953). Regnery and his staff continued, however, to print a diverse selection of works on world affairs and even fiction.[22]

Regnery saw his company as fulfilling an urgent need to speak truth to the world about the dangers of Communism and collectivism—and the benefits of pursuing conservative ideals. Accordingly, he initially sought to establish his firm as a nonprofit, "not because I had any ideological objection to profits, but because, as it seemed to me then and does still, in matters of excellence the market is a poor judge." He intended to function like a university press, publishing books for their ideas' merits and not their financial viability. Unfortunately for Regnery, the Internal Revenue Service felt differently. The Henry Regnery Co. incorporated as a for-profit publishing house in 1948—although

Regnery's continuing interest in publishing for the sake of ideas rather than profit meant it didn't make much of one, especially in its early years.[23]

BY FOCUSING on a single list, we become its authors' student, understanding where they placed their priorities in the anti-Communist struggle, including where and how they believed Communism should be fought. We can also see how print culture informed the development of an active conservative constituency in American life. Stormer's list in particular reveals how print developed and energized the anti-Communist movement. *None Dare Call It Treason* was more alarmist than some volumes, but Stormer's list was diverse, encompassing a broad spectrum of conservative takes on the Communist menace. Furthermore, *Treason* was published in 1964, well along in the Cold War-era conservative movement but before Goldwater's electoral defeat prompted reappraisal of the conservative cause and, in some circles, a greater focus on domestic social concerns. Combined, these volumes demonstrate the comprehensive education conservative print culture could provide. All but one were readily available in paperback form, rendering them an affordable source for education.[24]

Liberty Bell Press printed Stormer's list at the rear of his book, along with his information on how to obtain the volumes. The first place Stormer directed his readers to was "any American Opinion Library." These libraries were the official bookstores and reading rooms of the conservative John Birch Society, established around the country to further the Society's cause. By directing interested readers to a physical location, Stormer encouraged them to actively engage with fellow conservatives. This allowed the list to lead to an educational process very different from the casual practice of following a reading list put out by the Modern Library or keeping up-to-date with Book-of-the-Month Club selections. Stormer also notified his readers that the books could be obtained by mail from The Bookmailer, or Poor Richard's Book Shop of Los Angeles, providing mailing addresses and prices for each volume; a solo reading experience was better than none at all. He even included a list of relevant government documents to peruse, with prices and instructions on how to order them from the U.S. Government Printing Office.[25]

Because Stormer was self-publishing through a vanity press, his list was not constrained by the strictures of larger publishers seeking to promote their own products. Indeed, his list did not even include publisher information. Stormer noted only the title, author's last name, and the volume's price— and, significantly, whether the book was presently available in paper.[26] Stormer viewed his audience as price-conscious, and he wanted to make the acquisition process as easy as possible. Even his referral of readers to American

Opinion Libraries had financial as well as organizational importance; if readers picked up volumes directly from a storefront, they would pay no shipping fees, and they might even be able to obtain lending copies or purchase used books.

The quantity discounts and group dynamics that authors like Stormer encouraged made print an exceptionally viable source for anti-Communist education. Print led concerned citizens to meet and discuss conservative ideas because they could share and distribute printed materials easily. One activist recalled that since "newsletters were copied and spread around, if you didn't have the money to order a newsletter from the Christian Anti-Communism Crusade or *Human Events* . . . people just shared all these things." Historians such as McGirr have collected anecdotes describing the ways in which books and tracts were shared. One woman, for example, recounted how a relative offered to care for her two young children while she recovered from an illness—if she agreed to read several conservative books.[27] The print format of many books also encouraged widespread distribution. While handsome, hardcover first editions were often available from conservative publishers like Henry Regnery Co. or mainstream houses like Prentice-Hall, the bulk of readers paged through inexpensive, pocket-sized paperbacks containing small print, narrow margins and lightweight interior pages and covers.

Stormer's book list took readers through five subthemes. The first three—"Communist Philosophy, Strategy and Tactics," "Communist Infiltration in Government," and "The Decay in Basic Institutions"—were geared toward telling readers what was *wrong* with the United States and the world in light of the Communist threat. Most books sounded warning bells of danger on the horizon—or closer. Stormer went on, however, to suggest another two series of volumes—"The Positive Approach" and "On the Offensive"—designed to establish a positive alternative to the gloomy world liberal and collectivist triumphs would create. This list would therefore educate readers in the basics of Communism and the menace it posed to government and society, and then teach them how society *should* function and what could be done to restore America to the right path.

Three key lessons surfaced throughout this body of literature. First, the liberal establishment of the period was making Communists' work far too simple. Second, the collectivist menace bore in its deepest assumptions the seeds of its own destruction: collectivists fundamentally misunderstood the orientation of human nature. And finally, if the United States was to be saved, educated action was absolutely essential. Along these lines, most argued that traditional American beliefs were in jeopardy, faltering under the weight of an unengaged populace blind to the dangers of creeping socialism. Different authors accused the era's most popular public figures, from Franklin Roosevelt to John Foster Dulles, of playing suspicious roles in an organized pattern of Communist subversion.

However, authors' positions varied widely on the specifics. Stormer, for example, dismissed most unionism as collectivism under another name, while Louis Budenz argued that since Soviet Communism was in reality a chief foe of free trade unionism, it was impossible to combat Stalinism effectively without supporting trade unions.[28] Authors came down on both sides of important contemporary questions like civil rights for African Americans. Still, central concerns held fairly constant. These themes help us understand the overall impression a reader would gain by reading the recommended books.

Perhaps the most common frustration voiced by the authors on Stormer's list was that of liberal naiveté. Some authors believed well-meaning liberals were inadvertently guiding the United States toward Soviet-type slavery. Rosalie Gordon, on the other hand, felt this process was deliberate. In her view, Franklin Roosevelt was "architect and first leader of America's slide into a European-type authoritarian system of government."[29] Gordon's *Nine Men Against America* (1958) castigated those Supreme Court members who had joined the court since the Roosevelt administration for their lack of judicial experience and excoriated Court decisions for their legislative intent, including the decision in *Brown vs. Board of Education*.[30] Her commitment to civil libertarianism, however, led her to also attack the Court's decision to uphold Japanese internment during World War II, calling it "perhaps the greatest assault on real civil liberties in our history."[31]

The Texas radio commentator and newsletter publisher Dan Smoot also insinuated that liberals were more than just unwitting accomplices in the work of the Communist conspiracy. In *The Invisible Government* he argued that the Council on Foreign Relations, a well-connected nonpartisan interest group dedicated to promoting a "positive" foreign policy, was little more than an "invisible government" dedicated to converting America into a participant in a one-world socialist system of governance.[32] The Council's membership from its founding in 1921 had included such American statesmen as Edward Stettinius, John Foster Dulles, John J. McCloy, Nelson Rockefeller, Adlai Stevenson, and Ralph Bunche—as well as a few infamous figures like Alger Hiss.[33]

Others made more modest claims. The young conservative pundit and *National Review* editor William F. Buckley, Jr., publicly repudiated John Birch Society founder Robert Welch for developing conspiracy theories that accused Dwight D. Eisenhower of being a Communist.[34] Even so, in *Up from Liberalism*, Buckley explained that danger lurked in the "passion for modulation" characteristic of Eisenhowerian "Modern Republicanism."[35] Buckley argued this lack of vigor endangered American freedom: "In seeking out the bland, the modulated approach, in blurring distinctions, and in acclimatizing men to life without definition, we erode the Western position; and that, take or leave a few bombs and airplanes, is all we have got."[36]

Liberal reluctance to see collectivists as dangerous Soviet allies led to problems both at home and abroad. Robert Morris, Republican counsel to the Tydings Committee, was frustrated by how partisan political considerations trumped an opportunity to truly investigate the validity of Senator Joseph McCarthy's 1950 accusations of Communist infiltration in the State Department. Morris explained that the committee's chief counsel was instructed to conduct a quick investigation and exonerate the State Department of all subversion charges, despite very concerning evidence to the contrary.[37] Buckley and L. Brent Bozell, a senior editor at *National Review* and Buckley's brother-in-law, made similar charges in *McCarthy and His Enemies* (1954). In the foreign sphere, reformed American Communist Nathaniel Weyl pointed out that the "full and romantic coverage" of Cuban leader Fidel Castro by liberal journalists such as Herbert Matthews and Edward R. Murrow lulled most Americans into complacency about the menace confronting them just ninety miles off shore.[38]

Several authors explained that many liberals were led astray because of Communists' skill in appropriating positive terms to describe nefarious aims. Dr. Fred Schwarz, an Australian physician who founded the Christian Anti-Communism Crusade, explicated common Marxian double-speak in his *You Can Trust the Communists (. . . to Do Exactly as They Say!)* (1960). "Righteousness," for example, meant for Communists any conduct that would advance world conquest. "Love," as well, meant anything that would further Marxism. By this definition, then, Stalinist purges could be termed "loving." "Peace" referred only to Communist victory. In short, Schwarz concluded, when Americans insisted on interpreting Communist phraseology in Christian terms, they ended up aiding and abetting them.[39]

Despite their fears, authors on Stormer's list took comfort in knowing that America and its Founding Fathers understood that humans were spiritual creatures, not materialist machines. Louis Budenz was one of many disillusioned revolutionaries laboring to awaken Americans to a danger they knew all too personally. Budenz had served for a number of years as the managing editor of the Communist *Daily Worker.* Arguing that most Americans had not been equipped with the technical understanding necessary to repel Soviet Communism, he offered *The Techniques of Communism* (1954) as a textbook for analytical and critical study. Communism marked the climax of the philosophy of materialism—denial of the existence of God or a world of the spirit. In this philosophy, humans were animals, motivated by materialistic considerations. History progressed through a series of class struggles, a cycle of conflict between the ruling class supported by the state and an oppressed proletariat. Marxists called this process of reaction and stasis "dialectical materialism." Once this cycle ended in the creation of a socialist utopia, humans would attain perfection: a classless society where "new man" would be so perfect that the dictatorship would voluntarily wither away. This was Communism's version of a messianic message. Utopia could be reached, however, only through worldwide Soviet dictatorship, so Soviet triumph was all-important. This, Budenz stressed, was the danger of the Communist message.[40]

Budenz exposed numerous holes in the Communists' theory. First, he argued, the proletariat of which Marx and Lenin spoke was largely fictitious. Workers in the twentieth century had not suffered progressive disintegration of their working and living conditions. Second, the present Soviet structure did not in fact constitute a dictatorship of the proletariat, but rather, the dictatorship of an oligarchy *over* a proletariat.[41] Third, and most significant, Budenz noted that Communists' philosophy of economic determinism evaded the fundamental issue raised and answered by Thomas Aquinas in his *Summa Theologica*: that the existence of motion requires a First Mover. Marx and Lenin never answered the question "what, or who, put the dialectical process in motion in the first place?" By setting Lenin or Stalin up as interpreter or proclaimer of correct Soviet doctrine, Budenz argued, Communists made a tacit admission that their "scientific" process of historical progression was in fact unscientific.[42]

If Communists neglected to take account of the spiritual origins of existence, they also, in businessman Henry Grady Weaver's opinion, failed to contend with the God-given qualities of human nature that made humans fundamentally individualistic.[43] Weaver compared Communists to collectivists throughout history who have believed that human society should be organized like a beehive, where the "common good" is more important than that of the individual. Instead, he argued, humans' purpose in society was to "exchange one good for another good more desired." This system of mutual aid and cooperation for the gain of *each*—a world composed of decisions made by people, not societies—was the true foundation of human interactions.[44] Weaver drew on Jewish and Christian scripture to reinforce his argument.[45]

Barry Goldwater repeated similar concerns about human nature to turn his *Conscience of a Conservative* into one of the most influential books of the

1960s. As the historian Jonathan Schoenwald has noted, Goldwater's slim volume took already-extant ideas, "clarified them, and added examples with which a mainstream audience could identify." The result was a "short primer" that "inspired thousands of Americans to join the still-young conservative movement." The Arizona senator received significant writing help from Bozell, the coauthor of *McCarthy and His Enemies*. At the height of its popularity the book reached the number six spot on the *New York Times* nonfiction bestseller list.[46] Young activist Lee Edwards later recounted that "[for us,] the '60s began not with a bang but with a book."[47] *Conscience* helped stimulate a Goldwater for President movement in 1960 and provided the basis for the Draft Goldwater movement culminating in his presidential run in 1964. A 1962 report on the conservative youth movement Young Americans for Freedom revealed that over 60 percent of the members had read *Conscience*.[48]

Goldwater took the debate over the essence of humanity into the political arena, seeking to correct what he believed was a fundamental misunderstanding of conservative political ideology. "I have been much concerned," he wrote, "that so many people today with Conservative instincts feel compelled to apologize for them. Or if not to apologize directly, to qualify their commitment in a way that amounts to breast-beating." Goldwater mentioned Vice President Nixon's statement that "Republican candidates should be economic conservatives, but conservatives with a heart," and Eisenhower's comment that he was "conservative when it comes to economic problems but liberal when it comes to human problems." Still other GOP leaders, Goldwater pointed out, insisted on referring to themselves as "'progressive' Conservatives." "These formulations," he argued, "are tantamount to an admission that Conservatism is a narrow, mechanistic *economic* theory that may work very well as a bookkeeper's guide, but cannot be relied upon as a comprehensive political philosophy."[49]

Goldwater was out to reclaim conservatism as a viable, admirable, comprehensive philosophy. "The Conservative approach," he proclaimed in his foreword, "is nothing more or less than an attempt to apply the wisdom and experience and the revealed truths of the past to the problems of today. The challenge is not to find new or different truths, but to learn how to apply established truths to the problems of the contemporary world."[50] Other politicians' waffling did a "great injustice" to conservatism. In fact, they had the situation completely reversed: "it is Socialism that subordinates all other considerations to man's material well-being." By contrast, "Conservatives take account of the *whole* man." Furthermore, conservatives understood that the economic and spiritual aspects of human nature were "inextricably intertwined. He cannot be economically free, or even economically efficient, if he is enslaved politically; conversely, man's political freedom is illusory if he is dependent for his economic needs on the State." A true conservative was offended by any debasement of an individual person.[51]

The authors on Stormer's list agreed that conservative, Judeo-Christian American values could save the United States and civilization itself from Communist enslavement. This was possible, however, only if educated Cold Warriors took concerted action. Most volumes encouraged their readers to read because reading allowed them to understand the positions of their enemies—Communists and, by extension, the liberal establishment—and fortify themselves with anti-Communist information drawn from government reports and conservative sources. Books armed educated anti-Communists and charged them with a moral duty to become activists in the cause of freedom. Halfhearted dedication was not enough; in the words of James Burnham, "To win we must also resolve to *endure*. We must have the will to survive and to be free."[52]

Throughout *The Techniques of Communism*, for example, Louis Budenz told his readers where to find information necessary to combat Communism. He advocated reading the books Communists themselves used to indoctrinate members.[53] He frequently cited the published reports of the House Committee on Un-American Activities and the Senate Subcommittee on Internal Security, as well as noted anti-Communists like J. B. Matthews, former HUAC counsel.[54] Budenz also recommended that anti-Communists guide their reading with bibliographies prepared by Wisconsin Representative Charles E. Kersten, Vice President Richard M. Nixon, and E. F. Tompkins of the Hearst newspapers. Finally, Budenz's own weekly column and *Counterattack* newsletter were "essential" reading.[55] Once educated, readers needed to do more. The United States was in dire need of intelligent and continuous action by community leaders. After all, a member of an infiltrated organization could believe him or herself entirely loyal and yet be influenced by the Communist in control of his local organization. To ensure their security, Americans *must* know the current Communist Party line; they *must* expose it to their elected officials, they *must* support patriotic organizations and they *must* maintain vigorous support of congressional inquiries and other government action.[56]

Stormer's list made it clear that reading had to lead to action. While Stormer believed the chances of survival were slim because collectivism had progressed too far, he called for a last-ditch effort to fight. He agreed with Budenz that dedicated Americans must first get the facts on the Communist conspiracy through his list, and then enlist others to take coordinated action. Stormer encouraged his readers to read at least two daily newspapers with opposite editorial viewpoints, as well as at least one weekly newspaper or magazine specializing in in-depth coverage of conservative activities. Possible candidates might include *Human Events*, *The Wanderer* (a Catholic publication), and *The Dan Smoot Report*. Readers should join organizations like the American Legion, the Daughters of the American Revolution, the John Birch Society, the Cardinal Mindszenty Foundation, the Christian Anti-Communist Crusade, Americans for Constitutional Action, Young Americans for Freedom, and the Foundation for Economic Education. Committed anti-Communists must get into politics and organize, organize, organize— and above all, they must make a spiritual commitment to fight Communism based upon their religious faith.[57] "The choice is yours," Stormer warned. "You can throw out your chest with pride and say, 'It can't happen here.' But nearly every one of the 800-million people captured by the communists since 1945 doubtless said the same thing."[58]

Books addressing problems in specific institutions also advocated civic education. Augustin Rudd, chairman of the New York Chapter of the Sons of the American Revolution's Educational Committee, warned that statist, pro-collectivist academic curricula had taken over many American public schools. Indoctrination of American children posed a clear and present danger to the future of the United States. Even so, Rudd sustained his faith that if books like his *Bending the Twig* (1957) revealed the truth, "there can be no question as to the ultimate outcome of this fight."[59] American parents would take back their educational institutions. Much water had passed under the historical bridge since Arthur Bliss Lane, former ambassador to Poland, wrote his *I Saw Poland Betrayed* (1948), but his memoir continued to offer instructive advice to aspiring foreign policy activists. The United States, he wrote, must demonstrate strident resolve to defend itself and its allies. The Soviet Union believed that even if the United States objected to an international incident, once initial public fervor died down Americans would lose interest and move on. The end result of such shallow commitment was a world where the Soviets could act with impunity.[60] If Americans could maintain their passion for their own free institutions through education, perhaps the tide might turn.

Only one author concluded that the last vestiges of American freedom could no longer be preserved. In *The People's Pottage* (1953), the libertarian financial journalist Garet Garrett argued that the New Deal constituted a revolution in American history from which there was no turning back. "There are those who still think," he argued, "they are holding the pass against a revolution that may be coming up the road. But they are gazing in the wrong direction. The revolution is behind them. It went by in the Night of Depression, singing songs to freedom." Even the most dedicated American could not "defend a world that is already lost."[61] Garrett, however, offered a way out. A painful counterrevolution would be necessary to overturn the new order, but with strong enough leadership it might be possible. "No doubt the people know they can have their Republic back if they want it enough to fight for it and to pay the price. The only point is that no leader has yet appeared with the courage to make them choose."[62] This was a stirring indictment for those who felt charged with the mission of taking back the United States from Communists and slippery-slope liberals.

ANTI-COMMUNIST conservatives who read the books on Stormer's reading list would emerge with a thorough education in the dangers currently confronting their world. They would also, however, have gained the tools to go out and take back their country from creeping liberalism-*cum*-collectivism. They knew what the Communists were up to, and they understood where they could go to learn more. Above all, they knew they were not alone. M. Stanton Evans recalled in *Revolt on the Campus*, a 1961 account of the growing conservative youth movement, that his own experience as a Yale student in the early 1950s was of a university where "liberalism, among faculty and undergraduates alike, ruled virtually without challenge." Late in his freshman year, however, Evans was told of two new organizations, the Intercollegiate Society of Individualists and the Foundation for Economic Education, that thought "along lines like yours." From ISI, Evans received books by the conservative nineteenth-century philosopher Frederic Bastiat, as well as contemporary thinkers like Chodorov. He also received *Human Events* and booklets from the Foundation for Economic Education. He learned of conservative publishers like Regnery and Devin-Adair. But the "discovery beyond price" was that "I was no longer alone. Here were men of reputation— scholars, journalists, publishers—who shared my uneasiness, and who brought factual support and theoretical subtlety to the conservative cause."[63] Not all of the volumes on Stormer's list could be termed "subtle," but as a whole they offered the same sense of belonging.

Readers may have found this journey through the perils of the Cold War scary, but it was also profoundly empowering. Conservatives used the educational networks they developed through reading groups and other ventures to take on future opponents. Over the course of the 1960s conservative activists moved beyond Communism to new concerns like liberal "permissiveness," law and order, big government, and the perceived social excesses of the era.[64] While specific entities waned and new ones grew to replace them, conservatives took advantage of the organizational tools they built in the anti-Communist struggle to take on new issues and arenas. In some cases, they even moved beyond movement politics and into institutional roles where they could directly influence public policy. McGirr tells the story, for example, of Jan Averill of La Habra, California, who moved from participation in Dr. Fred Schwarz's Schools of Anti-Communism in the early 1960s and membership in a study group to become increasingly involved in local education issues. By 1972, she was sufficiently motivated to run for and win a seat on the school board in her district. She told McGirr that without the background provided by her years of participation in a "Tuesday morning study club," she would never have had the confidence to contemplate public office.[65]

The books on lists like Stormer's provided an anti-Communist education that became a profoundly *positive* force for the development of a well-informed and motivated conservative electorate. Stormer himself went on to pen a number of additional volumes under the Liberty Bell Press imprint.[66] In recent years, he has delved into the world of multimedia, creating DVDs and videos on a variety of topics.[67] Today, of course, the Internet has supplanted many of the roles once played by small presses and distribution networks like those described above. As long as American politics remain contentious, however—which is to say, indefinitely—there will be a role for media of some kind in creating educational networks like the ones Stormer and his contemporaries so urgently advocated.

Notes

1. Robert Alan Goldberg, *Barry Goldwater* (New Haven, Conn.: Yale University Press, 1995), 139.

2. John Stormer, *None Dare Call It Treason* (Florissant, Mo.: Liberty Bell Press, 1964), copyright page.

3. Ibid., advertisement at rear of book.

4. Roger Lea MacBride, *Treaties versus the Constitution* (New York: Constitution and Free Enterprise Foundation, 1955), copyright page. One copy of the book cost $1.00; two to eight cost 80 cents apiece; ten to 25 cost 75 cents; 40 to 80 cost 70 cents; 100 to 700 cost 60 cents; and 1,000 or more cost 50 cents apiece.

5. Lisa McGirr, *Suburban Warriors: The Origins of the New American Right* (Princeton, N.J.: Princeton University Press, 2001), 60, 100–101.

6. Mary C. Brennan, *Turning Right in the Sixties: The Conservative Capture of the GOP* (Chapel Hill: University of North Carolina Press, 1995), 61.

7. McGirr, 62, 95.

8. Jonathan M. Schoenwald, *A Time for Choosing: The Rise of Modern American Conservatism* (New York: Oxford University Press, 2001), 38.

9. "The Bookmailer News," October 15, 1961, 3, 7, 20, 21. Manuscript Collection 207, McChord Williams (Mrs.) Collection, University of North Carolina at Charlotte Library.

10. "Bibliography of Major Communist 'Classics,'" in J. Edgar Hoover, *Masters of Deceit* (New York: Pocket Books, 1958), 328–32.

11. Sara Diamond, *Roads to Dominion: Right-Wing Movements and Political Power in the United States* (New York: Guilford, 1995), 38.

12. John A. Andrew III, *The Other Side of the Sixties: Young Americans for Freedom and the Rise of Conservative Politics* (New Brunswick, N.J.: Rutgers University Press, 1997); Chip Berlet, "The Write Stuff: U.S. Serial Print Culture from Conservatives out to Neo-Nazis," *Library Trends* 56 (Winter 2008): 570–600; Brennan; McGirr; Gregory L. Schneider, *Cadres for Conservatism: Young Americans for Freedom and the Rise of the Contemporary Right* (New York: New York University Press, 1999); Schoenwald.

13. For Victor Publishing information, see Rick Perlstein, *Before the Storm: Barry Goldwater and the Unmaking of the American Consensus* (New York: Hill and Wang, 2001), 61. These figures assume that The Bookmailer, despite its diverse offerings from other publishers, constituted an interest group as far as its own publications were concerned. The vast majority of the organization's catalog is dedicated to anti-Communist literature, and it even developed a "Freedom Library" in the late 1950s to aid in distribution of "the literature of freedom" ("The Bookmailer News," October 15, 1961, 31. Manuscript Collection 207, UNC Charlotte). A publisher called Talbot Books first released Henry Grady Weaver's *The Mainspring of Human Progress* in 1947. The Foundation for Economic Education released subsequent editions of Weaver's book. As no information is available on Talbot Books, *Mainspring* is categorized as an interest-group publication. Frederic Bastiat's 1850 work *The Law* constitutes a special case, given its age; the Foundation for Economic Education provided most reprints during this era, so it also is categorized as an interest-group publication.

14. *National Review*, November 3, 1964; Alice Payne Hackett and James Henry Burke, *80 Years of Best Sellers: 1895–1975* (New York: R. R. Bowker Co., 1977), 14, 18, 38, 174, 180. Figures are from the *Publishers Weekly* bestseller records for the periods given. *Conscience* is listed as selling 3,007,000 copies combined through 1975; whether the discrepancy between this figure and the one cited in the introduction is due to sales after 1975 or reflects a lack of accounting by *Publishers Weekly* of the Victor Publishing Co. copies is unknown. *Masters of Deceit* sold 2,192,133 copies. *Conscience* also made the all-time paperback list with 2,500,000 copies sold. The Liberty Bell Press web site claims that 7.2 million copies of *None Dare Call It Treason* have been sold since 1964 (Liberty Bell Press publications page, www.libertybellpress.com/publications.htm, accessed 26 September 2007).

15. *National Review*, November 3, 1964.

16. McGirr, 135; Stormer, 120.

17. Rosalie M. Gordon, *Nine Men Against America: The Supreme Court and Its Attack on American Liberties* (New York: Devin-Adair, 1958), 83–84.

18. Diamond, 93.

19. Henry Regnery, *Memoirs of a Dissident Publisher* (New York: Harcourt Brace Jovanovich, 1979), xi.

20. Ibid., 15–18.

21. Ibid., 31, 38–39.

22. Ibid., 107. Much of the fiction Regnery published did address anti-Communist themes.

23. Ibid., 44–45.

24. Only Augustin Rudd's *Bending the Twig: The Revolution in Education and Its Effect on Our Children* (1957) was unavailable in paperback.

25. Stormer, 254. The government documents Stormer listed included the Senate Internal Security Subcommittee's "The New Drive Against the Anti-Communist Program," "The Bang-Jensen Case," "Interlocking Subversion in Government Departments" and "The Communist Party, USA, What It Is, What It Does: A Handbook for Americans"; the House Committee on Un-American Activities' "The Ideological Fallacies of Communism," "Communist Target—Youth," "Issues Presented by the Air Reserve Training Manual," and "Guide to Subversive Organizations and Publications"; and the House Record's "Permit Communist Conspirators to Be Teachers?"

26. Stormer, 254.

27. McGirr, 62–63, 97.

28. Stormer, 169–71; Budenz, 204. Stormer did laud George Meany for his anti-Communist statements. Budenz explained that Communists did not believe in labor unions; they believed in *using* them to gain the dictatorship of the proletariat. They allowed Communists to show interest in the problems of the working class, and they also allowed them to gain influence in organizations essential to the American economy and military. Once the dictatorship of the proletariat had gained control, however, free trade unions would be barred just as they were in the Soviet Union (181–82).

29. Gordon, 10. Little information is available about Gordon.

30. Ibid., 85–86.

31. Ibid., 60.

32. Dan Smoot, *The Invisible Government* (Dallas: The Dan Smoot Report, Inc., 1962), iii–iv.

33. Ibid., 5. All of these individuals were among the 40 members of the United States delegation to the United Nations founding conference in 1945 who were members of the Council on Foreign Relations.

34. Buckley and the other editors of *National Review* attacked Welch and his conspiracy theories in the magazine's February 13, 1962 issue, taking care to distinguish between Welch himself and well-meaning John Birch Society members (Schoenwald, 137).

35. William F. Buckley Jr., *Up from Liberalism*, 1959 (New York: Bantam Books, 1969), 77.

36. Ibid., 87.

37. Robert Morris, *No Wonder We Are Losing* (New York: The Bookmailer, 1958), 100, 111. Morris also served as assistant counsel to the New York State Legislature's Rapp-Coudert Committee investigating Communism in the New York City Schools in 1940, in U.S. Naval Intelligence during World War II, and as counsel to the Senate Internal Security Subcommittee in the 1950s.

38. Nathaniel Weyl, *Red Star over Cuba: The Russian Assault on the Western Hemisphere* (New York: Devin-Adair, 1960), 148–51.

39. Fred Schwarz, *You Can Trust the Communists (. . . to Do Exactly as They Say!)* (Englewood Cliffs, N.J.: Prentice-Hall, 1960), 7, 13–16.

40. Budenz, 7–14.

41. Ibid., 9–10.

42. Ibid., 15,19.

43. Weaver was the head of General Motors' Customer Research staff. He also authored many articles in the field of psychological research (Leonard E. Read introduction

to Henry Grady Weaver, *The Mainspring of Human Progress*, orig. pub. 1947 [Irvington-on-Hudson, N.Y.: The Foundation for Economic Education, 1953], unnumbered front matter).

44. Weaver, 39–40.

45. Ibid., 80, 85. Weaver argued, for example, that the Ten Commandments were the "first and greatest document of individual freedom in the recorded history of man." Jesus' new commandment to "love thy neighbor as thyself" was the "foundation of intelligent self-interest and practical cooperation."

46. Schoenwald, 126.

47. Andrew, 17.

48. Ibid., 146.

49. Barry Goldwater, *The Conscience of a Conservative*, 1960 (New York: Macfadden Capitol Hill, 1961), 9.

50. Ibid., 5.

51. Ibid., 10–13.

52. James Burnham, *The Web of Subversion*, 1954 (Boston: Western Islands Publishing, 1965), 203.

53. Budenz, 64, 74.

54. Ibid., 211.

55. Ibid., 310. Nixon wrote his bibliography during his years in the House.

56. Ibid., 301–2.

57. Stormer, 229–34.

58. Ibid., 236.

59. Augustin G. Rudd, *Bending the Twig: The Revolution in Education and Its Effect on Our Children* (New York: New York Chapter of the Sons of the American Revolution, 1957), 9.

60. Arthur Bliss Lane, *I Saw Poland Betrayed* (Indianapolis.: Bobbs-Merrill, 1948), 311–12.

61. Garet Garrett, *The People's Pottage* (Caldwell, Idaho: Caxton Printers, 1953), 15, 18.

62. Ibid., 174.

63. M. Stanton Evans, *Revolt on the Campus* (Chicago: Henry Regnery Co., 1961), 6.

64. McGirr, 16.

65. Ibid., 265.

66. *The Death of a Nation*, 1968; *Growing Up God's Way*, 1984; *None Dare Call It Education*, 1998; *Betrayed by the Bench*, 2005.

67. *The Bible, the Declaration, and the Constitution, What Are "Dead" Communists Doing in Today's World*, and *The War Against Our Culture Through Our Schools*. Liberty Bell Press publications page, www.libertybellpress.com/publications.htm, accessed 26 September 2007.

II ESTABLISHING A BEACHHEAD

3 Literature and Reeducation in Occupied Germany, 1945–1949

CHRISTIAN KANIG

Writers as "Engineers of the Human Soul"

IN 1948, THE Soviet Union's most respected writers—including Stalin Prize laureates—wrote an open letter to the Soviet government to complain about the quality of the publications in which their works appeared. These books were printed on poor paper, they argued, and the binding was inferior. Although the writers received some promises of improvement, the open letter went largely unnoticed. At the same time, a former schoolteacher then serving as a Soviet officer at a Red Army publishing house in Germany sent a letter to the Soviet government. His letter quickly found its way to Stalin, who took time to answer it and see to it that all the letter's requests received prompt responses.

It is easy to determine the reasons for the unequal treatment of the two letters: Germany was the front line in the Cold War. On German territory, the Soviet Union and the United States engaged each other in a dialogue about the advantages of their respective political ideologies. The former Allies publicly compared their competing models of modernization before a German audience because they perceived the Germans as detached observers whose allegiance had to be won. In this battle for German minds, print was the weapon of choice. Thousands of books and several newspapers aimed at the Germans celebrated Western freedom or, alternately, Soviet egalitarianism.

To keep up with this "arms race" of books and newspapers, the Soviet Occupation Forces in Germany founded the publishing house ISVA. As tensions between the Allies grew, so did ISVA. By 1948, ISVA had mushroomed into the largest publishing enterprise in the Soviet empire and dominated the German book market. In four years, ISVA printed over 500 million books and eliminated every competitor. It also conducted studies to ascertain the impact Soviet literature had on German minds and used sophisticated PR techniques to win the population's allegiance. ISVA even employed the Red Army to force bookstores and libraries to advertise and stock its books. Red Army officers patrolled bookstores, libraries, and reading rooms to ensure that Germans were reading Soviet novels. ISVA became a primary ideological base in the print war: the Soviets flooded the Western occupation zones with Marxist books and Stalinist brochures, while the Americans fired back with Gulag atrocity stories, defector narratives, and free-speech pamphlets. Both sides developed elaborate control and censorship procedures to stave off hostile literature.

The escalating Cold War did not just affect the content of literature. Ideological warfare forced drastic changes upon the mode of producing printed matter. New methods of publishing millions of copies within weeks inflicted long-term structural changes upon Germany's cultural landscape and altered the material reproduction of Germany's print culture. Within three years, the Red Army publishing house fundamentally changed the way books had been produced in Germany. ISVA wiped out almost any other independent publishing house in Soviet-occupied Germany; and when it ceased to exist in 1949, ISVA had homogenized a sizable component of Germany's culture.

Soviet policy toward print culture in Germany was a response to the Allies' ambition to transform German culture as a whole. When in 1944 reports of American reeducation designs reached Moscow, the Soviets began to consider reeducation plans of their own. In January 1944, the Soviet ambassador in London wrote to Stalin that it was "absolutely necessary to seriously reeducate the German people.... At the moment, there are many projects about reeducation in England and America that are not only strange but outright dangerous."[1] As a result, the Soviet leadership set up its own panels to consider reeducation. In March 1944, a Soviet official informed a panel that "in America, at several universities commissions have been created that are working on the problem of reeducating the Germans.... Thus far, they have not put forward any useful proposals. The proposals are going in the direction of flooding Germany with foreign teachers and schoolbooks. These are pointless measures."[2] Soviet officials felt that American reeducation designs would fail because from a Marxist-Leninist viewpoint, American attempts to transform the German education system were doomed to insufficiency. Stalin had, after all, defined fascism as an outgrowth of capitalism, and in the Soviet view rooting it out required altering Germany's economic base.

At the end of the war the Soviets decided to propose a reeducation plan of their own that capitalized on their post-revolutionary experience as a template for postwar Germany. In April 1945, an article in the influential journal

Bolshevik emphasized the Soviet experience in using literature as an instrument for reeducation.[3] Reeducating a people from bottom to top would not ensure success. It would be easier to take power first, and then use the state to transform the society and its mentality from the top down while simultaneously altering the economic base. In conceptualizing a new culture for a new society, intellectuals should draw on the progressive strains of all cultures. Naturally, Soviet culture—the most progressive of all cultures—would have the strongest influence.

The Sovietization of the German Publishing Industry

In summer 1945, the Soviet Military Administration (SMA) founded the Soviet Military Administration Publishing House (ISVA). SMA pursued a radical policy toward printed matter, compiling bibliographies of "fascist, militarist, and reactionary literature" to be removed from private and public libraries. Within a year, the Soviets had examined 300 libraries in 112 towns and confiscated more than one million books.[4] The libraries' gaps were to be filled with ISVA publications.

ISVA was also meant to serve another purpose: the Kremlin intended to utilize German publishers to produce books for the Soviet market. The war had inflicted damage not only on the Soviet landscape, but also on the political outlook of Soviet citizens; a considerable segment of Soviet citizenry hoped for more liberalism after the war.[5] A Soviet officer remembered a conversation with a professor in 1944 in which the officer voiced his hopes for a political relaxation after the war. But the professor dashed his hopes. "Remember my words; it is going to stay that way," he said. "As soon as the war is over, they will preach more diligence on the ideological front, the triumph of Marxist-Leninist science, about the extraordinary contributions of Comrade Stalin to dialectical materialism; they will publish 10 million copies of Stalin's *Problems in Leninism* and 20 million copies of Stalin's *Short Course of the History of the VKP(b)*."[6] The professor was right. After the war, the Kremlin intended to compensate for the ideological relaxation that the war had necessitated, but Soviet publishers were not up to the task. Therefore, in fall 1945 ISVA received the order to print in Germany 6.2 million copies of the *Short Course* within eight months. Devastated by the war, no German publisher was capable of issuing 6.2 million books within the short period of time the Soviets desired. Moreover, the German publishing industry did not quite match Soviet desires. German publishers operated on free-market principles: they consisted only of an office that took on manuscripts and dealt with finances and public relations. Upon accepting a manuscript, a German publisher would outsource the job to a printing workshop and a bookbinder. Very few publishers issued books in quantities of 100,000 copies, let alone millions. Only when all copies sold out would a German publisher consider another edition. In contrast, Soviet publishers were state institutions where consumer demand was secondary to political decisions. In an ideologically driven state, Stalin's and Lenin's books had to be bestsellers, or at least the most-printed books. Soviet publishers edited, printed, and bound millions of copies in one facility. They then passed on all copies to the state institution KOGIz, which distributed the books throughout the Soviet Union according to a fixed pattern, regardless of demand.

At first, to fulfill the Kremlin's order for 6.2 million copies of the *Short Course*, SMA ordered the Red Army to screen East Germany for printeries and bookbinders.[7] ISVA began printing different pages at different printing facilities, transporting the pages by army trucks over great distances to binderies, where Germans who did not speak Russian bound the books. Sometimes the German binders bound the wrong pages in a book or left pages out. Such oversights were dangerous. After all, the *Short Course* had been partially written by Stalin himself, and mistakes like these could easily lead to arrest. To avoid this problem, ISVA's director decided to fuse printing and binding by dismantling previously independent bookbinders and printeries and integrating them into large factories for industrial book production: "To overcome the defects of the capitalist publishing landscape, we enabled the printeries to do the entire labor."[8] Close to large printing facilities, ISVA set up machine parks, and trained 5,000 employees in bookbinding. As a result, ISVA raised monthly output from three million books in early 1946 to nine million books by July 1946. In May 1947, ISVA announced its completion of printing the 6.2 million copies of the *Short Course*, and sent several trainloads of books to Moscow.

By that time, ISVA's *Short Course* had inflicted tremendous damage on the German publishing trade. ISVA had wiped out hundreds of small publishers and independent printing workshops and, thereby, had done more to homogenize the intellectual discourse in the zone of Soviet control in Germany than any ideological measure could have. ISVA's new chain-work facilities were ill suited for a free market and soon developed a self-interest in large output quantities and ideologically driven government orders. The *Short Course* had brought Sovietization in its wake and triggered the integration of culture into the socialist plan of production. ISVA's director proudly claimed that ISVA had "helped to overcome the defects of a capitalist mode of production and, thereby, created the preconditions to transfer the large [publishing] companies into people's property."[9] Indeed, when ISVA ceased production in 1949, almost all publishers in the Soviet zone were large, state-run enterprises that conformed to ideological dogma.

According to Soviet statistics, in 1946–47 ISVA delivered 169 million and in 1948 105 million books to the Soviet Union.[10] Forty percent of all books available in the Soviet Union were produced by ISVA in Germany. Within three years, 6,600 boxcars with books had crossed the Soviet border.[11] In 1948, the Soviet leadership allocated ISVA 34,000 tons of paper, whereas all Soviet publishers together received only 20,000 tons.[12] The Soviet military publishing house had not just conquered Germany; it had mushroomed into the largest publisher in the Soviet empire.

Literature for Reeducation

In fall 1945, ISVA began publishing Soviet books for German readers, intending to buttress the reeducation effort. Major Aleksandr Dymshits, a friend of the president of the Soviet Writers Union, headed SMA's Literature Unit and was charged with choosing manuscripts for publication. He remembered: "Besides its controlling function, SMA had the task of aiding the democratic and socialist forces among the German people. In regard to culture, art and literature, SMA was an adviser to leading representatives of progressive German culture. . . . Translations of works by Soviet writers played a role . . . for the democratic education of the German reader."[13]

From 1945 to 1946 the Soviets produced the classics of Marxism in two formats: 4.3 million books and 540,000 political brochures. During that time, the Soviets issued 13.5 million pieces of printed matter, outproducing the Allies several times over.[14] Even though the Potsdam Treaty had stipulated that the Allies would refrain from interfering in each other's zones of control, ISVA flooded all of Germany and Austria with cheap paperback editions. To expand the reach of Soviet ideology into the Western zones, ISVA employed German Communists camouflaged as "experts in Soviet Literature" to distribute its books in West Germany. One of these "experts" remembered a mission into the American zone: "A truck from the Soviet zone, packed with crates of books—dirtied and stamped on by the Americans at the demarcation line! Here we saw it with our own eyes. We were so glad to be receiving Marxist literature and belletristics—and the Americans are delightedly stamping on it."[15]

ISVA published acclaimed Soviet novels such as Maxim Gorkii's *Mother*, Nikolai Ostrovskii's *How the Steel Was Tempered*, and Alexei Tolstoi's *The*

Ordeal, and books deemed appropriate for a German audience. For instance, ISVA published Mikhail Sholokhov's *Virgin Land* because its depiction of Russia's rural life after the revolution matched the situation of German farmers after the Soviet-imposed land reform. Soviet officers hoped that German writers would emulate their style and content, and alter this Soviet genre for German conditions.

From a Soviet perspective, Germany was passing from the capitalist stage in history to a higher socialist one. As the historian Jan Gross shows for postwar Poland, Soviet propagandists perceived it as their duty to hasten Germany's transformation from capitalism to socialism as "a revolution from abroad."[16] Similarly, SMA officers in Germany felt obliged to stage a German revolution "just like a small Red October Revolution," as one prominent officer claimed.[17] ISVA officers repeatedly complained about the manuscripts sent by Moscow. Novels about the accomplishments of Stalin's Five-Year Plans, they felt, would neither buttress Soviet reeducation designs nor conjure up revolutionary sentiments. ISVA officers preferred literature about the 1917 watershed, the first post-revolutionary years, and the Communists' struggle against bourgeois remnants. They asked for novels showcasing Russian intellectuals and workers who had chosen to side with the Bolsheviks during the revolution.[18]

While ISVA was printing its first novels, Red Army officers lectured Germans on such topics as "Soviet Literature and Its Educational Significance," and "Soviet Culture and Its Influence on Western Culture."[19] The manuscript of a lecture titled "Soviet Culture and Its Influence on the World" survives.[20] The Soviet lecturer explained to his German audiences that Soviet culture was uniquely attractive because of its Russian and Soviet components. Because of Tsarist repression, Russian literature mirrored the suffering of the oppressed and, therefore, echoed the sentiments of the working class in capitalist societies. Soviet literature, in turn, had already leaped beyond the revolution and revealed what a victorious working class could achieve.

To increase consumption of Soviet literature, SMA imported Soviet post-revolutionary modes of distribution to Germany. It ordered Soviet-controlled newspapers to print ISVA novels in installments. SMA also introduced newspaper boards at marketplaces to enable people to stop by and read the paper on their way to work. Often, they posted undercover agitators next to these boards who would "translate" highbrow articles into colloquial language and engage readers in political debates.[21] The Soviets also imported reading barracks that provided books and newspapers and located in them town squares or near factory gates, In bombed-out Germany, these reading barracks were often the only warm places, and usually crowded with people reading or warming up.[22]

Literature as a Weapon in the Cold War

Everything changed in the spring of 1946. Churchill's "Iron Curtain" speech in Fulton, Missouri, made the simmering tensions between the Allies explicit and triggered German fears of an impending clash between Western and Soviet troops on German territory. Immediately, the Soviet zone buzzed with rumors about the Cold War turning hot. It was rumored that when American forces advanced into the Soviet zone German collaborators would face reprisals. A secret Soviet report echoed many others: "German intellectuals are afraid of a new war. Recently, their fear has dramatically increased because of Churchill's speech."[23] In light of an impending war, even stout German Communists became uncertain about their loyalties.

German intellectuals became suspicious of literature issued by the occupiers' publishing house and did not want to be associated with ISVA. After all, at the moment the possession of Nazi literature was considered illegal in all of Germany, and many Germans were uncertain what would happen if advancing American troops discovered Communist literature on one's bookshelf. German Communists distributing ISVA books in the Western zones repeatedly complained about Allied interference. ISVA's director suggested to his Moscow superiors that ISVA should publish literature under two different labels to overcome German suspicions. As a result, SMA ordered the German publisher Aufbau, a German-run spin-off of ISVA, to publish ISVA novels under its own name.[24] ISVA decided it would publish only Marxist-Leninist literature and works about the USSR.

> Everything else, first of all classical and Soviet literature and books about current political issues should be published under the brand of another, neutral publisher. Founding that publisher (with our participation, but without a formal connection between this publisher and SMA) would broaden the publication of Soviet translations and employ more Germans . . . (for political reasons, some German authors don't want to be published by the official publisher of the SMA). There are reasons to believe that books without the brand ISVA would be easier to distribute in the West.[25]

ISVA's director also asked that "our political tasks in Germany in 1947 be taken into consideration." He proposed to publish "books offering sophisticated critiques of [Western] bourgeois philosophy and sociology." The director later remembered that "in 1946 . . . we emphasized works unmasking German imperialism and fascism."[26] But by 1947, an anti-American focus had surpassed the previous antifascist one. An analysis of the 220 titles issued by ISVA between 1945 and 1949 shows the Cold War had found its way into ISVA's publishing portfolio.

Soviet literature published by ISVA in the initial stage of the Cold War fell into two distinct categories. On the one side, books like Sergei Koselskij's *The Fabrication of Lies: The Ways and Manners of the American Press* (Berlin, 1948) and *Falsifiers of History: The Real History of the Preparation and Development of Hitler's Aggression and the Second World War* (Berlin, 1948), and O. Kurganow's *Americans in Japan* (Berlin, 1948) condemned the West for American war crimes, capitalist oppression, manipulating public opinion, and support for anti-Communist and proto-fascist groups. On the other hand, books like Andrei Vyshinskii's *For Peace and Friendship among the Nations* (Berlin, 1948), Ilja Konstantinowskij's *The People's Democracies of Europe* (Berlin, 1948), and N. Popowa's *Women's Equality and the Position of the Woman in the Soviet Union* (Berlin, 1948) praised the Soviet Union and East

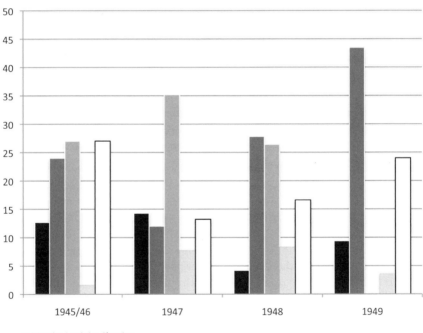

■ Marxist-Leninist Classics

■ Political Literature

▦ Literature about the USSR

▢ Russian Classics

☐ Soviet Literature

Table 3-1. Number of Titles Published Annually by ISVA, by Category

European "People's Democracies" as a window into the future and emphasized Soviet humanistic convictions.

After Churchill's speech, Moscow assessed the accomplishments of SMA's propaganda efforts. A report to the Soviet Communist Party Propaganda Administration specified that SMA had become a "valuable tool to control and guide the social and political life in the Soviet Zone in Germany."[27] However, the output quantity of Soviet literature did not correspond to Moscow's expectations. Moreover, SMA failed to combat Western propaganda. Particularly damaging was the American-licensed press because of its popularity. In order "to strengthen our influence, and weaken the Anglo-American influence," the report urged ISVA to increase its personnel and its output of literature.

Confronting its weaknesses, in May 1946 SMA began to assess the influence of Soviet and Western propaganda on German minds. The conclusions drawn indicated that many Germans complained about all-too-rosy portrayals of life in the Soviet zone. Analyzing Allied propaganda, SMA concluded: "Enemy propaganda contains . . . distortions of the socialist system as one where freedom of speech, the press, individual liberty and initiative have been abolished in favor of dictatorship, bureaucratism, and a police regime; it attempts to prove that the Soviet occupation regime is introducing 'socialization,' the abolishment of private property and lower living standards . . . no family values, no freedom of worship." To counter Allied accusations, SMA chose to step up anti-Western publications while simultaneously increasing pressure on German newspapers to publish anti-Western articles. "It is crucial not to allow a liberal relationship to the German reader; some [editors] are striving to contact Anglo-American agents, and [we need to] ensure strict control over them."[28]

The assessment of German public opinion was disappointing: most Germans preferred the West to the USSR and constantly compared living standards between the occupation zones. In May 1946, reports about Germans looking up to the West found their way to Stalin's ideologue, Andrei Zhdanov. Allied propaganda, the report to Zhdanov claimed, would "undermine the authority of the USSR in German eyes [and] raise the authority of the Allies as benefactors." The Soviet reaction was "late, and clumsy. It lacks fighting spirit and activity. We have no counterpropaganda. . . . Our inappropriate fear of 'insulting the Allies' has made the Americans so nasty that they openly use German police forces to shatter Communist organizations. We don't respond to the Americans' nasty pranks appropriately."[29] The report demanded that SMA directed all media toward a single purpose.[30] Foreign Minister Molotov was charged with setting up a German news agency "with an independent appearance to outside observers to allow [us] to introduce more of our propaganda into the press. A German news agency under our control would allow us to . . . supply our information to the press, to ward off anti-Soviet propaganda, and to engage in fast and thoughtful counterpropaganda."[31]

The first postwar elections in September 1946 tested German loyalties and the power of the Soviet media blitz. The Soviets supported the Communists with massive quantities of printed matter. A circular titled "Enemy Propaganda in the Soviet Zone before the Communal Elections" warned that "illegal newspapers and literature from the Western zones" would seep into the Soviet zone and urged propaganda officers to step up counterpropaganda against newspapers based in West Berlin.[32] Indeed, the American military government publicly announced the active distribution of printed matter throughout Germany.[33] Therefore, SMA ordered a drastic increase in its own publication of brochures with political content and prohibited the influx of Western newspapers.

The elections turned out to be a disaster for German Communists. The investigation commission Moscow formed to investigate the failure complained to Zhdanov that SMA "does not have a propaganda plan guiding the political line of all German and Soviet institutions."[34] ISVA's output of literature—particularly books depicting the construction of socialism in the USSR as a blueprint for Germany—did not meet expectations. A similar report to Stalin claimed SMA did not live up to its charges.[35] Although SMA controlled 37 papers, 5 radio stations and 52 journals, in the eyes of the Kremlin it insufficiently used these means.[36]

The Battlefields of the Print War

After their defeat at the polls, the Soviets intensified their efforts to seal off the Soviet zone from Western influences by limiting the influx of Western visitors, newspapers, and literature. A new SMA censorship circular urged newspaper editors to take "great care that no Anglo-American propaganda is finding its way into the papers."[37] SMA ordered printing workshops to accept only Soviet-licensed material and seal the printing machines after each workday, and it compiled lists of Western newspapers and journals prohibited from entering the Soviet zone.[38]

SMA also instigated a renewed cleansing campaign of German libraries. This time, libraries had to remove undesired foreign literature and books by Communist apostates.[39] Once more 2,670 libraries were screened, resulting in library holdings decreasing by 20–60 percent. A report specified: "The examination of public libraries instigated by SMA in late 1947 and early 1948 showed that the main source for the renewal of the library holdings are the publishers of the Soviet zone. These are the classics of Marxism, progressive political literature, Soviet, political, and contemporary literature."[40] As a result, only three years after the war, the entire stock of "fascist, militaristic, and reactionary literature" and foreign literature had been exchanged for "Communist and democratic literature." SMA also introduced the Soviet method of coercing librarians to guide the reading preferences of library patrons. Librarians had to undergo regular training sessions to "aid them with ways and methods to propagate books"; they were then expected to engage library customers in discussions about literature and promote certain novels and texts. In 1946 and 1947, 4,000 librarians went through these sessions.[41]

The first open battle in the Cold War in print occurred in April 1947. Soviets and Americans had long shot accusations at each other, but the staging of Konstantin Simonov's anti-American play *The Russian Question* at Berlin's prominent Volksbühne Theater led to the escalation of the print war. Simonov's play depicted an American journalist coerced by a newspaper mogul to compile anti-Soviet diatribes. The play suggested that a small clique of capitalists manipulated American public opinion for profit and employed anti-Communism to discredit American liberals. The American occupation authorities tried to prevent the play's staging by protesting to the Inter-Allied Control Council. Yet, the Soviets ensured the play would go on. SMA reported to Moscow: "The American Military Administration was unable to change anything. Its position confirmed only once more the motives underlying the *Russian Question*. Indeed, it really was similar to the position of the newspaper boss in Simonov's play who threatened the progressive journalist."[42] For weeks, the German press was filled with discussions about the play and the Soviet-American confrontation, and American and Soviet propagandists employed their German newspapers to support their cause.[43] In book form *The Russian Question* became a bestseller and sold out within days, and two Soviet-licensed newspapers printed the text in installments.

That same year, the American occupation authorities shot back by licensing the publication of Margarete Buber-Neumann's memoir *Under Two Dictators: Prisoner of Stalin and Hitler*.[44] Buber-Neumann had been married to a prominent German Communist. The couple emigrated in 1933 to the Soviet Union. During Stalin's purges Buber-Neumann's husband was shot, and she was deported to a gulag. Following the Hitler-Stalin Pact, the Soviet Union sent her back to Germany, where she spent four more years in camps. Her comparison of Soviet and German camps depicted German camps in much better colors. Moreover, she spoke very negatively about the Soviet Union as a whole and Communist intrigues in particular. Within weeks, the book became a bestseller and trickled into the Soviet zone.

Daily hardships in postwar Germany offered both Americans and Soviets many opportunities to blacken each other's credibility. Topics such as POWs, starvation, homelessness, ethnic cleansing, "denazification," expropriation, land reform, and frequent rampages of occupation soldiers figured prominently in propaganda appeals. The Americans escalated these recriminations, and they could build on preconceived notions of the Soviet Union as oppressive and backward by recycling older stereotypes. Moreover, as Americans raised living standards in the Western zones, they discredited Soviet promises of a bright future.

Wartime retrospectives also became a contentious topic. Soviets and Americans accused each other of having inflicted unnecessary suffering upon German civilians during the war. The Americans pointed to the atrocities committed by Soviet troops in Germany, while the Soviets put the blame for postwar destitution on American carpet-bombing of German cities. Articles in Soviet- and American-licensed newspapers clamored for an assessment of guilt. For instance, U.S. Ambassador Murphy complained about the Soviet brochure *Berlin—Worth a New War?*, which the U.S. Information Services Division believed was a Soviet response to the American-licensed magazine *You* issued to starving Berliners. Copies of the Soviet brochure had been found between issues of the American-licensed *Tagesspiegel*. The brochure was "intended to stir up anti-American feelings . . . the magazine shows the destruction and suffering caused in Berlin and other German cities by the 'first air bridge' during the war. The headline on one page reads: 'Yesterday phosphorus, today raisins, tomorrow atom bombs.'" ("Phosphorus" here refers to the incendiary bombs dropped by American bombers on German cities during the war, while "raisins" refers to the so-called "Rosinenbomber"— Raisin Bombers—a colloquial description of the American airlift bringing food into blockaded Berlin.) In Murphy's eyes, the publication was "an absolute low in Soviet propaganda. It represents an attack upon the Western Allies of an acrimony unprecedented in times of peace."[45]

With the unfolding of the Cold War, Soviet-American clashes in print multiplied. The 1945 Potsdam Treaty had urged all occupation forces to refrain from criticizing other nations' occupation policies and to allow the Germans free access to information on domestic politics. Directive No. 55 issued by the Inter-Allied Control Commission had stipulated the free exchange of printed matter among all occupation zones to ensure information freedom. Yet, with the unfolding Cold War, Americans and Soviets became increasingly suspicious of "enemy literature" entering their zones. Measures to prevent the distribution of printed matter multiplied on both sides in clear violation of Directive No. 55. American authorities worried that the influx of Soviet publications would lead to the emergence of fifth columns. Communists in the West, a secret memorandum read, planned to "import large quantities of pro-Communist literature from the east. . . . Production of books in the Western zones is very limited, in as much as paper is in extremely short supply. On the other hand, publishers in the Soviet zone offer German readers . . . a sizable selection of handsomely printed volumes at unusually low prices (e.g. Stalin's *Questions of Leninism*, 740 pages, 5 Marks). Such offers are naturally very tempting to book-starved readers here."[46]

The Soviets perceived Western literature as a threat to the socialist project and developed sophisticated measures to curtail distribution.[47] While measures to shut off the respective occupation zones multiplied, so did ways to circumvent them. In October 1947, a Soviet officer reported that the West had found a new way to smuggle newspapers into the Soviet zone, using waste paper to hide the American *Neue Zeitung*.[48] Similarly, an American intelligence report claimed that Soviet agents had placed anti-American brochures inside Western newspapers. To stave off the inflow of Western literature, in fall 1948 ISVA's director called for an escalation of the print war: "Much antidemocratic literature is currently being published in the Anglo-American zone. Suffice to say that a large part of that literature is listed in the German bibliographic bulletin under the section 'Religion, Theology, Service.' We have to withstand at any price the flood of religious, antidemocratic books with an even bigger flood of aggressive democratic literature."[49] Zhdanov discussed the plea in a Central Committee meeting with Stalin, and Stalin ordered 113 experienced propaganda cadres to be sent to Germany.

In the fall of 1948, the famous Leipzig book fair became the primary battleground in the print war. Leipzig had been the center of book publishing in prewar Germany, and its book fair had been a trendsetter for intellectual debates. In 1945, the Americans conquered the city, but due to wartime agreements, Leipzig ultimately fell under Soviet control. When American troops abandoned the city in summer 1945, a number of highly respected Leipzig-based publishers joined them. The Soviets were anxious to rekindle the spirit of the Leipzig fair and display the literary creativity and intellectual vibrancy of the Soviet zone by flooding the fair with Soviet-zone publications. The Americans, in turn, attempted to shred the book fair's credibility and economically cripple it by discontinuing rail traffic to Leipzig. In the end, 79 publishers from the Soviet zone and only eight from the West attended the fair. Before the opening, Red Army officers checked on each publisher and withdrew a number of Western publications. A Soviet report commented that Western publishers were unable to offer a single contemporary publication "showing visibly the policy of the Anglo-American occupation forces."

ISVA's booth left a particularly good impression on this Soviet agent: "The publisher convincingly demonstrated the broad development and the democratic content of the publishing industry in the Soviet zone. The Western zones looked poor in comparison, and . . . [Western publishers] seemed to be embarrassed about the small and greyish look of their booths."[50]

By spring 1948, about 6 million books by Soviet authors had been published in the Soviet zone, an area that had a total population of 19 million. Despite SMA's massive propaganda campaigns, the Soviets were losing ground. In a report to Moscow, SMA had to admit that competition for German intellectuals' allegiance was increasing.[51] A growing number of public intellectuals chose to relocate to the West, while political thought and literary conventions in the Soviet zone became increasingly monotonous.

To turn the tide, the Soviets employed their entire military machinery to distribute Soviet books to German readers. SMA placed reviews of its books in all Soviet-zone newspapers. The German Communist Party received large quantities of books for distribution.[52] About 400 copies of each ISVA book were sent to public intellectuals and newspapers in all of Germany. Soviet officers were charged with ordering book stores and libraries to investigate the ratio of Soviet to German books. Librarians had to report the circulation rate of Soviet novels. Dedicated Communist workers were encouraged to recommend Soviet novels to co-workers on lunch break. Finally in 1948, ISVA ordered an additional discount of 40 percent on all books to increase sales, making ISVA books very cheap. ISVA's director proudly claimed, "The chain production of ISVA books helped to make them cheaper while preserving good quality. This was possible because ISVA did not work for profit, and the books were published in masses and storage costs were low. That made ISVA books very affordable for German workers."[53] Indeed, ISVA books were mostly paperbacks of decent quality—a rarity in postwar Germany. Only the Marx-Lenin classics were hardbacks, and Lenin's and Stalin's books were of superior quality.[54] But because ISVA hoped to expand into the Western zones, even ISVA's paperbacks were of better quality than standard Soviet ones, triggering resentment in the Soviet Writers Guild.[55]

Although SMA conducted studies about the impact of Soviet literature, it is difficult to speculate about ISVA's real influence. In public perception, ISVA was omnipresent; it published twice as many titles as all other German publishers combined. Several voices gave positive assessments of the impact Soviet literature had on German minds. A student recalled the influence Soviet novels had on his group: "Back then, antifascist and socialist literature had a strong influence on our intellectual development. We read Soviet novels like

The Ordeal by Alexej Tolstoi and *How the Steel Was Tempered* by Ostrowski with great excitement."[56] ISVA's director believed that ISVA had accomplished its mission. Over time, "a widespread rise in consciousness sank in. . . . Interest in Soviet literature, consciously kindled by the party, grew."[57] Supposedly, Lenin's *Edited Volumes* (2 tomes with 1,954 pages) sold out within hours,[58] and the *Short Course* within three days.[59] Although this seems hard to believe, one has to bear in mind that in the immediate postwar years Communist ideas were widespread.

In October 1949, the Soviet Occupation Zone became formally an independent state. SMA ceased to exist, as did its publishing house ISVA. The German Communist Party maintained most censorship regulations, and no book would find its way into bookstores without the Party's consent. To many Germans, though, the German Communist regime appeared more liberal than the Soviet one. As a matter of fact, the perception of liberalism rested on earlier Soviet efforts to establish intellectual homogeneity. The blow delivered by Soviet officers to Germany's cultural framework shattered older methods of reproducing a culture's printed heritage. By eradicating outlets for critique, by closing hundreds of established publishing houses, and by controlling paper, printing machines, and printers, SMA created a publishing branch consisting of large state-run companies ill suited for a free market and unresponsive to demand. Ideological warfare in the dawning Cold War hastened the process of centralization. It took until the fall of the Berlin Wall in 1989 when independent publishers staged a comeback at the Leipzig book fair for the East German book industry to recover.

Notes

1. Jochen Laufer and G. P. Kynin, eds., *SSSR i Germanskii Vopros 1941–1949: Dokumenty iz Arkhiva vneshnei politiki Rossiiskoi Federatsii*, vol.1 (Moscow: Mezhdunarodnye Otnosheniia, 1996), 333–38.

2. Ibid., 450–45.

3. *Bolshevik* 3–4 (February 1945): 27–37.

4. Jan Foitzik, ed., *Politika SVAG v oblasti kultury, nauki I obrazovaniia: tseli, metody, rezultaty 1945–1949. Sbornik Dokumentov* (Moscow: ROSSPEN, 2006), 349–55.

5. On popular sentiment during and after the war and the Soviet government's response to it, see Vera Dunham, *In Stalin's Time: Middleclass Values in Soviet Fiction* (Durham, N.C.: Duke University Press, 1990).

6. Mikhail Koriakov, *I Will Never Go Back* (New York: E. P. Dutton, 1948), 30.

7. RGASPI F17/125/610, p. 207.

8. Ibid.

9. Ibid.

10. GARF 7317/43/13, p. 3.

11. Ibid., pp. 1–17.

12. RGASPI F17/125/606, pp. 22–24.

13. Aleksandr Dymshits, "Literaturbeziehungen zur Sowjetunion am Neubeginn," in Gerhard Ziegengeist, ed., *Begegnung und Bündnis* (Berlin: Akademie-Verlag, 1973), 64–66.

14. RGASPI F17/128/150, p. 70.

15. Franz Hammer, "Anfangen—ein Zauberwort in jenen Tagen" in Gerhard Ziegengeist, ed., *. . . einer neuen Zeit Beginn. Erinnerungen an die Anfänge unserer Kulturrevolution 1945–1949* (Berlin: Dietz-Verlag, 1981), 192.

16. Jan Gross, *Revolution from Abroad* (Princeton: Princeton University Press 2002).

17. Gerd Dietrich, "'. . . wie eine kleine Oktoberrevolution . . .' Kulturpolitik der SMAD 1945–1949," in Gabriele Clemens, ed., *Kulturpolitik im besetzten Deutschland 1945–1949* (Stuttgart: Steiner Verlag, 1994).

18. Foitzik, 343

19. GARF 7077/1/192, pp.153–58.

20. Ibid., pp. 202–6.

21. Ibid., pp. 39–43.

22. Ibid..

23. GARF 7133/1/273, pp. 305–10.

24. RGASPI 17/128/153, pp. 153–70.

25. Ibid., p. 150.

26. Mikhail Sokolow, "Bücher aus Leipzig," in Ziegengeist, *. . . einer neuen Zeit Beginn*, 470.

27. RGASPI F17/125/392, pp. 37–43.

28. Ibid., pp. 123–27.

29. RGASPI F17/128/153, pp. 1–7.

30. Ibid., pp. 8–16.

31. Laufer and Kynin, 620–21.

32. GARF 7077/1/201, pp. 8–16.

33. GARF F7371/2/5, p. 30.

34. Gennadii Bordiugov, ed., *Sovetskaia Voennaia Administratsiia v Germanii SVAG: Upravleniie Propagandy (Informatsii) i S.Tiulpanov, 1945–1949 gg. Sbornik Dokumentov* (Moscow: Airo-XXI, 1993), 243–51.

35. Ibid., 256–60.

36. Ibid.

37. Foitzik, 136–37.

38. Ibid., 133–36.

39. GARF 7133/1/253, pp. 25–26.

40. GARF 7133/1/251, p. 56.,

41. Ibid., p. 57.

42. Alexander Dymshits, *Ein unvergesslicher Frühling* (Berlin: Dietz-Verlag, 1979), 378.

43. GARF 5283/16/134, p. 52.

44. Margarete Buber-Neumann, *Als Gefangene bei Stalin und Hitler* (Munich: Europa-Verlag, 1948).

45. FW 861.20262/12-448, Henry J. Kellerman to George P.Allen and Ambassador Murphy, 24.12.48.

46. FW 861.00B/2-548, American Consulate A. Dana Hodgen, Stuttgart Germany to Secretary of State, "Communist Penetration of Cultural Activities in Württemberg-Baden," 5.2.1948.

47. GARF 7212/1/239, p. 8.

48. Ibid., p. 76.

49. GARF 7317/43/13, pp. 1–8.

50. GARF 7212/1/239, p. 35.

51. Foitzik, 262–75.

52. GARF 7317/43/1, p.1–17.

53. Ibid.

54. Renate Kruse, "Erste Manuskripte, neue Welten," in Ziegengeist, . . . *einer neuen Zeit Beginn*, 263.

55. RGASPI 17/125/611, p. 101.

56. Wolf Düwel, "Als Student im Kulturbund," in Ziegengeist, . . . *einer neuen Zeit Beginn*, 128.

57. Max Burghardt, "Die Ankunft," in Ziegengeist, . . . *einer neuen Zeit Beginn*, 116.

58. Sokolow, 470.

59. GARF 7077/1/192, pp. 275–84.

Bibliography

Primary Sources

Most of the archival sources cited in this chapter are files of the Soviet Military Administration in Germany [Sovietskaia Voennaia Administratsiia v Germanii: SVAG], declassified in 2001 and available at the Russian State Archive [Gosudarstvennoi Arkhiv Rossiskoi Federatsii: GARF] in Moscow. Some documents come from the former Archive of the Soviet Communist Party [Rossiiski Gosudarstvennoi Arkhiv Sotsialnoi i Politicheskoi Istorrii: RGASPI] in Moscow.

Bordiugov, Gennadii, ed. *Sovetskaia Voennaia Administratsiia v Germanii SVAG: Upravleniie Propagandy (Informatsii) i S. Tiulpanov, 1945–1949 gg. Sbornik Dokumentov.* Moscow: Airo-XXI.

Foitzik, Jan, ed. *Politika SVAG v oblasti kultury, nauki I obrazovaniia: tseli, metody, rezultaty 1945–1949. Sbornik Dokumentov.* Moscow: ROSSPEN, 2006.

Laufer, Jochen, ed. *SSSR i germanskii vopros. 1941–1949: Dokumenty is Arkhiva vneshnei politiki Rossiiskoi Federatsii.* Moscow: Mezhdunarodnye Otnosheniia, 2000.

Journals

Bolshevik

Secondary Sources

Clark, Katerina. *The Soviet Novel: History as Ritual.* Chicago: University of Chicago Press, 1986.

Dietrich, Gerd. *Politik und Kultur in der Sowjetischen Besatzungszone Deutschlands (SBZ) 1945–1949.* Bern: Lang, 1993.

Dietrich, Gerd. "'... wie eine kleine Oktoberrevolution ...' Kulturpolitik der SMAD 1945–1949." In Gabriele Clemens, ed.,: *Kulturpolitik im besetzten Deutschland 1945– 1949.* Stuttgart, 1994.

Dunham, Vera. *In Stalin's Time: Middleclass Values in Soviet Fiction.* Durham, N.C.: Duke University Press, 1990.

Gross, Jan. *Revolution from Abroad.* Princeton: Princeton University Press, 2002.

Hartmann, Anne, and Wolfram Eggelin. *Sowjetische Präsenz im kulturellen Leben der SBZ und frühen DDR.* Berlin: Akademie Verlag, 1998.

Naimark, Norman. *The Russians in Germany: A History of the Soviet Zone of Occupation, 1945–1949.* Boston: Harvard University Press, 1995.

Memoirs

Buber-Neumann, Margarete. *Als Gefangene bei Stalin und Hitler.* Munich: Europa- Verlag, 1948.

Dymshits, Alexander. *Ein unvergesslicher Frühling. Literarische Portraits und Erinnerun- gen.* Berlin: Dietz Verlag, 1979.

Koriakov, Mikhail. *I Will Never Go Back.* New York: E. P. Dutton, 1948.

Ziegengeist, Gerhard, ed. *... einer neuen Zeit Beginn. Erinnerungen an die Anfänge un- serer Kulturrevolution 1945–1949.* Berlin: Dietz-Verlag, 1980.

ISVA Publications Mentioned

Gorkii, Maxim. *Die Mutter.* Berlin, 1946.

Konstantinowskii, Ilia. *Die Volksdemokratien in Europa.* Berlin, 1948.

Koselskii, Sergei. *Geschichtsfälscher. Der tatsächliche Verlauf der Vorbereitung und Ent- wicklung der Hitleraggression und des zweiten Weltkrieges.* Berlin, 1948.

Kurganov, O. *Die Amerikaner in Japan.* Berlin, 1948.

Ostrovskii, Nikolai. *Wie der Stahl gehärtet wurde.* Berlin, 1947

Popova, N. *Gleichberechtigung und die Rolle der Frau in der Sowjetunion.* Berlin, 1948.

Sholokhov, Mikhail. *Neuland unter'm Pflug.* Berlin, 1946.

Simonov, Konstantin. *Die Russische Frage.* Berlin, 1947.

Tolstoi, Alexei. *Der Leidensweg.* Berlin, 1946

Vyshinskii, Andrei, *For Peace and Friendship among the Nations.* Berlin, 1948.

4   Democratic Bookshelf

American Libraries in Occupied Japan

HIROMI OCHI

AT THE END of World War II the American victors subjected Japan, along with other defeated nations, to a program of reeducation and reorientation. Hoping to demilitarize and democratize this country and its people, American authorities carefully selected cultural items, such as books, textbooks, periodicals, motion pictures, and radio programs, to be used to convey democratic ideas. Recent archive-based scholarship has clarified just how this cultural reeducation program worked. Reinhold Wagnleitner's study of postwar Austria is a case in point, while Kenji Tanigawa's work, for example, documents how motion pictures promoted Japanese democratization. In a series of works, Madoko Kon has examined gift books and information exchange through the system of CIE Information Libraries.[1] These studies show that the introduction of American culture alongside the installation of a new political system intended to connect the system of democracy to the lexicon of freedom, affluence, and equality. As a result, American authorities conflated the affluence and consumerism of the American way of life with republican democracy. These Western texts and images in turn reproduced the "containment culture" of the West, deploying both its geopolitical ideology and its gender roles through books selection and libraries.

Books had been a popular vehicle for promoting the American idea of democracy and the American way of life since the late 1930s,[2] and here I will focus on the selection of American books and periodicals provided to people in the initial stage of the postwar occupation of Japan through Civil Information and Education (CIE) book programs, especially the CIE Centers (later, US Information Centers). In particular, a careful examination of the actual selection of titles lays bare the negotiated and constructed nature of the "library" and the particular vision of democracy that the library intended to present in war-torn Japan. The first two sections of this essay trace the genealogy of book programs during the war, as well as the character of the "bookmen" involved in the programs, while the last two turn to the booklists used to create the library and the CIE library bookshelf to demonstrate the extent to which the idea of "democracy" as represented through the collection connected prewar, New Deal ideas of pluralism with Cold War anti-Communism and consumerism.

U.S. Libraries Overseas: Origins of Japanese CIE Libraries

The State Department's cultural-cooperation program began in 1938 as a limited program between the United States and Latin American countries. Troubled by Axis expansion in Europe, the Department hoped to encourage inter-American unity through travel and study grants, exchange of professors and books, assistance to United States cultural centers such as libraries, institutes, and schools, and distribution of informational motion pictures.[3] At that time, according to historian Henry James, Jr., officials hoped to use libraries to increase "friendly relations and understanding between the people of Mexico and the United States through the medium of books, periodicals, information services, and educational activities."[4] In this vision, the library was a place of exchange where printed materials could encourage friendship and understanding.

Cultural cooperation's purpose changed when the United States entered the war. From its founding in 1942, the Office of War Information (OWI) opened libraries in the Allied nations, beginning with England and its Commonwealth. The collections in these libraries were designed "to serve both as reference collections on the US and to augment the daily news report of the OWI," in the words of the Department of State. The initial collection had about 1,000 books consisting of "biography, history, travel accounts, classics of American literature, and Government reports."[5] According to Gary K. Kraske, initially OWI libraries put an emphasis on "sharing strategic information for the prosecution of the war," but, as more libraries opened in China, the Near East, and African nations, and as those libraries gained popularity, they took on the additional mission of "the diffusion abroad of American cultural values and technical information in preparation for the postwar spread of democracy." No longer confident that simple exchange of printed materials could ensure postwar development in the "proper" directions, libraries came to focus their materials on "information for rehabilitation and reeducation," although the amount of propaganda contained in these collections varied according to whether the country involved was allied, neutral, or enemy.[6]

Once the war was over, the U.S. government clearly expected that overseas libraries would play a critical role in shaping the direction of reconstruction and so maintained tight control over pre-existing libraries and information repositories. Immediately after the war, all the personnel, records, property, and appropriation balances of the libraries were transferred to the Interim International Information Service, then to the newly established Office of International Information and Cultural Affairs of the State Department.[7] At this point, with the exception of the Army's reorientation programs in Germany and Japan, the maintenance of American libraries abroad fell to the State Department. As Archibald MacLeish put it in 1947, the purpose of these overseas libraries was "to correct the image" of the United States abroad.[8] In 1948 the Smith-Mundt Act articulated this goal more clearly; these libraries should, in the words of the act, "promote better understanding of the United States in other countries" and beyond that, in a nod to fears about Soviet misrepresentation, create a "full and fair picture" of U.S. democracy. This act formalized the link between overseas libraries and U.S. foreign policy objectives. By 1950, in official language at least, attempts at balance had been replaced by a more militant "Campaign of Truth." These libraries, which had once been a source of exchange and information, were now engaged in the ideological conflict of the Cold War.[9]

Nonetheless, the collections prepared for CIE libraries in Japan immediately after surrender were less rigidly ideological than the language of the Smith-Mundt Act or other official statements might indicate. In one of her essays, Madoko Kon suggests that the promptness with which the CIE was able to set up libraries indicates that their origin was in the library programs instituted by the State Department, the OWI, and other private organizations such as the American Library Association.[10] One of the weekly reports of the CIE clearly says that in cooperation with "the Office of International Informational and Cultural Activities of the State Department," the library was "patterned after Information Libraries established by the former OWI."[11] As a result, the Army and the State Department collaborated so that in Japan these libraries contained works that reflected both earlier selection practices and the later, more propagandistic selections.

"Bookmen" as Home Front Warriors

During the war, a number of actors with differing ideas about the value of books and the meaning of democracy all had a hand in shaping the selection of books to be sent overseas for servicemen and women as well as books provided to foreign readers. This section explores some of the gender assumptions that shaped these book programs.

Traditionally, in the United States books and libraries had been associated with women. While Elaine Tyler May and other historians have focused on the way that containment affected women's roles once the war ended,[12] it is useful to see the way that "containment" of the dangerous power (or weaknesses) assigned to women came into play in the world of print. According to Kraske, the war increased "the importance of printed information as a strategic and psychological weapon" and changed "traditional perceptions of the functions of books and libraries as well as the hitherto limited role of American librarians."[13] While he mentions only librarians, Kraske's observations also reflect changes in the book industry as a whole—publishers, sellers, writers, and librarians. To many of these "bookmen" the "traditional perceptions of the function of books" called to mind a feminized image of books and reading. As F. Brett Cox has shown, in an industrialized society, to be a poet meant to pursue "the noncommercial, the impractical" and, ultimately to passively contemplate "the ideal" as the rest of society bustled. This image of passivity was easily associated with effeminacy.[14] In the familiar binary of masculine/feminine, people of the book world were marked as "feminine." Cox argues that as American literary studies emerged after World War I, newly professionalized literary critics and reviewers were eager to remove themselves from the realm of the feminine, using masculine vocabulary, for instance.[15] This was also the case with book publishers and sellers. In her study of the Council on Books in Wartime, Trysh Travis explains how the members of the Council saw their opportunity to participate in the war effort as returning an active, masculine power to the cultural realm. They created this air of masculinity by connecting books and reading to a culture of action, war, and democracy, which in turn allowed them to present themselves as masculine "bookmen."[16]

To give books so much power during the war—and, they hoped, beyond—librarians embraced this same militant, aggressive vocabulary at the ALA annual conference in Milwaukee in late June 1942. MacLeish, who had become assistant director of the OWI, urged librarians in his keynote address to create an "intellectual offensive" through "courageous and unrelenting attack." At the convention, the ALA adopted a policy statement reflecting the members' view of the "power of books and libraries in the war effort." As with the Council on Books in Wartime, speakers' papers were filled with the sense that librarians must act for the war effort to meet their newly forged "responsibility to educate for democracy."[17] As a result, the October issue of the *ALA Bulletin* was dedicated to the theme of libraries' home front efforts. The bulletin featured Roosevelt's message to the American Booksellers Association: "in this war, we know, books are weapons. And it is a part of your dedication always to make them weapons for man's freedom."[18] On the next page OWI director Elmer Davis described librarians as "combatants."[19] As with publishers and writers, the image of librarians was no longer feminine and passive: they were mobilized as combatants for freedom with their weapons, books. Their attitudes were totally in concert with that of the OWI book operation, which viewed books as "important weapons," citing Roosevelt's statement that "Books, like ships, have the toughest armor, the longest cruising range, and mount the most powerful guns."[20]

The war effort also demanded the services of critics, and as a result the OWI had an independent Advisory Committee on Books. This committee consisted of a number of distinguished authors and critics: Mark Van Doren, Harry Hanson of the *New York World Telegram*, Rosemary Benét, who was a writer herself and wife of Stephen Vincent Benét, Edward Aswell of *Harpers*; William Sloane of Henry Holt & Company, who was also one of the directors of the Council on Books in Wartime; Amy Loveman, editor of *Saturday Review of Literature* and secretary of the selection committee of the Book-of-the-Month Club; Joseph Margolies of the American Booksellers Association; and Jennie Flexner of the New York Public Library.[21] Although the committee lacked any of the emerging academic literary critics such as Norman Foerster or Cleanth Brooks among its members, it selected members who shared a vision of books as powerful weapons for transmitting the value of democracy.

Still, to create that vision of power, these critics needed to separate themselves from the genteel vision of culture associated with women. As Cox suggests, for many in the 1940s and 1950s, "masculinizing" criticism meant embracing modernists like Pound, Cummings, and Eliot.[22] Critics such as Van Doren belonged to the older generation of "genteel" literary critics and as such were often the target of criticism by this more professionalized group of literary specialists. In particular, as Joan S. Rubin and Janice Radway show, academic critics targeted such "middlebrow" critics, and institutions that promoted middlebrow reading such as the Book-of-the-Month Club and the *Saturday Review of Literature* for tainting culture with the feminized brush of consumer culture.[23] However, these middlebrow critics were precisely the critics most helpful to the OWI, which hoped to provide reading material to ordinary readers.

Despite the best efforts of academic critics to define the genteel or "middlebrow" critics as feminized, these critics too were able to appropriate the masculine rhetoric of wartime. According to Radway, both highbrow critics of the Book-of-the-Month Club and the club itself shared, or tried to appropriate, the idea of a public sphere which was supposed to be "pure, disinterested, and free from the exercise of undue influence." In analyzing the discourse of the public sphere, Radway refers to Michael Warner's argument on the discourse of republic, introducing the implicitly gendered notion of a public sphere that denied access to women and racial minorities.[24] In addition, as Rubin has argued, those critics who were effectively able to take on this republican mantle were able to bridge the gap between middlebrow genteel and highbrow masculine. For example, Amy Loveman, as an editor of *Saturday Review*, inherited Van Doren's journalistic, objective, and thus "disinterested" style through her self-effacement.[25] Seemingly using an ungendered voice, these studies suggest, the editorial members of the Book of the Month Club implicitly endorsed a masculine idea of their profession and, as a result, were also able to redefine their project as masculine for the purposes of the war.

The book program of the OWI thus brought diverse groups on the home front together in service to the nation, and its masculine rhetoric paved the way not only for uplifting the whole industry, but also for mobilizing men and women of letters, recreating them as "bookmen" and warriors. However, the definition of masculine book warriors reflected divisions in both politics and taste that would be central to divisions over book selection for postwar Japanese libraries. Those divisions led to different booklists and different senses of the power books could have as weapons.

Books as Weapons

Books for wartime OWI and State Department overseas libraries and gift book programs were carefully selected as "weapons" which could represent the might of the United States as well as the "American way of life." There were, however, a number of different lists of books compiled by different experts, which highlighted different versions of the "American way of life" and different attitudes about culture and democracy.

Immediately after the war, the two most accessible sets of books were the Armed Services Editions and the Overseas Editions that had been selected by the Council on Books in Wartime. The Armed Services Editions were a collection of reprinted books not for sale but for distribution to U.S. forces overseas. Representing a wide range of fiction and nonfiction as well as English and American literature, the series included a striking diversity in its selection: there were highbrow literary masterpieces, such as Herman Melville's *Moby-Dick* and Laurence Sterne's *Tristram Shandy*, as well as famous pulp Westerns by Max Brand and another pulp success, *Tarzan* by Edgar Rice Burroughs. While the selection committee might have preferred that servicemen develop a taste for highbrow classics, military observers believed that for soldiers in the battlefield, genre novels like Westerns and detective stories and even sentimental novels provided some release from the tension of their lives and therefore that those works were just as valuable as "better" books.[26]

These Armed Services Editions represented a diverse attitude toward America. Travis explains this diversity, citing Janice Radway's Book-of-the-Month Club study, as "planar logic," which avoided hierarchal judgments between books, seeing enlightenment and entertainment as different, coexisting categories.[27] After all, this series was not intended to inform foreign people about the United States and its democracy, but to boost morale. When applied to the task of reeducation, the planar logic of the collection created by the Council on Books in Wartime produced a vision of the United States that reflected the tastes of American G.I.s but had little to do with the foreign policy objectives of the United States.

The second set of books quickly adopted into Japanese libraries were the Council on Books in Wartime's Overseas Editions. These books were intended mainly for overseas libraries under the control of the OWI's Overseas Branch of the Bureau of Publications. The selection of titles to be published and translated into foreign languages was left to the OWI, with the help of its independent Advisory Committee. The books in the selection were still expected to function as "weapons," but the first selection of 40 books for the Overseas Edition shows another version of the United States in the year 1944, when it began to envision its postwar rehabilitation program.[28] Of the 40 titles,[29] books concerning the war account for 15, ranging widely from the official *American High Command Report* by Gen. George C. Marshall and *Prelude to Invasion* by Secretary of War Henry Stimson, to personal war narratives such as Max Miller's *Day Break for Our Carrier*. Probably information on the Pacific war was considered indispensable, and three books were included: Robert Sherrod's *Tarawa*, Joseph C. Grew's *Report from Tokyo*, and *Fortune*'s *Japan*. Two concerned postwar planning: *Preface to Peace*, a report of a symposium with speakers including Herbert Hoover and Wendell Willkie, and *How New Will the Better World Be?* by Carl Becker. Two dealt with U.S. international relations: *The Road to Teheran* by F. R. Dulles and Walter Lippmann's *U.S. Foreign Policy*. These books not only justified U.S. actions in the Pacific war, but also presented the argument for postwar orientation of the Japanese people.

Other books provided a picture of U.S. life: Stephen Vincent Benét's short national history *America*, written at the request of the War Department; *How America Lives* by J. C. Furnas, which originally appeared in *Ladies Home Journal* and showed the lives of ordinary American people; and *TVA* by David Lilienthal, a history of one of the major New Deal projects. In addition, to show the power of democracy and foundations of American life, Overseas

Editions included several biographies of Americans who could represent America's commitment to concepts such as freedom, judicial restraint, liberty, and innovation, including Benjamin Franklin, Thomas Jefferson, and Oliver Wendell Holmes, Jr. While biographies of Benjamin Franklin might be expected, Overseas Editions also included Howard Fast's *Citizen Tom Paine*, Lincoln Steffens's autobiography *Boy on Horseback*, and Rackham Holt's *George Washington Carver*. In addition, the one work of literary criticism included was *On Native Grounds* by Alfred Kazin, one of the representative figures of the so-called New York Intellectuals. The novels listed most are about the war in one way or another: *For Whom the Bell Tolls* by Ernest Hemingway, *The Human Comedy* by William Saroyan, and *A Walk in the Sun*, a story of World War II, by Harry Brown. Finally, science played a prominent role; alongside the biography of Carver there was a biography of Audubon by Constance Rourke, Bernard Jaffe's *Men of Science in America*, and John Ratcliffe's *Science Yearbook 1944*. In terms of postwar foreign policy, Overseas Editions as a whole put more emphasis on the U.S. overseas and domestic war efforts, justifying those efforts and the value of democracy, liberty, and technological innovation.

As the inclusion of Lilienthal and Benét might indicate, books selected for the Overseas Editions had a clear connection to the New Deal liberalism of the 1930s. Of the forty books, at least four were written by members of the Advisory Council of the Writers' War Board (John Steinbeck, Fletcher Pratt, S. V. Benét, Carl Van Doren).[30] The men involved in the selection of these texts and the texts themselves indicate the complex problem of representing "America" in overseas libraries. Some members of the Writers' War Board had joined after leaving the League of American Writers, a Popular Front group that many quit after the Moscow trials and the Hitler-Stalin Pact. Their participation in the Writers' War Board, as well as the Federal Writers' Project (FWP), grew out of their interest in social causes and their hope that the system of democracy in the United States would be best able to address those interests.[31]

A third source influenced the making of the CIE's booklist: the American Library Association (ALA). The ALA was involved with projects for exporting American publications: Books for Europe funded by the Rockefeller Foundation in 1942, and Books for Latin America under the Coordinator of Inter-American Affairs in 1942, for example. For these projects, the ALA used already circulated lists, such as *Book Review Digest*, the journal *Booklist*, and *Standard Catalog for Public Libraries*.[32] In addition, they compiled the *Selected List of Books in English by U.S. Authors* containing 1,279 titles and the *Selected List of Periodicals Published in the United States* containing 460 publications to assist the librarians in their selection.[33] Librarians creating these lists intended the books to "offer a representative picture of North American life to the intelligent layperson in other countries"[34] The selection in the *Selected List of Books* drew heavily on *Interpreting the United States,* a list that the ALA created (with help from Great Britain's National Central Library).[35] In fact, in his 1943 report on the Books for Europe Project, Young suggests that *Interpreting* would be useful for librarians. His endorsement made this text central to book selection for overseas libraries.[36]

Interpreting the United States was published in 1942 and 1943, the latter version subtitled "A List of Books Suitable for British Public Libraries" and intended for the use of local librarians. The title page of the 1943 version featured the message that the books in the list were chosen "to give a picture of America and American people as they are to-day." To see the characteristics of the United States represented in this list, let us first take literary criticism as our example, as the selection of criticism overshadows the selection of novels and poetry. Representative titles are: *The Flowering of New England* and *A New England Reader* by Van Wyck Brooks, *The Story of American Literature* by Ludwig Lewisohn, *American Renaissance* by Francis O. Matthiessen, *Main Currents in American Thought* by Vernon Parrington, and Carl Van Doren's *What Is American Literature?* The list did not include two influential academic books: Norman Foerster's *The Reinterpretation of American Literature* (1928), which presented the more academic approach to American literature formulated by the Modern Language Association; and the classic statement of New Criticism, Brooks and Warren's *Understanding Poetry* (1938).

Interpreting the United States created a booklist that reflected the tastes and ideals of America in the 1930s when the canon consisted of New England writers, romanticism, realism including local-color literature, and very little modernism. Indeed, the 1943 fiction list included neither F. Scott Fitzgerald nor William Faulkner (though Faulkner was listed in 1942). Generally the fiction list reflects almost all the novelists Carl Van Doren named in *What Is American Literature?*, the bibliography of which mentions only three twentieth-century novelists: James Branch Cabell, Theodore Dreiser, and Sinclair Lewis. Modernism was barely represented. The list in *Interpreting* also recommended Louis Untermeyer's *Modern American Poetry*, an anthology which did not include Pound or Eliot. At the same time, the fiction list contained bestsellers such as Margaret Mitchell's *Gone with the Wind, Drums along the Mohawk* by Walter Edmonds, and *The Yearling* by Marjorie K. Rawlings. The list avoided, however, the most lowbrow selections of the Armed Services Editions; there were no genre or pulp novels like *Tarzan*. This list showed the pre–New Critical canon of American literature, "modern" in that it had canonized nineteenth-century writers such as Poe, Hawthorne,

Melville, and Emerson while expelling genteel writers such as Longfellow, Lowell, and Bryant. It had not yet approved high modernists like Pound and Eliot, and alongside canonized authors were Book-of-the-Month Club favorites including Rawlings and Edna Ferber.[37]

This booklist was marked by New Deal liberalism in two senses: it reflected the liberal interests of Popular Front writers and showed the idea of what can be called multi-ethnic, progressive democracy. The selection of plays on the list reveals this focus. Most were the work of contemporary playwrights, and as the entry of the radio drama collection *Free Company Presents* shows, the selection foregrounded playwrights involved in the Free Company (a group of American writers advocating freedom of speech and of the press) and the Writers' War Board. Of the thirteen works selected, four were by members of the Free Company (Maxwell Anderson, Marcus Connelly, Paul Green, Robert Sherwood) and another four by members of the Writers' War Board Advisory Council (Norman Corwin, Clifford Odets, Eugene O'Neill). Like those of the War Board, many members of the Free Company were liberal writers, with a few formerly associated with the League of American Writers. The Federal Writers' Project of the New Deal, championed by the League, also served to channel former Communist sympathizers in acceptably liberal directions.[38]

The connection to the New Deal's commitment to a multi-ethnic democracy is explicit in the section of *Interpreting the United States* titled "American Regions and Their Cities," which went so far as to include the FWP's American Guide Series which described the different regions, states, and cities of the nation and attempted to present the diversity found within each of these divisions. Additionally the "Humor" section listed Constance Rourke's *American Humor: A Study of the National Character*. Rourke, later a director of the Works Progress Administration's Art Project, stressed in this book the "'folk' contexts of writers as different from one another as Poe, Whitman, Twain, and Henry James" and filled the gap between high and low cultures by covering diverse fields ranging from "African-American spirituals, cowboy songs, tall tales, myth" to "Melville and James."[39] In the sections on autobiography, fiction, and poetry, there was ethnic and regional diversity in classic local-color stories by Joel Chandler Harris, Bret Harte, and Hamlin Garland. The ethnic diversity of this guide ranged from Mary Antin's *Promised Land*, which evoked the idea of the American dream for immigrants, to Zora Neale Hurston's *Mules and Men*, and an anthology of verse by African American poets, *Caroling Dusk*.

In this sense, the selection in *Interpreting* shows the vision of America that had been central to foreign policy of the 1930s. This America was represented by a canon consisting of the mainly white, male authors selected by Van

Wyck Brooks and Carl Van Doren, alongside a smattering of immigrant and African American writers. Politically, the works were tinted with what William Cain calls a "muscular pro-Americanism,"[40] and New Deal liberal, progressive ideas. While hardly "diverse" in the way American scholars think of the word now, the selection of texts in *Interpreting* presented the world with a multi-ethnic, progressive image of the United States. As Werner Sollers argues, it was believed that this image of America could be an effective weapon in the fight against the racist, fascist axis.[41]

This liberal, multi-ethnic image, however, was not the only guide in the selection of books for the reeducation of formerly fascist enemies. The ALA's *Books Published in the United States 1939–1943: A Selection for Reference Libraries* (1945) was intended to inform reference libraries in war areas about important American books published during the conflict. Titles included in this list were carefully vetted first by the American Council of Learned Societies, and then by a staff drawn mainly from the New York Public Library.[42] Unlike *Interpreting*, this list was not meant to represent the United States, but rather to show the "best" books published during the war. As a result, the sections on history, political science, and language and literature contained works dealing with matters outside America and presented a very different vision of the type of culture found in a democratic and free nation.

Books Published's focus on "the best" signals its difference from earlier lists. Rather than supporting the type of "planar" logic that could include diverse authors and types of works to represent America, this list embodied the hierarchy that was coming to dominate the literary battles of the cultural Cold War. The selections in the literary section show this shift clearly. To begin with, the Modern Language Association (with its orientation against "genteel" critic-journalists and its valuation of professionalized, academic criticism) served as the outside adviser for this list. As the organization acknowledged, the aim of the literary section was "to select representative works of merit by authors of general importance," but that selection would "reflect the taste and critical judgment of the person making it."[43] The selection by the mainly academic professionals of the MLA does indeed show the obvious transformation of the American literary canon. The change from the canon presented by *Interpreting America* is most obvious in the section on poetry. American literature, as presented by *Interpreting*, relied heavily on fiction. Its list included only 4 poetry anthologies but 65 titles in fiction. *Books Published*, on the other hand, focused much more on poetry with 28 poetry collections, many by individual authors, and only 47 fiction titles. Though Untermeyer's *Modern American Poetry* fit into *Books Published*'s time range, it was not included. Instead, *Books Published* featured not just works by Benét and MacLeish but also more radical and experimental works by E. E. Cummings, T. S. Eliot, Wallace Stevens, Robert Penn Warren, and Yvor Winters. Indeed, twenty names including the above appear in *Sixty American Poets, 1896–1944* compiled by poet and New Critic Allen Tate, who was then commissioned as Consultant in Poetry in English for the Library of Congress under MacLeish.[44]

Indicating the shift in the U.S. cultural scene and literary canon, *Books Published*'s fiction list included southern modernists Robert Penn Warren and Carson McCullers. Ludwig Lewisohn and Vernon Parrington disappeared from the literary criticism section, replaced by New Critics Kenneth Burke and John Crowe Ransom, as well as the MLA's Norman Foerster. Considering that the WPA series was also excluded, this list reflected the gradual shift from New Deal multicultural liberalism and the American literary canon of the 1930s to an anticipation of the Cold War consensus and a literary canon that reflected the values of the 1950s. This canon championed artistic freedom and experimentation over realism and social engagement; it celebrated difficulty and ambiguity over accessibility and simplicity.[45]

Book programs, whether for publication or for libraries, and the work of preparing lists for the programs thus functioned as an arena where factions of various interests presented their vision of the United States, freedom, and democracy. They also served as a conduit for the ambitions of intellectuals and bookmen to participate in the national war effort on the home front. Using these lists, American leaders created a Japanese CIE library that conflated the pictures of the United States configured by those lists.

Democracy on the Bookshelf

As a program, the operations of the CIE in the occupied-Japan section of General Head Quarters/Supreme Command for the Allied Powers (GHQ/SCAP) were, although under the auspices of the War Department, an integral part of the State Department's Information and Educational Exchange program, which administered the worldwide operations of radio (VOA), press and publications, films, people-to-people exchanges, and libraries under the International Information Center Service. The United States established the Civil Information and Education Section as a Special Staff Section to advise the Supreme Commander on policies relating to public information, education, religion, and other areas posing sociological problems in Japan and Korea by General Order No. 183 on September 22, 1945. One of CIE's functions was "to expedite the establishment of freedom of religious worship, freedom of opinion, speech, press and assembly by dissemination of democratic ideals and principles through all media of public information."[46] Cultural policies of GHQ corresponded to those taken by the United States for West Germany and Austria. Unlike the Soviet Union, which established a special publisher in its occupied areas, GHQ kept existent Japanese publishing houses and through censorship controlled the contents of their output. Along with this, GHQ tried to disseminate American ideas through American cultural items such as books, magazines, and movies.[47]

CIE Libraries (later CIE Information Centers) were only one such "medi[um] of public information." Through the Gift Book Program, GHQ provided Japanese schools with storybooks mainly by American authors to introduce "Democratic America" and the American way of life. These books were meant to serve as models for the Japanese as they searched for new directions for their country and their individual lives. Initiated after the U.S. Education Mission and American librarians reported the condition of Japanese school libraries in 1946, this program proposed that the Japanese adopt the U.S. book classification system and selected well over 700 books that the program staff felt should be included in Japanese libraries. After an exhibition of these books in major cities, officials distributed the collections to school libraries in 1946.[48] Also, following the proposal of the U.S. Education Mission, GHQ embarked on the reform of Japanese public libraries and school libraries, believing that they would be instrumental in the reeducation of the Japanese people.[49]

The CIE Library, however, was the first of all these book programs. After the September 1945 General Order, the CIE opened its first library on a small scale on November 15, 1945, in Tokyo, to "supply Japanese public, editors, and writers with reference and background material on the war, international affairs, and American life in order to assist in carrying out the democratization of Japan in accordance with established policies of the Supreme Allied Commander."[50] Accordingly the CIE first planned to acquire books on World War II, international affairs, and the American scene, along with professional scientific and general publications, reference books, and newspapers, a collection largely modeled on the collection created by the Overseas Editions. This plan was somewhat derailed by the reality of what CIE leaders had access to. According to the weekly reports of the CIE,[51] it seems that at first they received small collections of books that, instead of having been carefully selected for the purpose of democratizing Japan, were random boxes of Armed Forces Editions.[52]

Gradually, however, the collection took shape. Among the 80 books received at the end of the year, ten are identified in the report and those, at least, are clearly focused on the reeducation aims of the CIE library program and reflect the New Deal liberalism of some of the library lists. The titles included Carl Becker's *Modern Democracy*, Walter Lippmann's *U.S. War Aims*, and

Henry Wallace's *Democracy Reborn*.[53] Of the ten books, Lippmann's was one of the titles of the Overseas Editions, and three books including Becker's were listed in *Interpreting the United States*.

The collection remained small; in February 1946 the library had only 320 books.[54] At that point, CIE leaders selected books from "certain confiscated libraries," access to which had been granted by the Washington Document Center. Again their report shows only ten titles of their selection of over 700 volumes, but what they chose to report on indicates their preferences: Samuel Peter Orth's *American National Government*, Isaac Lippincott's *Economic Development of the United States*, Vernon Parrington's *Main Currents in American Thought*, William Munro's *Government of the United States*, Edward Kirkland's *History of American Economic Life*, and S. E. Morison and Henry Commager's *Growth of the American Republic*. Of the ten, Morison and Commager's and Parrington's titles appeared on the *Interpreting* list. Finally, when the library reopened on March 13, 1946, for wider public use, it had more than 1,000 books, 110 magazines, 5 newspapers, and 2,000 pamphlets on the shelves,[55] and soon received 300 books from the Office of International Information and Cultural Affairs.[56] In 1948 it got a collection from a former OWI outpost for the Yokohama branch, again through the State Department. These collections proved invaluable and, as a result, the CIE requested the whole collection of the OWI inventory, saying, "They cover subjects which are in constant demand and will be an excellent addition to the present collection."[57]

This process shows that at the initial stage of the occupation, instead of having a complete collection of its own, the CIE accepted books already selected mainly by the State Department, which means the selection closely reflected the State Department's idea of democracy for Japan and the SCAP policy of "supplying reference and background material on a. World War II, b. International Affairs and c. American scene."[58] There was indeed a selection guide consisting of 1,495 books (including several overlaps). But even in 1946, the Library Unit of the CIE requested that each library add to its collection according to the list.[59] Considering this fact, the only complete booklist that the CIE weekly report presents—including the 300 titles donated and additional titles from the Department at the time of the reopening of the library in March 1946—has a great significance when one considers the real nature of the bookshelf of the CIE library. There are 490 titles, of which 480 titles overlap the "Publications for Occupied Areas" list.

Of these 490 titles, at least 110 are from the *Interpreting the United States* booklist, 10 are from Overseas Editions, 2 are from *Selected List of Books in English by U.S. Authors*, and 4 are from *Books Published in the United States*

1939–1943. Of the rest, about 20 titles concern World War II, and around 10 concern U.S. foreign policy. Additionally, there are many books about science and technology for the guidance of Japan's rehabilitation and introductory books about American regions including the Federal Writers' Project series. Considering Henry James, Jr.'s description that the collection in libraries in occupied areas emphasized publications from 1939 and later,[60] it can be said that the State Department collection based on the "Publications for Occupied Areas " list for the CIE library was not a random selection, but one modified for immediate postwar Japan. It presented the democracy described in *Interpreting the United States*: a multicultural, New Dealers' democracy whose idea of diversity and equality was still effectively posited against the racist and fascist ideas of Japan. Despite the association of those values with the American past, this democracy was characterized by contemporary books as well as Overseas Editions. Beyond the picture of democracy, this library also attempted to control the history that Japan might generate later. The materials donated by the OWI library focused on "information for rehabilitation and reeducation" to be achieved by providing books on war records, postwar planning including international affairs, and the prosecution of war criminals.[61] The CIE collection in the spring of 1946, then, signaled the new project of Japanese rehabilitation. Americans believed that by learning about democracy and a democratic world order representing a "pluralism of values," the Japanese would abandon their former system of feudalistic "obedient citizenry" and embrace the American way of life.[62]

These libraries, despite their limited collections, proved to be popular and soon spread throughout Japan. The "CIE Weekly Report" said that the first CIE Information Library enjoyed over 300 visitors almost every day after reopening to the wider public.[63] After September 1946, the CIE successively opened 22 branches in major cities in Japan including Nagoya, Kyoto, Osaka, and Fukuoka to offer local people a good selection of American books and periodicals, and to function as cultural centers offering English conversation classes, exhibitions, record concerts and so on, as was the case with "Amerika Häuser" in occupied Germany. A columnist in a major Japanese newspaper notes, looking back at the immediate postwar days, that the CIE libraries had been "oases" for intellectuals and technical people, especially when it was extremely difficult for people to acquire a journal or a book from overseas. The libraries, he continues, were popular among people who "craved" foreign books, and enjoyed more than 1,000 visitors a day.[64]

If the CIE library book collection stressed a certain kind of democratic, liberal pluralism at the initial stage of the U.S. occupation of Japan, another version of democracy was presented through the magazine collection of the

CIE library. While the first set of books was relatively small, in the same report the CIE libraries listed 107 different magazines, a vast collection which
had the advantage (to Japanese non-readers of English) of being brightly illustrated.[65] Especially before translated books were disseminated through
the Translation Program from 1948 onward, American magazines functioned
as a popular vehicle that conflated democracy and affluence. Several pictures
of the Tokyo library show the placement of the magazine racks in the center
of the reference room, where they were used to attract visitors. Along with
journals for professionals, there were a number of popular American magazines for the general public such as *Colliers, Fortune, Reader's Digest, Newsweek, Time, Life, Look, Ladies Home Journal, Good Housekeeping, Harper's
Bazaar,* and *Vogue.*[66] In the year 2002, former workers and visitors at the CIE
Information Center in Osaka held a reunion and published a memoir in which
they favorably recall the days they frequented the library. It was "a place full of
the flavor of culture," presenting visitors with information, music concerts,
English classes and so on. Japanese employees were very impressed with the
Christmas gifts from American librarians, and the place was always filled
with enthusiastic visitors who turned the pages of the latest issues of *Vogue,
Life,* or *Time,* amazed at the sights of American life.[67] In a time of scarcity,
when Japanese publishing houses were struggling with paper shortages and
strict censorship and people were lining up in front of the bookstore to get a
copy of *Reader's Digest,* those "beautiful gravure pictures" on the pages and
the high quality of the paper strongly impressed Japanese visitors with their
abundance and affluence. In the pages of those magazines were many advertisements featuring happy housewives dressed beautifully in kitchens full of
electric appliances. One of the frequent visitors says that she always ran to the
center to spend her lunchtime enjoying the magazines and music records.[68]
She was not an exceptional case: in the Tokyo library, 22 percent of the visitors were women and were "chiefly interested in American fashions." Indeed,
those magazines were especially attractive to young women "yearning for
Dior's New Look." In April 1949, *Asahi Shinbun* featured a huge picture cap-
tioned "Fashion Season," explaining that "Tokyo's CIE library is very crowded
with young women because of its American fashion magazines."[69] At a time
when few Japanese people could understand English, the visual images of the
United States in the magazine pages served as a vehicle to present the brand-
new idea of democracy as affluence. Postwar Japanese were expected to model
themselves after this.[70]

That image of an affluent society was coupled with the image of the United
States as a place of freedom and equality, but in these magazine spreads the
equation of affluence and democracy appeared to demand profoundly un-

equal gender roles. As Elaine Tyler May points out, the model home and white middle-class suburban families, complete with "distinct gender roles for family members . . . with a male breadwinner and a full-time female homemaker," represented the "essence of American freedom," serving as a Cold War ideological foundation of American superiority.[71] In postwar Japan, the installation of democracy went hand in hand with this postwar American gender reconfiguration under the name "equality of the sexes." Every issue of the *CIE Report* shows the way vigorous campaigning using radio and newspapers promoted equality of the sexes as one of the symbols of this newly installed institution, "democracy," even as the magazine collections revealed that the definition of "equality" presented to the Japanese people implicitly endorsed the U.S. postwar gender roles. Indeed, while *The Report of the U.S. Education Mission to Japan* declared in 1946 that one of the ways to exterminate "feudalism, and militarism" and to implement democracy was to lead the Japanese people to transform their society from one based on a "cohesive" family system to one founded on "the worth and dignity of the individual" and women were given the vote after the war, in the same report they were encouraged to endorse the idea "that to be 'good' wives, they must be good" and that to be "wise mothers, they must be wise." Men, on the other hand, were encouraged to behave as "an active animal" and in that way become the type of individual "who has fully found himself in his job." In the case of Japan, a former ultra-nationalist, ultra-masculine country, explicit masculine discourse such as George Kennan's insistence, in his "Long Telegram," on "cohesion, firmness and vigor" was not to be utilized to fight against the threat of the Soviet Union, especially when the Soviet Union was one of the Allies.[72] Instead the masculinity of Japanese men was contained within the framework of the Cold War domestic gender roles, indirectly sustaining Cold War domestic policies.[73]

While pictures could effectively convey much about the United States, as the Cold War came increasingly to be defined by ideological positions, the fact that few Japanese could read English at this time became an important difficulty in the effort to contain Communism. To meet this challenge, GHQ created a translation program in 1948, which operated under the control of the SCAP Translation Program. Through this program, 3,550 titles were translated into Japanese, the majority of them American books. The titles selected by the CIE were intended to "contribute to fulfillment of the obligations and needs of the Japanese people under the Potsdam Declaration," and not to be based on "entertainment value or literary superiority."[74] When the translation program was augmented in 1948, however, the CIE's book selection reflected the emerging Cold War scheme of "democracy versus totalitarianism." For example, classics such as *Huckleberry Finn* and *Tom Sawyer* were translated as they were thought to present model democratic heroes symbolizing individual freedom.[75] On the other hand, recent classics such as Steinbeck's *Grapes of Wrath* that showed Americans experiencing hardship and suggested more collective social organization were not translated. (The motion picture section of the CIE also omitted John Ford's film of the novel since the film version depicted the extreme poverty of the 1930s.)[76] *Animal Farm*, which the CIE libraries did not carry at first, was strongly recommended "with enthusiasm" for those "befogged by the utopian claims of authoritarian ideology."[77] The development of the translation program for CIE libraries shows that their original New Deal liberal tone was gone. Books by Cold War intellectuals such as Arthur Schlesinger, Jr., and Lionel Trilling were introduced to the Japanese people, as were biographies of American heroes like Babe Ruth and Abe Lincoln. In fact Edwin Reischauer's lecture featured in the November 10, 1948 issue of the "CIE Bulletin" describes the implicit logic of these collections. The types of works being translated could connect the containment of Communism to the containment of women. These texts indicated the importation of what Suzanne Clark calls the Cold War hypermasculinity of intellectuals such as Trilling, avoiding extremes and appealing to apparently "unmarked, neutral positions of superior reason," which characterized the masculinity of intellectuals.[78] Like the ideas of those intellectuals, Reischauer's distaste for "a rush toward the ideological extremes," "totalitarianism," or the state of "enslavement" of "man" went hand in hand with the CIE selection policy and its adoption of Cold War "anti-totalitarian" rhetoric.[79]

Book programs offered a discursive arena in which the Japanese could create a new "democratic" subjectivity. By the 1950s, books and magazines disseminated the Cold War idea of democracy directly and indirectly through the image of an affluent society, or through American heroes like Huckleberry Finn or Abe Lincoln. This newly introduced notion of "democracy" was culturally translated through terms as "wealth," "freedom," "freedom of choice," "equality of people" and "equality of the sexes." The visual images of magazines, the multiculturalism present in the library book collection, and the strong anti-Communist ideas and individual freedom found in translated books all indicate that these terms were imported in complex and multivalent ways. Democracy as promoted in postwar Japan had to be reshaped so that it would be understandable to the Japanese people, and yet, to meet American foreign policy objectives, it had to be strongly imbued with Cold War containment rhetoric. The image of the affluent society in particular presented a very understandable model toward which ordinary Japanese could strive. Especially in the process of breaking down the old authoritarian, militarist ideology, the equation of freedom with affluence, as well as a seeming equality of the sexes, promised a new style of life for the Japanese people. At the same time, the most accessible images and all-male heroes of freedom replicated old patterns, which eased Japan into an alliance of Cold War policy from within.

Notes

1. Reinhold Wagnleitner, *Coca-Colonization and the Cold War: The Cultural Mission of the United States in Austria after the Second World War*, trans. Diana M. Wolf (Chapel Hill: University of North Carolina Press, 1994); Kenji Tanigawa, *America Eiga to Senryou Seisaku (American Motion Pictures and Occupation Policy)* (Kyoto: Kyoto Daigaku Shuppankai [Kyoto University Press], 2002); Madoko Kon, "America Kyouiku Shisetsudan no Okurimono (Giftbooks from the U.S. Education Mission)," *Kiyo Shakaigakka (Journal of the Faculty of Literature. Department of Sociology)*, 6 (1996): 121–49, and "America no Jouhoukouryu to Toshokan: CIE Toshokan to no Kakawari ni Oite (American Information Exchange Programs and Libraries: In Terms of CIE Libraries)," *Kiyo Shakaigakka (Journal of the Faculty of Literature. Department of Sociology)*, 4 (1994): 29–42.

2. Gary Kraske, *Missionaries of the Book: The American Library Profession and the Origins of United States Cultural Diplomacy* (Westport, Conn: Greenwood Press, 1985).

3. Department of State, *The Cultural-Cooperation Program 1938–1943* (Washington, D.C.: Department of State, 1944), 3.

4. Henry James, Jr., "The Role of the Information Library in the United States International Information Program," *The Library Quarterly* 23:2 (April 1953): 82–83.

5. Department of State, *The Cultural-Cooperation Program*, 27.

6. Kraske, *Missionaries of the Book*, 144.

7. On the orders concerning the institutional transformation, see "Establishment of the Interim International Information Service," *Department of State Bulletin* 13:325 (September 16, 1945): 418 and "Plans for International Information Service," *Department of State Bulletin* 13:340 (December 30, 1945): 1045–46. On the changing emphasis of OWI library operations, Kraske, *Missionaries of the Book*, 144; on the involvement of War Department in the cultural policies in the occupied areas, see Wagnleitner, *Coca-Colonization*, 50–55.

8. Archibald MacLeish, "Introduction," in Ruth Emily McMurry and Muna Lee, eds., *The Cultural Approach: Another Way in International Relations* (Chapel Hill: University of North Carolina Press, 1947), ix.

9. James, "The Role of the Information Library," 77–78.

10. Kon, "American Information," 29–40.

11. "CIE Weekly Reports, Library Division" 24 February–2 March 1946 (NARA II College Park MD: RG 331 SCAP UD 1651 Box 5117). The nature of CIE libraries is totally different from that of the community libraries in U.S. concentration camps for Japanese Americans during World War II. The aim of the camps was Americanization of potential enemies in the United States, but selection of the book for the camps was not really a selection; rather, they were discards of local libraries and the rejected books of the Victory Books Campaign. For further information on these libraries, see Andrew B. Wertheimer,

Japanese American Community Libraries in America's Concentration Camps, 1942–1946 (UMI Dissertation Services, 2004).

12. Elaine Tyler May, *Homeward Bound: American Families in the Cold War Era* (New York: Basic Books, 1988).

13. Kraske, *Missionaries of the Book*, 39.

14. Brett F. Cox, "What Need, Then, for Poetry?: The Genteel Tradition and the Continuity of American Literature," *New England Quarterly* 67:2 (June 1994): 220.

15. Ibid., 219–33.

16. Trysh Travis, "Books as Weapons and 'The Smart Man's Peace': The Work of the Council on Books in Wartime," *Princeton University Library Chronicle* 60 (Spring 1999): 353–99.

17. Patti Clayton Becker, *Books and Libraries in American Society during World War II: Weapons in the War of Ideas* (New York: Routledge, 2005), 96–97.

18. Franklin D. Roosevelt. "Weapons for Man's Freedom." *ALA Bulletin* 36:11 (1942): 582.

19. Elmer Davis, "A Message to American Librarians," *ALA Bulletin* 36:11 (1942): 583.

20. "Basic Plan for Books. Aug 18 1944" (NARA II College Park, MD: RG208 (OWI) NC148 Entry 464 Box 2949 Folder "Book Selection-Operations").

21. "Procedure for selection of books for inclusion in Overseas Editions series. May 31, 1944" (NARA II College Park, MD: RG208 NC148 No.464 Records of the Bureau of Overseas Publication, Box 2949 Folder7). On August 15, 1944, the members of the outside Advisory Committee were partly changed. In place of Rosemary Benét, poet and critic Louis Untermeyer is listed. "Overseas Editions. August 15, 1944" (NARA II College Park, MD: RG208 NC148 No.464 Box 2949 Folder "Book Section-Operations").

22. Cox, "What Need," 226–33.

23. Janice Radway, *A Feeling for Books: The Book-of-the-Month Club, Literary Taste, and Middle-Class Desire* (Chapel Hill: University of North Carolina Press, 1997), 221–57; Joan Shelley Rubin, *The Making of Middlebrow Culture* (Chapel Hill: University of North Carolina Press, 1992).

24. Radway, *A Feeling for Books*, 230.

25. Rubin, *Making of Middlebrow Culture*, 87.

26. *A History of the Council on Books in Wartime* (New York: Country Life Press, 1946), 101–24.

27. Travis, "Books as Weapons," 387–88.

28. *A History of the Council on Books in Wartime*, 125–26; "Book Section Material Monthly Progress Report June 10, 1944–July 10, 1944" (NARA II, College Park, MD: RG208 NC148 No.464 Records of the Bureau of Overseas Publication, Box 2951 Folder "Monthly Progress Report, Bureau of Overseas Publication"); "OWI-Council on Books in Wartime Overseas Book Project June 6, 1944" (NARA II, College Park, MD: RG208 NC148 No.464 Box 2951A Folder" Overseas Editions Contract: Council's Letter to Members").

29. "Basic List of Approved Books. Sept 22, 1944" (NARA II, College Park, MD: RG208 NC148 No. 464 Box 2951A Folder "Memos re Selection").

30. *Writers' War Board: Third Annual Report* (New York: Writers' War Board, 1944) (NARA II, College Park, MD: RG208NC148 Entry 339 Box 1695 Folder "Books and Magazines Bureau Liaison with Writers' War Board").

31. Judy Kutulas, "Becoming 'More Liberal': The League of American Writers, the Communist Party, and the Literary People's Front," *Journal of American Culture* 13:1 (1990): 71–80.

32. Ellsworth Young, *Report of the Books for Europe Project of the American Library Association* (New York: American Library Association, 1942), 2.

33. Department of State, *The Cultural-Cooperation Program*, 32.

34. Kraske, *Missionaries of the Book*, 159.

35. Books for Latin America Project, American Library Association, *Selected List of Books in English by U.S. Authors* (Chicago: American Library Association, 1942), 5–6.

36. Ellsworth Young, *"The Books for Europe Project: A Résumé,"* *ALA Bulletin* 37:2 (1943): 48.

37. According to Rubin, Henry Seidel Canby of the Book-of-the-Month Club favored Rawlings and Ferber, but criticized Thomas Wolfe and William Faulkner. Rubin, *Making of Middlebrow Culture*, 121.

38. On the member list of the League, see Franklin Folsom, *Days of Anger, Days of Hope: A Memoir of the League of American Writers 1937–1942* (Niwot: University Press of Colorado, 1994), 265–331. On the shifting attitudes of the League members, see Kutulas, "Becoming 'More Liberal.'" On the members of Writers' War Board, see their 1st to 3rd *Annual Reports* (1942–44) (NARA II, MD: RG208,NC148, Entry 339, Box 1695 Folder "Books and Magazines Bureau Liaison with Writers' War Board"). On Free Company, see xroads.virginia.edu/~1930s/RADIO/Free/main.html.

39. William E. Cain, "Inventing American Literature," in *The Cambridge History of American Literature,* vol. 5, ed. Sacvan Bercovitch (Cambridge: Cambridge University Press, 2003), 389.

40. Ibid., 376.

41. Werner Sollers, "Ethnic Modernism," in *The Cambridge History of American Literature,* vol. 6, ed. Sacvan Bercovitch (Cambridge: Cambridge University Press, 2003), 512–28.

42. Committee on Aid to Libraries in War Areas, International Relations Board, American Library Association, *Books Published in the United States 1939–1943: A Selection for Reference Libraries* (Chicago: American Library Association, 1945), viii–ix.

43. Ibid., x.

44. Allen Tate, *Sixty American Poets, 1896–1944: Selection, Preface, and Critical Notes by Allen Tate, Consultant in Poetry in English, 1943–1944* (Washington, D.C.: The Library of Congress, 1945).

45. On the transformation of American literary criticism and academism, see Gerald Graff, *Professing Literature: An Institutional History* (Chicago: University of Chicago Press, 1987), and Kermit Vanderbilt, *American Literature and the Academy: The Roots, Growth, and Maturity of a Profession* (Philadelphia: University of Pennsylvania Press, 1986).

46. "General Order No.183, 22 Sept.1945" (GHQ/SCAP Records, Economic and Scientific Section ESS(E) 00761, National Diet Library, Tokyo, corresponding to NARA II: RG331 SCAP Records Economic and Scientific Section Box 6392 Folder 10).

47. For the publishing policies of the Soviet Union for the occupied areas, see Christian Kanig's essay in this collection.

48. Kon, "Gift," 121–50; Tsuyoshi Ishihara, *Mark Twain in Japan: The Cultural Reception of an American Icon* (Columbia, MO: University of Missouri Press, 2005), 63.

49. On the need for library reform, see the *Report of the United States Education Mission to Japan*, 30 March 1946 (National Diet Library, Japan: GHQ/SCAP CIE CIE(C)01776–01777, corresponding to NARAII: RG331 Box.5348 Folder3) 48–49. For a summary of library reform, see Philip O. Keeney, "Reorganization of the Japanese Public Library System I," *Far Eastern Survey*, February 11, 1948: 32–35, and "Reorganization of the Japanese Public Library System II," *Far Eastern Survey*, January 28, 1948: 19–22. More on school library reform can be found in Theodore F. Welch, *Libraries and Librarianship in Japan* (Westport, Conn: Greenwood Press, 1997), 99–110.

50. "Organization of CIE, 19 October, 1945." (NARA II, College Park, MD: RG 331 SCAP UD1647 CIE Box 5059 Folder "Organization of CIE, 1945").

51. CIE weekly reports show only some of the titles. Unfortunately, the initial collection has long gone from the first CIE library in Tokyo (now American Center). The only collection preserved is that of the Yokohama branch, but the library cards don't show the dates of receipt by the library until 1950.

52. "CIE Weekly Reports, Library Division," 8–15 December 1945 (NARA II College Park, MD: RG 331 SCAP UD 1651 Box 5111).

53. "CIE Weekly Reports, Library Division," 3–10 January 1946 (NARA II College Park, MD: RG 331 SCAP UD 1651 Box 5111).

54. "CIE Weekly Reports, Library Division," 24 February–2 March 1946, 3 March–9 March 1946 (NARA II College Park, MD: RG 331 SCAP UD 1651 Box 5117).

55. "CIE Weekly Reports, Library Division," 10–16 March 1946 (NARA II College Park, MD: RG 331 SCAP UD 1651 Box 5117).

56. "CIE Weekly Reports, Library Division," 31 March–5 April 1946 (NARA II College Park, MD: RG 331 SCAP UD 1651 Box 5117).

57. "CIE Intra-Section Memorandum. Sept 15, 1948," (NARA II, College Park MD: RG331 SCAP UD1671 Box 5328 Folder "Books, Shipping Lists, Incoming").

58. "Organization of CIE, 14 November 1945" (NARA II, College Park MD: RG 331 SCAP UD1647 CIE Box 5059 Folder "Organizations")

59. "Book Order for Branch Libraries, 2 December 1946" (National Diet Library, Tokyo: GHQ/SCAP Records CIE(C) 01541–01542, corresponding to Nara II, College Park MD: RG331 SCAP Records CIE Box 5328 Folder 11).

60. James, "The Role of the Information Library," 84.

61. Kraske, *Missionaries of the Book*, 144.

62. *Report of the United States Education Mission to Japan*, 11.

63. "CIE Weekly Reports, Library Division," 17–23 March, 23–30 March 1946 (NARA II College Park, MD: RG 331 SCAP UD 1651 Box 5117).

64. About America Houses and their activities, see Wagnleitner, *Coca-Colonization*, 128–49; "The CIE Libraries," Jihyo (Editorial Comments), *Asahi Shinbun*, March 1, 1952; "Oshimareru Kyu CIE Toshokan (Passing of Former CIE Libraries)," *Asahi Shinbun*, February 8, 1953.

65. "CIE Weekly Reports, Library Division," 24 February–2 March, 1946 (NARA II College Park, MD: RG 331 SCAP UD 1651 Box 5117).

66. About the openings of the branches, see *CIE Bulletins* issued between September 1947 and October 1949 (NARA II College Park, MD: RG 331 SCAP UD 1651 Box 5117). Also see Kon's summary in Kaiko Bunshu Iinkai (Editorial Committee for Memoir of the CIE Library), *CIE Toshokan wo Kaikoshite* (Memoir of the CIE Library) (Toyonaka, Osaka: Kaiko Bunshu Iinkai, 2003), 4–5. On their cultural activities, see Akira Shigeno,

"Beikoku-Seifu no Nihon ni Okeru Kouhou-Bunka Katsudou ni Tsuite (Informational and Cultural Activities of the U.S. Government in Japan)," *Cosmica* 14 (1985): 10–40. For the pictures of CIE Information Library Tokyo, see NARA II, College Park, MD: RG331 UD1651 Box 5111. On the magazine lists of CIE Information Library, see "CIE Weekly Report," 9–15 Feb 1946 (NARA II College Park, MD: RG 331 SCAP UD 1651 Box 5117). On America House and its activities, see Wagnleitner, *Coca-Colonization*, 128–49. There Wagnleitner names as "the most-read American authors: Ernest Hemingway, Louis Bromfield, John Steinbeck, Sinclair Lewis, John Marquand, William Saroyan, and Pearl S. Buck," and also names the popular American magazines: *Life, Time, Newsweek, Reader's Digest, Saturday Evening Post, Colliers, Look, Vogue, Harper's Bazaar, Ladies Home Journal, Good Housekeeping,* and *Better Homes and Gardens* (135). The names and titles overlap those of Japanese centers.

67. Kaiko Bunshu Iinkai (Editorial Committee for Memoir of the CIE Library), *CIE Toshokan wo Kaikoshite* (*Memoir of the CIE Library*) (Toyonaka, Osaka: Kaiko Bunshu Iinkai, 2003), 13–14, 22.

68. Ibid., 30.

69. "Passing of Former CIE libraries," *Asahi Shinbun*, February 8, 1953; "Oshare Season (Fashion Season)," *Asahi Shinbun*, April 27, 1949. *CIE Bulletin* 11 May 1949 (NARA II College Park, MD: RG 331 SCAP UD 1653 Box 5172), 5.

70. In his *America Eiga to Senryou Seisaku*, 448–49, Kenji Tanigawa cites the statement of movie director Nagisa Oshima that the message he got from Hollywood motion pictures during the occupation was not about democracy; instead he saw America as an industrial, progressive land filled with heroes fighting for progressive causes and heroines who love them. But at the same time, the affluence and the happy couples themselves also were a phase of democracy. As Tanigawa points out, motion pictures presented the visual image of American society as a model for postwar Japanese people.

71. May, *Homeward Bound*, 11–13.

72. *The Report of the U.S. Education Mission to Japan*, 3–7, 12–13.

73. On George Kennan and the discourse of containment culture, see Alan Nadel, *Containment Culture: American Narratives, Postmodernism, and the Atomic Age* (Durham, N.C.: Duke University Press, 1995), 15–17; Frank Costigliola, "Unceasing Pressure for Penetration: Gender, Pathology, and Emotion in George Kennan's Formation of the Cold War," Journal of American History (March 1997): 1309–39.

74. On the program, see *CIE Bulletin*, 26 May 1948, 13, and 12 October 1949, 5 (NARA II College Park, MD: RG 331 SCAP UD 1653 Box 5172).

75. Ishihara, *Mark Twain in Japan*, 65–66.

76. Tanigawa, *America Eiga*, 444–45; Wagnleitner, *Coca-Colonization*, 270.

77. *CIE Bulletin* 22 June 1949 (NARA II College Park, MD: RG 331 SCAP UD 1653 Box 5172), 7. Ishihara also cites the *Bulletin*'s comment on *Animal Farm* in his note on page 62 of his book.

78. Suzanne Clarke, *Cold Warriors: Manliness on Trial in the Rhetoric of the West* (Carbondale: Southern Illinois University Press, 2000), 3.

79. Edwin Reischauer's lecture featured in the *CIE Bulletin* 10 November 1948 (NARA II College Park, MD: RG 331 SCAP UD 1653 Box 5172), 3, 7.

5 The British Information Research Department and Cold War Propaganda Publishing

JAMES B. SMITH

THAT COVERT elements of Western governments were intimately involved in the publishing culture of the Cold War has long been established, with the most famous incident being the revelation, in 1967, of the CIA's involvement in the Congress for Cultural Freedom and funding of the Congress's cultural journal *Encounter*. Over the past decade the activities of the British government in the field of Cold War propaganda have come under increasing scholarly scrutiny, with the release of files from the Information Research Department (IRD) of the British Foreign Office to the British National Archives allowing a detailed picture of the agency to emerge.[1] Officially founded in 1948 under the Attlee Labour government and the anti-Communist Foreign Secretary Ernest Bevin, and ostensibly tasked with the "compilation of information report for H.M. Missions abroad,"[2] the IRD operated as the Cold War propaganda unit of the British government, disseminating a range of non-attributable material to select politicians and journalists in Britain and overseas.

Initially designed to carry out the comparatively benign purpose of highlighting the benefits of British social democracy compared with American capitalism or Soviet Communism, the IRD soon supplemented this with the production of a range of aggressively anti-Communist material. The department took an active stance in the propaganda battle against the Russians and their Communist allies, at a time when Western governments' intelligence assessments concluded that the coming conflict with the USSR would not necessarily involve direct military activity but rather overt and covert ideological actions, with the production and distribution of propaganda material a key tactic used by both Soviet and Western powers in extending and contesting influence in regions such as the British colonies. The IRD would continue to grow, under Labour (1945–51, 1964–70, 1974–79) and Conservative (1951–64, 1970–74) administrations alike, to become one of the Foreign Office's largest departments, until its closure in 1977. While the initial productions of the IRD consisted largely of background papers and briefs, intended for select distribution and not designed for direct public consumption, a key aspect of the department's output would soon come in the form of covertly subsidized publishing ventures. This chapter intends to overview this development, starting from the early maneuvers by IRD officials to entice commercial publishers into carrying IRD material, through to the successful series of books secretly funded by the IRD that ran through the 1950s and '60s.

Recruiting Publishers

By 1949, spurred by the initial success of its papers and the growing demands for more substantial material to distribute, as well as an international political climate dominated by events such as the Berlin Blockade that suggested a long-term struggle against Communism, the IRD had embarked upon concerted attempts to instigate a book-publishing program. This program began with the identifying and recruiting of suitable authors and independent publishers deemed both trustworthy and politically sympathetic to the IRD's aims. Most famously, the department attempted to recruit George Orwell, who declined to write for the IRD himself, but allowed the department to distribute his extant work and provided a list of intellectuals he considered to be crypto-Communists and thus not suitable for IRD commissions.[3] While Orwell's relationship with the IRD has captured newspaper headlines over the past decade, it was only one incident in the wider effort to approach authors, editors, and independent publishing houses in this period.

The story of the relationship between the IRD and Penguin Books, instigated by the department's Leslie Sheridan, provides a detailed example of exactly how the organization attempted to recruit commercial publishers for the purpose of "grey" propaganda (or information material that, while factually accurate, was selectively chosen, arranged, and distributed without official attribution). Sheridan, a wartime officer with the British Special Operations Executive, had been brought into the IRD in 1949 to run the Editorial Section, while maintaining a separate office at 47 Essex Street, in Westminster, London. Thus, while he was clearly intimately involved in the operations of IRD, he could nonetheless operate at arm's length, ostensibly describing his role in correspondence as merely that of an "adviser" to a branch of the Foreign Office, and therefore able to act as the liaison between commercial publishers and the IRD. As a result, the Foreign Office could influence the editorial direction of major British firms without appearing directly involved. This arrangement drew on established British governmental opinion, gained over the course of propaganda campaigns in the two world wars, that propaganda was a crucial tool and most effective when overt links to its origin were removed. Britain, as a democracy, wanted to ensure that it did not appear to be using the same strategies as those of the totalitarian governments it sought to oppose.[4]

Such was the case in Sheridan's negotiations with Allen Lane, the publisher who pioneered the marketing of cheap paperback editions with the establishment of Penguin Books in 1935, and whose Pelican imprint carried an influential list of mass-market nonfiction. Lane's recruitment would have represented a major coup for the IRD. In a minute circulated through the IRD, Sheridan reported that during a meeting with Lane he used his "usual cover story," implying that Lane did not realize the exact nature of Sheridan's employment.[5] He reported that Lane, recently returned from a trip to America, was "much impressed—and depressed—by the crudeness of anti-Soviet propaganda and the lack of balance with which the American people were viewing this problem." Sheridan saw an opening to encourage Lane in the directions advocated by the IRD. Lane had already acquired an internal IRD information document, "Foundations of Stalinism," via a contact at Reuters, and Sheridan encouraged him to rework it from its current report-like form into one that would interest a general commercial readership, provided that "it was not quoted as an official document," and that "there was no suggestion that the paper contained the views of HMG." Sheridan equally stressed that he did not regard such arrangements as propaganda, adding in the minute that "I must make it clear, this paper was not propaganda, it was simply a collection of facts."

On the basis of Lane's initial interest in this document, Sheridan hoped to use Lane as a conduit for other publications, requesting departmental approval to pass to him a series of "basic papers" from the IRD with titles such as "Forced Labour in the USSR" and "Training the Young for Stalin." It was clear that Sheridan intended this material to find its way into a Penguin book; he stated that "this will be sufficient for him to brief any author . . . [e]specially if I tell him he can ask me for further information on specific points." At the head office, the IRD balked at this request to provide Allen Lane and Penguin Books such an uninhibited degree of access to restricted material without knowing the identity of the receiving author. IRD staff raised questions concerning the security implications, as well as noting that such basic papers might be too propagandistic for an independent author's taste.[6] Nonetheless, the staff remained enthusiastic about acquiring the services of such an influential publisher. They used their desire for secrecy as a way to control in advance the authors Lane was authorized to employ.[7] Hence, as he requested further meetings with Lane, Sheridan offered both the prospect of access to restricted material and the possibility of being brought into the circle of this shadowy Whitehall organization as bait: "If the Department of the Foreign Office I advise were convinced that a satisfactory job would be done by some selected author, they might be willing to put a great deal of additional material at his disposal; I think I can say that some of this material would be very difficult if not impossible to obtain except with some official help."[8]

While it appears that nothing came, in this instance, as a result of these meetings (with Lane postponing further interaction due to business commitments), other officers of the IRD were pressing forward with a wider and more ambitious project of attempting not just to influence the direction of individual publishers, but to establish a more direct conduit for publishing and distributing pamphlet and book-length material. In a letter the head of the IRD, Ralph Murray, explained to the Labour Foreign Office minister, Christopher Mayhew, that while it was now regarded as a "necessity" to ensure that "publishing firms [were] interested in IRD subjects," with approaches made "to a few firms, particularly the Oxford University Press," such "suggestive and tentative" methods still only frustratingly presented the "promise of results" rather than more concrete arrangements that could ensure a steady flow of material.[9] In response, the IRD envisaged a larger and more concrete publishing enterprise, over which they would exert more direct control. The department had already attempted to mobilize the resources of existing center-left political organizations for this end, but had found these organs manifestly inadequate, noting the level of "small cooperation" that it had achieved from the Labour Party (such as the use of Labour Party literature in Burma) and the "dismal experience" of working with the central British union body, the Trades Union Congress (TUC), while trying to prompt the TUC to generate their own political literature for overseas political use. Not deterred by the limited results of this enterprise so far, the IRD was now looking for "a dynamic solution" to allow it to step up its activity and produce a "flow of literature, either in this country or abroad, which can compete with the Communist propaganda machine."

Background Books and Ampersand

The IRD's quest to find a publisher reached fruition in 1951 with the launch of the Background Books series—a series that would run to over one hundred titles, and one that would feature the work of many of the major British authors in the fields of philosophy, politics, trade unionism, and Sovietology. The Background Books, in the lifetime of the series, would be produced by three separate publishers. The initial run would be carried by Batchworth Press, an obscure London publishing house which, before its involvement in government propaganda work, had produced such titles as *Snuff and Snuff-Boxes* and *On Railways at Home and Abroad*. After the closure of Batchworth in 1955 the series switched to Phoenix House. Finally, the Bodley Head under Max Reinhardt took the series over after 1960.[10] Throughout these shifts Stephen Watts, another of the IRD's network of ex–wartime intelligence officers now operating as a supposedly freelance publisher's editor, commissioned books for the series, liaised with the IRD regarding choice of titles, and dealt with the publishers, some of whom would later state that they were unaware of Watts's connection with the Foreign Office or IRD.[11]

Besides this editorial control exercised through Watts, the books were also directly financially supported by an arrangement between the IRD and the publishers. H. H. (Tommy) Tucker, a journalist who joined the IRD in 1951 and stayed until its closure during the 1970s, described the mechanism as a formal "see-safe" agreement (or agreement that the publisher would be financially "safe" on the venture due to a pre-order of a certain number of volumes by the IRD, which thus guaranteed the run would reach at least the break-even point). The IRD would "suggest authors [and] suggest themes" and then guarantee to "buy the end product" (typically on the order of 15,000 copies), leaving the publisher "quite happy because that covers their costs and distribution and everything and anything above that is sheer profit for them." The front company Ampersand (with Sheridan and Watts on its board of directors) provided the intermediary through which these funds were released.[12]

The first publications in the Background Books series were simple pamphlets with bright red paper covers, a large question mark across the front title the sole illustration. They were stapled rather than bound, costing either one shilling or one shilling and sixpence, and normally from thirty-two to forty-eight pages in length: a format that was clearly designed to facilitate the cheapest possible production, distribution, and reproduction of works in the series. With topical titles, such as the first book's *What Is Communism?*, these texts appeared innocuously factual, offering a commonsensical take on contemporary issues. The self-deprecating description on the back cover further conveyed this sense:

> These little books are designed to provide ordinary people, interested in what is going on in the world to-day, with some background information about events, institutions and ideas.

They will not interpret current history for you but they will help you to interpret it for yourself.

Background Books range widely in subject dealing with what lies at the roots of the questions thinking people are asking, filling in the background without which world affairs to-day cannot be properly seen or judged.

By the time of the publication of Russell's pamphlet *What Is Freedom?* in 1952 there were ten of the series in print, among them *What Is Peace?* by the Dean of Chichester, *What Is NATO?* by Andrew Boyd, *What Is Titoism?* by Cicely and Christopher Mayhew, and *The Law—Servant or Master?* by L. B Schapiro. As the series continued, the works were often more substantive, with the occasional "Background Specials" presenting substantially longer and more detailed works (the 1952 *How Did the Satellites Happen?* by "A Student of Affairs," for example, ran to over 300 pages). For its final incarnation, the Bodley Head created a more substantial format of concise, clean hardback editions running to around 100 pages. Considerably more elegant than the initial booklets of 1951, the Bodley Head's books demonstrate that the IRD's marketing strategy for the series had undergone an interesting shift, away from cheap pamphlets and toward volumes that would not look out of place on the shelves of university libraries. What, then, was the ideological position adopted in these works, given the covert support of the IRD? Paul Lashmar and James Oliver have characterized the Background Books as predominantly "anti-Communist" in their subject matter and argument, describing much of the output as "rather simple anti-Communist propaganda."[13] While this simple anti-Communism is often apparent, books in the series reveal a spectrum of positions—from uncompromising anti-Communism to a more positive, progressive vision of social democracy—a range that reflects the IRD's shifting propaganda roles between that of anti-Soviet and pro-"Third Force," and shows a sometimes surprisingly diverse range of political views that found voice in the IRD-backed series.

At one extreme, the works did present "red scare" material, using dire pictures of Communist threat rather than factual analysis. Particularly notable in this regard was the book by the Labour politician Francis Noel-Baker entitled *The Spy Web: A Study of Communist Espionage*, published by Batchworth Press in 1954, which presented the details of four espionage cases involving Communist Party members. Using these cases, Noel-Baker suggested that every member of the Party in the West was on an inevitable trajectory toward becoming a spy:

Even when a communist is associated only with the open, legal side of his party's work, he lives in an atmosphere of constant conspiracy and absolute

> discipline. . . . And because no rank-and-file member may ever discuss policy
> or express a political opinion which is not simply a repetition of slogans passed
> down to him from above, he longs . . . for some practical way of demonstrating
> his loyalty and faith—whether it be selling the *Daily Worker* on a street corner
> or becoming a Russian spy.[14]

This simplistic psychological profiling thus beat a propaganda drum but, in
presenting the Communist as an undifferentiated drone, failed to offer any
new intervention in the debate, reinforcing existing anti-Communist opinion rather than asserting the value of social democracy.

The Spy Web represents an example of Background Books at their most
manifestly anti-Communist; such stridency was by no means uniform. Other
works attempted to adopt a tone of scholarly neutrality, as was the case in the
Glossary of Political Terms (1966) edited by Maurice Cranston and containing
entries from many prominent British political scientists; while presenting
an alphabetically arranged discussion of terms ranging from Anarchism to
Trade-Unionism, it managed to offer a concise and useful discussion despite
the obvious constraints of the need for brevity and simplicity. The most interesting and original proportion of the Background Books expressed a positive,
if still critical, vision of Britain. C. M Woodhouse's *Post-War Britain* (1966),
for example, presented the history of Britain after 1945 as "a story partly of
successful adjustment and partly of maladjustment,"[15] offering a cautious account of the progression and reform in British society and concluding with
the question "Will the social forces which prevail be those which are directed
forwards and outwards, or those which are directed backwards and in-
wards?"[16] The book optimistically suggests that it would be the former. Also
notable in this regard was Bryan Magee's *The Democratic Revolution*, released in 1964, which openly criticized capitalism and Communism alike,
stating that "the ideologies of Capitalism and Communism were products of
the nineteenth century, and neither of them is applicable to the world we live
in. Although both sides of the Cold War still go on mouthing the old theories, their practice has long ceased to accord with them, if it ever did."[17] Magee clearly sympathized with the West, holding that it had progressed beyond
capitalism into a state of social democracy, unlike the repressive Soviet system. Nonetheless, he criticized the "extreme inequality" prevalent in the West.
He also made statements such as "Everyone on the Democratic Left should be
on the rampage to smash for ever the class structure that is the root of most of
the remediable evil in our society," sentiments which no doubt were at odds
with the more trenchant Cold Warriors in the Foreign Office.[18]

The IRD's interest in the Background Books extended to ensuring that the
works were distributed worldwide, and particularly ensuring that they reached
opinion influencers in areas of British interest. The early books in the series

carried a note stating that others in the series were available "from booksellers and newsagents," and indeed Tucker confirmed that "they sold well on the commercial market." However, this market was only one target. Once books reached print, Tucker explains, the IRD bought 15,000 copies, "which we then distributed to Foreign Office posts around the world who wanted them and put an order in for them, we sent them out and they presented them to their local contacts and anyone who then [*sic*] thought would be interested in them."[19] Thus, the see-safe agreement was more than just a subsidy to stimulate a publishing market; it resembled a laundering exercise. The IRD funneled authors, ideas, and research material through an outsourced publishing organization, then bought the product and distributed the books abroad, at which point it encouraged overseas posts to reproduce, translate, and distribute the material—now disguised as having independent origin.

As the IRD distributed large numbers of Background Books, it kept close tabs on the recipients. For instance, in November 1953 the "Regional Servicing Centre" in the British Embassy in Mexico reported the distribution of copies of four early Background Books (*A Press in Chains* by Dennis Bardens, *What Was the Russian Revolution?* by "A Student of Affairs," *What Is Democracy?* by Bertrand Russell, and *What Is Culture?* by T. R. Fyvel) in Central America. This report contained lists of the recipients of each individual title, including senior government officials, church leaders, and press editors in El Salvador, Honduras, Cuba, Guatemala, the Dominican Republic, and Nicaragua.[20] The IRD distributed Russell's *What Is Democracy?* to forty-two recipients. In some countries the distribution appears to have favored direct government sources, as in El Salvador where the list included contacts in the Ministries of Culture, Defense, Interior Relations, and Exterior; whereas in other countries the list showed a more concentrated effort to place Russell's work among press contacts, with entries recording names such as Enrique Roman of *La Estrella de Nicaragua* and Isberto Montenegro of *Diario de Costa Rica* (both of which had a capital "P" alongside in the margin, presumably to distinguish members of the press).

While the Background Books represented the IRD's most sustained foray into propaganda publishing, other publishing projects were developed during the lifetime of the department's operation. The most important of these was Ampersand, previously noted as the company IRD contract staff directed and used to funnel money to the Background Books. Sheridan registered the Ampersand company name as early as 1946, and Ampersand was involved in publications such as the Bellman Books series in the mid-1950s.[21] After Hugh Carless, a member of the Foreign Office who served as a first secretary in the IRD from 1958 until 1961, introduced Leslie Sheridan to Rayner Unwin, son of Sir Stanley Unwin, an agreement was reached with the major publishing company Allen and Unwin to distribute a series of Ampersand books.[22] By 1966, Allen and Unwin Ampersand Books listed fifteen publications in the series, ranging in price from three shillings for the shorter works, up to 30 shillings for the substantial editions of academic bibliographies. This series appeared to have been designed to target a university readership. For example, one of the most militantly anti-Communist Ampersand works, *Outlines of Communism* (edited by the conservative political scientist Gerhart Niemeyer, adapted and released by Ampersand in 1966), carried a subtitle proclaiming itself an "essential textbook for students of politics."

Ampersand also published works of formidable scholarship, the most notable being the annotated bibliography *Books on Communism*, which went through three heavily revised editions. The first edition, released by Ampersand in 1959, was by ex–MI6 officer R. N. Carew Hunt and covered about 1,900 bibliographic entries; the second edition, edited by Walter Kolarz after Hunt's death, had expanded to around 2,500 entries, running to 568 pages in length and costing 30 shillings. These were studies clearly intended for research libraries and for shaping the work of Sovietologists. Indeed, an academic reviewer of the Kolarz edition was moved to praise the work as a volume that "deserves to be brought to the attention not only of scholars and students interested in communism but of a large part of the academic community in general."[23] Notably, the Kolarz edition was released the next year in the United States by Oxford University Press—an interesting example of a work initially dependent on covert funding from a governmental propaganda department filtering through to one of the world's premier university presses.

This filtering process indicates the differences between the IRD's approach and that taken by the Soviet Union. Whereas Soviet propaganda efforts often worked with scales and controls that dwarfed any of the IRD's efforts, as Christian Kanig illustrates in the present volume,[24] the IRD did not seek to completely saturate the market. Instead it adopted a strategy which could be characterized as top-down, devising publications that would be of interest to opinion-formers (whether to politicians and journalists overseas, or students and academics at home), who would then adapt and disseminate the ideas in their own work. Thus the actual influence of the IRD's books, while difficult to judge, perhaps lies less in propaganda coups achieved by the works themselves than in their attempts to steer paradigms of debate, stimulating suitable publications on otherwise financially unrewarding topics such as Sovietology to ensure that pro-Western views, in key areas, were contesting the intellectual field. That Background and Ampersand titles were often reviewed (and praised) in scholarly journals shows that their viewpoints achieved circulation and credibility.[25]

But whose views were represented? Was the IRD subsidizing a market for topical political and historical studies, and granting full intellectual and academic freedom for its authors. Or did its involvement extend into the shaping of what these ostensibly independent books would contain? Ex-IRD official Tucker defended the integrity of the intellectual material produced by authors, and described the output as being "entirely their own thoughts. . . . All we did was identify an author who obviously we thought had views not dissimilar to our own—but who then took a subject and wrote about it as he would normally."[26] Scholars assessing IRD-funded works have generally concurred with such a position, with Lyn Smith suggesting, after reviewing most of the works in the Background series, that "there is no evidence that writers' views were trimmed to particular political lines" and that "rather it was the case that if their independent opinions fitted in with IRD's requirements then their output would be used."[27]

This, however, does not account for the more ambiguous systems of controls that existed in many cases. While the IRD officers themselves may not have directly intervened in the formation of the text, the books subsidized by the IRD were nonetheless subject to a series of subtle mechanisms to ensure that the end products presented material acceptable for the IRD's purpose. And, of course, material that was not useful was not subsidized. Indeed, given that the IRD, via its network of contract staff such as Sheridan and Watts, vetted the publishers and editors, controlled the see-safe funding, identified sympathetic authors to be approached for a particular title, and in many cases provided research material for the authors to base their study upon, it is not surprising that few "direct steers" needed to be given; the end product could likely be ascertained long before a draft of the work reached an IRD officer's desk. In many cases, the authors were clearly aware that the work they were producing was done at the instigation of the IRD, and thus would have, from the outset, been conscious of the desired coverage and arguments of the books. For example, Christopher Mayhew, the Labour politician and junior Foreign Office minister instrumental in the founding of the IRD, was well aware of the IRD's desires when he and his wife Cicily wrote one of the earliest Background volumes, *What Is Titoism?*, and later also wrote *Coexistence Plus: A Positive Approach to World Peace* for the Bodley Head in 1962. However, as Lashmar and Oliver have ascertained, other authors appear to have been genuinely in the dark about the IRD's backing of the works. For example, Bryan Magee, whose study was above noted to be one of the most positively social-democratic, subsequently stated that he had no knowledge of the IRD's involvement in the scheme, and expressed his anger at the fact that such an involvement existed, giving credence to Tucker's suggestion that many of the Background authors were indeed unaware of the arrangements in place.[28]

Despite these claims, there is evidence that the IRD shaped the actual intellectual content of works it funded, controlling the scope of what the commissioned books covered, and asking for revisions if some political point was not suitable for the aims of the series. This appears to be the case in the work of Bertrand Russell, an author who produced several of the Background Books, and undoubtedly one of the most intellectually respected authors that the IRD co-opted. In a recent study seeking to clarify Russell's involvement with the IRD, Andrew G. Bone examined the archival record regarding the genesis of Russell's publications, providing an illuminating picture of how these works were commissioned and shaped. Russell's *What Is Freedom?*, for example, was commissioned after an approach by the literary agent Colin Wintle—yet again a figure who had previously worked in the Special Operations Executive. That Wintle approached Russell was itself unremarkable; more notable, Bone suggests, was that Wintle provided Russell lengthy specifications as to what would be required in the publication: "Inherent in the discussion would be the contrasts between the freedoms enjoyed outside and those enjoyed inside the Communist world. . . . Full allowance should be made for the imperfections of the non-Communist world, but a firm stand taken about absolute standards of individual freedom—a point upon which one could well afford to dogmatise."[29] After he reviewed the manuscript, Wintle requested further substantive alterations, including modifications of Russell's criticisms of American anti-Communism. Bone suggests that such intervention and specificity as to what a publication should carry stands out as highly unusual, and that Russell "was not used to following such precise editorial or ideological directions."[30]

Nonetheless, Wintle's suggestions can be seen throughout *What Is Freedom?*, as Russell constantly punctuates what could otherwise be an abstract topic with direct links to contemporary political scenarios. Russell, as suggested, avoided a one-sided presentation (although it is unlikely an intellectual of Russell's calibre needed specific editorial directions to achieve this), drawing attention to Western hypocrisy over the idea of individual freedom by noting that exercising such rights as divorce by mutual consent or abortion as a medical necessity would still result in severe repercussions: "If you are a teacher at an American college you will very likely not be allowed to go on teaching. If you are a politician, you will not be elected. . . . The forces of organised cruelty, disguised as morality, will crush you if they can."[31] Nonetheless, these points are only minor compared with the denunciations of the Soviet system with which Russell constantly punctuates his argument. He repeatedly attacks the USSR, saying, "I do not think that there has ever in past history been so little freedom anywhere as there is in present day Russia"; and "We used to think the Czarist government a tyranny [b]ut what an ineffectual and feeble tyranny it was compared to what now exists!"; and "If one could imagine the Soviet government lasting for three thousand years . . . it would be obvious that no important new ideas could ever arise in Russia"; and "I do not think there has ever in human history been such a vast organised hypocrisy as the pretence that the Soviet government represents the interests of the proletariat."[32] Russell had ample grounds to criticize the USSR for its repression of freedom, but this constant resort to hyperbole in the discussion seems an uneasy element of the book—a heavy-handed attempt to link his philosophical arguments with the contemporary political scenarios that Wintle had specified should be the prime target of the work.

Russell's book highlights the uncomfortable nature of the IRD's relation to British publishing. That the British government should seek to encourage the publishing of topical and informed works by noted intellectuals was, in itself, benign (many contemporary academics, dependent on governmental research grants, would no doubt welcome more such support). Yet the fact that this support remained covert, buttressing supposedly independent authors and presses, raises further questions about the IRD's position within British intellectual culture during the Cold War. Hugh Wilford has argued that potentially the "most disturbing" aspect of the activities of the IRD was that "throughout the Cold War period, the Foreign Office was involved in a covert intervention in internal British political life," and that the "IRD's domestic operations enjoyed the voluntary support of a number of ostensibly autonomous institutions and groups: not just labour elites, but opinion-forming national media such as the BBC and major newspapers as well."[33] The fact that the books subsidized by the IRD even today remain on the shelves of libraries, in Britain and abroad, suggests that the organization's involvement in British publishing may prove to be one of the most enduring examples of the IRD's domestic intervention.

Notes

1. There is a small but growing body of scholarly work concerning the IRD, with this present chapter particularly indebted to the following: Andrew Defty, *Britain, America and Anti-Communist Propaganda 1945–53: The Information Research Department* (London and New York: Routledge, 2004), which is the most comprehensive single study of the IRD; Paul Lashmar and James Oliver, *Britain's Secret Propaganda War* (London: Sutton, 1998), which offers an investigative account of the IRD with good insight into its modes of operations; Foreign Office Historian, *IRD: Origins and Establishment of the*

Foreign Office Information Research Department 1946–48, Foreign Office History Notes, No. 9, 1995; Richard Aldrich, *The Hidden Hand: Britain, America, and Cold War Secret Intelligence* (London: John Murray, 2001) esp. chapter 5; Hugh Wilford, *The CIA, the British Left, and the Cold War: Calling the Tune?* (London: Frank Cass, 2003); Lyn Smith, "Covert British Propaganda: The Information Research Department: 1947–77," *Millennium: Journal of International Studies* 9:1 (1980): 67–83, which contains some detailed analysis of the IRD's book output; W. Scott Lucas and C. J. Morris, "A Very British Crusade: The Information Research Department and the Beginning of the Cold War," in Richard J. Aldrich, ed., *British Intelligence, Strategy and the Cold War, 1945–51* (London and New York: Routledge, 1992), pp. 85–110; Francis Stonor Saunders, *Who Paid the Piper? The CIA and the Cultural Cold War* (London: Granta, 1999), which gives brief attention to the IRD amidst the wider investigation of CIA activity in this field. A more comprehensive survey of available literature can be found in the introduction to Defty's study.

2. As described in the yearly diplomatic lists published by the British government.

3. The file containing IRD discussion of this approach, and the material that Orwell provided, can be found in PRO FO1110/189. For a detailed (if slightly sensationalized) overview of this material, see Timothy Garton Ash, "Orwell's List," *New York Review of Books*, September 25, 2003.

4. See Valerie Holman, "Carefully Concealed Connections: The Ministry of Information and British Publishing, 1939–1946," *Book History* 8 (2005): 197–226.

5. Sheridan, circular minute, 12 May 1949. PRO FO 1110/221. My attention was drawn to this file via Hugh Wilford's brief reference to it in *The CIA, the British Left, and the Cold War*, p. 76, n. 41.

6. Runacres, circular minute, 13 May 1949. PRO FO 1110/221.

7. Adam Watson remarked: "I think Mr Sheridan can easily mention to Mr Lane how coy the FO are about giving out research material etc unless they know just who is going to see it." Watson, circular minute, 14 May 1949. PRO FO 1110/221.

8. Sheridan, letter to Allen Lane, 2 June 1949. PRO FO 1110/221.

9. Ralph Murray, letter to Christopher Mayhew, 10 April 1949. PRO FO 1110/221.

10. As Lyn Smith has previously noted, the exact number of works in the Background Books series is almost impossible to trace, with no complete publisher's list available. Smith was able to trace 108 separate works.

11. See Richard Fletcher, George Brock, and Phil Kelly, "How the FO Waged Secret Propaganda War in Britain," *The Observer*, January 29, 1978, p. 2.

12. H. H. Tucker, interview by J. Hutson on 19 April 1996. British Diplomatic Oral History Programme, Churchill Archives Centre, Cambridge, U.K. Transcript available online at www.chu.cam.ac.uk/archives/collections/BDOHP/Tucker.pdf. With regard to Ampersand's role in these transactions, Richard Fletcher was the first person to publicly connect the dots linking the company Ampersand Limited (founded in 1946) to the operations of the IRD. See the introduction to Lashmar and Oliver for discussion of how these investigations unfolded in the 1970s.

13. Lashmar and Oliver, p. 101.

14. Francis Noel-Baker, *The Spy Web: A Study of Communist Espionage* (London: Batchworth Press, 1954), p. 12.

15. C. M Woodhouse, *Post-War Britain* (London: Bodley Head, 1966), p. 9.

16. Ibid., p. 94.

17. Bryan Magee, *The Democratic Revolution* (London: Bodley Head, 1964), p. 8.

18. Ibid., p. 25.

19. The 15,000 copies purchased by the IRD, as mentioned by Tucker, appears to have been standard practice, as it tallies with the number of copies of the first book, *What Is Communism?*, which Defty (p. 166) identified as having been acquired and distributed abroad via British missions (5,000 via the Foreign Office, 10,000 via the Colonial Office). If, as Lashmar and Oliver state (p. 101), the total print run for this work was 20,000 copies, it is evident that the IRD purchase accounted for three-quarters of the total volumes printed.

20. Regional Servicing Centre, British Embassy Mexico, to Information Research Department, London, 18 November 1953. PRO FO 1110/573.

21. Lashmar and Oliver, p. 100.

22. Hugh Carless, interviewed by Malcolm McBain, 23 February 2002. British Diplomatic Oral History Programme, Churchill Archives Centre, Cambridge, U.K. Transcript available online at www.chu.cam.ac.uk/archives/collections/BDOHP/Carless.pdf.

23. Witold S. Sworakowski, review of *Books on Communism: A Bibliography*, *Slavic Review* 24:2 (1965): 363–64.

24. Kanig's essay highlights the Soviet publishing house ISVA in occupied Germany, which "printed over 500 million books and eliminated every competitor" in the short period of 1945–49.

25. For example, Ivo Lapenna's *Soviet Penal Policy* (London: Bodley Head, 1968; also released Chester Springs, Penn.: Dufour Editions 1968), would attract several reviews in British and American journals, with the reviewer for *International and Comparative Law Quarterly* 18 (1969) stating that it was "remarkable that we have in so small a compass so complete and so highly critical an account of the Soviet penal theory, law and practice" (p. 507); a reviewer in *Russian Review* 29:2 (1970) called the work "an indispensable analysis of the theory and practice of Soviet criminal law and procedure" (p. 235). It is beyond the scope of this present chapter to offer a more comprehensive account of the reviews such Background books received in scholarly organs, but it can be noted that similar review attention was by no means unusual for other books sponsored by the IRD.

26. Tucker, interviewed by Hutson.

27. Smith, p. 77.

28. Lashmar and Oliver, pp. 101–3.

29. Andrew G. Bone, "Bertrand Russell as Cold War Propagandist," *Bertrand Russell Society Quarterly* 125–26 (February–May 2005), 9–33. Available online at www.lehman.cuny.edu/deanhum/philosophy/BRSQ/05feb.bone.htm.

30. Ibid.

31. Bertrand Russell, *What Is Freedom?* (London: Batchworth, 1952), p. 12.

32. Ibid., pp. 15, 19, 23, 25.

33. Hugh Wilford, "The Information Research Department: Britain's Secret Cold War weapon revealed," *Review of International Studies* 24 (1998): 353–69. Reference on p. 369.

6 Books for the World

American Book Programs in the Developing World, 1948–1968

AMANDA LAUGESEN

SCHOLARS HAVE paid much attention to the cultural Cold War in Europe,[1] but less to its battles in other parts of the world. As writers such as Odd Arne Westad have demonstrated, the developing and non-aligned regions of the world played a vital, if not central, part in the cultural politics of the Cold War.[2] However, material and political differences between Europe and the developing nations resulted in culture—especially books—being used differently in those regions. Many emerging nations undergoing the process of decolonization and nation-building faced significant problems in terms of political stability, economic underdevelopment, and exploitation, and lacked much of the basic infrastructure to facilitate economic and political success. As the old imperial powers slowly faded from the world stage, the United States and the Soviet Union made these developing nations battlegrounds, further impeding their progress toward stability. In response, the superpowers (but particularly the United States) framed their engagement with the developing world as motivated by the desire to help those nations "modernize"—and thereby undergo the development necessary to make them stable and "free."

Despite the challenges that American book programs faced abroad—such as low rates of literacy, limited publishing and distribution infrastructure, and political instability—U.S. Cold Warriors saw libraries, books, and print as powerful means for waging the cultural Cold War in the developing world, just as they were in Europe. Books were conceived of and used as propaganda weapons to win allegiances. This tallied with a general desire to have some kind of propaganda program as an integral part of American foreign

126

policy, and was especially strong in the foreign policy discourse of the 1950s.[3] Kenneth Osgood demonstrates in his recent volume *Total Cold War* (2006) just how important the psychological and ideological war was to the Eisenhower administration, and comprehensively chronicles the various government programs developed to wage this "total war."[4]

A variety of programs came to politicize books and reading during the Cold War by working within this government discourse of books as propaganda weapons, and had an impact in the developing world. The United States Information Agency (USIA), established in 1953, was the main, but by no means the only, government agency created in the early Cold War to promote America's image and American values such as "freedom," "democracy," and "private enterprise" abroad. Reading rooms and the distribution of books—in English and in translation—were important, but sometimes controversial and even problematic, parts of the government's mission to mobilize culture as foreign policy.

While it is perhaps unsurprising that the Cold War saw governments mobilize books to win hearts and minds around the globe, private citizens—as individuals and as professionals—also participated in their own Cold War offensives. The American government relied on such support and participation, which Osgood argues helped to "camouflage" the agendas of the state that informed this work undertaken by private citizens.[5] Undoubtedly, the participation of private citizens in the cultural Cold War helped to legitimate it, but it also needs to be acknowledged that these people saw the work they did as important and significant—they too were engaged with (in their view) "defending America" and fighting for 'freedom," sometimes with an aim of promoting their professional interests and status at the same time. In the example of Freedom House's "Books USA" program, we can see how such private book programs operated, what they sought to achieve, and what image of the United States was being projected by them, and even trace some evidence of how recipients viewed and utilized these programs.

The final section of this essay is devoted to a discussion of Franklin Book Programs, a quasi-governmental, not-for-profit program which began its life in 1952 as an organization devoted to helping translate and distribute American books abroad, but which evolved into an agency that sought to promote a global modern book industry while downplaying or camouflaging its links to the U.S. government. Franklin's work raises perhaps some of the most interesting questions about the role of books in America's global work during the Cold War. Franklin embraced an idea of books as tools of modernization. Modernization theorists argued that if emerging nations could develop along lines deemed acceptable by the Western nations, their sympathies would tend naturally toward democracy, capitalism, and freedom. This discourse became popular in the 1960s, especially in government programs and agencies such as the Peace Corps and the United States Agency for International Development (USAID), and was enthusiastically embraced by organizations such as Franklin.

What these various book programs illustrate is not simply American cultural imperialism or the ascendance of U.S. military and financial interests. Granted, when one sees them in the light of U.S. military interventions and covert operations, and the hypocrisy of American race relations, it is difficult not to be cynical about American motivations. Book programs turn up in countries like Egypt, Iran, Iraq, Nigeria, and Indonesia through the 1950s and 1960s—all nations deemed strategically and commercially important for the United States, and this was not coincidental. A rhetoric of universal values and world peace, often articulated by people working in book programs, is put into ironic relief when we look at the whole picture, from the Vietnam War to the projects of the CIA (which was undermining democracy in Iran, the Dominican Republic, and Guatemala even as U.S. cultural diplomats preached democracy).

However, to dismiss these book programs as simple propaganda—as most scholars have so far done—is inadequate. Rather, the histories of these programs suggest the complexity of American cultural diplomacy efforts, and of the soul-searching that American involvement abroad provoked for some of the parties involved. Librarians, publishers, and other purveyors of books abroad saw book programs as a means to bring the world together in an "imagined community" of those who valued print, and this community would in turn promote world peace; such faith in books was surprisingly strong in the years between the devastation of the Second World War and the violence of the late 1960s, which undermined such ideals. Many participants genuinely desired to try and counteract the darker aspects of American foreign policy, but remained blind to the fact that their own values and beliefs might not be the ideal to which new nations aspired. Acknowledging that the story of American book programs abroad is complex and perhaps compromised is not to apologize for them—indeed, their story can provide some valuable insights that can inform present understandings of American engagement with the world. This seems particularly pertinent when we look at current "book aid" programs the United States funds. As the United States continues to send American books to countries with which it seeks to cultivate good relationships, revisiting the programs of the past is a valuable exercise.

Books as Propaganda Weapons: USIA and the Book Abroad

During the Second World War, books, libraries, and reading were mobilized by the American government, publishers, librarians, and intellectuals to fight fascism. Books were to be "weapons in the war of ideas," as the Council for Books in Wartime put it.[6] After the war ended, it was unclear what the future of book and library programs abroad would be, especially in terms of government support. Funding was scaled back and wartime agencies were dissolved. However, the wartime experience set important precedents for the Cold War period: government would rely on the support of private industry, non-government organizations, and professional associations for cultural programs, and the ideology that conceived of books as weapons to "win hearts and minds" would be transferred to the global fight against Communism.

The 1948 Smith-Mundt Act made education and information an integral part of American foreign policy, responding to increased tensions with the Soviet Union as the decade moved to its conclusion. Culture, information, and education were all to be weapons in a new war. In 1953, the United States Information Agency was established, assuming responsibility for the "information" side of official cultural diplomacy, although educational exchange programs remained under the control of the Department of State. While radio, film, and other so-called "fast" media were prioritized in much of the agency's activity, USIA believed books and libraries could be used to fight the Cold War and win people over to the American way of life.

A Department of State press statement in that year declared that a book and library program was important "for a simple reason that can be simply put: It is the vital responsibility of the American Government to protect the good name of the American people, no less than their vital interests."[7] Books would be vehicles for providing basic information on America, its people, and its policies; they would work to disseminate scientific and technical information that would build up friendships abroad; and they could help persuade peoples abroad (who might think otherwise) that America had a distinctive and valuable cultural tradition.[8] USIA inherited the many reading rooms across the world that had been set up under the United States Information Service during the Second World War,[9] and sponsored numerous programs that involved books, reading, and libraries. By the early 1950s, USIA was responsible for some 196 information libraries in 64 countries, with holdings of over two million volumes.[10]

Befitting an information library, USIS bookshelves were lined with appropriate reading material that matched foreign-policy imperatives and the image that America sought to project of itself. Books fitting into USIA priority areas such as "free choice" and the "pursuit of peace" were expected to be obtained and promoted by librarians and field officers. For example, William O. Douglas's *The Anatomy of Liberty* was deemed to meet the objective of "free choice," and was seen as suitable reading because it spoke "to all nationalities and races in pointing out that liberty and justice are keystones to survival in a world threatened by a nuclear holocaust."[11]

However, as a 1951 readership survey of the USIS Library in Baghdad noted, USIA reading rooms in many places reached only a small percentage of the local population. This library averaged about forty patrons daily, and about 4,000 books were actively read from the library collection. Scientific books were the most popular, suggesting that local students and professionals were not necessarily looking for a crash course in "American values." While the library held 95 books in the Dewey Classification range for the United States of America, their average usage index was low compared to the subject classifications for Calculus, Chemistry, and even Pakistan. An observer in 1953 noted USIS libraries in the Middle East as "far from realising their potentialities."[12]

USIA saw books and print as performing a variety of functions within American cultural diplomacy, but promoting the interests of the United States was the priority. A list of pamphlets and documents "distributed to the field" in 1964 suggests that USIA posts used print to transmit a number of different messages about America's global role, and that the printed material they distributed matched the political and economic interests of the United States. Included on the list were government pamphlets on the "world Communist movement" (authored by the House Un-American Activities Committee), the election of union officials, the American interest in UNESCO, and U.S. participation in the International Atomic Energy Agency; also distributed were 2,275 Sears, Roebuck and Company catalogs. Journal publications donated to the USIA for worldwide distribution included the *American National Red Cross Annual Report*, the *Standard Oil Bulletin*, and *The School Library*.[13] These selections underscore the criteria cultural diplomats used to choose books for distribution or for USIS reading-room collections: that they endorse or highlight anti-Communism, American participation in international organizations, American consumerism and commercial interests, and the importance of science and education.

USIA also used books in various person-to-person diplomacy efforts, such as the presentation of volumes to foreign institutions and individuals. Mostly, this activity targeted local elites whom USIA judged to be key opinion-makers. Dan Lacy of USIA noted that his organization had presented some one and a quarter million volumes around the world by 1954.[14]

USIA further sought to distribute American books through local publication and translation programs. The organization had subsidized the publication of 44 million copies of 4,400 American titles in 50 languages by 1960.[15] These books reflected the diverse aims of USIA, and varied from translations of American classics such as Louisa May Alcott's *Little Women* to basic science books such as Herman Schneider's *Your Telephone and How It Works* to Frederick Lewis Allen's *The Big Change* (a popular history of the first fifty years of America's twentieth century) to accessible biographies of American presidents such as Lincoln and Jefferson.[16] However, while United States agencies did engage in translation and distribution programs around the world, they were far outpaced by the Russians. In the first half of 1957 alone, the USSR published 15,631,700 copies of 372 titles in 12 languages, mostly through the Foreign Languages Publishing House in Moscow.[17]

USIA book programs and libraries politicized books and print in that they conceived of them primarily as propaganda weapons, turning them into manifestations of American power abroad. But this caused problems. The United States faced considerable anti-Americanism in many places, and programs to distribute American books and magazines in translation were often viewed with suspicion. Egyptian journalist Samy Dawood, writing in *Al Gomhoria* in 1955, denounced such programs as a form of cultural imperialism. Writing of the Arabic publication of foreign magazines, he declared: "We look upon it as part of the foreign propaganda which employs in our country different ways and means . . . we always sound the warning against this methodical and foreign cultural invasion which penetrated [*sic*] the country."[18]

USIA book programs also faced challenges from within the United States, and even within the agency itself. Just before USIA was established, and while book programs were still part of the International Information Administration, Joseph McCarthy's accusations against the State Department caused books to be removed and banned from USIS bookshelves. Authors with left-wing associations as well as authors who presented a less-than-positive image of the United States were targeted—examples of these include John Steinbeck, Howard Fast, and even Albert Einstein.[19] Ongoing issues over censorship in U.S. libraries abroad continued well into the Cold War period, with a *New York Times* article noting in 1958 that USIA was banning certain books and movies from its reading rooms "on the grounds that they would hurt the nation abroad."[20] Books thus raised significant questions of intellectual freedom and its compatibility with state interests during the Cold War. Books often seemed to be, from the point of view of many USIA staffers, open to misuse and misinterpretation, and therefore a sometimes less than effective weapon for the Cold War arsenal. This ambivalence led to ongoing battles within and against USIA over funding for, and the impact of, book programs.

Continuing support—financial and moral—for USIA book and library programs was ultimately in short supply. Thomas Sorenson, USIA's deputy director in the 1960s, much preferred the power of advertising, the "fast" media, and direct targeting of groups abroad.[21] Book programs failed to provide the kind of rapid results that could be effectively gauged and quantified in a way that politicians who secured funding liked.[22]

At the other end of the spectrum, professional and non-governmental organizations often viewed overt propaganda as a threat to intellectual freedom and ultimately counterproductive. Many Americans harbored real concerns about just how far government should go in waging a propaganda war. While the USSR operated massive print operations through the instrument of the state, the United States declined to do so. In a country that exalted private enterprise, and in which wariness of excessive federal power went back to the founding of the nation, it was impossible simply to use government to produce masses of print propaganda. One result of this was to encourage at home and abroad the kind of covert funding and support for private organizations that would so taint the U.S. government by the end of the 1960s.[23]

The governmental approach thus came to rely heavily on the support of private citizens and private organizations. As Arthur Edwards, president of Books USA, a private organization that distributed books to "worthy" recipients around the globe, put it, "I feel that it is important for private enterprise to undertake tasks of this nature rather than depending on government to assume all such responsibilities."[24] Thus fears surrounding government-directed propaganda programs might be allayed; such collaboration, however, ultimately served the ongoing politicization of books, libraries, and reading in the Cold War.

Bookshelves Abroad: Private Book Programs in the Cold War

As massive state-sponsored propaganda campaigns were incompatible with the pro–free enterprise message *carried* by such campaigns, USIA and other cultural-diplomacy agencies welcomed private efforts to supplement their own work. USIA representative Guy Davis lauded one such effort, the Bookshelf project, as being "the only privately-operated program in the country [which] actually manages to get responsible, authoritative pro-democratic (and anti-Communist) books into the hands of the leadership class in the new nations."[25] Freedom House aimed Bookshelf USA at potential and actual elites in countries it targeted, including students, trade union leaders, social workers, and government officials; Books USA aimed at a somewhat broader readership. Both programs claimed to take books to the world as philanthropy, patriotism, and part of the pursuit of world peace.

Through Bookshelf USA, packets of selected books were sponsored by a variety of organizations, which in 1960 included the American Society of African Culture, the American Association of University Women, the YWCA, the Carnegie Endowment for International Peace, and the Near East College Association. Bookshelves went to a number of African countries, including Nigeria, Ghana, and South Africa, the Middle East (primarily Israel and Turkey), and countries across Asia from India to Vietnam. Latin America and the Caribbean also received book packets. Until 1960, the bulk of these book packets went to libraries or university professors, although students, labor leaders, and social workers were also recipients, and the grateful letters of some became evidence of the program's value. While the letters in the archive do not reveal the range of responses to the program—they are uniformly positive—they do provide insight into how some recipients viewed such efforts. Whatever the donors' intentions might have been, books were used by recipients for their own purposes, much in the way of USIS libraries.

Several recipients wrote to Freedom House asserting their own concerns, as well as praising the United States. "An intellectual" in India wrote that "the gift leads me to greater understanding between the two great democracies, India and America," while another from Kerala noted the defeat of the "Red raj" in that region and how important it was "to wage a relentless war of ideas against the dire dangers of Communism." The Minister for Social and Co-operative Development in Tanganyika (soon to be Tanzania) wrote that "Tanganyika is about to face the future as a very new and young country, and we are most anxious to avail ourselves of all the advice we can from other countries. . . . What a treasure trove of classics in political writing you have sent."[26] While these people were probably pro-American intellectuals and government figures targeted because of their sympathies, recipients had agency in the relationship—they could use the books to shore up their friendship with the United States for a variety of political and other purposes. The Indian intellectual praised America, but saw his country, recently independent, as a similar beacon of world democracy. For the politician in decolonizing Tanzania, books offered information and ideas that could be adapted to his country's search for political and cultural identity.

As with other book programs, the issue of whether books were to be subordinated to propaganda aims provoked debate at home. In 1960, a Freedom House Bookshelf Committee evaluated the program to find ways to make it more effective. They consulted a number of intellectuals and academics, many of whom worried about the program putting too much weight on propaganda rather than addressing real problems that developing nations faced. Lucian Pye, the political scientist, modernization theorist, and Asia expert, concluded his advice to the committee with, "I believe what I am suggesting is that freedom requires not only faith in democratic values, but also knowledge for solving ordinary problems of government."[27] Justice William O. Douglas noted that most people in the world did not, in fact, want to be just like Americans, and a far better approach for Bookshelf USA would be to find common strands of humanity between peoples.[28] A broader range of books was required, these experts suggested, and recipients should be given the opportunity to select what they wanted for their libraries or for themselves.[29]

Bookshelf USA packets thus came to include a variety of nonfiction and fiction. Nonfiction ranged from political classics such as Tocqueville and the *Federalist Papers* to more recent publications such as Theodore White's *The Making of the President 1960* and John F. Kennedy's *Profiles in Courage*. More general nonfiction works believed useful for developing nations, such as Dr. Spock's *Baby and Child Care* and E. Sheldon Smith's *The Atom and Beyond*, were also available in selected packets. Fiction ranged from Sinclair Lewis's *Main Street* and J. D. Salinger's *The Catcher in the Rye*, both somewhat critical of American society and culture, to popular American classics such as Owen Wister's *The Virginian* and Jack London's *The Call of the Wild*. "The Personal Bookshelf," a selection of books for individuals deemed to be "potential leaders," included Orwell's *Animal Farm* and Solzhenitsyn's *One Day in the Life of Ivan Denisovich*, both critiques of totalitarianism, alongside Booker T. Washington's *Up from Slavery* and Richard Bardolph's *The Negro Vanguard*, African-American texts that expressed a moderate and accommodationist view on race relations.

These selections presented an America of the early 1960s willing to be critical of itself, but not too radical in its self-analysis. Race posed a significant public relations issue for the United States abroad, as a number of writers have shown.[30] It was difficult to convince many developing (and often decolonizing) nations that American goodwill was sincere (or that America was the ideal to emulate) when images of racial violence in the American South appeared in the international press. The U.S. government and book programs such as these worked to present an America attempting to grapple with its social shortcomings, but the inclusion of books such as Washington's reflected the ultimately moderate liberalism of the people involved in these book programs. This in turn shaped the image America projected through programs like Bookshelf USA.

Books USA, initiated by Edward R. Murrow not long before his death in 1965,[31] was similarly "designed to improve understanding of America abroad by distributing good American paperbacks through Peace Corps volunteers and United States Information Services to students and teachers, schools, colleges and libraries."[32] A letter requesting financial support for the program put it this way: "We send, so to speak, CARE packets of the mind, food for thought. Our books counteract anti-American propaganda, and correct misinformation and misunderstanding of the United States worldwide."[33] By 1963, the Books USA program had thousands of orders from Peace Corps volunteers and USIS libraries across the world.[34]

Support for Books USA came from major paperback publishing houses including Doubleday, Pocket Books (which had a close relationship to USIA and, before that, to the Council of Books in Wartime), and the New American Library, all of which supplied discounted paperbacks for book packets. Publishers who sold their books to Books USA could claim a tax deduction, thereby ensuring a subvention for their patriotism while also promoting their commercial interests globally and at home (Americans were encouraged to use the book lists as a basis for their own reading choices).[35] The publishers, no less than the donors of the books, believed they were helping to "tell the truth about America and bridge the dangerous book gap which separates us from other nations."[36]

How did people respond to Books USA, as donors and recipients? Responses were diverse, suggesting that such programs addressed people's concerns from anti-Communism (U.S. resident Dorothy W. Mallis wrote: "SOMETHING CAN BE DONE!!! . . . we can help bring PEACE to these misguided friends of communism"[37]) to the desperate desire to read books (Samuel Oba of Nigeria wrote that he lived too far from any library to obtain books to read and was grateful for anything[38]). Many Peace Corps volunteers requested books from Books USA because of the dearth of books in their postings, appreciating the books not because they were particularly American in nature, but because they were in English and could be used for teaching purposes.

As USIA recognized, books were not easily subordinated to propaganda uses. Books could disseminate ideals and values, but they did not pack the immediate punch of a radio broadcast. While book selections in these privately run programs did to some extent shape the image that America presented abroad, recipients used books in ways that suited them. Conflicts over exactly which books should be used to represent America reveal that many Americans struggled over the image they wanted to project, and over the use that their programs could have for people in developing nations. Privately run book programs therefore did play an important part in the American cultural Cold War offensive, and undoubtedly helped publishers profit, along with helping government achieve its aims. Yet they ultimately confirmed the ongoing subordination of books and reading to American foreign policy aims.

Books and Modernization: Franklin Book Programs and the Cold War

Through the 1950s and 1960s, books were increasingly invested with the power to modernize, educate, and bring to democratic values to the peoples of the developing world. As USAID noted in its statement on its use of books: "books are one of the major factors in building the human resources required for political, economic, and social development of a nation."[39]

USAID, the successor to the International Co-operation Administration, and part of a new approach to developing nations implemented by the Kennedy administration with the Foreign Assistance Act of 1961, focused on the importance of education and technical aid to help nations modernize. Modernization theorists argued that processes such as industrialization, urbanization, education, and democratization went hand in hand.[40] All emerging nations faced a common problem, they argued: how to become modern.[41] It was important therefore to help these nations achieve modernity. For modernization theorists, Nils Gilman argues, "modern" frequently meant "American," although "modern" was presented as "universal."[42] Gilman also persuasively argues that the language of modernization effectively masked anti-Communism and made it respectable by embedding it within intellectual discourse ostensibly about the "neutral" processes that all nations inevitably went through.[43] Michael Adas puts it more bluntly, writing that, after the Second World War, "the modernization paradigm supplanted the beleaguered civilizing mission as the pre-eminent ideology of Western dominance."[44]

The discourse of modernization infiltrated American book programs in the 1960s, with USAID becoming a major source of funding. In 1966, the agency articulated its mission as the "promoti[on of] US foreign policy by assisting peoples of the world in their efforts toward economic, social and political development." To this end, it sought to help "establish and expand overseas book industry capabilities through technical assistance grants and loans for writing, printing, publishing and distributing books abroad," and to secure the "overseas distribution of US books (especially textbooks) and related educational commodities in the basic professions and trades and the learned disciplines." These books were to go to libraries of educational institutions and other relevant organizations.[45]

Franklin Book Programs, Inc., was an early recipient of USAID support. Established in 1952, and primarily sponsored by USIA in the 1950s as a not-for-profit agency tasked with translating and distributing American books in the Middle East and Southeast Asia, Franklin quickly came to focus its efforts on the development of the entirety of the "book industries," including printing, publishing, book distribution, and library development. As early as 1952, Franklin's president, Datus Smith (former director of Princeton University Press) wrote: "Modernization and Westernization are on the march in the Middle East in any event, and not much that Franklin might do would halt them or indeed accelerate them greatly. The question is not whether the forces will continue but whether modernization will be accomplished constructively or destructively."[46] By 1967, Franklin's language was firmly positioned within the modernization paradigm: "books are the basic tools of education," declared the Franklin Annual Report that year. "Quite aside from the social and intellectual contributions that local book-publishing can make to any country, it is a key to the effort of emerging nations to take their place in the modern world."[47]

To this end, Franklin conceived of itself as a project, moral and humanitarian in nature, that could also support the broad aims of the U.S. government and even the commercial interests of book publishers through helping to establish a global culture of modern commercial publishing. Hiring local people to run Franklin's programs abroad was central to this plan. Franklin employed local intellectuals to head up its regional offices, and to act as writers and translators. Franklin asserted that its emphasis on employing local people to work in its offices and in encouraging a "turning away from the sahib-native relationship of the past" was the greatest contribution that America could make in fighting Communist influences in emerging nations (and was clearly an attempt to mark the American approach as different from that of the old imperial powers). "No Soviet enterprise and virtually no other business or educational project sponsored by the West," read a Franklin report, "has given the emphasis to self-respect and human dignity that Franklin has tried to maintain in all its work."[48] For local intellectuals, working with Franklin offered opportunities not only to demonstrate solidarity with the West, but to gain valuable skills and training in the publishing industry.

Franklin quickly worked to distance itself from being seen as a "purely propagandistic agency," despite its early funding from USIA, and found USAID, among other sources of funding, a more appropriate fit for its work. In 1966, Smith, interviewed in the *Wilson Library Bulletin*, argued that Franklin responded primarily to the needs of "the local people" rather than the demands of the American government. "I should emphasize," he went on, "that Franklin is not a politically-oriented organization. We have not published any American propaganda, nor have we published books that are propagandistic in terms of the local politics in the countries where we are represented. We are very proud of the fact that in two places where American relations were very strained, the Franklin program has gone ahead."[49] Franklin programs received financial support from target nations, perhaps because a country wished to demonstrate solidarity with the United States, but more often because those countries took advantage of the technologies and textbooks that could help them modernize. If the United States saw modernization as desirable for its own geopolitical purposes, many developing nations were keen to use the American programs to further their own goals of nation-building. For example, in writing a preface to the Arabic edition of Edward Bernays's *The Engineering of Consent* (1955), Egyptian intellectual Dr. Mohamed Tewfik Ramzy stressed the need to develop the profession of public relations in the Middle East. He extolled the progress already made in Egypt, and encouraged readers to embrace the value of "important scientific and intellectual methods that do not clash with the basic structure of Arab society." To do this would "testify to our inherent capacity for achieving all-round progress."[50]

Increasingly, Franklin was critical of USIA's emphasis on heavy-handed propaganda and its narrow, ideological view of the purpose of books, despite the fact that Franklin had helped distribute thousands of USIA-approved books in the 1950s. USIA's pressure to have a say in book selection rankled Franklin's leadership—and challenged their objective status; however, it is also evident that the views of Americans involved with cultural programs such as these were evolving, at times away from USIA orthodoxy. A 1965 personal note from Datus Smith in the Franklin correspondence, for example, complains that "the American idée fixe about 'communism' (real or imagined) is one of our greatest handicaps in world relations."[51]

Modernization offered, then, a much more acceptable way for those who ran Franklin's programs to think about their work. As Gilman argued, Cold War imperatives were no less important in this than in the earlier propaganda efforts; however, for those who engaged with book work abroad, helping developing nations through aid and education was a goal far more compatible with their view of themselves. In 1958, Smith had commented that it was necessary to counter the "ugly American" perception of Americans abroad—the book by William Lederer and Eugene Berwick depicting arrogant and corrupt Americans in Southeast Asia was published that year—and he called for Americans to open their hearts and minds to various peoples around the globe, something he deemed "essential for our spiritual health."[52]

Alongside their emphasis on employing locals, Franklin sought to encourage indigenous book industries as part of a general promotion of private enterprise. In setting forth a "plan for worldwide development" in 1962, Franklin noted: "A basic concept in all of the work is that publishing and printing are key factors in both economic as well as educational development. Book industries themselves are effective examples of small-scale development projects."[53] In Iran, for instance, Franklin engaged in various activities to encourage a commercial publishing and book trade, including setting up a "Model Bookshop" in Tehran in 1963[54] and a book distribution program (*Ketabhaye Jibi*), referred to as the "wire-rack project." This latter aimed to introduce retailers to the U.S./U.K, custom of displaying inexpensive books in wire racks alongside various other goods.[55] Other work that Franklin undertook ranged from assistance in the development of printing plants (for example, Franklin created the S.S. Offset Press in Tehran with the assistance of local private funds, which produced most of Iran's textbooks) to training book-industry workers in promoting book selling and book awareness (for example, assisting in the organization of a national book week in Kenya in 1967 and 1968).[56]

Appropriately, the theme for the 1967 Kenyan National Book Week was "Books Build Nations," and another major theme of Franklin's work was nation-building.[57] The development of national identity was believed to be a necessary precondition for modernity, according to theorists such as Lucian Pye.[58] A number of Franklin's activities not only spread American values, but aimed to encourage nation-building (if along American lines). The basic goal of creating an "indigenous" publishing industry and employing and training locals was clearly linked to the project of nation- and state-building, but was also important in the genesis of a number of cultural projects, such as the creation of national bibliographies and the development of national encyclopedias and dictionaries.[59] Dictionary and encyclopedia projects were initiated by Franklin in Iran, Egypt, and Indonesia in the 1950s and early 1960s. The encyclopedias were modified versions of the Columbia-Viking Desk Encyclopedia, a well-known and popular American encyclopedia, with "purely Western" items deleted and entries of local significance added.[60] Such work undoubtedly was supposed to help forge national identity—as such works do; Franklin argued the projects had value for increasing intellectual horizons and providing an important base for the development of education.[61]

Thus we can identify a final major theme in how Franklin thought about its work, and how this linked to modernization: Franklin aimed to promote education and libraries as a means both to create a consumer base for books and to help in the overall project of development. The promotion of libraries became an increasingly important part of Franklin's work in the 1960s.

Franklin had come to realize, in line with development thinking, that libraries (complementing education) played a central role in creating the kind of market and readership that American books needed. A 1966 Franklin newsletter noted that their aim was "to strengthen libraries, both for the sake of spreading education and literacy, and in the belief that book industry development depends to a large extent on the existence and activities of adequate libraries . . . next to schools, they do more than any other institution to develop the interest in reading that eventually produces educated citizens and informed book buyers."[62]

Franklin supported a number of international library development programs, such as the Afghan School Library Project, begun in 1966, and sponsored by (among others) the Asia Foundation and the Royal Afghan Ministry of Education. Books were selected by the ministry from lists supplied by Franklin and suggested by American librarians; the books were then supplied to newly created libraries in schools across Afghanistan. The majority of the books were to be in Persian, a language that Franklin presses published in, but these were supplemented by Arabic and English volumes. The project aimed to provide "a balanced collection of books which would be attractive to young people eager to broaden their intellectual horizons."[63] Franklin similarly sponsored library programs in other countries, including Indonesia, Korea, Nigeria, and Pakistan.[64] It further sought to address the needs of new literates as part of its education agenda. Projects undertaken by Franklin that sought to provide reading material for new literates included a Persian-language magazine for Iranian children, *Paik* ("Messenger"), which had a circulation of some 250,000 in 1967. *Paik* was supplemented by a series of easy-to-read books, with print runs of some 50,000.[65]

The work that Franklin did to promote a book industry and a culture of book reading and commercial "modern" publishing had several often inseparable motivations, including humanitarianism, patriotism, and commercialism. Franklin's leaders may have seen their work primarily as humanitarian, but they sold it to government as patriotism (or, increasingly, as aid for modernization which served state interests) and to publishers (who subsidized translation rights for the books published) as paving the way for American commercial expansion. They certainly promoted American interests abroad, but they did so in a more complex way than as simple propaganda. By embracing the ideas of modernization, they found a way to further America's goals, without feeling that they were contributing to an "ugly American" image of the United States abroad.

In 1963, Thomas J. Wilson, chairman of Franklin's Board of Directors, wrote to McGraw-Hill's Curtis Benjamin that Franklin had sought to help substitute "the image of a book for the image of a soulless machine which America's enemies have tried to fasten on us."[66] The book programs of the 1960s aimed to show a different face of America—one that sought to speed developing nations on their path to modernity, thereby helping to win the Cold War and make the world more like America. Ultimately, the programs did not have the success that was hoped for—but they do reveal American motivations and views at a crucial period of the Cold War.

THESE BOOK programs did not end with the conclusion of the Cold War. In 2005, USAID launched the Egypt National Book Program for Schools, which as of 2007 had delivered over 21 million books to schools around Egypt, the country where Franklin Book Programs first opened an office.[67] Aimed at primary school readers, these books are selected by both American and Egyptian publishers on the basis of criteria laid out by a committee based in Cairo which includes prominent intellectuals and educators. Books selected must be "attractive and interesting" and should "promote creativity, environmental awareness, and gender sensitivity." Books to be found on Egyptian school bookshelves thanks to this program, reports the *Christian Science Monitor*, include *The Lion King*, *The Wright Brothers*, and *A Girl Named Helen Keller*.[68]

The program was initiated by USAID as part of a public diplomacy initiative of the George W. Bush administration aiming to encourage reform in the Middle East and North Africa, with a focus on democracy, political and economic reform, and gender equity;[69] at the same time, the United States faced and still faces considerable anti-Americanism and hostility not least because of a war being waged in Iraq and other actions linked to the so-called War on Terror. Although the Cold War between the United States and the USSR is now over, cultural diplomacy continues to be an important part of American foreign policy, and book programs continue to be significant, as this Egyptian project demonstrates. Historical perspectives are therefore vital, if such programs are to continue. However, history does not offer any clear lessons as to their effect; rather, it suggests the complex issues raised when a country seeks to politicize books for the purpose of foreign policy, and perhaps serves as a warning against embarking on such programs without very careful consideration as to their motivations and impact.

Notes

1. For example, see Volker R. Berghahn, *America and the Intellectual Cold Wars in Europe: Shepard Stone between Philanthropy, Academy, and Diplomacy* (Princeton: Princeton University Press, 2001); Walter L. Hixson, *Parting the Curtain: Propaganda,*

Culture, and the Cold War, 1945–1961 (New York: St Martin's Press, 1997); Giles Scott-Smith and Hans Krabbendam, eds., *The Cultural Cold War in Western Europe 1945–1960* (London: Frank Cass, 2003).

2. Odd Arne Westad, *The Global Cold War: Third World Interventions and the Making of Our Times* (Cambridge: Cambridge University Press, 2005). Another important recent contribution to shifting the focus to a "global Cold War" are the essays in Kathryn C. Statler and Andrew L. Johns, eds., *The Eisenhower Administration, the Third World, and the Globalization of the Cold War* (Lanham, Md.: Rowman and Littlefield, 2006).

3. S. J. Parry-Giles, "The Eisenhower Administration's Conceptualization of the USIA: The Development of Overt and Covert Propaganda Strategies," *Presidential Studies Quarterly* 24:2 (Spring 1994): 263.

4. Kenneth Osgood, *Total Cold War: Eisenhower's Secret Propaganda Battle at Home and Abroad* (Lawrence: University Press of Kansas, 2006).

5. Osgood discusses primarily the "People-to-People" programs of the 1950s in exploring this theme. Ibid., 215.

6. An interesting account of the work of the Council is Trysh Travis, "Books as Weapons and 'The Smart Man's Peace': The Work of the Council on Books in Wartime," *Princeton University Library Chronicle* 60:3 (Spring 1999): 353–99.

7. Press release, Department of State, July 8, 1953, Library of Congress Central Files (MacLeish-Evans), Box 871, Folder 18, Library of Congress Archives, Washington D.C.

8. Ibid.

9. United States Information Service (USIS) remained the name for USIA offices outside of the United States.

10. Dan Lacy, "The Overseas Book Program of the United States Government," *Library Quarterly* 24:2 (April 1954): 178.

11. "Information Center Service Monthly Progress Report," February 1964, 4, Franklin Book Program Records, MC057, Box 72, Folder 4, Mudd Manuscript Library, Princeton University, Princeton, N.J. (hereafter referred to as FBP).

12. Datus Smith, "Report and Recommendations," January 11, 1953, FBP, Box 3, Folder 5.

13. "Information Center Service Monthly Report," 6–7.

14. Lacy, 179.

15. "Report on USIA Book Programs," 1960, 1, Freedom House Records, MC187, Box 82, Folder 7, Mudd Manuscript Library, Princeton University, Princeton, N.J. (hereafter referred to as FHR).

16. "Memorandum," January 15, 1953, 12–14, FBP, Box 3, Folder 5.

17. "Background report," October 1957, 2, FBP, Box 38, Folder 4.

18. "We are not enemies of culture," *Al Gomhoria* November 3, 1955, translated by Franklin Book Programs, FBP, Box 3, Folder 4.

19. For a discussion of the "overseas libraries controversy," see Louise S. Robbins, "The Overseas Libraries Controversy and the Freedom to Read: US Librarians and Publishers Confront Joseph McCarthy," in Hermina G. B. Anghelescu and Martine Poulain, eds., *Books, Libraries, Reading and Publishing in the Cold War* (Washington D.C: Library of Congress, 2001), 27–39.

20. *New York Times,* April 26, 1958, 23.

21. Richard J. Arndt, *The First Resort of Kings: American Cultural Diplomacy in the Twentieth Century* (Washington, D.C.: Potomac, 2006), 157.

22. S. J. Parry-Giles notes how the USIA was under pressure to provide "quantitative evidence to establish the effect of American propaganda" ("Propaganda, Effect, and the Cold War: Gauging the Status of America's 'War of Words,'" *Political Communication*, 11 [April–June 1994], 211), and that the impact of books, reading, and libraries did not lend themselves to "fast" and "quantitative" impacts.

23. CIA funding for various cultural programs and philanthropic foundations was first openly reported in the *New York Times* in 1968.

24. Arthur Edwards to Mrs. Archie K. Davis, March 31, 1966, FHR, Box 88, Folder 7.

25. Guy Davis to Harry Scherman, June 9, 1964, FHR, Box 82, Folder 3.

26. "Report on USIA Book Programs," 5–7.

27. Lucian Pye to Freedom House Book Committee Conference, July 28, 1960, FHR, Box 82, Folder 6.

28. "Report on 1960 Conference," 78, FHR, Box 82, Folder 8.

29. "Committee Program Prospectus," FHR, Box 82, Folder 11.

30. Penny M. Von Eschen, "Who's the Real Ambassador? Exploding Cold War Racial Ideology," in Christian G. Appy, ed., *Cold War Constructions: The Political Culture of United States Imperialism, 1945–1966* (Amherst: University of Massachusetts Press, 2000); Thomas Borstelmann, *The Cold War and the Color Line: American Race Relations in the Global Arena* (Cambridge: Harvard University Press, 2001).

31. Murrow, aside from being a noted journalist, was also director of the USIA from 1961 to 1964. A book based on his radio series *This I Believe* was one of the most popular works translated into foreign languages and distributed by USIA/Franklin Book Programs abroad.

32. Arthur R. Edwards to Samuel Meek, FHR, Box 83, Folder 14.

33. Shura Massey to Bruce P. Wilson of the Carling Brewing Company, September 1, 1966, FHR, Box 89, Folder 1.

34. "Books USA Annual Report September 16 to December 31, 1963," 8, FHR, Box 83, Folder 2.

35. Summary Minutes, Executive Committee Meeting, September 18, 1963, FHR, Box 88, Folder 9.

36. Arthur Edwards, September 25, 1964, FHR, Box 83, Folder 2.

37. Dorothy Mallis to Books USA, February 14, 1966, FHR, Box 89, Folder 8. Emphasis in the original.

38. Samuel A. Oba to Books USA, August 22, 1966, FHR, Box 89, Folder 8.

39. "The Use of Books in the A.I.D. Program," Policy Determination 12, AID Executive Secretariat, September 17, 1962, FBP, Box 61, Folder 10.

40. Nils Gilman, *Mandarins of the Future: Modernization Theory in Cold War America* (Baltimore: The Johns Hopkins University Press, 2003), 5.

41. Ibid., 34.

42. Ibid., 14.

43. Ibid., 13.

44. Michael Adas, "Modernization Theory and the American Revival of the Scientific and Technological Standards of Social Achievement and Human Worth," in David C. Engerman, Nils Gilman, Mark H. Haefele and Michael E. Latham, eds., *Staging Growth: Modernization, Development, and the Global Cold War* (Amherst: University of Massachusetts Press, 2003), 35. This is also a point emphasized by Michael E. Latham's *Modernization*

as Ideology: American Social Science and "Nation Building" in the Kennedy Era (Chapel Hill: University of North Carolina Press, 2000).

45. "Summary of Book and Library Activities Being Administered by Members of the Interagency Book Committee," 1966, FBP, Box 127, Folder 1.

46. "Policy Memorandum," 3, September 18, 1952, FBP, Box 3, Folder 5.

47. *Franklin Book Programs Annual Report for the Year Ending 30 June 1967* 1, FBP, Box 15, Folder 6.

48. "Franklin Book Programs Annual Report," September 1959, 18, FBP, Box 15, Folder 8.

49. *Wilson Library Bulletin*, February 1966, 535.

50. "Memorandum on Publication of Edward Bernays, *Engineering of Consent*, in Arabic," 1958, FBP, Box 192, Folder 30.

51. Handwritten note by Datus Smith to Shirley B. in response to reading manuscript of *The Radical Papers*, August 9, 1965, FBP, Box 76, Folder 10.

52. Datus Smith, "American Books in the Non-Western World," *New York Public Library Bulletin* 62 (April 1958), 174.

53. Franklin Book Programs, "Plan for Worldwide Development," [4], January 29, 1962, FBP, Box 5, Folder 3.

54. Don Cameron to Mr. B. S. Arnold of Prentice-Hall, January 17, 1966, FBP, Box 116, Folder 12.

55. Documentation on this project can be found in FBP, Box 116, Folder 1; it was launched in 1961.

56. *Franklin Book Programs Annual Report for the Year Ending June 30, 1968*, 10–11, FBP, Box 15 Folder 6.

57. *Franklin Book Programs Annual Report for the Year Ending June 30, 1967*, 20, FBP, Box 15, Folder 6.

58. Pye's advocacy of the importance of national identity is mentioned by Gilman, *Mandarins of the Future*, 170.

59. *Franklin Book Programs Annual Report for the Year Ending June 30, 1968*, 13, FBP, Box 15, Folder 6.

60. "Memorandum re. Arabic Encyclopaedia (Egypt)," March 27, 1953, FBP, Box 91, Folder 2.

61. "Proposal for an English-Arabic Dictionary," July 25, 1963, FBP, Box 93, Folder 5.

62. Franklin Newsletter #35, March 1966, 1, FBP, Box 39, Folder 1.

63. Franklin Newsletter #38, November 1966, 2–3, FBP, Box 39, Folder 1.

64. *Franklin Book Programs Annual Report for the Year Ending June 30, 1968*, 10, FBP, Box 15, Folder 6.

65. *Franklin Book Programs Annual Report for the Year Ending June 30, 1967*, 7, FBP, Box 15, Folder 6.

66. Thomas J. Wilson to Curtis Benjamin, 1963, FBP, Box 2, Folder 9.

67. "Egypt National Book Program for Schools—Fact Sheet," USAID website, egypt.usaid.gov/Default.aspx?PageID=447 Viewed November 22, 2007.

68. *Christian Science Monitor*, March 8, 2006.

69. As set out on USAID's website: www.usaid.gov/about_usaid/presidential_initiative/diplomacy Viewed November 21, 2007. This was part of a Presidential Initiative under the George W. Bush administration.

7   Impact of Propaganda Materials in Free World Countries

MARTIN MANNING

THIS ESSAY describes the propaganda collection amassed by the United States Information Agency (USIA) during the Cold War. Originating in World War II, the collection had as its first focus anti-American propaganda created by the Axis countries. After World War II, the U.S. Department of State established a propaganda collection in its information division to keep track of the ever-changing Cold War propaganda appeals of the Soviet Union and other Communist nations. The statutes originally intended to protect Americans from Nazi propaganda were retooled to empower the State Department to control and confiscate materials created by Communist countries for distribution in the United States. The resulting collection reveals much about how propaganda entered and was distributed in the United States, as well as providing evidence of the actual content and major themes of pro-Communist printed materials. While this collection is useful now for historians of the Cold War, it may also have had some role in the generation of counter-propaganda in the United States and may even have played a role in establishing American priorities in the cultural Cold War.

The State Department's collection does not encompass all pro-Soviet propaganda or "cultural diplomacy" materials, of course. Under an official 1956 cultural agreement, for instance, the two Cold War antagonists officially exchanged glossy magazines designed for each others' markets; the United States offered *America Illustrated* and the Soviet Union provided *Soviet Life*. However, a great deal of printed material, created on both sides of the Cold War, circulated throughout the Eastern and Western blocs both legally and illegally. As a result, the USIA, organized in 1953, began to keep and organize the propaganda it confiscated. This propaganda collection became an

145

important tool of USIA in the 1950s and early 1960s and was later used by other agencies (FBI, CIA, FBIS, Defense, etc.) as well.

History of the Collection: World War II, the Foreign Agents Registration Act, and Cold War Background

The Office of War Information (OWI) was created by President Franklin D. Roosevelt to handle domestic propaganda and to promote the Allied war effort. During World War II, OWI began to collect propaganda samples from the Axis countries. These were quite valuable as policy materials, as they made it possible for the Allied countries to monitor how they were being portrayed and thus craft their own propaganda to hit back accordingly. This collection was enabled by the Foreign Agents Registration Act (FARA), a bill enacted in 1938 in response to lawmakers' fears about the potentially damaging effect of Axis propaganda. FARA required persons acting as agents of foreign principals in a political or quasi-political capacity to make periodic public disclosure of their relationship with their foreign principal, as well as of any activities, receipts, and disbursements in support of those activities. Disclosure of the required information facilitated evaluation by the government and the American people of the statements and activities of such persons in light of their function as foreign agents.

The act originally required sources to be properly identified to the American public in response to German propaganda in the lead-up to World War II, in an attempt to limit the influence of German agents in the United States. Among its provisions, the act required people under foreign control to register with the Department of Justice before attempting to sway public opinion. Persons or organizations had to register if they:

a. Engaged in political activities;
b. Acted in a public relations capacity for a foreign principal;
c. Solicited or dispensed any thing of value within the United States for a foreign principal;
d. Represented the interests of a foreign principal before any agency or official of the U.S. government.

The act also required that material entering the country that is clearly propaganda must be clearly labeled as political propaganda. "Political propaganda" is defined in section 1(j) of the Foreign Agents Registration Act.[1] The term included any form of communication (printed or not) and gave the broadest possible definition of the ways that propaganda might influence individuals or "any section of the public." In fact, something was included as propaganda under this law even if the person disseminating only *believed* that the material would influence people. The direction of influence was somewhat clearer. That part of the definition explained that the influence would be labeled propaganda if it was made "with reference to the political or public interests, policies, or relations of a government of a foreign country or a foreign political party or with reference to the foreign policies of the United States or [to] promote in the United States racial, religious, or social dissensions." In addition, the definition paid special attention to the possibility of violent overthrow of the state, stipulating that a communication would be defined as propaganda if it included a message "which advocates, advises, instigates, or promotes any racial, social, political, or religious disorder, civil riot, or other conflict involving the use of force or violence in any other American republic or the overthrow of any government or political subdivision of any other American republic by any means involving the use of force or violence." FARA's broad definition of propaganda was removed from the law in 1966, and the word "propaganda" was replaced throughout with the words "information materials." In 1995, FARA was repealed entirely.

At the end of World War II, a widespread belief that good relations with the Soviet Union would continue briefly diminished the concern over alleged Communist and other subversive infiltration of the federal government so that FARA statues appeared not to apply. However, the rapid intensification of Cold War tensions after 1945 and concerns about possible Communist infiltration of the government drastically changed the political climate in the United States. In late 1946 President Truman appointed a commission to study governmental employee loyalty, which eventually led him to inaugurate a sweeping new federal loyalty program in March 1947. The rapid, major deterioration in the civil-liberties climate and the reemergence of the "subversives in government" issue that marked the period between the end of World War II and early 1947 led to a renewed interest in propaganda aimed at the United States from Communist countries and a new use for FARA.

This development resulted from four factors. Of primary importance was the drastic postwar deterioration of relations with the Soviet Union and the beginning of the Cold War. Second, Americans were increasingly obsessed with perceived dangers posed by internal subversion in general, and Soviet and Communist Party espionage in particular, fueled by reports (some public and some held within the government) of Russian spy operations in North America, along with a new Communist hard line that reflected general Cold War tensions. Postwar economic tensions and frustrations in the United States, including massive inflation and a major wave of strikes in 1946, also fostered a general sense of anger and anxiety. Finally, renewed fears about propaganda resulted from deliberate attempts to ignite a domestic Red Scare by a powerful coalition of American conservatives—notably the FBI, the business community, the Catholic Church, and, especially, an increasingly politically desperate Republican Party.

As a result the State Department began making inquiries concerning foreign propaganda material arriving in the United States from abroad in the mails and in freight. The Department of Justice, in a March 2, 1951, letter, held that, in the opinion of the Attorney General, certain Communist propaganda publications are un-mailable. This opinion rested on a 1940 holding (39 Op. Atty. Gen. 535) that sending of propaganda to the United States by an unregistered agent of a foreign principal (usually another country) in violation of FARA constituted a violation of a penal statute; furthermore, the Attorney General stated that under authority of section 1717 of title 18, United States Code, the Postmaster General might bar such propaganda from the mails under conditions that (1) propaganda was mailed to this country by an unregistered foreign agent, and (2) the propaganda aided a foreign government.

It was this climate that fostered the growth of the State Department's propaganda collection, partly as an attempt to study and to monitor Communist activities. The collection started small but became an extensive operation in the early 1950s. It had particular importance during the McCarthy period, especially as it dealt with materials intended for the free world, and sent from Soviet front organizations.

The collection's value to McCarthy and his group resulted from the Attorney General's rulings that suggested that the bags of propaganda material could be controlled by the post office. Section 305(a) of the Postal Service and Federal Employees Salary Act of 1962 provided that "mail matter, except sealed letters, which originates or which is printed or otherwise prepared in a foreign country" and which is determined by the Secretary of the Treasury to be "Communist political propaganda" can be detained by the Postmaster General when it arrives in the U.S. domestic mails.[2] The propaganda had to list country of origin and be properly labeled. The addressee had to be notified that this material was received and could get the material delivered only by returning an attached card; otherwise the mail would be destroyed. The statute further defined "Communist political propaganda" in terms similar to FARA's by outlining what constituted political propaganda and by noting an exemption from its provisions for such mail addressed to governmental agencies and educational institutions or sent pursuant to a reciprocal cultural international agreement.

The post office was not the only agency involved; the U.S. Customs Service also had some responsibility in intercepting the propaganda that came to be archived at the State Department. Customs dealt with two classes of propaganda material: items that came directly into the United States from Communist countries, and material developed in non-Communist countries and sent into the United States. Most of these were subject to scrutiny and, in certain cases, to the provisions of FARA. Irving Fishman, the government official who dealt with Communist political propaganda as it came through customs, kept an extensive correspondence with the Chicago, San Francisco, and New York ports of entry. His letters indicate that USIA had a contract with Treasury to deal with the nearly nonstop arrival of these materials. USIA renewed this contract up until the mid-1970s, when the collection was discarded because of disuse.

Distribution and Quantity

The amount of material Fishman and his staff dealt with is staggering and averaged at least 15,000 to 20,000 individual pieces of printed matter monthly. Twelve to fourteen men in Fishman's office, working with post office personnel, were tasked with handling this material, and they unpacked, sorted, and screened every item that came in from the Soviet Union and from Soviet-bloc countries from more than 200 mail bags daily. In the process, they learned that three main methods were used to bring propaganda material into the United States:

1. Some material, especially newspapers and periodicals, was mailed directly to an individual within the United States. This could be as a result of a subscription to the particular publication purchased by the individual within this country or as a result of mailing lists obtained by the publisher.
2. A considerable amount of material arrived in bulk, consigned to various bookstores, newsstands, and other purveyors of literature for resale. These stores were located in most of the large metropolitan centers of the country, and the character of the shipments varied according to the language communities within the metropolitan area.
3. An extensive amount of material was ordered at the request of government agencies, universities, libraries, and schools for research purposes. In this connection, it should be noted that the Soviet Union and its satellites shipped considerable scientific and educational material into the United States, which upon examination usually revealed the presence of some political propaganda regardless of how objective and scientific the particular work purported to be.

Some propaganda also entered the country intended for embassies, through the so-called diplomatic pouch. Although FARA applied to "a diplomatic or consular officer of a foreign government who is so recognized by the Department of State," Communist political propaganda material could be received and distributed through, for example, the Soviet embassy in Washington without falling under Fishman's scrutiny.

Overall, at least 25,000 groups and organizations on the mailing lists received propaganda materials. A sampling of them indicates that a wide range of Americans may have had some interest in these materials. Unsurprisingly, many were organizations openly connected to the Soviet Union—such as the Chicago Council of Friends of the Soviet Union or the Massachusetts Council of American-Soviet Friendship. In addition, some unions such as the National Union of Marine Cooks and Stewards received some of these materials, alongside university libraries from Harvard's to the University of Hawaii's. Libraries of other organizations such as the United Nations also accepted propaganda into their collections. Some bookstores that received these materials—such as the Progressive Book Store of Los Angeles and the Modern Book Store in Chicago—appear to have had close links to the Communist Party. Both bookstores were named as distribution points for Communist literature during HUAC's investigations.[3] Nonetheless, some indication of the range of recipients is the fact that Addison-Wesley, a publishing house founded in 1942 to create textbooks for a wide market of American schools and which appears to have had no links to the Communist Party, also received Communist materials.

Another source of distribution was ethnic groups themselves. In fact, certain types of language materials were designated by vicinity based on ethnic jurisdictions. For example, Philadelphia received many Hungarian, Czechoslovakian, Russian, Polish, and Croatian publications. New York, because of its generally wide assimilation of nationalities, received almost all the language publications. Chicago was heavy on materials in Polish. However, national origin was not always limited to certain locations; materials received by ethnic groups in one location might be forwarded to friends throughout North America. Many individuals who visited Iron Curtain countries smuggled propaganda materials back into the United States when they returned. Although smuggling such materials might be considered a blatant violation of FARA and postal regulations, many of these materials were created to look as though they were produced in America, especially those that were similar in format, size, and appearance to popular magazines like *Time* and *Life*. Both the Post Office Department and the Bureau of Customs experienced considerable difficulty in barring from entry into the United

States or eliminating from the mails material which circumvented FARA because they did not have available competent translators or political analysts to assist them in determining its political or propaganda nature. Also, although it might be illegal to carry Communist propaganda into the United States, FARA did not prohibit an individual from reading a pamphlet or a booklet or any periodical emanating from Communist countries, provided the individual evaluated it properly by knowing its source (not always an easy task).

On August 7, 1952, the Commissioner of Customs requested the collector of customs at each of the ten principal ports of entry (New York, San Francisco, Los Angeles, Honolulu, Boston, Baltimore, Minneapolis, Chicago, Seattle, New Orleans), to furnish as much information as possible relative to the arrival in the United States, in the mails or otherwise, of propaganda publications. These reports reveal a good bit about how location and demographics determined the types of propaganda that might target that location. The New Orleans office reported no receipt of propaganda from Communist-controlled countries. Honolulu, on the other hand, received such magazines as *Peoples China, China Reconstructs*, and *China Monthly Review*; newspapers such as *For a Lasting Peace, For a People's Democracy, Shanghai News, Pyung Book Ilbo,* and *No Doug Shin*; and such pamphlets as *The Communist Party, Leader of the Chinese Revolution*. Boston made particular reference to technical periodicals in Russian, periodicals commenting on world events, and picture magazines with stories on life in the Soviet Union. Chicago noted in its report that some of the propaganda channeled through that office had contained some disparagement of the United States and other Western countries.

Because the Post Office Department in Washington received copies of material that was mailed directly to the recipient within the United States only on occasion, no estimate could be made of the amount of propaganda sent directly to people living in America. Registered mailings were held for six months, during which time notice was given to the postal administration of the country of origin in accord with the Universal Postal Convention. At the end of six months the material was destroyed if no other disposition had been made.

A considerable proportion of the Communist propaganda arriving in the United States was consigned to the New York City book distributors Imported Publications and Products and Four Continent Book Corporation, both of which were registered with the Department of Justice under FARA. The owners of both companies were investigated by HUAC. The owners of Four Continent Book Corporation estimated that it had imported over one million dollars worth of printed material into the United States between 1946 and 1960. Interestingly the committee also noted that Four Continent exported half a million dollars of printed material back to the USSR, serving as what the committee called a "legal intelligence agency."

The customs service and the mailbags were only one channel of distribution for propaganda. Importers such as New York's Brandon Films brought films into the United States from the Soviet Union, Poland, and Czechoslovakia. Thomas Brandon, its president, was subpoenaed by HUAC on June 12, 1958, to answer charges that he was distributing Communist propaganda films. In his testimony, Brandon noted that he had a contract with Artkino Films, Inc., which specialized in the importation of films from the Iron Curtain countries. While Artkino was registered as a foreign agent under FARA, Brandon Films was not because it was not acting as a principal for another country. Other firms, as well, fell under that exemption.

Nature and Content of the Propaganda Found in USIA's Collection

An examination of propaganda samples determined that the content for the most part was typical of Chinese or Soviet publication. Generally speaking, the material was devoted primarily to praise of these countries and their "peaceful" objectives, as well as descriptions of the "improved way of life" in the various satellite countries that had come under Communist domination. They also expressed severe criticism of the United States—claiming, for instance, that under the direction of Wall Street, U.S. foreign policy focused on war-mongering. In addition, in the early 1950s materials contained atrocity stories designed to illustrate the barbaric methods by which the United States and other UN countries conducted hostilities in the Korean War, with particular emphasis on the indiscriminate bombing of civilian populations, germ warfare, and mistreatment of prisoners of war. These policies were contrasted with the enlightened, humane treatment accorded UN prisoners held by the Communist forces. Finally, there was considerable material devoted to the theoretical aspects of Marxism, Leninism, and Stalinism, and extolling the accomplishments and virtues of the leaders of the Soviet Union, China, and the satellite countries (at least until those leaders fell from grace). Concentrated efforts were made to appeal to the various ethnic minorities within the United States—in fact, in 1962 Senator Hubert Humphrey specifically requested to see this collection's materials regarding American race relations.

Communist propaganda arrived in the United States in the form of magazines (some copiously illustrated), books with hard bindings, paperbacks, pamphlets, newspapers, films, and music both sheet and recorded. Foremost in terms of quantity and frequency of shipment were newspapers and magazines. In addition, there was a considerable quantity of pamphlets devoted to a single subject. The Soviet Union transmitted its newspapers, such as *Pravda* and *Izvestia*, along with a number of magazines, pamphlets, and bound volumes in the Russian language that, because of the lack of translators, could not be properly analyzed as to propaganda content. From the nature of the illustrations and cartoons, however, agents determined that they contained either material designed to extol the Soviet Union and its leaders or excoriate the United States as "aggressive" and "imperialistic." The Soviet Union transmitted in considerable quantities an English-language weekly entitled *New Time*, with book reviews, editorials, and articles on Soviet foreign policy and on its relations with its satellite countries and the Western democracies. The propaganda material fell into the following categories:

1. Books, pamphlets, printed letters, leaflets, brochures, bulletins, printed and distributed by international front organizations; publications with an appeal to specific groups of people, such as youth, teachers, women, labor; periodicals such as *The Democratic Journalist* (International Organization of Journalists), *World Student News* (International Union of Students), *News Bulletin* (IUS), *Teachers of the World* (World Federation of Teachers' Union), *World Youth* (World Federation of Democratic Youth).

2. Publications of Sino-Soviet bloc countries published in "free world" languages, especially English. Periodicals such as *Poland* (printed in Warsaw), *China's Sports* (Peking), *Korea Today* (Pyongyang), *Vietnam* (Hanoi), *Hungarian Review* (Budapest), *Prague Newsletter* (Prague); other publications published in orbit countries aiming at audiences in the free world.

3. Publications of Communist orientation, published outside the Communist orbit in "free world" languages. Periodicals such as *Revolution* (Paris), *Northern Neighbors* (Gravenhurst, Ontario).

4. Any examples of, or information about, new Communist-sponsored periodicals or other publications regardless of where they are published.

5. Periodicals in orbit languages, especially satirical magazines such as *Szpilki* (Warsaw) and *Perets* (Kiev). Other orbit-language publications that contained statistics on conditions within orbit countries.

6. Orbit-language newspapers, especially those in Soviet minority languages such as Armenian, Lithuanian, Latvian, Georgian. Russian-language newspapers were of less interest since most were already received on subscription.

7. Children's books, posters, exhibit material, and other printed matter disseminated in connection with Communist-sponsored world or regional conferences or local events.
8. Communist agitator handbooks or similar material.
9. Lexicons, dictionaries, and other reference volumes on technical and scientific subjects (such as medicine, physics, outer space, engineering, nuclear fusion) in Russian and East European languages.
10. Materials addressed to Soviet émigré populations.
11. University literature and catalogs from schools in all Communist countries, including Cuba.
12. Publishers' catalogs of Communist material.
13. Bulletins, magazines, and other publications of Communist-nation embassies and legations in the United States and in other capitals.
14. Korean Communist materials published in Japan.
15. Cuban Communist materials of any description, intended for consumption in North or South America, or in Africa.
16. Material on Albania and Rumania.
17. Indigenous Communist and other anti-American propaganda obtained from Africa, Latin America, Near East, and Southeast Asia.

Certain types of propaganda material were in special demand. According to a June 10, 1964, USIA cable, these included publications of bi-national organizations or friendship and cultural societies; publications of local or international Communist front organizations; ornate, prestige publications; posters and other graphic media; trade and trade fair publications. In addition, USIA included a catchall category, "other publications," that revealed the topics of most interest to readers searching for propaganda: materials that exploited current events, contained an anti-American tone, included bibliographical information on Communist publications (including booklists, ads, and reviews), and specifically appealed to certain groups, especially women, children, or teachers.

The two largest Communist nations, naturally, accounted for most of this material. The Soviet Union sent a considerable number of pamphlets, in both Russian and English, devoted to single issues or aspects of Soviet foreign policy. A monthly magazine, *News*, which described itself as a "Searchlight on World Events" and was printed in English, arrived in the United States in large quantities. Communist China transmitted English-language magazines entitled *People's China, China Reconstructs,* and *China Monthly Review,* as well as a newspaper entitled *Shanghai News* and a bulletin, *Daily News Release.*

However, the satellite nations also produced a good bit of the material in the collection. Czechoslovakia, for example, produced considerable quantities of printed material for export, including twenty to twenty-five newspapers and an equal number of magazines. These periodicals fell roughly into the same categories as those from the Soviet Union—that is, newspapers and magazines devoted to trade union activity, youth affairs, or women's affairs, and publications containing comments and expressions of views on the political situation. Poland also sent to the United States about fourteen different newspapers and six magazines, all in Polish, devoted to informing the Polish-speaking population in the United States of the "wonderful" conditions in Poland since it had come under Communist control and, in comparison, the decadent, peace-disrupting position of the United States and other Western democracies. Publications arriving from Hungary, Rumania, Bulgaria, Albania, and East Germany followed the same pattern. The Rumanian government transmitted an illustrated monthly, *Bulletin of Information of the Working Youth of the Rumanian People's Republic,* devoted to extolling the position of workers and youth in Rumania since coming under Communist control. Like the Soviet Union, Rumania transmitted pamphlets or magazines devoted to a single subject, such as, for example, one issued by the Romanian Institute for Cultural Relations with Foreign Countries—*The Congress of the Intellectuals of the Rumanian People's Republic for Peace and Culture*—proceedings of a 1949 conference in Bucharest.

The propaganda collection shows the importance of two particular groups to the messages of the Communist Party: women and youth. There were at least thirty-six Communist and Communist front magazines for women circulated in free world countries. The major source was the Women's International Democratic Federation (WIDF), founded in December 1945 as an international Communist front organization; its stated aim was to prevent the recurrence of war and the resurgence of fascism for the sake of the well-being of women and children. It published and distributed materials such as the book *I Want to Live, Ban Atomic Weapons.* However, WIDF also published reports of its annual congresses which supported a wider role for women and asserted their multiple functions in society. For example its 4th Congress, held in Vienna in 1958, resulted in the report "The Creation of Conditions Which Will Enable [a] Woman to Fulfill Her Role in Society as Mother, Worker, and Citizen."

Illustrated magazines in the Russian language included *The Soviet Woman,* which depicted the major role played in Soviet life by women as compared to the minor and "oppressed" position of women in the United States and other Western democracies. A similar quarterly, *Czechoslovak Woman,* was published in Czechoslovakia in English from 1954. In the second issue, an article entitled "For a World without Wars and Weapons" described a meeting of women from all European countries in Prague and focused on the "menace" of the remilitarization of West Germany.

Targeting youth groups with print material seems counter-intuitive, since most people believed that youth during the Cold War were more interested in other forms of popular culture such as music and TV. Nonetheless the youth audience has always been a prime target of foreign propaganda because of its potential as future leaders and citizens. In fact, much of the USIA's work was geared toward future leadership programs. Additionally, in the 1950s and the 1960s, especially, print was an effective, cost-efficient way to deliver information quickly. Aware of the competition, propaganda for the youth market was bright, colorful, and very visual. These materials took the form of posters, comic books, and glossy periodicals.

In his June 1958 testimony before the House Committee on Un-American Activities, Fishman told Congress that the Kremlin-controlled international Communist-propaganda machine was bombarding student and youth groups in the United States and throughout the free world with a flood of multilingual propaganda.[4] Although over a half-million pieces of Communist propaganda destined for such groups entered the United States monthly, none of this material was labeled as Communist, or registered as required under FARA, because the Soviet apparatus channeled it into the United States through non-Communist countries or, in some cases, through front organizations.

During the height of the Cold War, the World Federation of Democratic Youth (WFDY), another international Communist front organization, was the dominant producer of propaganda material for the youth market. WFDY was an international organization of Communist and socialist youth organizations, founded in London on November 10, 1945 (in its own words) after "the anti-fascist victory of the people, as an anti-imperialist, progressive, democratic and massive international youth organization that gathers more than 150 organizations from more than 100 countries." It published periodicals such as *World Youth*, a monthly issued from Budapest beginning in 1946, which focused on the ever-changing habits and lifestyles of youth in Communist countries—a sort of *Tiger Beat* for leftists. However, WFDY did not focus on lifestyles alone. The Budapest-based *WFDY News*, begun in 1959, contained a far more political message. Printed in English, French, and Spanish, *WFDY News* documented the ways that the Communist countries were trying to bring about a peaceful world.

In fact, U.S. "warmongering" remained an important theme and, given developments in the youth culture of the 1960s and 1970s, may have had a good bit of appeal. For example in the early 1970s, WFDY published *With Vietnam to the Final Victory*, a pamphlet that proposed a peace settlement for the Vietnamese conflict and depicted the United States as the enemy of this peace process. Finally, as late as 1982, WFDY created the pictorial work *WFDY for Peace, Détente and Disarmament 1945–1982*, which contained glossy images showing the political activity of young adults.

Case Study: China

Examining the collection's Chinese holdings reveals the specifics of how one country's propaganda apparatus worked. During the Cold War period, domestic propaganda was crucial to the formation and promotion of the cult of personality centered around Chairman Mao Zedong. It also served as a useful tool for mobilizing popular participation in national campaigns such as the 1958 Great Leap Forward and the 1966–76 Cultural Revolution. Following the death of Mao in 1976, propaganda was used to blacken the character of the notorious Gang of Four, who were blamed for the excesses of the Cultural Revolution. Past propaganda also encouraged the Chinese people to emulate selfless model workers and soldiers such as the famous Comrade Lei Feng, suicidal Civil War hero Dong Cunrui, self-sacrificing Korean War hero Yang Gensi, and Dr. Norman Bethune, a Canadian doctor who assisted the Communist Eighth Route Army during the Second Sino-Japanese War. It also praised Third World revolutionaries and close foreign allies such as Albania and North Korea while vilifying both the American "imperialists" and the Soviet "revisionists."

China also produced a great deal of propaganda for export. The popular-style presentation of most of these magazines was sufficiently attractive to enable them to compete with other publications, and they were so heavily subsidized by the Chinese Government that they were often much cheaper than their rivals. Thus, in developing countries, especially in Africa, China exploited the rising demand for reading matter by selling literature at minimal prices. If a nation banned Chinese publications as subversive, Beijing tried to introduce them from non-Communist countries whose postmarks were not likely to excite the interest of the authorities. When thousands of copies of *More on the Nehru Philosophy in the Light of the Sino-Indian Boundary* (a supplement to *China Reconstructs*) were seized in Bhavnagar, India, it was found that they had been posted from Tokyo.[5] Rome's *L'Epoca* reported on October 13, 1963, that an intensive Chinese propaganda campaign was being directed against France and Italy from Berne. Publications entered these countries by diplomatic bag and were then distributed by post. Moscow Radio on June 23, 1964, quoted the *West African Pilot* saying that Chinese literature intended for Africa was being sent from Paris.

One typical example of external Chinese propaganda is *Women of China*, an English bi-monthly that first appeared as a quarterly in 1956, produced by the National Women's Federation (also called the All-China Democratic Women's Federation) of the People's Republic of China. While it sometimes included items not specifically concerning women, the magazine espoused the views of Chinese women on current international questions: the contributions they had made to industry, agriculture, culture, education, and art under Socialism; their rights and place in politics, economic life, education, and other fields; their loves, marriages, family life, and their children's education; and their experiences in the struggle for national liberation and women's emancipation. *Women of China* also carried stories on Chinese literature, fine arts, handicrafts, cookery, household affairs, films, and sports activities.

The Chinese also sent magazines to a variety of influential people in non-Communist countries. For example, the *New York Times* reported on July 6, 1963, that *Peking Review*, a staple in many academic libraries during the Cold War, was being sent to the United States in increasingly large numbers. One issue had been received by editors of college newspapers "from coast to coast."

Throughout the 1950s and 1960s the Chinese increased the number of languages in which their magazines were published. *China Pictorial* appeared in six languages in 1952, and in nineteen different languages in 1965. Within eighteen months of its first publication *Peking Review* added five new language editions to the original English version and became a major vehicle for propaganda about the Sino-Soviet schism. Chinese propaganda periodicals were usually produced on good-quality paper with excellent photographic reproduction. Even in the worst days of paper shortage in China, when magazines for the home market were printed on the poorest paper, foreign-language periodicals were as well produced as ever. Chinese periodicals, always violently anti-Western, catered to a variety of interests, ranging from the arts to science, from trade to youth activities—and from revolution to guerrilla warfare.

Uses of Propaganda Material

The main users of the propaganda collection were the research analysts who incorporated facts and figures into surveys that they compiled, usually for congressional committees and individual senators and representatives. Budget analysts and senior agency management also used the materials in testimony before Congress.

Of particular interest to government users were the two Russian special collections that USIA maintained: the propaganda collection and a collection of Cyrillic-alphabet books, which originated in the early 1950s. Material came from catalogs of some fifteen state publishing houses and other sources in the Soviet Union and through a Russian book supplier in the United States. The Cyrillic collection actually supplemented the propaganda collection in that much of its material was undoubtedly propaganda; in fact, it included in its holdings about 200 volumes of English-language propaganda periodicals, published in the Soviet Union, from the 1960s through 1978. These included *New Times, Soviet Military Review, Soviet Union, Soviet Woman*, and *Sputnik* as well as encyclopedias, dictionaries, reference books, and titles of interest to the research analysts. The collection was strongest in history, Soviet foreign policy and international relations, economics, and literature.

The major users of the propaganda collection were the research analysts in USIA's Office of Research and Intelligence, who drew heavily on the collection for use in their public opinion polls and research surveys. The collection could even inform policy development, especially regarding the crafting of messages intended to refute Soviet claims about the United States and the West. It also had a number of other uses both within USIA and outside the agency. For example, it provided important information on topics that might be difficult to research otherwise, such as the relations between the Chinese and Indonesian Communist Parties, which could be found by studying the *Peking Review*. Its anti-American posters were used by USIA lecturers, and some of its graphic illustrations showing attacks on U.S. businesses in Asia were used in textbooks by the publisher Hill and Knowlton.

The collection was also useful for exhibitions, and its materials were often put on display to warn Americans about appeals that might influence their thinking. For example, in 1961, the Chicago public-relations firm Burston-Marstellar Associates requested background information and propaganda materials for its "Sights and Sounds of Communism." They used materials to create a display that would clearly indicate the dangerous nature of Communist propaganda. In the same spirit, in 1966 Voice of America used anti-American posters in an exhibit in its hallways. Not all of the uses of the collection were negative; the U.S. Embassy in Moscow borrowed materials for a friendly exhibition illustrating U.S.-Russian contacts.

Printed propaganda materials also clearly shaped some anti-Communist activism in the United States, and this anti-Communist propaganda was also collected by the State Department. This type of propaganda was often less professionally produced than Communist propaganda, and in some instances its anti-Communism is so hysterical that it may be a Communist-produced forgery. Once such booklet was *The Communist Gospel of Peace According to Marx, Mao Tze-tung, Lenin, and Stalin*. The booklet, privately published in Tokyo in 1952, lists Richard Lawrence-Grace Deverall, an American Federation of Labor Asia representative and a Catholic activist, as its author. Clearly, whoever wrote it used Communist propaganda images to counter Communist propaganda. The author took selections from three pamphlets published

Figure 7-1. Cover of the anti-Communist pamphlet *The Communist Gospel of Peace According to Marx, Mao Tze-Tung, Lenin and Stalin*, by Richard L.-G. Deverall (Tokyo, 1952).

Figure 7-2. Chinese propaganda image glossed by Deverall as "Doubtless a delegate to a 'Communist Peace Conference'!"

Figure 7-3. Chinese soldiers charging in a 1940s–50s image glossed by Deverall as "Partisans of Peace rushing to sign a Communist Peace Pledge!"

by what he calls "Soviet Chinese for either Red China or the Overseas Chinese." Claiming that these illustrations present a clear vision of Communist China's real message of "peace," this booklet attempts to show that China's true aim is a new militarism in Asia. The cover pictures, including a man holding a gun (central image), a young man blowing a horn, and a boy thinking of Mao Zedong, come from a crayoning book for children. Such illustrations of youth and innocence might indicate "peace" and "love" but the author of the booklet felt they revealed a far more insidious intent in a book for children, urging them to make their choice: the paratroopers, the army, or the navy.

Most important, the propaganda collection at the State Department made a selected, but important, audience aware of the shifts and tides in the Cold

War panorama. Government officials in the free world needed to understand and appreciate the Cold War menace and be able to translate those dangers to U.S. citizens and those of other states. Unlike Sino-Soviet bloc publications produced for internal use, and thus distributed to a captive audience, the same output for free world countries needed to reach an audience accustomed to a wide variety of views.

Finally, this collection indicates the shifting winds of the Cold War. The years immediately following the end of World War II, when Truman met Stalin at Potsdam, were a period of hard lines in many of our initiatives toward the Soviet Union. This sense of hardness was reflected in the propaganda that both sides issued. By 1954, one sees a shift to a soft approach in the propaganda battles and a more positive attitude (with regular exceptions) of extolling bloc activities in preference to unreasoned attacks upon free world leadership, a shift that produced a far more sophisticated and consequently more effective propaganda output from the Sino-Soviet bloc countries. In 1961, Kremlin publicists used their vast propaganda machine to project the image of a vigorous but peace-loving Soviet Union intent on protecting

Figure 7-4. Deverall took Chinese Communist images and used captions to undermine their (untranslated) pro-Communist messages. Here he writes: "The Chinese militarists indoctrinate the children and give them their choice of being a paratrooper, a soldier, or a sailor. In such manner are the Chinese children prepared as potential blood donors for Moscow and cannon fodder for the military adventures of the Peking bandits."

mankind from "imperialist" inroads. With the tensions of the American involvement in Vietnam, attacks on the United States as "war-mongers" appeared in Soviet-bloc propaganda beginning in the mid-1960s. However, when President Nixon visited China in 1972, Chinese propaganda, at least, moved toward a more favorable approach to the United States. With the hard-line attitude of the 1980s, propaganda battles between East and West intensified but USIA, at least, was unable to supply the samples of material to its staff and other agencies as it had since the beginning of the Cold War. In the late 1970s, the propaganda collection was disbanded due to lack of space and staff.

Now, after the end of the Cold War, it is difficult to assess just how effective these USIA/State Department campaigns were (or were not) solely from the materials in the propaganda collection. It will fall to another scholar to examine whether U.S. policymakers focused too much on responding to certain kinds of Communist accusations just because they were reflected in these materials, or if this collection demonstrates that the Communist nations actually intended to frame their propaganda to appeal in the specific ways I have conjectured. Today the propaganda collection seems like a relic of the Cold War, known only to later generations through history books, but in its time, its relevance was critical to its function.

Notes

1. 22 U.S.C. 611(j).
2. 39 U.S.C. Section 4008-A.
3. Testimony of LeRoy Herndon, March 27, 1953. Investigation of Communist Activities in the Los Angeles Area in 1953 (part 2), p. 505. In the hearings: U.S. Congress. House. Committee on Un-American Activities. Investigation of Communist Activities in the Los Angeles Area in 1953; hearings held in the 83rd Congress, First Session, March 23, 24, and 25, 1953.
4. *Communist Propaganda, pt. 9: Student Groups, Distributors, and Propagandists*; hearings (HUAC, June 11–12, 1958). Washington: GPO, 1958.
5. *Statesman* (Delhi). February 4, 1963.

Research Sources

Correspondence in the files about the propaganda collection includes acquisitions lists of materials received, showing the types of material, listed under country of designated origin and requests to use the collection for interests as varied as exhibitions, budget hearings statistics, reports, and evaluations. There is also substantial material on Irving Fishman, the Deputy Commissioner of Customs, U.S. Treasury Department, in New York, and in charge of a special project dealing with control of political propaganda for the entire country; he had an agreement (called contract in the letters) to deliver the bags of propaganda to the USIA Library. Much correspondence details the problems the staff, usually one person, had in keeping ahead of the bags, which arrived at least bi-weekly. Once they arrived, the contents had to be sorted and some type of bibliographic control attempted. Ultimately this proved futile, and the collection was finally neglected in the mid-1970s when there was no staff in place to handle it and USIA priorities shifted. A feeble attempt was made to keep the collection up, but it proved too difficult. By the time I arrived at USIA in 1978, there were unopened bags waiting to be processed and bits and pieces of what was once a substantial collection, physically and intellectually.

Primary

Most of the information in this chapter came from the files of the former USIA Propaganda Collection, now in the author's custody. However, there are archives and libraries that contain propaganda materials from the Cold War period and earlier. There is a list of such collections in the Martin Manning and Herbert Romerstein, ed., *Historical Dictionary of American Propaganda* (Westport, Conn.: Greenwood, 2004). Other significant collections of primary-source propaganda include the Library of Congress's Manuscript Division (particularly for Communist Party USA records microfilmed from the Soviet archives); the Hoover Institution Library and Archives in Palo Alto, Calif.; California State University at Fresno's Sanoian Special Collections Library (especially the War Propaganda Collection); New York University's Tamiment Library (for the papers and photographs of the Communist Party USA); the German Propaganda Collection at the University of Minnesota library; and the Communist Propaganda from North Vietnam Project at the University of Wisconsin library.

Government Documents

U.S. Congress. House. Committee on Un-American Activities. *Communist Propaganda, part 9: Student Groups, Distributors, and Propagandists*; hearings. Washington, D.C.: Government Printing Office, 1958.

U.S. Congress. House. Committee on Un-American Activities. *Investigation of Communist Propaganda in the United States, part 1: Foreign Propaganda; Entry and Dissemination*; hearing, 84th Congress, 2d Session. Washington, D.C.: Government Printing Office, 1956.

U.S. Congress. House. Special Committee on Un-American Activities. *Investigation of Un-American Propaganda Activities in the United States*; [hearings held] on H. Res. 282; 76th Congress, 3d Session. Washington, D.C.: Government Printing Office, 1940.

U.S. Congress. House. Special Committee on Un-American Activities. *Investigation of Un-American Propaganda Activities in the United States*; [hearings held] on H. Res. 282; 77th Congress, 1st Session. Washington, D.C.: Government Printing Office, 1941.

U.S. Congress. House. Special Committee on Un-American Activities. *Investigation of Un-American Propaganda Activities in the United States*; [hearings held] on H. Res. 282; 78th Congress, 1st Session. Washington, D.C.: Government Printing Office, 1943.

Secondary

Banghoorn, Frederick C. *Soviet Foreign Propaganda*. Princeton: Princeton University Press, 1964.

Delaney, Robert F. *The Literature of Communism in America: A Selected Reference Guide.* Washington: Catholic University of America Press, 1962.

Evans, F. Bowen, ed. *Worldwide Communist Propaganda Activities.* New York: Macmillan, 1955.

Fried, Richard. *Nightmare in Red: The McCarthy Era in Perspective.* New York: Oxford University Press, 1990.

Frye, Alton. *Nazi Germany and the American Hemisphere, 1933–1941.* New Haven, Conn., and London: Yale University Press, 1967.

Gertz, Elmer. *Odyssey of a Barbarian: The Biography of George Sylvester Viereck.* Buffalo, N.Y.: Prometheus Books, 1978.

Goldstein, Robert J. "Prelude to McCarthyism: The Making of a Blacklist." *Prologue,* 38, 3 (Fall 2006). Online: http://www.archives.gov/publications/prologue/2006/fall/agloso .html

Griffith, Robert, and Athan Theoharis, eds. *The Spectre: Original Essays on the Cold War and the Origins of McCarthyism.* New York: New Viewpoints, 1974.

White, Joseph J. "Sino-Soviet Bloc Periodicals Published in Free World Languages." MSLS thesis. Catholic University of America, 1964.

III PRINT AS A TOOL TO SHAPE DOMESTIC ATTITUDES

8 "How Can I Tell My Grandchildren What I Did in the Cold War?"

Militarizing the Funny Pages and Milton Caniff's *Steve Canyon*

EDWARD BRUNNER

No OTHER comic strip artist could match the prestige of Milton Caniff at the end of World War II. Ron Goulart's pronouncement that "quite possibly, Caniff was the most popular comic strip artist in America in 1947"[1] seems indisputable. Identified with a victorious war, his nationally syndicated *Terry and the Pirates* strip had charted a boy's coming of age as a fighter pilot under circumstances that captured the meaningless brutality and desperate emotions of wartime. And from 1943 to 1946, he had voluntarily furnished to armed forces weeklies a humor strip, *Male Call*, that used the conventions of pin-up art to present the war from an enlistee's perspective. When an item in a 1945 Walter Winchell column announced that Caniff had signed a contract with Chicago *Sun* publisher Marshall Field to develop a new comic strip at the end of 1946, Caniff's fame enabled him to strike distribution agreements with 96 Sunday and 162 daily newspapers, before a single detail of the new feature was available. (Caniff was still under contract to produce *Terry and the Pirates*, and anything he put on paper legally belonged to his syndicate.) When the first episode of *Steve Canyon* appeared on January 13, 1947—a debut heralded by a *Time* magazine cover story—it had an estimated readership of 31 million.[2]

If any comic strip belonged on the cover of a 1947 newsweekly, it was surely *Steve Canyon*, a feature that emerged just as the divisions that defined the Cold War were forming. Caniff's new feature would become a remarkable

169

mass-culture product that addressed the anxieties of an America that had acquired world hegemony with disconcerting ease. *Steve Canyon* transplanted the material of a melodramatic male adventure tale, with its attraction to dangerous situations and glamorous *femmes fatales*, to global hot spots. For many readers, these narratives would offer a relatively coherent and comprehensible version of events that were unfolding grimly and confusingly on the newspaper's front pages. In a 1948 article, Caniff explained that his main character was not a "plainsman" but an "airplanesman" who carried on the tradition of the scout posted to cavalry units who were settling the frontier. As an "ex-Army lad, as an Air Transport Joe who had hauled VIP's . . . to all parts of the world," Steve Canyon would "function in the manner of the old-time plainsmen who guided wagon trains from the Mississippi and the Missouri to the coast. . . . Those scouts knew the Indians and their lore; they knew where the 'friendly' water-holes were located, where buffalo could be found for food, where the best trails ran."[3] In Steve Canyon readers saw the decidedly expansive American presence as benign and comforting, while lone operative Steve Canyon served as a guardian for others.

Caniff addressed an America that had come to dominate the world but then found the environment to be flawed, inhabited by aliens with their strange "lore." The mission of *Steve Canyon*, then, was to lead its readers across this new wilderness, among other things acclimatizing them to a vision of America that intertwined industrial, commercial, and military interests, viewing them all as implicated in dangerous ventures at crucial points on the globe. In this disconcertingly large world, the straightforward good-versus-evil conflicts that had defined World War II adventuring gave way to nuanced oppositions that called for delicate maneuverings and savvy compromises. A successful outcome could turn on avoiding a direct confrontation. Glimmers of the military-industrial complex appeared in episodes where Canyon works for U.S. industrialists wrangling to co-opt Russian interests in the Middle East, or undertakes espionage operations to protect the vast global holdings of beautiful Wall Street magnates, or discovers underground insurgency groups marshaled against societies traditionally engaged in exporting raw materials to the United States. As a result, *Steve Canyon* must be counted among other examples of print culture that did more than simply reflect a postwar moment. Caniff helped constitute a Cold War mentality—in a general sense, by purveying a global imaginary in which America's reputation was under siege even in remote locations by an undeclared enemy whose exact identity Caniff's feature played a role in defining, and in a specific sense, by portraying oppositions most effectively resolved not by brute violence but through ingenious maneuvers that controlled representations, adjusted images, and altered perceptions.

NEWSPAPERS WERE still powerful delivery systems for information and entertainment in the opening years of the Cold War, and the most popular site in the newspaper, as opinion polls of newspaper readers had been confirming since 1930, was still the funnies page—the one place visited by almost every reader, young or old, urban or rural, rich or poor, overeducated or uneducated. Twenty years later, this situation was virtually unchanged. Indeed, a 1950 New York University poll indicated that more college-educated readers (82.1 percent) turned to the comic strips than did readers with an eighth-grade education or less (69.3 percent).[4] The very structure of the medium, as recent theorists have argued, enhanced its accessibility. The basics of the comic strip—sequential images with accompanying dialogue—provided a user-friendly form whose audience could self-tailor its consumption. Unlike the film or play or radio program, which unrolled in its own time, the comic strip was consumed at each user's own pace. Its popularity turned on this asymmetrical relation with its audience: it never intimidated its users with time constraints. Comics qualified as that "highly creative activity with potential for high satisfaction" that, according to Wayne A. Wiegand, defined print culture at its most pleasurable.[5]

The satisfaction associated with comic strips helps explain their value during 1939–45. Daily and Sunday newspaper comic strips (and their déclassé offspring, the newsstand comic book) contributed to the war effort by presenting familiar characters successfully coping with disturbing situations. Many strips sent their principal characters to military settings, even to the front lines. Comic books, available in all PX stores, featured simple humor or offered a morale boost through tales of good triumphing over evil in spectacularly super-heroic fashion. When newsprint rationing ended with the war, several newly proposed comic strips were predicated on the assumption that adults would be loyal to a medium associated with the most dramatic experience of their lives.

Among new offerings, none was anticipated more eagerly than Caniff's. Readership for *Terry and the Pirates* quadrupled during the war, and the weekly strips of *Male Call* had been collected in 1945 in a bound hardback that rapidly passed through four printings. (Caniff arranged to send free copies of the *Male Call* volume to newspaper editors who carried *Terry and the Pirates*, many of whom would soon be approached by syndicate salesmen with contracts for Caniff's new strip.) Taken together, these strips earned Caniff celebrity status, establishing his credibility as one who grasped both civilian and military points of view. Letters to Caniff in the weeks following the 1947 launch of *Steve Canyon* emphasize how widely his work had circulated during the war, how fondly it was remembered, and how important it had been.

In a 1946 essay Caniff suggested that the interchange between producers and consumers of comics is always brief, intense, and private, playfully observing that the "cartoonist makes love to his reader a meager minute or two each day."[6] Caniff's correspondents remembered, however, the very public settings where readers consumed his latest production. When Caniff's correspondents recalled *Terry and the Pirates* or *Male Call*, his work was rarely remembered as a device to entertain or distract: it was an important site of exchange around which many could gather. Beyond that, readers associated *Terry and the Pirates* with the public values for which the war was being fought. One ex-G.I. wrote that "[*Terry*] helped considerably during the bulge when all our papers stopped coming, because the krauts had us cut off," as if Caniff's strip represented the freedom and mobility under threat both locally and globally. Another wrote of finding *Male Call* pin-ups in unlikely places, spotting them in "a castle in Holland, a pup tent in Normandie, or a blasted cellar in Germany"—a list with a triumphal edge to it, as if these drawings marked the advancing American presence in the European theater of war, even in the enemy's quarters. As the war began to wind down, with American success increasingly assured, Caniff's Miss Lace started to appear almost exclusively in what Caniff had called at one time her "uniform": a low-cut sheath dress, usually with elbow-length gloves and heels, all in formal black, that insistently colonized the female body as confidently as American troops had dominated the war's two fronts (fig. 8–1). In the weeks after launching *Steve Canyon*, letters confirmed that Caniff's new strip was being used in similar ways, and by writers not just from the military: a student at the New Jersey College for Women explained that the strips were now posted on the bulletin board of her sorority house. A sailor on the USS *Cebu* summed up the esteem *Steve Canyon* enjoyed (on his ship the bulletin board in the mess hall was where crew gathered to read the strip): "You'd be surprised to see the number of 'old salts' who are constantly gathered around, taking it all in," adding: "I guess Steve Canyon has long since ceased to be a kiddies strip."[7]

Caniff worked hard to distinguish his work from that done for children. Readers associated his strips with detailed military hardware, accurate official dress, and correct protocol. During the war, the military assigned an officer to act as his liaison for acquiring information and declared his studio a site where classified documents could reside. In the postwar years, Caniff re-

Figure 8-1. *Miss Lace:* "Global Strategy—'So Round; So Firm . . .'" (July 22, 1945). Used with the permission of the Milton Caniff estate, all rights reserved. (Caniff titled each strip for copyright purposes; he invokes the first half of a current slogan for Lucky Strike cigarettes that ends "so fully packed.") Earlier in the war, Miss Lace was always attired in a new outfit that showed impeccable taste. As the war drew to an end, she increasingly appeared only dressed in what Caniff called her "uniform"—an erotically charged arrangement that universalized her looks and underscored the idea that the American Girl was the prize that troops had been protecting from enemy aliens. But this strip neatly reminds its readers that the war is over, the time for conflict has passed, and long-unavailable pleasures are now in reach.

mained in touch with powerful military representatives, beginning with the Commanding General of the Army Air Forces. He joined the Air Force Association at its founding in 1946 and continued responding to requests from military units for posters, insignias, or other service. But no source could have been as useful as the correspondents with whom he had been working over the years, many of them men and women who had been or were still in the armed services. Examining Caniff's archived letters, the cultural critic Jennifer Hayward noted the "enormous amounts of time" that Caniff spent "reading and responding to audience suggestions," pointing out "many cases of multiple letters from the same persons." Caniff's biographer Robert C. Harvey charted the increase in the time Caniff set aside for handling correspondence; an arrangement that required a "chunk of the week" in 1935 had expanded, by 1943, to "most afternoons." Caniff made a point of never discouraging a correspondent. He replied graciously even to negative letters. He kept information flowing by answering most letters with at least a two- or three-sentence note, and at times by responding in detail, offering professional-level advice to those who requested it, including examining the work of aspiring cartoonists. Above all, he perfected a method for supplying individualized drawings to those who requested them (fig. 8–2). In the 1930s, he had begun producing pre-printed drawings of various characters on high-quality paper that could be customized by hand-coloring, with space available for a personalized greeting and his signature. One-of-a-kind drawings could always be sketched for dignitaries or when occasions demanded them. Some of Caniff's exchanges, Hayward points out, developed into extensive correspondences that stretched over years.[8]

Contact with letter writers enabled Caniff to appear less as inspired inventor than knowledgeable collaborator. His adult audience came to expect an emphasis on actual events. In the late 1930s, he disengaged from the exoticism of a pulp-tale Orient and substituted the verisimilitude of a China besieged by Japanese invaders. Wartime followers of *Terry and the Pirates* knew from press releases in newspapers that Caniff brought into his storyline the exploits of a handful of actual military personnel; they appeared in gently caricatured drawings, their names slightly distorted. For example, "Flip Corkin" was based on Colonel Philip Cochran, and when Cochran carried out a maneuver in March 1944 in Burma, the planning process was dramatized in an episode of *Terry and the Pirates*. "Dude Hennick" was based on Frank "Dude" Higgs, a fighter pilot who had resigned his military commission to serve as a civilian flight instructor for Chinese air cadets. When Higgs died in a plane crash in China in October 1945, newspaper headlines connected him with his fictionalized character, and photographs showed him reading with amusement his comic strip exploits. Caniff had a visible record of making contacts with heroic figures at the center of the war.

In a 1960 interview, Caniff proposed that the formula for his strips could be reduced to "Boy-meets-girl against a gigantic news story."[9] This relation between the boy-girl plot and the "gigantic news story" would undergo marked change in the postwar years. During World War II, that story involved clearly defined enemies fighting over specific targets, but in the postwar years, at least

Figure 8-2. *Miss Lace* (circa 1945–46). Used with the permission of the Milton Caniff estate, all rights reserved. Letter writers identifying themselves as veterans requesting a drawing of Miss Lace might be sent this, one of several that Caniff had pre-produced for correspondents. Lace's elegant dress and flower-bedecked coiffure contrasts sharply with battle fatigues and the unshaven faces of the two recruits, but her eagerness to be escorted by rough-hewn troops signals her trust in them and their devotion to her.

in its details, that story was considerably less certain. *Steve Canyon* resembled *Terry and the Pirates* in offering a version of front-page news events that processed them in a manageable, even amusing form. But those front-page events were now dramatic in a different way, with stakes that were stranger, more elusive.

CANIFF BEGAN *Steve Canyon* as an "optimistic strip," Goulart observed, pointing to the name of the "fledging charter airline [Canyon] was trying to start": Horizons Unlimited.[10] The name resonated with a handful of entrepreneurs who wrote to Caniff, seeking permission to use it for their own charter flight organizations. The idea of starting up a brand-new business struck a positive note, and one reader even proposed an improvement on the company motto. Caniff's slogan—"You furnish the reason, we'll furnish the ride"—was critiqued as long on alliteration but short on rhyme, and what was recommended instead was "You tell us where, we'll get you there." The name, in fact, had achieved enough recognition only six weeks after the strip's beginning that a letter addressed to "Horizons Unlimited / Salt Lake City Air Port" could reach Caniff, forwarded by the U.S. Postal Service.[11]

Steve Canyon also began as an adventure strip with special appeal to veterans adjusting uneasily to civilian life. Originally, it centered on ex–Army Air Force pilot Steve Canyon's picaresque adventures as he nurtured a charter airline that would allow him and a cohort of wartime buddies to travel to remote corners of the world and meet exotic maidens, sweet women, and bad girls. Caniff's initial outlines and story sketches, as he relayed them in an interview with *Editor & Publisher* in 1946, included a New York headquarters for Steve Canyon, a second-in-command who would be "a fixer, a brilliant guy," and a girlfriend whose professional career as an actress kept her and Canyon apart.[12] None of these possibilities ever materialized. Though Caniff planned to leave behind *Terry and the Pirates* and begin with fresh characters suitable for a world so new it was still being formed, he soon found that his readership was not receptive to radical change. Female readers especially found Caniff's choice of a new hero unsettling. One remarked that the youthful Terry was "the type of boy we will look up to," the type of boy it would be perfect to marry, unlike the "rugged fellow that Steve Canyon will be." Another wrote that Terry was "naïve enough to make you worry about him. . . . Whereas Steve Canyon's face is 'harder' looking, so you don't feel you *have* to worry about his welfare. He looks more experienced." Another writer thoughtfully pursued her disquiet: "At least a quarter of the enjoyment I get from my favorite comics comes from familiarity with the characters, from the feeling that they are my friends, and from the delight of trying to foretell their future reactions on the basis of their past behavior. In Steve Canyon, I feel awkward and ill at ease, homesick in fact, and view the stranger characters with a suspicious and critical eye instead of the tolerant friendly one I had for the old characters"[13] Caniff's success in accustoming his readers to the characters in *Terry and the Pirates* posed a threat to his desire to begin over. Since Caniff's previous syndicate had commissioned a new artist to continue *Terry and the Pirates*, using the very characters he had carefully developed, he was also under siege from his own inventions.

Caniff's strip was not a year old before it underwent a distinctive swerve. In March 1947, the president announced that the United States must extend support to Greece and Turkey to thwart Soviet efforts to establish influence there, and in July 1947, George Kennan's "long telegram" analyzing Soviet history and motivations and urging a policy of containment was published in *Foreign Affairs*. As these events set the stage for the Truman Doctrine, a representative of military intelligence approaches Canyon and, as both men address each other by their military rank, "Captain Canyon" is asked informally to keep his eyes open and report on what he might observe in the region where his job would next take him, the Middle East. The exchange is notable for the military spokesman's insistence on deniability; "There's no undercover angle to this!" he says, in a panel in which his face is nonetheless shrouded in darkness (December 4, 1947) (fig. 8–3).[14] This strip represented a departure from the narrative of romance and global adventure. From this point on, Caniff's feature not only acknowledges the necessity of postwar militarism but unquestioningly assumes its importance. In his new role, Canyon became guarded, losing the swagger of the strip's opening episodes. Early on when he disapproves of a prospective client, he tells him to "go fry your hat" (January 13, 1947). In the next few years, he becomes a more thoughtful, even vulnerable figure, in need of caring, like the America that he "unofficially" represents with its enemies seemingly everywhere.

That siege mentality is less evident in the plot-lines of the strip, which often turn on melodramatic reversals and unlikely coincidences, than in background details, in offhand dialogue, and in oblique references. Caniff adjusts his initial vision of *Steve Canyon*, who at times takes on the role of a secret agent. *Steve Canyon* strove for a realism that few comic strips aspired to. Numerous characters, even sympathetic figures, died in the course of various episodes.[15] But its notable feature would be its underlying atmosphere of confusion, deception, even distrust, and an uncertainty that sometimes advances and sometimes retreats, often in ways related to current events. In the months just before the outbreak of war on the Korean peninsula (June 1950) but after the revelation that Klaus Fuchs had supplied the Russians with information

Figure 8-3. *Steve Canyon* (Thursday, December 4, 1947). Used with the permission of the Milton Caniff estate, all rights reserved. Canyon's first direct contact with a military intelligence officer unfolds across several daily episodes and assumes a readership that can appreciate a sequence filled with dance-like dialogue in which unstated messages pass with complete success. In previous dailies, Franklin was notably silent, replying to inquiries with a single word or a grunt. When he becomes voluble, as he is here, his face is plunged in shadow, and so is Canyon's, temporarily.

that may have helped them develop their atomic bomb (February 1950), Caniff presented an episode in which, as it unfolded over the course of several weeks from March 25 to June 3, almost all the principals were in disguise, including Canyon himself (unidentifiable behind a beard he had grown after an adventure that had taken him out of civilization for months), but it became impossible for any of them to know whether their disguises had been penetrated. In this episode, Canyon must play a role, substituting in the place of a Russian spy who had been traveling incognito to a port in China to escort an American scientist who is defecting from the West. In the process Canyon encounters two women he knows from his past but who may not recognize him behind his masquerade. Notable for its lack of action and its emphasis on verbiage (Canyon, who knows neither Russian nor Chinese, must contrive excuses for everyone to converse in English), the sequence ends with a dramatic moment of bluffing in which the bluff is exposed as having no danger: a Canadian submarine, of all things, has been hovering at the edges of a seagoing hostage exchange and guaranteeing security. As the plot twists and turns, with masks removed only to be worn again, and authority passing abruptly from one figure to another, the unfolding sequence nearly collapses under its excessive ingenuity. In fact, ambiguity dominates all efforts; no one appears heroic because no one is free from the taint of evasion.[16]

Caniff's plot-lines construct a new kind of enemy, devious, manipulative, duplicitous—threatening the United States not by invading its territory but by undermining its confidence and diminishing its prestige. "The mutant enemy appeared everywhere—in foreign lands and at home," Ron Robin writes in his history of the development of what he calls "the military intellectual complex" as he traces the work of "public opinion leaders" who "participated in the transformation of assumptions, fears, and selective information into a plausible, widely accepted construction of the enemy."[17] While the two sequences that launched *Steve Canyon* in 1947 were set in South America and in the American southwest (both areas, Goulart speculated, that "had the advantage of having no unpleasant war atrocities and no bombed-out cities"[18]) later sequences sent Canyon to locations where wartime oppositions continue to play out and where events, even in faraway regions, had an impact on domestic life in America.

In a sequence from October and November 1948, Canyon and a sidekick are shipwrecked and wash up on a shore in the Indian Ocean, where they discover "local subversive interests" determined to disrupt the harvest of a crop bound for the United States. Not only will the disruption weaken the exporting country, but also as Canyon blurts out: "That stuff is needed in America!" (October 17, 1948). This "stuff" is nominally a shipment of food, but also simultaneously the battle to keep open shipping lanes for stuff is figuratively a battle to sustain both freedom and prosperity. A similar sequence from November 1947 to January 1948 presented an agent of a foreign country masquerading as a Middle Eastern sheik who attempts to sabotage American medical supplies badly needed by the local populace with the specific aim of injuring "American prestige" (December 31, 1947). Both of these sequences demonstrate the manipulative nature of America's new enemies and the stakes in postwar conflicts. As David Ryan observes, the Truman Doctrine cast America as "the guarantor of Western security, the regenerator of its economy, and the instigator of a period of freedom and prosperity."[19] Avenues of commerce between countries must stay open, in part to serve nations in need, in part to register a strong American presence. When problems arise, what looms is a hydra-headed enemy working to frustrate American national interests, forcing the country into retaining its military posture.

In the months leading up to the Korean War, Caniff agitated for increased military awareness. For example in 1949, an elderly Chinese scholar points to a map and tells Canyon: "If the China coast is controlled by another power, *your* main line of defense suddenly shifts to the Western hemisphere—Alaska to Cape Horn!" (July 24, 1949). What initially appears to be dry and scholarly explication becomes a subtle drumbeat of persuasion. As the story evolves over the next months, various characters voice identical sentiments, sometimes as direct comments, or vivid slogans, or down-home words of salty wisdom: "I'd rather fight you at the end of my lane than my front yard!" (August 9, 1949); "It makes sense to settle any fight as far from home as possible, before your antagonist has his foot in your front door!" (October 16, 1949); "It is said they fought in China in the hope they would not one day be backed to the wall on their own soil" (January 11, 1950); ". . . the time to lock the barn is *before* they heist the horse!" (May 20, 1950); and "The place to defend your house is as far down the road as possible" (October 19, 1950). The enemy remained undefined, but the repetition confirms an enemy exists. Caniff's argument justifies extensive military intervention far from any native soil, recasts aggressive acts as wisely defensive gestures and shows that an extensive commitment to a standing military is a benign form of foreign policy.

WARREN I. COHEN contends that the Korean War "alter[ed] the nature of the Soviet-American confrontation, chang[ing] it from a systematic political competition into an ideologically driven, militarized contest."[20] But Caniff's eagerness to translate political difference into ideological confrontation predates the June 1950 entry date of North Korean troops into the South. A substantial involvement in public relations gave Caniff the confidence to devise stories that identified the skill of self-promotion as an American virtue that would help define future conflicts.

Caniff was a master of sophisticated ballyhoo. When asked once to choose his ideal alternate career, he immediately answered: head of a large advertising agency.[21] Along with a cover story in *Time*, Caniff was featured in a story in *Newsweek* (January 20, 1947), an article in *Life* (February 3, 1947), and a piece in the April 1947 *Coronet*. In 1948, he was discussing *Steve Canyon* in *Collier's* (November 20), and readers of the December *Better Homes & Gardens* were given a tour of his "rugged modern home . . . [p]erched on High Tor Ridge in Westchester, just outside New York City," where the color scheme in Caniff's bedroom is "as masculine as his comic-book characters—heavy beige and rust draperies, rust-colored bedspread, beige rug."[22] In later years, Caniff would make guest appearances, in cartoon form "visiting" a Sunday 1947 episode of Al Capp's *Li'l Abner* (in a complex joke, he was attempting to find a job in Capp's strip for a noble character from *Terry and the Pirates* who had been left without a role in the strip's current incarnation); speaking as a guest on radio shows broadcast from New York, including *Town Meeting of the Air*; appearing on the cover of *Newsweek* for April 24, 1950; and endorsing various brands in full-page advertisements in national magazines: Rheingold beer (1951), Hiram Walker bourbon whiskey (1955), Thom McAn shoes (1955), and Sheaffer pens (1958).[23]

Caniff demonstrated that the syndicated newspaper strip participated in the network of interlocking media that comprised the postwar cultural apparatus. Yet for Caniff, such widely circulating image-making was not simply a self-promotional gesture but an action that defined the confidence and inventiveness that marked American superiority. Publicity was America's secret weapon: outsiders were drawn to the prosperity, glamour, and mobility that popular culture in the United States presented. When Canyon is captured by the beautiful Russian submarine commander Akoola (in Russian, "shark"), he finds her attractive. She provokes his flirtatious inquiry (with its ominous air of decades of ongoing warfare): "How can I tell my grandchildren what I did in the Cold War?" By coincidence he learns that Akoola, behind the locked door of her quarters, secretly dresses Western-style and poses before her mirror in a strapless form-fitting gown with opera gloves and heels (a precise copy of Miss Lace's "uniform"). Murmuring to her one evening on the deck of her submarine, he describes the success that could lie before her if she would recognize that she "could do better in silk than on a submarine": "You'd be a real sensation in America, and you know it! . . . I know some friends in Hollywood who could take it from that end!" (August 22, 1948). The ability to adorn oneself, to enhance one's attributes and use them to become a "sensation" is a form of self-invention fundamental to the American sense of possibility.

The cold war that Caniff presented involved "scripts and actors," as Christian G. Appy has written, in which "the struggle for the world" is also a "struggle for the word."[24] The image, in such a struggle, is different from propaganda. The image is acceptable, profoundly real, because paradoxically it openly acknowledges and embraces itself as image. Propaganda is different: it is developed in secret, cloistered from sight, and untrustworthy. Akoola's flaw is that she poses behind a locked door, admiring herself in a single mirror. In an American paradise of images, there are no locked doors and mirrors are everywhere. This differential is fundamental to the Cold War as Caniff envisioned it, and in one particular narrative, he invited his readers to join him as publicists and image-makers. In a March 1949 sequence, a sheltered Asian teenager who is the royal heir to the throne of a country like Tibet and whose name translates as Princess Snowflower is wavering in her allegiance to the United States, a country about which she knows very little. In an aside to his readers, Caniff proposes a contest for them to nominate the one film she might see to provide the best view of America. The invitation mobilized old correspondents and created new ones. The contest-winner, *The Best Years of Our Lives*—a 1946 film tracing the lives of three war veterans whose transition to civilian life poses distinct problems for each—not surprisingly reveals just how close a majority of Caniff's audience felt the war to be three years after its end and how sensitive they remained to problems of adjustment.[25]

Caniff's contest was a multi-level feat of promotion—one that enhanced the strip's credibility while underscoring the power of media image-making to represent America. Over three thousand letters arrived, with nominations often accompanied by comments. Some praised the winning film for showing "how the poor and the better situated families got along" even as others questioned (in the words of archivist and scholar Lucy Shelton Caswell) whether "REAL life as they knew it ever was shown on the screen."[26] Caniff anticipated that skepticism and smartly incorporated it in an ingenious plot-twist. The fortress city in which Princess Snowflower reigns is surrounded by armed rebels, and when she must escape the city to save herself, she never gets to view *The Best Years of Our Lives*—but the invading rebels do. Their screening allows Caniff to select scenes from the film and portray the reactions of the rebels and their commander. The commanding officer derides the film as sheer propaganda, mocking an actor who is holding a good-size ice cream sundae, but even this simple sign of American abundance astonishes

Figure 8-4. *Steve Canyon* (Thursday, April 21, 1949). Used with the permission of the Milton Caniff estate, all rights reserved. Caniff's staging of diverse audience response to *The Best Years of Our Lives* demonstrates the strength of the comic strip medium. Caniff can juxtapose antipathetic viewpoints using word-balloon conventions that distinguish audible remarks from subdued whispers. Since the movie is in a language unintelligible to the rebels they respond only to its visuals, a process that illuminates details the movie's American audience may have failed to notice or admire.

the rebels, who consider a common drug store a "fairy tale bazaar" (fig. 8–4). The commanding officer, striving to retain his authority, calls attention to a scene in which damaged combat aircraft are spread out across a field—here is a sign that even these Yankees are imperfect. Yet one rebel soldier whispers to another: "But this film was made to show to other Yankees—not to *us!* Do they not have to be constantly assured that they are invincible?" (April 21, 1949). Of course this staging also addresses readers in America, endowing them with a superior position from which to view these backward outsiders— who, as they watch, grow increasingly astute at reading the images presented to them.

The belief that America has no ideological message to sell—that it need only display its unmediated "real" image—drove an ingenious twist that pre-ceded this episode. Earlier in the sequence, Americans who are inside the besieged fortress worry that their plan to fly in a copy of *The Best Years of Our Lives* to show to the princess will never penetrate the rebel embargo. One of them proposes that movies of his hometown sent by his wife might serve as an alternate. With this twist, Caniff displays everyday life in small-town America as filmed without an agenda. Readers following this episode view this home movie with its "ordinary" sights within a new conceptual frame. They are placed in the position to judge the home movie's effect on the prin-cess, an outsider unfamiliar with the United States. The home movie's vi-gnettes condense everyday life into a celebration of educational opportuni-ties, mobility, health care, access to justice and free speech—all of which the film's narrator, commenting anecdotally, admits he failed to appreciate at the time he enjoyed them: "This is the railroad station where you can take a train to any place in the U.S.—over any state border—and you don't need a pass-port or visa, health certificate, vaccination certificate, letters of introduction to your consul showing financial status and good character, or police permit— and you don't need a round-trip ticket" (April 6, 1949). To a group trapped in a fortress under siege, of course, such mobility seems particularly enticing.

As it happens, the princess does see this "unmediated" glimpse of Ameri-can life when she slips into the back of the room, and she is impressed. Caniff crafted the third of the three daily episodes that feature these home movies so that its final panel is a shot of the rebels invading the city—a striking contrast to the calm newspaper office portrayed in the first panel (fig. 8–5). With this display of hometown placidity interrupted by rebel-engineered chaos, Caniff allegorizes domestic peace as endangered by foreign policy failures. With such staging, Caniff has mediated an "unmediated" arrangement in which we inhabit a stance of innocence even as we awaken to discover simple, com-mon values that we take for granted. Caniff's images gained power because

Figure 8-5. *Steve Canyon* (Friday, April 8, 1949). Used with the permission of the Milton Caniff estate, all rights reserved. Caniff's ability to convey nuance through detail is on display in this complicated sequence whose opening panel affirms the social equality that exists in everyday life even as the viewing arrangement for the home movies reveals that immensely wealthy magnate Copper Calhoon is seated by herself at the front, occupying a whole sofa as if entitled to extra space. When the projectionist mentions that his personal life holds no interest, it is the foreign princess who objects to his appraisal, disclosing her presence even as Calhoon's turning head and sneering profile dominate the panel.

he constructed them as if they were *not* created images but slices of reality. In this strip, he suggests that the "real" America is free from ideology. At the same time, Caniff's episodes are contrived to portray an America that needs neither publicity stunts nor Hollywood movies to proclaim its unique strengths (even as this assertion is elaborately staged within a comic strip as a self-conscious act of publicizing America to an outsider). Caniff's audience may appreciate the various filters that they peer through, always aware that staging within staging is occurring, or they may simply enjoy what appears to be an unpremeditated documentary record of American life.

CANIFF WAS shrewd at staging narratives that appeared to be offhand digressions or slight diversions but which in fact embedded value-laden messages. Twice a year, on Christmas Day or near it and on Armed Forces Day (mid-May), he halted his story-line either to address his readers in a voice that was close to his own or to show his characters on break, and in their down time discussing what mattered to them. These interludes were, so to speak, Caniff's "home movie" offerings, even as they paralleled developments in Canyon's career; he had re-enlisted at the outset of the Korean War and remained a military man for the duration of the strip, though his orders often took him behind enemy lines, in disguise, on special assignment.

No other cartoonist so successfully spoke to the comic-strip audience in these episodes that appeared to be intimate and unguarded.[27] When Terry earned his pilot's wings in October 1943, he listened to Flight Officer Flip Corkin speak of the sacrifices of those who made it possible for him to be a fighter pilot. Much admired and widely distributed, this Sunday page was read into the *Congressional Record*, duplicated in numerous publications, and posted on military bases around the world.[28] It was a powerful example of Caniff's ability to dramatize deeply held connections that unified a diverse America at a time of high tension. Over the years, Caniff's audience wrote warmly of these stand-alone episodes, comparing the latest to the previous. The dialogue in the 1949 hometown movie sequence, one correspondent wrote, "should be read into the Congressional Record as it was with Flip Corkin's 'red, white and blue' speech."[29]

When Caniff presented a stand-alone strip on a Sunday page, he took advantage of a powerful forum. The color printing of the Sunday supplement brought depth to drawings otherwise seen only in diagrammatic black-and-white, and the space for story-telling tripled in size. The audience for Sunday pages, moreover, was especially receptive, according to a 1955 study commissioned by the Hearst newspapers. Sunday comics, the study maintained, were "assimilated in an environment of relaxation, sometimes privacy or withdrawal, and reflect a feeling of communion with the printed word and colored pictorial episode that offers unparalleled opportunities for exploration by the advertiser."[30] While elements in this study are open to suspicion—it draws conclusions with appeal to advertisers—not all its material is distorted. Comments by several interviewees attest that Sunday pages are not read in a gulp on the way to work but perused, even returned to throughout the day. The study indicates that Sunday page reading has become "ritualized," Jennifer Hayward concludes, noting interviewees who were quick to "attest to the fixity of their consumption patterns: they read the Sunday page in the same time, place and circumstance every week."[31]

James Kavanaugh has argued that ideology is likely to be transferred most successfully when it appears as inconsequential. That which seems real or ordinary is "the paradigmatic form of ideology," for its aim is to produce "an *obvious* 'reality' that social subjects can assume and accept, precisely as if it had not been socially produced and did not need to be 'known' at all."[32] When the Sunday episode of an adventure strip, which usually features fast pacing and tight action, temporarily embraces a more casual narrative, one that depicts the strip's characters as if they are in between adventures, relaxing, talking among friends, then the readers—themselves in a similarly casual situation—are likely to believe that these remarkably ordinary strips are convincingly "real," and the events they unfold are a glimpse of actuality. Caniff was well aware of this principle. When asked by a professional group of high school teachers in 1947 to insert morally uplifting messages in his strip, he explained that "the best results in matters of this sort are obtained by indirection in such an idiom as the comic strip."[33]

Caniff's Sunday stand-alone strips around Christmastime in the late 1940s and early 1950s emphasized the value of a strong military in ways that made this Cold War doctrine appear natural and unquestionable. A Sunday episode for December 23, 1951, reveals Canyon visiting a university chapel with plaques on several walls that honor students who have died in various wars (fig. 8–6). Where Canyon pauses longest and most thoughtfully, however, is before an area with no plaque. Of course readers in 1951 would be quick to realize that the next space is "empty" only temporarily, as the suddenly unpopular Korean War drags on. Yet a larger message is also present: war is endless, and there will always be a need for more space, additional room on another wall. Peace is the aberration. Knowing this all too well, Canyon is the dedicated military man, representing those serving in far-off locations. If America is under siege, his pose suggests it is also well guarded. At Christmastime a year later, the holiday fell in between two Sundays and Caniff created two strips, December 21 and December 28. Both together aroused anxieties only to

Figure 8-6. *Steve Canyon* (Sunday, December 23, 1951). Used with the permission of the Milton Caniff estate, all rights reserved. The Korean War had entered a period of stalemate in mid-1951, with opposing troops on either side of the 38th parallel and armistice negotiations on and off throughout the fall, so Caniff's Sunday strip appears at a moment when the war has lost support but with no ending in sight. The wall's blank spot also represents an unknown future, even as the Asian man who docilely holds a broom and listens to the chapel's caretaker reminds us of America's responsibility for global peace.

allay them. In the first, Caniff commented on civilians living near military airports who complained of noisy jet aircraft flying at odd hours. They learn that these annoying interruptions signal the security Americans enjoy. In the second, he staged a fantasy moment in which the conversation between a cook and a customer in a late-night diner is joined by Uncle Sam, who recalls other darkest-before-the-dawn moments in American military history to assure his audience that all will be well. The patriotic spirit of the country never rests, it can be found in even unlikely places, and such vigilance can only be reassuring. If civilians only knew a bit more military history, they might realize how well they are protected.

For a full minute each day, for a few minutes each Sunday, Caniff held the attention of twenty to thirty million readers and influenced public opinion in the subtlest of ways. For alternative and oppositional comic strips that effectively question the militarism of the opening years of the Cold War, it is necessary to look beyond syndicated strips in mainstream daily papers to African-American weekly newspapers. Although the *Chicago Defender*'s *Speed Jaxon* feature, written and drawn by Jay Jackson, was ending its run as Caniff was beginning his new strip, the *Pittsburgh Courier*'s *Jive Gray* feature, written and drawn by Oliver Harrington, would continue to trace the postwar adventures of its eponymous hero, one of the Tuskegee Airmen, into 1951. Harrington unfolds a narrative not just different from Caniff's but so diametrically opposed that Gray could only have inhabited one of Canyon's adventures as his nemesis. In two sequences, one set in Central America in 1947, the other in South Africa in 1950–51, Gray and friends are hired by nameless "rebels" who are mounting a guerrilla war against outsiders intent upon colonizing them to extract valuable natural resources. At war's end Gray, unlike Canyon, is so thoroughly unemployable as a pilot that at one point in Harrington's strip, he abandons a career as an airmen and takes work as a journalist. He is kidnapped and left to die after attempting to expose corruption in big business.[34]

Caniff and Harrington saw the postwar era differently. At a moment in postwar history when politicians were divided about the extent to which America should play a role in world leadership, Caniff's daily episodes dramatized a Middle East and an Asia infiltrated by "subverts" and "undies" bent on undermining American interests in regions that supplied the United States with vital resources, from oil to foodstuffs to uranium. Caniff sketched a scenario that called for outposts of American investment to be established far from home, based on the readiness of a highly mobile U.S. military, and he supported a network of agents who performed surveillance on an enemy that was aggressive and untrustworthy. Caniff engaged his readership in what he carefully represented as collaboratively based plotting which allowed him to effectively purvey an idea of a war no longer fought on conventional battlefields but with tactics that involved public relations, imagery, and representations—tactics that incidentally demanded a new valuation of the contributions that mass or popular culture could make to the national defense. In unsolicited letters endorsing Caniff's productions, readers uncritically embraced a world of Cold War oppositionality in which it would be unthinkable to question the idea of a standing military guarding an American presence in virtually any point in the globe as a reasonable norm.

Notes

My grateful thanks to Lucy Shelton Caswell, Jennifer Robb and Susan Liberator for their scholarly guidance in the Ohio State University Cartoon Research Library.

1. Ron Goulart, *The Funnies: 100 Years of American Comic Strips* (Holbrook, Mass.: Adams, 1995), 172.

2. While all sources agree that an unusually high number of newspapers contracted for Caniff's feature, numbers vary according to source. I err on the side of the conservative, drawing on newspaper numbers from Carl Horak, *A Steve Canyon Companion* (Mountain Home, Tenn.: Manuscript Press, 1996), and estimates of circulation from *Time* magazine, "Escape Artist" (January 13, 1947), 59. But see Robert C. Harvey, *Meanwhile . . . : A Biography of Milton Caniff* (Seattle: Fantagraphics, 2007), 536, for an explanation that indicates a total of 238 newspapers ran first episodes of either the Sunday or the daily *Steve Canyon*. The strip appeared in so many papers because, though Fields contracted with Caniff to produce a new strip, it was distributed in tandem with King Features, a vast nationwide network of papers.

3. Milton Caniff, "Secrets of a Comic-Strip Artist," *Coronet* 21:6 (April 1947), 138.

4. Lawrence Farrant, "NYU Study Finds 4 of 5 Adults Read Comics," *Editor & Publisher* 83:20 (May 13, 1950), 12.

5. Wayne A. Wiegand, "Introduction," *Print Culture in a Diverse America*, ed. James P. Danky and Wayne A. Wiegand (Urbana: University of Illinois Press, 1998), 3.

6. Milton Caniff, "How to Be a Comic-Strip Artist," in "John Paul Adams" (Clark Kinnaird), *Milt Caniff: Rembrandt of the Comic Strip* (Philadelphia: David McKay, 1946), 60.

7. General Correspondence, January 1947, February 1947, Milton Caniff Papers, Ohio State University Cartoon Research Library.

8. Jennifer Hayward, *Consuming Pleasures: Active Audiences and Serial Fictions from Dickens to Soap Opera* (Lexington: University Press of Kentucky, 1997), 105; Harvey, *Meanwhile*, 334–35.

9. Mary Anne Guitar, "Close-up of the Artist: Milton Caniff," *Famous Artists* 8:3 (1960), n.p., and reprinted in *Milton Caniff: Conversations*, ed. Robert C. Harvey (Jackson: University of Mississippi Press, 2002), 50–58, p. 53.

10. Goulart, *The Funnies*, 172.

11. General Correspondence, February 1947, Milton Caniff Papers, Ohio State University Cartoon Research Library.

12. Helen M. Staunton, "Milton Caniff Unveils His New Strip with Hero 'Who Has Been Around,'" *Editor & Publisher* (November 23, 1946); rep. in Harvey, *Conversations*, 31–34.

13. General Correspondence, January 1947, February 1947, Milton Caniff Papers, Ohio State University Cartoon Research Library.

14. The date on which individual strips were first published appears parenthetically in the text. A collected edition of the first six years of the strip is currently in print. See Milton Caniff, *Steve Canyon, 1947–1953* (Centerville, Ohio.: Checker Publishing, 2003–2007).

15. It is not just unusual but extraordinary when fairly significant players in a comic strip sequence unequivocally die; the convention is that death, if it occurs at all, happens offstage, or under circumstances that allow for the character to someday return. In 1947, the head bodyguard of the tough female entrepreneur (who has employed the Horizons Unlimited team) gives up his life to save his boss, with whom he is clearly in love. A few years later, the presence of the Korean War may be evident in a series of sequences in which a number of characters are caught in circumstances that lead to their death, including one of Canyon's earliest companions, Breck Nazaire (in a January–April 1951 sequence), the "Duchess of Denver" (April–August 1951), and Nimbus Neil's father, a Department of Commerce weather observer (April–July 1952).

16. The sequence is among the most intricate of Canyon's productions. Not only does it reintroduce and counterpose two powerful women who have been absent from the strip for several years (Madame Lynx, a formidable Russian spy, and Feeta-Feeta, Canyon's Girl Friday from the strip's opening episodes), but many of the players are linked through a theme of divorce and separation, which plays on issues of loyalty that are threaded through the sequence. At the same time, Canyon himself is swept into the morass, as though such masquerades threaten to corrupt all who play them. Perhaps the somewhat unusual appearance of a Canadian submarine at the close would signal that espionage was not unique to America: readers with long memories might recall the trial of Allan Nunn May, a Canadian convicted in 1946 of providing atomic secrets to Russia.

17. Ron Robin, *The Making of the Cold War Enemy: Culture and Politics in the Military-Intellectual Complex* (Princeton: Princeton University Press, 2001), 3, 4.

18. Goulart, *The Funnies*, 173.

19. David Ryan, "Mapping Containment: The Cultural Construction of the Cold War," in *American Cold War Culture*, ed. Douglas Field (Edinburgh: Edinburgh University Press, 2005), 61.

20. Qtd. in Robert J. McMahon, *The Cold War: A Very Short Introduction* (Oxford: Oxford University Press, 2003), 51.

21. Qtd. in Lucy Shelton Caswell, "Milton Caniff, American Master," in *Milton Caniff: A Celebration of His Birth* (Columbus: Ohio State University Libraries, 2007), 19.

22. Esther Hansen McTighe, "Milton Caniff's Modern Home," *Better Homes & Gardens* 27:4 (December 1948): 114.

23. The information presented here has been culled from various bibliographies; the most interesting, however, may well be the material in the *Profili* ("Profile") series, edited by A. Becattini and A. Vianovi, and translated as *Milton Caniff: American Stars and Stripes* (San Casciano: Glamour International, 2001), pp. 73–92, which reflects coverage in both America and Italy and indicates a portion of Caniff's influence abroad. For examples of Caniff's endorsements, see *Steve Canyon Magazine* 14 (February 1986), 22–25.

24. Christian G. Appy, "Introduction," *Cold War Constructions* (Amherst: University of Massachusetts Press, 2001), 3–4.

25. The proportion of readers opting for this film was considerable—one out of four. The movie is notable for emphasizing the role women will play in the aftermath of the

war, but Caniff downplays the theme of the wounded male who requires female care and emphasizes instead prosperity, as if impoverished rebel outsiders could best relate to a land of abundant food, so wealthy it could discard whole airplanes.

26. Lucy Shelton Caswell, "America in Seven Reels," *Steve Canyon Magazine* 7 (September 1984): 21.

27. These "stand-alone" strips are numerous enough to have been collected as *Milton Caniff's America: Reflections of a Drawing Board Patriot*, ed. Shel Dorf (Forestville, Calif.: Eclipse, 1987).

28. The "Creed of the Pilot" became the unofficial title of the October 17, 1943, Sunday panel which, Caniff's biographer Robert C. Harvey reports, was "widely reprinted and circulated to Army bases and flight schools all around the world" (Harvey, *Meanwhile*, p. 439). Harvey examines in detail the Sunday strip and the tales surrounding it, including the anecdote in which Representative Carl Hinshaw of California read the material into the *Congressional Record* to preserve it in a national archive, and his version cites excerpts from half a dozen correspondents, one of whom was the current Army Air Forces Commanding General, H. H. Arnold (a long-time admirer of Caniff's work). See *Meanwhile*, pp. 435–39.

29. General Correspondence, April 1949, Milton Caniff Papers, Ohio State University Cartoon Research Library.

30. Robert P. Davidson, "Introduction," Science Research Associates, *The Sunday Comics: A Socio-Psychological Study with Attendant Advertising Implications* (N.p.: n.p., 1956), n.p. This hefty booklet—nearly 200 pages—presents itself as a "report" by "Science Research Associates" produced in consultation with the New York–based "Advertising Research Foundation." It is presented as an in-house professional document: its pages are typewritten and double-spaced, and none are set in typeface. However, it is also prefaced by a note on the letterhead of *Puck, The Comic Weekly* (the Hearst syndicate's comics supplement), and signed by *Puck's* General Manager. And most of the comic strips mentioned by the subjects interviewed are titles syndicated by Hearst. This appears to be a product commissioned and distributed by the Hearst syndicate to persuade advertisers that the Sunday comics supplement competes successfully with television for audience loyalty.

31. Hayward, *Consuming Pleasures*, p. 107. She is summarizing data found in the Science Research Associates study on pp. 37–39.

32. James Kavanaugh, "Ideology," in *Critical Terms for Literary Study*, ed. Frank Lentricchia and Thomas McLaughlin (Chicago: University of Chicago Press, 1990), 311.

33. General Correspondence, February 1947, Milton Caniff Papers, Ohio State University Cartoon Research Library.

34. See Edward Brunner, "'This Job Is a Solid Killer': Oliver Harrington's *Jive Gray* and the African-American Adventure Strip," *Iowa Journal of Cultural Studies* 6 (Spring 2005), 36–57.

9   Pineapple Glaze and Backyard Luaus

Cold War Cookbooks and the Fiftieth State

AMY REDDINGER

IN 1967, AN upstate New York housewife, Elizabeth Ahn Toupin, authored *The Hawaii Cookbook and Backyard Luau*, which was published that year by the tiny Silvermine Press in Norwalk, Connecticut. By the time Toupin's book appeared on shelves, cookbooks fully or partially dedicated to the study of Hawai'i were a regular part of a booming Cold War cookbook market, and the sales history of Toupin's own book attests to the Hawai'i fad.[1] Silvermine sold the rights to the book to Doubleday's imprint Bantam Books (which ordered an initial print run of 50,000) and Doubleday's Cookbook of the Month series, which sold 90,000 copies in the first month, "outselling anything before, including James Beard," according to Toupin. She adds, "Doubleday ended up selling about 120,000 and removed the book as an option after learning that they had exclusive rights [to] and were the publisher of [the competing] Trader Vic's cookbook."[2] In addition to its remarkably high sales, this cookbook bears notice as an indicator of the Hawai'i fad because it was published in conjunction with the 1966 release of the movie *Hawai'i*, based on James Michener's 1959 novel, and because Michener wrote the cookbook's introduction. It is also notable in that it is substantive, well researched, and authored by an Asian American woman raised in Hawai'i.

It is also significant that Michener, a white Quaker novelist from rural Pennsylvania, does the work of "introducing" the reader to a book about Hawaiian cooking and culture. Introductions provide the reader with an overview of what to expect in the coming pages, but also work to authorize the text—to give it validity, accreditation, and endorsement. The dust jacket photograph features Toupin, a woman experienced in entertaining scientists and diplomats, smiling tentatively at the camera while the tall, lanky, Michener

Hawaiian Luau

Oysters Rumaki

"Pig" Roast on the Turnspit

Teriyaki Steak

Sweet Potatoes with Coconut

Baked Bananas

Chinese Peas

Tahitian Salad

Aloha Baked Pineapple

Blossom Tea

Have a potluck party, Hawaiian style. Invite your friends or neighbors to bring their barbecue grills and cook alongside you for a real feast. To prepare this luau, you will need two brazier-type grills and one grill with a rotisserie attachment. Aloha Baked Pineapple can be cooked while the main course is being enjoyed.

Oysters Rumaki

To get the party off to an exotic start.

12 slices bacon, cut in half	½ teaspoon salt
24 large oysters, fresh or frozen	¼ teaspoon pepper

Fry bacon 2 minutes on each side. Drain oysters; dry on paper towels. Sprinkle oysters with salt and pepper. Wrap each with bacon slice; secure with wooden pick. Grill on hibachi or in hinged grill 2 inches from hot coals 12 minutes, or until bacon is crisp, turning once. *24 appetizers.*

looks down toward her with a vague smile on his face. The photograph visually articulates what Michener's introduction implies: this book is written by a housewife (who brings knowledge of Hawai'i) and endorsed by an *expert*. Michener's paternalistic posture synecdochizes his authority as a white American male and as an "expert" on the islands, and thus lends Toupin his gendered and racialized credibility.

In his introduction, Michener explains that Hawaiian food is worth experiencing for the pleasure of *difference*, reassuring the mainland reader that "just as the islands are a tasty blend of many different peoples, so Island cooking is a blend of many different cuisines. This book tells you how to achieve that culinary balance." Toupin follows Michener's introduction with a preface first positing that "'Hawaiian cooking' can become a way of life for it opens the mind and, more important, the palate to different tastes, cooking techniques, to cultures and the people themselves," and then outlining a history of immigration and colonization and cataloging the diverse foods and culinary practices of these immigrant groups.[3]

This rich and detailed contextualization of Hawaiian food and eating is notable for its rarity among Cold War Hawaiian cookbooks—a sub-field of publishing dominated by vacuous, cheap, poorly researched volumes presenting an ambiguous "Polynesian Cuisine." These cookbooks share, however, a deep engagement with the geopolitical terms of the Cold War through the gendered work of cooking and entertaining and thus must be understood as part of the complex geopolitical matrix of the period as disseminated through the ever-changing gendered terms of its domesticity. Reciprocally, these cookbooks show how the gendered discourse of Cold War domesticity is central to the articulation of Hawai'i, and what comes to be seen as *Hawaiian-ness* in the mainland consciousness. Several factors bring Hawai'i into the forefront of the cultural imagination: the emergence of the islands as a key strategic location after Pearl Harbor; the geographic role of the region as the "gateway to the Pacific" from the Japanese occupation to the 1970s; commercial air travel making Hawai'i a readily accessible vacation destination for those in the continental states; and the economic effects of postwar reconsolidation and suburbanization on (mainland and island) U.S. homes and families. It is within the shifting terms of U.S.-Hawai'i relations that we can read these cookbooks as doing similar work to the travel literature of Vietnam explored by Scott Laderman elsewhere in this volume: aiming to make an area, in the words of South Vietnam's National Tourist Office, "better known and thus better loved."

From Hearth to Test Kitchen: A Historical Overview of American Cookbooks

Mid-century American cookbooks emerged from a tradition of collaboratively authored household manuals and community texts intended to contribute to the practical, everyday know-how of housewives and cooks. From Amelia Simmon's 1796 *American Cookery* to nineteenth-century commonplace books in which "receipts" for popular dishes were jotted down or held for safekeeping to the 1931 publication of Irma S. Rombauer's seminal *Joy of Cooking,* American cookbooks have historically circulated recipes that, in effect, constituted the very idea of "American" cuisines.[4] The cookbook genre is so deeply linked to a passing on of *shared* knowledge that well into the mid-twentieth century, cookbooks often used shorthand notes to communicate a recipe that would need much more elaboration by contemporary standards. The cookbook as a site of communicating practical knowhow relied on a shared cultural understanding of the kitchen, cooking, and foodways.[5]

Cookbooks are inherently collaborative; even those texts authored and published under a single name contain recipes that are often the product of generations of domestic work. The American cookbook tradition adds to this history of collaboration the widespread and deeply rooted community cookbook. Generations of churches, synagogues, aid societies, and community homemakers' clubs published (most often via non-professional printing) collections of recipes authored by the group. While the proceeds of community cookbooks almost always go to charity or group fundraising, the publication of the text also serves to build community through a shared food-knowledge. In the case of the Maui Home Demonstration Council's 1963 publication of *Our Favorite Recipes,* we can see that the cookbook functions as a vehicle for community education, providing practical tips for such things as survival during wartime hardship and safe handling of food in the humid Mauian climate.[6]

Corporate-sponsored cookbooks form a very different branch of the American cookbook lineage. Descending from early magazine advertising in which flour, baking powder, or condensed milk producers would offer a recipe, corporate-sponsored cookbooks in the 1920s and '30s began as small pamphlets offering recipes and general home-management advice. The 1934 publication *The New Art of Buying, Preserving, and Preparing Foods* is a neat, 112-page volume published by General Electric with a cover price of one dollar.[7] It includes a generous offering of recipes, but also dedicates front matter to the importance of upgrading one's home with a "modern," electric kitchen.

The blending of corporate advertising and recipe instruction is central to the development of corporate cookbook publication.

While early cookbooks were often collaborative, community, or family efforts, these mid-twentieth-century cookbooks introduce an anonymous, corporate author. General Electric's small volume does not have a single author listed on the cover or the title page; instead, the cover explains the text was "created by the General Electric Kitchen Institute." Corporate-authored cookbooks become increasingly prevalent during the Cold War, especially with the Betty Crocker and Better Homes and Gardens series published by General Mills and Meredith Press, respectively. Both companies had published highly successful conventional cookbooks (the *Better Homes and Gardens Cook Book* and *The New Betty Crocker Cook Book*) prior to moving into the serialized cookbook market. For both companies, cookbooks were a secondary venture, subsidiary to the parent companies' main production (magazines for Meredith and cereal and baking supplies for General Mills). Nonetheless, it soon became apparent that the serialized cookbook market was lucrative and popular, and production was expanded to include a wide range of serialized cookbooks with fewer recipes and many more color photographs than their predecessors.[8]

These serialized texts shared with many cookbooks of the period a heightened focus on food of foreign cultures and countries—recipes couched in cookbook introductions as *opportunities* for experimentation and expansion of taste and experience. In the introduction to the 1967 *Hostess Cookbook* the reader is greeted by the customary note from Betty Crocker, declaring that "if you're like most women, giving a party means many things to you. It provides an opportunity to entertain close friends, to let people you like discover each other. It offers you a chance to prove your prowess as a cook, to display your talent for decorating, to demonstrate your diplomacy, to give your children firsthand knowledge of the social world."[9] The responsibility of the housewife and hostess is complex: she must entertain and please while also educating and introducing new foods and traditions within what the 1959 *Holiday Cookbook* explains to the reader are the constraints of gender difference: "as a rule, men like simple food and women take to 'something different.'"[10] It can be argued, then, that the housewife-as-diplomat and social coordinator is responsible for making guests and family members *comfortable* while gently encouraging them to try "something different." The designation for new and unusual foods becomes the ubiquitous Cold War "foreign food" sections, which most often include Mexican, Italian, Indian, Japanese, Chinese, and Polynesian or Hawaiian recipes. Whereas many of the "ethnic" sections within the Betty Crocker and Better Homes and Gardens series present a series of à la carte recipes, the Polynesian and Hawaiian section often appears as a set of coordinated recipes described as a luau.

The Cold War–era "appearance" of Hawai'i as a regular feature within the pages of the American cookbook marks a shift in the U.S. relationship to Asia and the Hawaiian Islands, one directly linked to Hawaiian statehood. A series of political and economic developments brought the long-waged fight for full political inclusion of the islands into the "mainland" of U.S. political representation.[11] In the Hawaiian Islands, statehood was bolstered by a master-narrative of Americanness, but the mainland narrative created about the Hawaiian and Asian "other" now poised on the cusp of citizenship was rooted in the idea of *difference*. Arguably, cookbooks of the period respond to the appearance of a mostly non-white state by taking the idea of Hawai'i and what Hawaiian culture means to the mainland U.S. home and family.[12] The backyard luau becomes the site of a complex mediation of the perceived difference of Hawai'i and the homogeneity of mainland suburbia, creating a mode of better understanding the region—a region that had in the past been treated, at best, with ambivalence.

Cold War Americans responded with a hearty interest in Hawai'i and readily took up the cookbooks' instruction on how to reproduce their own little corner of "paradise" in their suburban mainland homes. Hawai'i as a new state and a much-heralded "gateway to Asia" was celebrated and consumed far and wide. It didn't take long, however, for the trend to become overly familiar. According to Jane and Michael Stern, everyone jumped on the tiki trend: "By the late fifties nearly every middle-class American suburban home with a patio had become a site of unsophisticated luaus; and to the average (non-gourmet) housewife, 'Polynesian Cooking' had become little more than a synonym for dumping chunks of pineapple, banana, and maraschino cherries on otherwise humdrum food."[13]

How to Cook a State: A Closer Look at the Serialized Texts

Hawai'i begins to figure in the Better Homes and Gardens and Betty Crocker series in two ways—as a type of cooking and as a mode of entertaining.[14] First, we see the rise of foods that claim to be Hawaiian-influenced: pineapple is added to every possible recipe, which then becomes "Hawaiian." These recipes tend to be dispersed throughout non-Hawaiian food chapters that are often dedicated to a part of a meal (e.g., main courses, salads) rather than to an ethnic or entertainment theme. For example, we can see recipes such as *Aloha Pineapple Punch* among drink recipes, and *Pineapple Upside Down Cake* becomes a regular feature in the desserts and cakes section. These recipes are assimilated into the pages of the serialized cookbook, working to offer an interesting alternative to more common, everyday recipes.

Hawai'i also begins to appear in the serial cookbook as an *occasion*. According to these cookbooks, the housewife's role includes entertaining and is deeply linked to creating fun and enjoyment for family, friends, and neighbors as well as—and this is key—fun for the hostess herself. As the anonymous corporate author of *Best Buffets* explains: "Buffet-style serving is fun, whether supper is for 5 or 50! Begin with a buffet centered around good food and an attractive table. You, the hostess, will fairly glide through dinner! You can enjoy your party without shuttling back and forth to the kitchen: you'll have time to chat with guests and they'll relax and have a good time."[15]

The emphasis on the housewife's imperative to entertain stretches across all of the books in these series. The cookbooks' concern with modes of entertaining highlights one of the paradoxes of Cold War domesticity—the complicated ease promised by domestic life. This paradox can perhaps best be understood in the intersection of American exceptionalism within the terms of consumption and capitalism—a phenomenon readily visible in the oft-used example of the 1950 Nixon-Khrushchev "Kitchen Debate." Nixon's claim for social and political superiority comes in terms of the efficiency and modernization of the American home and the subsequent simplification of the housewife's daily labor.[16] And yet, as is clearly visible in the pages of any of the Better Homes and Gardens or Betty Crocker cookbooks, ever-expanding technology did little to make women's work easier; expectations and responsibilities simply shifted.[17] As Erika Endrijonas further argues, the paradox of technology's impact on the home was very evident in cooking trends of the era; women were encouraged to be very creative—in very controlled ways.[18] In the 1950s the role of *hostess* was added to the homemaker's role of mother and wife: "the late 1940s and 1950s witnessed the emergence of not only a reinvigorated consumer culture and a child-centered culture but also a food-centered culture. . . . Time saved on household tasks through technology meant more opportunities for women's personal development. Such development was tempered, however, by powerful messages that women should not neglect their domestic obligations to the family."[19]

The push to entertain is readily taken up by serialized cookbooks; entire volumes are dedicated to all possible modes of entertainment encountered by the newly minted Cold War "hostess," and luaus become one piece of a larger assemblage of ideas (or, as one text claims, the "jackpot" of ideas) for entertaining family and friends. The luau is distinguished among the many options of a vast repertoire as a type of relaxed and fun entertainment for the whole family and an *exotic* option for entertaining guests. According to the

logic of these texts, certain holidays call for propriety and tradition (e.g., Easter dinner) while other occasions require something more fun, relaxed, and *unusual*—this is often where the luau comes into play. In the *Holiday Cookbook* the luau is in the "Foreign Fare" section along with "Chow mein dinner," "Sukiyaki supper," and "Italian specials." While all of the recipes in these texts are highly Americanized (the recipe for fried rice calls for a package of pre-cooked rice, bacon, and canned mushrooms) they are still labeled as different and placed in a context marked "foreign."

The opening page of the *Holiday Cookbook* luau features a large color photograph of a man in a suit surveying a table laden with luau foods. The page has been given the title "Polynesian hospitality—the luau," a title that promises the hostess the opportunity to create an event that will make her guests feel welcome and at ease; in fact, "the luau" is written as an appositive in this title and literally becomes synonymous with "Polynesian hospitality."[20] The use of "Polynesian" makes general reference to the Pacific Islands, without any geographic (or political, historical) specificity and, in effect, obscures the connection of food and cultural practices for a specific people and place. The man in the accompanying photograph is Victor Bergeron, and the luau is presented as "Trader Vic's" style, referencing Bergeron's highly successful chain of Polynesian-themed restaurants featuring "south seas" food.[21] According to Victor Bergeron's own accounts, he made a fortune and a career out of making the unpalatable palatable—domesticating and "Americanizing" native Polynesian food. The explicit and unabashed appropriation of

Polynesian cuisine is essential to the project of discerning the mainland's postwar relationship to Hawai'i. Bergeron's appearance in the Better Homes and Gardens' *Holiday Cookbook*, moreover, highlights these serialized texts' concern with the marketing and promotion of the parent company and its commercial partners. The Betty Crocker series referenced the company's products with recipes that called for Bisquick, Gold Medal Flour, or Betty Crocker cake mixes, layering the texts with advertising and product placement.

The 1963 *Better Homes and Gardens Best Buffets* instructs readers to "Bring Hawaii to your table!" As an imperative, this sentence calls upon the implied reader/homemaker and cook to "bring" Hawai'i home to be reproduced on her table in the form of the luau.[22] This sentence enacts and authorizes the ongoing metonymy through which the highly popular "luau" comes to mean "Hawai'i" and an entire history and population is erased. If Hawai'i can be enacted and constructed through the creation of a luau—which includes the preparation of nine recipes and decoration with flowers and plants—then, according to the logic of the text, Hawai'i is *easily* replicated.

If we extend the metaphor of *ease* to suggest that the luau offers the housewife-as-diplomat foods that are new and interesting and yet easy for the family to *digest,* even those (male) family members who, we have been told, prefer the familiar will find this meal agreeable. The literal and symbolic consumption of Hawai'i is the imperative embedded within the command *bring*; the consumption of "ethnic food" as consumption of and participation in culture is similar to the logic furthered by Donna Gabaccia's claim that Americans' multi-ethnic eating should be read as a redemptive and hope-filled act.[23]

In the epigraphic welcome note to General Mills' 1967 *Betty Crocker's Outdoor Cookbook*, "Betty" writes that there is nothing quite like the "change-of-pace pleasure of cooking and eating outdoors," and the luau is found in a chapter entitled "Patio Parties—with a Cross-country Flair" that explains that parties with a regional American theme are particularly fun.[24] The *Outdoor Cookbook* begins with fourteen pages of general barbeque instructions and tips, including strategies for keeping the coals lit, instructions for working with different kinds of grills, and a checklist of necessary tools and utensils. The setting for the luau is crafted further with the suggestion: "What about treating your guests to the Hawaiian Luau? Have the man of the hour wear his splashiest sportshirt and say 'Aloha' to each guest with a paper lei. Perhaps you'll even ask all of the women to wear muumuu-style dresses."[25]

Despite the apparent enthusiasm for a Hawaiian theme, this luau is one of the more basic and stripped-down; the minimalist title "Hawaiian luau" indicates, perhaps, what Jane and Michael Stern refer to as the tiredness of

the luau by the end of the 1960s.[26] The photograph accompanying this luau is a two-page-wide close-up image of a buffet table. The faux luau pig (a glazed ham with raisin eyes and an apple at its "mouth"), salad in an enormous clamshell, decorated drinks, and ample foliage are flanked by two identical, small statues which represent the "primitive and unusual" native Hawaiian culture and tradition. The coconut cups can be imagined as the crude, premodern containers from which native peoples, represented by statues, drink exotic drinks.

As luaus, presumably, had become familiar to this target audience by 1967, the *Outdoor Cookbook* declines to explain them, instead jumping right into instructions for hosting one. The first two sentences command and instruct: "Have a potluck party, Hawaiian style. Invite your friends or neighbors to bring their barbeque grills and cook along side you for a real feast."[27] While all three luaus examined in this essay are intended to be parties, this luau creates a heightened sense of the communal and the casual. It is intended for the out-of-doors, the backyard or patio. This luau—within a text printed in 1967—represents the later end of the serialized cookbook obsession with Hawai'i. The larger project of familiarizing and producing knowledge of Hawai'i through the luau has been successful: Hawai'i is familiar and *known* and has, apparently, been brought to the table time and time again. The familiarity of Hawai'i is evident in the fact that this luau will be *not* Hawaiian, but "Hawaiian style," which seems to be self-consciously inauthentic mimicry of the luau—like the "pig" in the photo.

The descriptive flourishes found in these cookbook luaus are quite remarkable. The *Outdoor Cookbook* luau is described as exotic, mainland, Island, traditional, pan-Pacific, glistening, luxuriant, imaginative, plentiful, glamorous, and floral-scented. This luau uses a sexual language that calls on the senses (glistening, floral-scented), while invoking relative geographic locations (mainland, island, pan-Pacific), and highlighting excess (plentiful, luxuriant). These adjectives provide a lexicon for an understanding of Hawai'i as exotic and pleasurable; they also provide explicit instruction to the housewife/homemaker for creating these pleasures within her home. The descriptive language used to introduce the recipes stands in sharp contrast to the highly directive, imperative-filled, and adjective-barren cooking instructions found beneath the title and subtitle. The subtitles seem to remind the reader that the work of producing each individual recipe functions as a part of the larger project of creating the luau, which, the reader is reminded, will be "luxuriant" and "glamorous." These brief sentences and phrases mediate the labor of preparing the food and refocus the preparation toward the pleasure to come.

"We're So Glad You Could Come" and Other Lessons from the Table

Glossy, colorful, and lacking any historical contextualization, the Betty Crocker and Better Homes and Gardens series represent Hawaiian food and the luau variously as an unusual way to throw a party (*Holiday Cookbook*), an occasion to bring Hawai'i home (*Best Buffets*), or a familiar but still fun way to entertain guests on the patio (*Outdoor Cookbook*). The texts produce Hawaiian food and the luau as attractive, luxuriant, and *easy* modes of entertainment through which the participants have a safe and mediated experience of the foreign and which operate, simultaneously, to consume and assimilate *difference*.

It is the popular, Americanized, pedestrian nature of the serialized cookbooks and their promotion of Hawai'i as interesting, exotic and worth replicating that makes these texts an important site of investigation; the proliferation of the "unsophisticated luau," passed off as an exotic opportunity, is one of the ways in which the *practice* of Hawai'i is enacted on the mainland and coordinated through the texts of popular domestic culture. It is precisely because of the mainstream, middle-class accessibility of the Betty Crocker and Better Homes and Gardens cookbooks that the luau becomes an important and widely disseminated mode of Cold War entertainment. Difference, as it is constructed in the luaus, is both fixed and manageable, providing pleasure and entertainment.

The serialized cookbooks of the Cold War are different from their genre predecessors not only because they were corporate-sponsored and authored, but also because they were published within the Taylorized, Book-of-the-Month Club–inspired model in which parts of each cookbook were used in combination to produce "new" texts. (For example, in the Better Homes and Gardens series the same recipe for Japanese Sukiyaki can be found in *Meals with a Foreign Flair* and the "Foreign Fare" section of the *Holiday Cookbook*.) Janice Radway brings us an apt critique of this publishing method through the words of Dorothy Parker: "a book-like non-book, a pseudo-book which afflicts the field of cookbooks with a chunk of merchandise that is likely to disappear as suddenly as it appeared in the first place. Another 'bright' idea blown away on the gusty wind of the next 'bright' idea."[28]

What Parker describes as the "bright" and empty process of this mode of Cold War cookbook publishing dislodges an understanding of cookbooks in the terms of the feminist critical theory of the last decades of the twentieth century in which scholars focus significant attention on the texts of women's everyday lives as repositories of social and cultural information. As Cold War

American cookbooks begin to focus on instruction in cooking "ethnic" and "foreign" foods they also become cheap, poorly researched, and textually inferior to the texts that came before. These thin texts, in their wide circulation, effectively charged American housewives with the responsibility of introducing Hawai'i to their families and friends. Subsequently, the housewife-as-diplomat emerges from these pages as the tentative arbiter of Hawai'i responsible for engaging and even highlighting the vague terms of difference while simultaneously familiarizing that difference.

As the reader is reminded in the introductory pages of the *Holiday Cookbook*, the luau is one of the easier, "self-service" types of meals of which any savvy hostess will want to take advantage.[29] When creating events for the enjoyment of friends, neighbors, or her husband's colleagues, her work, at the ideological level, is to prepare the family and community to *consume* the idea of Hawai'i. If, as the *Holiday Cookbook* suggests, men prefer the usual foods while women take to "something different," then women are necessary arbiters of the new and unfamiliar "foreign" foods that comprise the luau. The reader is promised that her family will respond well to the interesting new foods and the pleasant surroundings. Her pleasure, however, is derived not primarily from the food, beverages, and décor of the luau, but instead from the promised ease of this kind of an event.

Placing serialized cookbooks, as the products of corporate test kitchens and anonymous authors, within the tradition of cookbooks challenges some of the key feminist-historical assumptions about cookbooks as a woman-authored folk-genre. The corporate texts offer sanitized and pared-down versions of the Hawaiian food that authors like Elizabeth Ahn Toupin worked diligently to preserve and record. Betty Crocker and Better Homes and Gardens offer plasticized luaus lacking any historical or material context, stripped down for easy digestion, authored not by a group of women with a specific geography and history but by a corporation, a brand, a spokescharacter. And yet, it seems uncanny that both the anonymous corporate texts and texts such as Toupin's *Hawaii Cookbook* are subject to the same terms of operation. While Toupin's text is "authorized" by Michener as a valid and useful source of knowledge about Hawai'i, the corporate cookbook takes up the same relationship of arbitration and mediation. In the corporate texts, more of the burden of replication is placed on the shoulders of the housewife/reader as she ventures out to teach her family and friends how to love Hawai'i.

Cold War American cookbooks play a crucial role in the production of knowledge about Hawai'i—helping readers make sense of the emergent state—through food instruction, the promise of pleasure, and occasional histories of migration (as with Toupin).[30] Rather than the serialized-textual reproduction of Hawaiian cuisine simply being a moment of acculturation, or kitsch, it seems that the rapid publication and distribution of these texts point to a complex and contested conversation about consumption, race, and the possibility of incorporating Hawai'i as a part of the United States through a process of literal and figurative domestication and consumption that was taking place in 1960s political discourse and popular culture. The housewife—the cookbooks' real audience—is charged with the grave responsibility of managing the racial and ethnic differences presented within the text, a responsibility packaged for her not as work but as an occasion to produce entertainment and pleasure. In the relationship between the housewife and Hawai'i, work becomes pleasure, the foreign becomes familiar, and food and entertainment become the means by which the housewife, and the nation for which she stands, bring Hawai'i home.

Notes

1. In this article I use the Hawaiian spelling "Hawai'i" whenever the words are my own. However, as was common practice at the time, most of the publications referenced use the Anglicized "Hawaii" in titles and quotations.

2. Elizabeth Ahn Toupin, e-mail correspondence with Greg Barnhisel, October 16, 2008.

3. Elizabeth Ahn Toupin, *The Hawaii Cookbook and Backyard Luau* (Norwalk, Ct.: Silvermine, 1967), 9, 13.

4. Rather than attempting to make an argument for a homogenous "American food" I am highlighting the fact that historically the American cookbook was concerned with passing on the knowledge of familiar foods. These cookbooks participate in the cultural foodways of regional and ethnic groups, providing an important link to group identity and culture.

5. It is not until well into the twentieth century that we begin to see a sustained trend in which all of the minute steps of a recipe are spelled out in great detail, a textual feature that suggests a shift in the cultural know-how assumed in cookbook readers. This is a textual shift that Erika Endrijonas traces as both a result of efforts at standardization (reforms led by food experts like Fannie Farmer) and the assumption that important training of housewives had lapsed during wartime and other periods of national and economic upheaval (e.g., the Great Depression): Endrijonas, "Processed Food from Scratch: Cooking for a Family in the 1950s," in *Kitchen Culture in America: Popular Representations of Food, Gender, and Race*, ed. Sherrie A. Inness (Philadelphia: University of Pennsylvania Press, 2001), 162.

6. The Maui Home Demonstration Council books have been published regularly since 1939.

7. Many of the pamphlets from this era were free to consumers. For instance, *New Magic in the Kitchen* is a small booklet published in 1930 by the Borden (Condensed Milk) Company that was mailed to consumers upon written request. The National Kitchen Modernizing Bureau (affiliated with the "Edison Electric Institute") distributed its 1937

booklet *Meals Go Modern Electrically* as part of the campaign to convert consumers from gas to electric kitchen appliances.

8. It is important to note that General Mills was experiencing significant expansion during this period and was well on its way to becoming the multinational corporation it is today. (For more on the history of General Mills Corporation, see James Gray's *Business without Boundary. The Story of General Mills* [Minneapolis: University of Minnesota Press, 1954].)

9. The fictional figure "Betty Crocker" began as a pen name for the General Mills employees who would respond to notes and questions from housewives in the 1920s. The "Betty" persona took many forms over the years, including the warm, personalized note (printed in a handwritten-style typeface) in the opening pages of the cookbook.

10. Better Homes and Gardens, *Holiday Cook Book* (New York: Meredith, 1959), 5.

11. The success of the 1950s statehood movement—a movement which had been unsuccessful in the past—can be attributed largely to the coming-of-age of Nisei veterans who used the G.I. Bill to obtain educational, professional, and law degrees. This political power contributed to the 1954 Democratic overthrow of the Republican oligarchy that had dominated island politics for decades. These island political powers still had to negotiate statehood with the U.S. Congress, which had in the past expressed tremendous hesitation at the incorporation of a state with a largely non-white constituency; this racism and hesitation were successfully combated by the creation of a master narrative of Japanese American (and particularly Nisei veteran) patriotism. For a thorough discussion of the history of the Hawaiian plantation economy and the sugar and pineapple corporations' role in the process of statehood, see Gavan Daws, *Shoal of Time: A History of the Hawaiian Islands* (New York, Macmillan, 1968), and Lawrence H. Fuchs, *Hawaii Pono: A Social History* (New York: Harcourt, Brace & World, 1961).

12. Jane and Michael Stern, *A Taste of America* (Kansas City: Andrews and McMeel, 1988); Fuchs, *Hawaii Pono*, 381.

13. Stern and Stern, *A Taste of America*, 56.

14. Subtitle with apologies to M. F. K. Fisher's seminal *How to Cook a Wolf.*

15. Better Homes and Gardens, *Best Buffets* (New York: Meredith, 1963), 6.

16. A claim that Khrushchev notably responded to by stating, "I still think women should get on their hands and knees and scrub the floor." Kathi Ann Brown, *Meredith: The First 100 Years* (Des Moines: Meredith Books, 2002), 75.

17. Ruth Cowan, *More Work for Mother: The Ironies of Household Technology from the Open Hearth to the Microwave* (New York: Basic Books, 1983), 15.

18. Endrijonas, "Processed Food from Scratch," 159.

19. Ibid., 157.

20. Photo from Better Homes and Gardens, *Holiday Cook Book* (New York: Meredith, 1959). The word "Polynesian" is a term deeply rooted in colonization. According to the OED, the origins of the word "Polynesia" are French. First used by De Brosses in 1756, it became a popular term with traders and explorers, used to describe the islands of the South Pacific.

21. In 1932 Victor Bergeron opened his first restaurant in San Francisco. By 1936 this restaurateur would be known as "The Trader," and by the 1950s his restaurant had expanded to a national chain known as "Trader Vic's." While this essay does not focus on the phenomenon of Trader Vic's, I find it an important starting point in the investigation of mainland America's mid-century fascination with Hawaiian food. From the outset,

Victor Bergeron was clear that his specialty was *Americanized* Polynesian food—the restaurant's attraction was, admittedly, more about the exotic décor and its signifiers than the food itself. Bergeron noted that the success of his business lay in the fact that the South Pacific theme "intrigues everyone. You think of beaches and moonlight and pretty girls. It is complete escape" ("Trader Vic"). In a 1958 interview in *Newsweek* Bergeron stated: "The real, native South Seas food is lousy. You can't eat it."

22. While no direct mention of audience is made in the body of these texts, the beginnings of the cookbooks (especially the Betty Crocker line) often included a letter addressed to "home maker" or "housewife."

23. Donna Gabaccia, *We Are What We Eat: Ethnic Food and the Making of Americans* (Cambridge: Harvard University Press, 2000), 231.

24. Betty Crocker, *Outdoor Cookbook—Barbeques* (New York: Golden Press, 1967), 100.

25. Ibid.

26. Stern and Stern, *A Taste of America*, 56.

27. Betty Crocker, *Outdoor Cookbook*, 110. Photo courtesy of the General Mills Archives.

28. Janice Radway, *A Feeling for Books: The Book-of-the-Month Club, Literary Taste, and Middle-Class Desire* (Chapel Hill: University of North Carolina Press, 1997), 84–85.

29. Better Homes and Gardens, *Holiday Cookbook*, 4.

30. Both Elizabeth Ahn Toupin's *Hawaii Cookbook* and the 1963 publication *Hawaiian Cuisine*, published by the Hawaii State Society, include detailed histories of labor and migration that deeply influence contemporary Hawaiian culture.

10   Mediating Revolution

Travel Literature and the Vietnam War

SCOTT LADERMAN

FOR HARVEY S. OLSON, the Republic of Vietnam's political predicament was simple. The author of one of several popular guidebooks to Asia whose appearance coincided with a post–World War II tourism boom, Olson saw in Vietnam none of the imperialist ambitions from Washington that had earlier characterized French policy in Indochina. The Viet Minh, he informed his readers in 1962, was in no way a genuine nationalist movement; its undeniable popularity, he explained, was the result of a Communist "ruse." The organization "perpetrated a cruel hoax on the Vietnamese people when, under the guise of fighting for freedom and independence for all of Viet Nam, they were, in reality, doing their utmost to lead the country into the open arms of communism [and] enslave the entire population." As for the Republic of Vietnam (R.V.N.), the southern state that was daily convulsed with political unrest, its "hardy citizens" were "democracy's greatest friends and communism's greatest foes." And these hardy citizens' view of the United States, the chief benefactor of the authoritarian government of Ngo Dinh Diem? "They love us," Olson gushed.[1]

While *Olson's Orient Guide* may have been more effusive than a number of its competitors, such sentiments were by no means unique. In the 1950s and early 1960s, as Vietnam sought to place itself on the global tourism map, travel writers—guidebook authors, prize-winning journalists, even freelancers for the Department of Defense—undertook the cultural work of mediating for Americans the history and politics of the conflict in Vietnam. Rejecting the notion of an indigenous struggle for national liberation, these writers situated the Vietnamese insurgency within a simplistic Cold War frame of reference. Support for the Diem regime and its successors was support for freedom and democracy. Internal opposition to the Saigon government was

209

evidence of international Communist subversion. American intervention in this faraway land was a matter of national defense. The discursive framework would hardly seem surprising to scholars of Cold War culture. What is unusual, however, is its context: literature extolling the touristic marvels of Vietnam, from the colonial ambience of Saigon and the imperial architecture of Hue to the golden beaches of Nha Trang and the world-class hunting of the interior highlands.

While for most Americans today the word "Vietnam" conjures a war rather than a country, such was not always the case. In the late 1950s, as commercial jet travel became possible and Americans took a greater interest in visiting the Far East, the government of the Republic of Vietnam, like several of its Asian neighbors, sought to place Vietnam on the global tourism map. Now that the country had, it was hoped, moved beyond the Viet Minh's bloody war with France that consumed most of the decade following World War II, the time seemed right to promote travel to the fledgling Indochinese state.[2] The reasons for this undertaking were several. At the most basic level officials hoped tourism would assist with economic growth, pumping foreign currency into a corner of Southeast Asia battered for years by unrelenting warfare. Yet it was not simply a matter of capturing dollars and francs. As the director of the National Tourist Office suggested in a 1958 report to Diem, tourism's contribution to improvements in technology, transportation, and commerce would aid the state's development in multiple ways, providing not just economic but political, social, and cultural benefits as well.[3]

For a government facing both internal and external questions about its political legitimacy, this was an important consideration. Born out of the 1954 Geneva accords that explicitly precluded the seventeenth parallel from serving as a permanent "political or territorial boundary," the Republic of Vietnam— or what became known colloquially as "South Vietnam"—was essentially a U.S. creation.[4] That a Catholic despot—one who enjoyed little popular support and routinely employed terror as his preferred method of suasion— ruled an overwhelmingly Buddhist nation only added to the authorities' difficulties. International tourism thus came to assume a unique role in the Saigon government's cultural diplomacy campaign. In particular, tourism— and, importantly, the burgeoning literature associated with it—possessed the potential to generate positive sentiments about the southern state that would translate into popular support and diplomatic goodwill, serving the interests of both America and its client in a variety of ways. Indeed, a motto of the National Tourist Office was "to make the country better known and thus better loved."[5]

Tourism publications, whether state-generated or independently produced, offered an ideal means of achieving this objective. Such publications
could be provided not only to the thousands of foreign travelers journeying
to the new southern republic—nearly 40,000 by 1962, according to official
statistics—but they could also be distributed to persons abroad—from schoolchildren to armchair travelers to members of civic organizations—through
travel agencies, the Republic of Vietnam's network of embassies and consular
offices, or the most influential member of the Vietnam lobby, the American
Friends of Vietnam.[6] While the number of visiting foreigners remained relatively small when compared with more popular Asian destinations such as
Japan and India, tourism in Vietnam was never merely about luring tens of
thousands of sun-seeking visitors to the fledgling southern state. Rather, the
cultural work performed by international tourism and its vast literary output
could contribute to the government's quest for political legitimization, thus
helping to fulfill one of the R.V.N.'s chief diplomatic objectives.[7] And when one
considers that many readers would have been influential shapers of American
opinion—diplomats, intelligence officials, missionaries, journalists, corporate executives, NGO workers, and the like—the travel literature's significance was only compounded.

At the same time that important periodicals such as *Holiday* and *Travel*
began to extol the touristic virtues of the "stripling Asian nation," Vietnamese officials in the late 1950s and early 1960s attempted to reinforce their
country's popular appeal through a colorful assortment of guidebooks, pamphlets, posters, and brochures that constructed southern Vietnam as an exotic paradise rather than a site of budding insurgency and state repression.[8]
Distributing the materials not only within the south but also through the
R.V.N.'s diplomatic offices overseas, the authorities sought to have their literary corpus, at the most elementary level, highlight southern Vietnam's hundreds of miles of beautiful coastline and coral reefs, its thrilling big-game
hunting in the mountainous interior, and its cosmopolitan capital as the
"Pearl of the Orient." In doing so, the tourism documents provided alternative representations of Vietnam from those beginning to appear more regularly in the West, from press coverage of R.V.N. politics to Hollywood films
and television dramas that relied on the visual excitement of violent conflict.
Precisely how many copies of these materials were printed by Saigon's National Tourist Office is uncertain, but the number was sufficiently large that
the documents can be found today in the archival collections of not only
American ex–military personnel but also non-governmental organizations
and important U.S. intelligence officials, such as the former C.I.A. director

William Colby, who had served as the Agency's Saigon station chief from 1959 to 1962.

The outwardly tourist-oriented language of these materials could not mask their simultaneous discursive appeal for political legitimacy.[9] Cognizant that tourists were often interested in history and cultural heritage—and, importantly, that the materials could be distributed abroad to influence foreigners with no immediate plans to visit Indochina—the authorities subtly suggested that the Saigon regime, as opposed to the revolutionaries challenging it, was the true inheritor of Vietnam's patriotic tradition.[10] The materials' narratives were written in such a way that readers could easily believe the U.S.-created and -supported government to be the sole indigenous force fulfilling Vietnam's historical mandate of national independence. By portraying Hanoi or the southern revolutionaries as Communist interlopers seeking to violently spread the "foreign ideology" of China and the Soviet Union, Vietnamese travel writers presented the R.V.N. authorities as valiantly defending against this unprovoked aggression.

If Western guidebooks and U.S. military publications in the 1960s generally felt compelled to address the reality of an escalating Vietnamese war, as will be seen later, the tourism literature generated in the Republic of Vietnam from the late 1950s through 1975 was more ambivalent in confronting the conflict. On the one hand, war is generally bad for tourism—most travelers do not wish to flirt with death while spending their holidays abroad—so the authorities largely sought to mask its presence in their touristic representations of the south.[11] But, on the other hand, the Saigon government faced a severe crisis of legitimacy, and tourist literature could be one way of spreading its political message to a global audience. What one therefore found in many Vietnamese pamphlets, guidebooks, and brochures as the war escalated was an effort to achieve a precarious balance: a minimization of the conflict's undeniable omnipresence in much of the south coupled with a nod—sometimes subtle, sometimes not—to the Saigon government's critical struggle against supposed Communist aggression.

Tourism authorities and the regime's supporters constructed this balance through a variety of means. Revealing their transnational sensibilities, for example, tourism publications described the Republic of Vietnam as committed to modernization—a concept increasingly crucial to American policymakers' objectives for the Third World, as Amanda Laugesen also shows in this volume—while not devaluing the traditions still governing daily Vietnamese life. "Vast programs of community development, construction, social reform, education, and modernization" were contributing to "a transformation that is taking place so rapidly that it is impossible for the visitor to remain unaware of it," an official pamphlet insisted in 1961. At a time when the Saigon regime was receiving large quantities of U.S. aid, foreign tourists—including visiting congressmen and Washington insiders—were assured by the R.V.N. authorities that the southern state, "under the leadership of President Ngo Dinh Diem," was "emerging as one of the most stalwart members of the family of Free Nations."[12]

Yet, it was clear, modernization alone would not entice tourists. Why travel to Southeast Asia, after all, to witness what could be seen in the United States? The Republic of Vietnam's rapid modernization had to therefore be conjoined with the exoticism of Vietnamese traditional life if the authorities hoped to lure pleasure-seeking international visitors. Whereas modernization and anti-Communism may have endowed travel to southern Vietnam with political virtue, the conjunction of Vietnamese "tradition" and the region's colonial French heritage would provide its visual appeal. The literature provided a ready means of marketing this facet of southern Vietnam, from cover photographs or illustrations of strikingly beautiful women clad in traditional *ao dai* costumes to encomiums to cosmopolitan Saigon, a city of "broad, shady boulevards bisect[ed by] modern business centers" and "big, luxurious cars compet[ing] with horse carts."[13] This visual combination of the traditional and the modern, then, revealed Vietnam to be an exciting destination for foreign travelers while, importantly, confirming for Americans that the Vietnamese embraced the modernization project espoused by the United States.

While in some instances the political nature of the era's tourism publications could be quite subtle—referring to the southern Vietnamese regrouping zone as "Free Vietnam," for example—at other times their political underpinnings were unabashedly explicit.[14] *Visit Fascinating Vietnam*, a pamphlet published by the National Tourist Office to coincide with 1961's designation as "Visit the Orient Year," was emblematic of the former. Like other publications, this one spoke glowingly of the "Free Republic of Vietnam," including, importantly, the welcome it offered to "about one million happily resettled refugees" from the north.[15] For Americans exposed to the harrowing plight of these mostly Catholic northerners in the mid-1950s—whether in *Reader's Digest*, secular and Catholic newspapers, Tom Dooley's best-selling book *Deliver Us from Evil*, or the television drama *Navy Log*—the allusion to the happy resettlement of the "refugees" served to link the southern government to the humanitarian impulse that most Americans believed drove U.S. foreign policy.[16] Travel to the Republic of Vietnam could thus be considered a demonstration of one's patriotic commitment to a like-minded Cold War ally. "Vietnam has lived through more than her share of kingdoms and dynasties, colonization and internal partition," the *Visit Fascinating Vietnam* authors asserted, "but today, under the leadership of President Ngo Dinh Diem," the southern state was emerging as a devoted member of the American-led "family" of free peoples.[17] For those in the West, venturing to the south could thus serve as a symbolic gesture of support for the anti-Communist struggle.

To entice foreigners, locations were described as attractively exotic yet safely familiar—a slice of Europe in Asia. The highland resort of Dalat was "rather like . . . Geneva, with stately hotels and fashionable villas" as well as "several exclusive little inns of strictly European style" that served food "in the Savoy tradition." Yet in the midst of this Old World comfort, one could

Figure 10-1. The placement of attractive women on the covers of materials produced by the National Tourist Office, as with this pamphlet for the highland resort of Dalat, was a not unusual strategy of the R.V.N. government in promoting Vietnam to sometimes weary foreign travelers. *Dalat* (Saigon: National Tourist Office, n.d.).

still find in the central market "numbers of the many hill tribe people who live deep in the forests."[18] Vung Tau, which "preserves a certain continental charm on its picturesque streets, in its restaurants, and on its beautiful beaches," has, like Nha Trang, "been likened to the Rivera."[19] Similarly, Saigon, where women "patter in French with a Parisian accent," was the "Paris of the Far East" or "the most Parisian city east of the Suez Canal."[20] The R.V.N. capital was "sophisticated" and beautifully adorned; its newest hotel was "decorated with France's St. Gobain glass and Italian marble," and one of its public spaces was constructed like "a typical, spacious French square." And yet: "Everywhere are the street scenes of Oriental life so compelling to foreigners—the rush hour traffic jam, made not by cars, but by scooters; the service station for unlucky bicycles, equipment hanging on a tree or a street corner; the vendors of soup, dried meat, sugar cane juice; the coster mongers with their colorful wares and, *above all, the doe-eyed shapely Vietnamese girls dressed in the most gracious way.*"[21] Saigon was, in short, a city whose "face is French but whose heart is Oriental."[22] With the Republic of Vietnam thus a fascinating blend of the Orient and the Occident, as well as, importantly, a state occupying a "strategic position in Southeast Asia," as the authorities were sure to note, travel there merited tourists' support.[23]

An earlier volume even more blatantly politicized its travel guidance. Appearing in 1957, *A Glimpse of Vietnam*, a 100-page book full of enticing imagery and background information, identified neither a publisher nor place of publication, but it did note that its "photographs and graphic materials" were provided by the Ministry of Information and the United States Information Service–United States Operations Mission Photography Laboratory.[24] Among the three people identified as authors, the one listed first, Gene Gregory, was the husband of Ann Gregory, editor of the English-language *Times of Viet Nam*, which served as an important organ of R.V.N. propaganda. Whatever the volume's origins, its contents read like an unrestrained brief for the Saigon regime. Diem's one-time rival, Bao Dai, was characterized as a naïve tool of the French colonialists who sought to "rule through the institution of the monarchy" by "molding it to their designs," rendering the emperor "putty in their hands." The Viet Minh revolutionaries, on the other hand, rode "the shirt tail of the nationalist movement" and attempted "to exploit it to their own advantage." Their undeniable popular support was explained away as rooted in local ignorance.

The strength of the Viet Minh [immediately after World War II] was in its appearance as essentially a nationalist movement. French power had been broken and the people were predisposed to support such a successful effort to establish independence. The Communists had gone through the motions of abolishing the Communist Party and making the pretense of pristine nationalism, a fiction which they maintained until 1951 when the Communist apparatus reappeared openly well entrenched in command of the Viet Minh which they had exploited as a front.

It was to a nationalist movement that Bao Dai thought he was rendering the supreme power when he abdicated [to the Democratic Republic of Vietnam in 1945] and it was to such a regime that men like Tran Trong Kim thought they were lending their support. Many found almost too late that they had been duped; some like Bao Dai had a rude and sudden awakening; others realized the true situation only after 1951.

One of those who recognized that the Viet Minh was only "posing as a purely nationalist movement," the authors suggested, was Ngo Dinh Diem. This embattled premier of the south had to contend not only with Communist aggression but also with "a gang of brigands and river pirates" deployed by the French "whose purpose was to thwart and destroy" him. Despite the gravity of the threat, Diem succeeded in overcoming these obstacles while also resettling approximately a million northern Vietnamese who "made their way to freedom in the South," thus "showing their contempt for the Communists."[25]

In its foreign policy, the volume explained, the Republic of Vietnam, under Diem's leadership, had committed itself to "resistance to the Red peril which menaces all free peoples." Domestically, the Saigon authorities had established peace throughout the south, taking over, in "*Operation Liberation*," "vast areas of Viet Nam . . . which had been occupied by the Viet Minh," "completely annihilating" the Binh Xuyen rebels, defeating the Hoa Hao sect, and, "in a peaceful way," conducting a "successful all-out campaign against the Communist underground." Declaring itself a stabilizing presence, the government had established "peace and security . . . for all the territory south of the Seventeenth Parallel, in many instances for the first time since 1945." As a result, "people have drifted back to their villages which they had left years before to begin once more a normal and productive life."[26]

Of course, at an obvious level the R.V.N.-produced travel literature sought to market southern Vietnam as a land of exotic charm and touristic pleasure, and it did so ably. Yet the literature's deeper purpose in rhetorically bolstering the Saigon government's legitimacy was unmistakable. Travel publications might be considered a particularly effective tool in the R.V.N.'s broader cultural propaganda campaign, as their seemingly apolitical subject matter—tourism and tourist sites—fascinated readers interested in Asia while cloaking the literature's political nature. Toward this end, Vietnamese officials created tourism documents that were widely used for non-touristic purposes, such as *A Guide to Viet-Nam*, a 40-page booklet published in 1959 or 1960 by the R.V.N.'s embassy in the United States.[27] Ostensibly a guide for tourists visiting southern Vietnam, in fact the document appears to have been used principally to publicize the appeal of the fledgling state to the American public, thus promoting its political legitimacy while cultivating support for the large amounts of aid being provided at the time by Washington.

A Guide to Viet-Nam was a broad overview of southern Vietnam and its points of interest to Western tourists. It contained information on festivals, hunting, and beaches, and considerable background on the Vietnamese people and Vietnamese culture. It was also, however, an explicitly political document intended to bolster the Diem regime; the text was bookended, for example, with references to the government's anti-revolutionary struggle. Locating Vietnam "at the juncture of East and West," the authors initially distinguished "Communist North Viet-Nam" from the "Free Republic of Viet-Nam in the South," and they concluded their narrative by insisting on the southern state's important role in the global Cold War. "This pamphlet deals primarily with the physical aspects and the picturesque side of Viet-Nam," they wrote. "There is, however, another aspect of Viet-Nam which cannot fail to captivate the tourist: the stimulating picture of the Free Republic of Viet-Nam which remains attached to its ancient heritage while working for economic and social progress." Readers should not dismiss Vietnam as a distant locale of no concern to them, the authors suggested, for "placed at the crossroads of the Far East, and for the time being divided between a Communist regime in the North and a free democratic system in the South, Viet-Nam plays no small part in the ideological contest between the Communist and the Free Worlds."[28]

R.V.N. diplomats cooperated with American Friends of Vietnam (A.F.V.), which spearheaded the Vietnam lobby in the United States, in disseminating the booklet to the largest possible audience. Its gratis availability was announced in *New York Mirror Magazine*; it was distributed to "several hundred" teachers and schoolchildren in 1961; and it was included in "A Kit for Teachers" created by the A.F.V.[29] Notice of the "Kit for Teachers" appeared in the Asia Society Calendar, *Social Education, Intercom*, and the UNESCO magazine *Orient-Occident*, as well as over the New York radio station WNYE.[30] Copies were distributed to the Summer Institute for Asian Studies at the State College of Iowa, which administered a summer program for teachers in the Hawkeye State, and to dozens of influential Americans and Vietnamese.[31] By the close of 1962, reported the A.F.V.'s executive secretary, sales of the kit had "picked up," with over seventy sold.[32] The guide's inclusion in the teaching kit was certainly ingenious, as the booklet was generously sprinkled with photographs that, unlike the more stale verbiage that characterized much overseas propaganda, helped to bring Vietnam to life for school-age children.[33] Finally, the *Guide to Viet-Nam* proved beneficial to R.V.N. boosters through people-to-people contacts: a Vietnamese student enrolled in a course in the United States titled "Education for Mutual Understanding," for example, requested multiple copies with which to educate others "anxious to know more about Viet Nam."[34]

While the Republic of Vietnam generated numerous tourism-related documents intended not only to encourage foreign travelers but to buttress the state's fragile international legitimacy, the Saigon government was by no means alone in producing tourism materials that sought to cast Vietnam's political predicament, as well as the West's relationship with it, in terms favorable to an American and global audience. So, too, did Western guidebook authors. Travel writing has long played an important role in helping to map tourism's cognitive terrain. As early as the 1830s, guidebooks began to identify for tourists not just what could be seen but, perhaps more important, "what ought to be seen."[35] This included not only the identification of tourism sites but also intellectual direction as to how they should be interpreted. In the case of Indochina, well before the R.V.N.'s National Tourist Office began developing its literature in the 1950s, non-governmental travel writers had sought to sanitize or even erase France's imperial dominion over the Vietnamese people. In 1926, for example, author Lucian Swift Kirtland conceded that "French power and authority [in Indochina] are as absolute as any one might care to demand," but added that "the hand of administration wears a velvet glove." Kirtland's view was that French colonialism was essentially benign. Considering the "diabolical character of the [region's] climate," he wrote in a discursive reflection of the environment's presumed role in racialized cultural hierarchies, France's "progress of less than a half century [in developing Indochina] is really remarkable."[36]

Even more generously, in 1930 the author of a guidebook to Saigon depicted nineteenth-century Vietnam as a place ravaged by "conflicting forces" until benevolent foreigners acted to put an end to the chaos in 1859. It was in that year that "the French, together with a handful of Spanish volunteers, had to intervene in order to restore peace under the French flag."[37] The action apparently marked the end of Vietnamese history, as, despite seventy years having passed since the intervention, the sentence was the last in the volume's synopsis of the past.

Little changed with the global increase in anticolonial sentiment after World War II; while guidebook authors may have begun to acknowledge that the French occupation was in fact despised by the bulk of the Vietnamese people, they were careful to distinguish the American intervention from that of its European predecessor. This adoption of Cold War ideology was evident among civilian travel writers. Like Harvey S. Olson, whose glowing praise for the Republic of Vietnam opened this chapter, Robert S. Kane, too, embraced the American mission. Kane's "A to Z" series of travel guides, which began with an Africa volume in 1961 and would be produced under the Rand Mc-Nally imprint after 1980, proved popular for their first-person narratives and easygoing style.[38] In *Asia A to Z*, Kane notified his touring readers in 1963 that the United States was "attempting to bring order out of the chaos in Vietnam." Vietnam, he wrote, was split in two; half was "in the hands of a Communist regime closely allied to that of neighbor Mao Tse-tung's," and the other half was "a sovereign state." Unlike Olson, however, Kane was quite critical of Ngo Dinh Diem, offering some praise but also rebuking his administration's authoritarianism and repression. In the latter's estimation, the anti-Communist perspective of exiled oppositionist Tran Van Tung, who accused the president of letting "the Communist Vietcong control and terrorize the country right up to the city limits of Saigon" by "purg[ing] himself of all capable anti-Communist leaders" in his broad crackdown on perceived dissent, provided "food for thought." If the United States were to succeed in defeating the southern insurgency, Kane approvingly quoted Tung, it would need to reappraise its "sink-or-swim-with-Diem policy." The author's concern, in other words, was entirely pragmatic.[39]

Among the most popular Asian guidebooks for the English-speaking world in the 1960s were those published by Fodor's. The imprint's naturalized American founder and namesake, Eugene Fodor, was a veteran of the Office of Strategic Services, the predecessor of the Central Intelligence Agency, and he allowed CIA operatives to work as travel writers for the series so as to furnish them with civilian cover. When the relationship was revealed in 1977, Fodor was unapologetic: "They were all highly professional, high-quality," he said of the agents. "We never let politics be smuggled into the books." It is unknown whether any of the writers who covered Vietnam were intelligence operatives, but that the guidebooks were ideological products is unquestionable.[40]

The company annually published regional volumes that covered Vietnam until 1974, and they were unambiguous in their representation of the Vietnamese conflict: "Vietnam" meant the Republic of Vietnam, a "nation" in which "Communist guerrillas" had been skirmishing with the "legitimate government" of the state "since it was born."[41] Although the rule of Ngo Dinh Diem was admittedly "often heavy-handed," he was an "honest man" who had "succeeded in cleaning up the country, imprisoning the racketeers and

warlords, many of whom had their own private armies, and outlawing some
of the more militant religions which had been created for the sole purpose
of terrorizing the superstitious peasants." Moreover, "brothels were closed,
opium-smoking cut down, land reform achieved, and an attempt made, with
massive injections of American aid, to put the country on a sound economic
basis." While the Republic of Vietnam was not a "democracy" because "personal rights and liberties" were by no means guaranteed, the Vietnamese accepted this temporary arrangement, particularly in light of "the Communists' well-known ability to utilize freedom of speech and freedom of political
opposition to undermine a free but economically weak country." "The people
of Vietnam obviously prefer their present form of government to [Commu-
nist] dictatorship," the guidebook claimed for years during the 1960s, "but
they are waiting for the day when a real democratic system will be inaugurated."⁴² That day had still not arrived as the end of the decade approached,
although the nature of the conflict remained clear: It was a "war between the
Communists and the Free World" in which the "Communist enemy in the
countryside" was attempting to "overthrow the free Vietnamese government
in Saigon."⁴³ The critical scholarship of the decade, which viewed the war not
in conventional Cold War terms but as a Vietnamese struggle for reunifica-
tion and independence, appears to have had no effect on Fodor's representations of the war.

In what must register as one of the most bizarre series of travel publications for the country to appear during this tumultuous era, and one which
indeed saw the U.S. position as historically exceptional, from 1963 through
the early 1970s the Department of Defense published a series of pocket guides
for Vietnam that were intended to be at once tourist guidebooks and helpful
introductions to Vietnamese history, society, and culture. Created by a branch
of the military known as the Office of Armed Forces Information and Education (OAFIE), the guides were published at a time of growing concerns that
personnel arriving in Vietnam were insufficiently persuaded about the gravity of the political situation. In 1962 officials were readily acknowledging that
some G.I.s were "not sure why they are in Viet Nam or why it is in the U.S.
national interest for them" to be there.⁴⁴ A "timeless indoctrination or orientation" would therefore be necessary, one that framed the struggle in Vietnam as an instance of global Communist aggression and not, to be sure, as
indigenous resistance to the Diem regime.⁴⁵ Yet it was important, officials
recognized, that their propaganda efforts not be identified as such. "Troops
tend to shy away from 'indoctrination,' particularly if formal, mandatory instruction is involved. They prefer 'information' and are sensitive to any hint
that it may be colored by propaganda."⁴⁶ The pocket guides authored that

same year thus seemed ideal instruments in this "information" campaign. Their seemingly innocuous purpose—providing information on where and how to enjoy oneself while serving in Vietnam—masked their insidiousness. While they hardly represented American troops' first exposure to Cold War ideology, they certainly helped to reinforce it.

The military's tourism publications, in other words, provided a context for the American presence that divorced it from the taint of French colonialism, associating it instead with the promotion of freedom and a righteous defense against Communist expansionism. The pocket guides' appearance followed years of attempted indoctrination by military officials as well as Hollywood's explicit connection in the 1950s of the American anti-Communist gospel to the political situation in Southeast Asia. The guidebooks thus emerged out of a political and cultural milieu that sought to mediate America's growing confrontation with revolutionary nationalism in much of the Third World while bolstering Washington's efforts to promote an international system consistent with the tenets of liberal capitalism.

At this broader analytical level, the travel documents fused the state's need to instill ideological conformity with the troops' desire for information on places to visit while serving overseas. The pocket guides therefore assumed an important role in the military's larger effort to properly educate Americans sent to Indochina. They were, in essence, an early and implicit acknowledgment of the manner in which travel literature—and its provision of information on the pursuit of leisure—could be embraced by the state to further crucial political and ideological ends.

The Pentagon's Vietnam guides were part of a larger series of such publications, dating to at least as early as World War II, produced by the Office of Armed Forces Information and Education; among the twenty titles in existence by 1963 were guides to Korea, the Philippines, Germany, and Japan.[47] The guides, OAFIE explained, were "illustrated booklets about a country (or group of countries) where a sizeable number of our Service persons are stationed or will visit frequently." They were conveniently small, literally of a size—approximately five inches by four inches—that could easily be carried in one's pocket.[48] Nearly 10,000 copies of the first Vietnam edition were prepared for military personnel.[49] Like all OAFIE publications, the guides radically simplified often complex matters, focusing on presenting information at an "eighth grade level of understanding."[50] The textual structure of each volume was the same. It included sections on history and geography, "information about the people, their religions and customs," and their "system of government" and armed forces. In addition to practical assistance in understanding foreign weights, measures, and monetary systems, as well as "pointers on conduct, hints on shopping, the most historic and scenic places to visit, hotels and restaurants, and suggestions about recreation," the pocket guides crucially included explanations of "why our military personnel are in the area."[51]

Figure 10-2. The U.S. Defense Department's pocket guide for Vietnam shared many of the characteristics of the civilian travel literature—women on the cover, flowery language, assistance with cultural mediation—while reminding military personnel that they were "grassroots ambassadors" for the United States as it struggled against international Communism. Office of Armed Forces Information and Education, *A Pocket Guide to Viet-Nam,* DoD PG-21, DA Pam 20-198, NAVPERS 93135, AFP 190-4-3, NAVMC 2593 (Washington, D.C.: Government Printing Office, 1963).

Touting the endless possibilities for sightseeing, diving, hunting, and water skiing along Vietnam's miles of breathtaking beaches and in its lush, cool mountains, the guides identified their readers' Southeast Asian service as nonetheless a geopolitical imperative. As tourists, the service members could avail themselves of Vietnam's abundant leisure opportunities, but as military personnel they were necessarily Cold War actors: "grassroots propagandists" and cultural ambassadors in the American campaign to defeat the revolutionary insurgency. It was their duty to "strengthen South Viet-Nam's defense against the Communist guerrilla aggression directed by the North" by aiding the "free nation" ruled by Ngo Dinh Diem. Yet pleasure remained a selling point. "The dangers of ambush and raid will make sightseeing impossible in some places," the Pentagon authors wrote, "but, when security restrictions permit, be sure to see something of the lovely country you are visiting and get acquainted with the charming—and tough and courageous—people who call Viet-Nam home."[52]

WHETHER IT was the Republic of Vietnam's booklets and brochures, the guidebooks published by Eugene Fodor and other popular travel writers, or the pocket guides produced by the U.S. Department of Defense, the printed texts attached to Vietnamese tourism provided an important contribution to the propaganda employed to bolster Washington's Cold War mission. Within these publications' ideological universe Communism had emerged as the gravest of international perils, the Diem regime perhaps its greatest opponent, and the Vietnamese people America's most loyal friends. In the annals of Cold War propaganda such discourses are hardly unique. What is remarkable, however, is the venue of their dissemination. Tourism publications have traditionally been associated in the popular imagination with the quest for leisure, cultural authenticity, and adventure. But in fact, the Vietnam-related materials reveal, the tourist literature used by thousands of pleasure seekers has—at least in some instances—been deeply embedded in the geopolitics of international relations.

Whether this literature was ultimately effective as cultural propaganda cannot be determined with any certainty. It would appear—judging from its broad reach, the lack of critical responses to it, and the more recent embrace by tourists of various guidebook discourses—that the authors of these documents enjoyed some success. This is probably truer, however, of the early years of the American war than its latter stages. It is difficult to believe, for instance, that cynical and disillusioned U.S. military personnel in 1971 would have accepted without question their pocket guide's claim that the corrupt, repressive, and unpopular government of the Republic of Vietnam was "fighting for . . . one of man's fondest dreams—freedom."[53] Yet in the early 1960s, when "the war hadn't really become a war yet," as one American veteran recalled that "simpler time," the Cold War ideology of the tourism literature was likely met with a broad popular embrace.[54] Those years before the Tonkin Gulf incidents were, after all, a very different time.

Notes

1. Harvey S. Olson, *Olson's Orient Guide* (Philadelphia: J. B. Lippincott, 1962), 972–73.

2. Unlike the government in Saigon, officials in Hanoi did not seriously enter the tourism business until relatively late, establishing a tourism department only in 1974. Michael Lynch, ed., *All-Asia Guide*, 10th ed. (Rutland, Vt.: Charles E. Tuttle Co., 1978), 573.

3. Matthew B. Masur, "Hearts and Minds: Cultural Nation-Building in South Vietnam, 1954–1963" (diss., Ohio State University, 2004), 165.

4. "The Final Declaration on Indochina," *Foreign Relations of the United States, 1952–1954,* Volume XVI: The Geneva Conference (Washington, D.C.: Government Printing Office, 1981), 1541.

5. Gene Gregory, Nguyen Lau, and Phan Thi Ngoc Quoi, *A Glimpse of Vietnam* (1957), 99. The volume identifies neither a publisher nor place of publication.

6. *International Travel Statistics: 1962* (Geneva: International Union of Official Travel Organizations, 1964), 109. Whereas 1957 recorded only 13,250 international arrivals, by 1960 that figure had nearly doubled to 24,256. The number of visitors increased even further—to 37,783 in 1961—before stagnating and then falling below 30,000 with the war's gradual escalation. *International Travel Statistics: 1957* (Geneva: International Union of Official Travel Organizations; London: British Travel and Holidays Association, 1959), 93; *International Travel Statistics: 1960* (Geneva: International Union of Official Travel Organizations, 1962), 102–3; and *International Travel Statistics: 1961* (Geneva: International Union of Official Travel Organizations, 1963), 124. The figure remained there until 1967, when the number of arrivals increased to 34,312. It increased further to 61,215 in 1969, and then surpassed 72,000 in 1970. *International Travel Statistics: 1967*, ITS/CIR/69(1), vol. 21 (Geneva: International Union of Official Travel Organizations, 1969), unpaginated; *International Travel Statistics: 1969*, ITS/CIR/70(3), vol. 23 (Geneva: International Union of Official Travel Organizations, 1970), unpaginated; and *International Travel Statistics: 1970*, ITS/CIR/72(1), vol. 24 (Geneva: International Union of Official Travel Organizations, 1970), unpaginated. The statistics may be somewhat misleading, however, because only a fraction of these international arrivals—especially after the Kennedy administration increased its military commitment to the R.V.N.'s preservation in 1961—were persons traveling to Vietnam solely for purposes of sightseeing. By the mid-1960s, it seems, most were coming because of their involvement in the war.

7. For an important overview of the R.V.N.'s cultural propaganda offensive, including tourism, see Masur, "Hearts and Minds."

8. Santha Rama Rau, "The Strange Beauty of Vietnam," *Holiday* (August 1957), 62–63, 114–19; Richard Tregaskis, "Vietnam Visit," *Travel* (March 1959), 41–47.

9. This was true, as well, of materials generated by the royal Vietnamese administration during the First Indochina War. See, for example, *Vietnam as a Tourist Centre* (Saigon: National Office of Tourism, 1953).

10. An example of this discursive construction is a short guide to Nha Trang published by the National Tourist Office in the late 1950s. While most visitors would have recognized Nha Trang for its coastal appeal and holiday atmosphere, which was partially acknowledged in the guidebook's statement that "the beach is the most attractive sight to the tourist just arriving to Nha Trang," most of the text was not, in fact, devoted to this obvious feature. Instead, much of the editorial comment recounted early history and legends or contextualized historical sites. In describing Mieu Sinh Trung, an old pagoda in a suburb north of the city, the authors noted that the "pagoda was built under the reign of Gia-Long to commemorate the valiant feats of officials and soldiers who had shed their blood for the unity of Viet Nam." The authors then added that the pagoda "receives every year a government allocation." *Nha-Trang* (Saigon: National Tourist Office, n.d.), 7, 20. In other words, the government in Saigon, by ensuring the survival of a temple commemorating those who had "shed their blood for the unity of Viet Nam," was itself, unlike the authorities in Hanoi, the genuine force of Vietnamese nationalism for which patriots had historically fought. After all, the regime did, like its northern counterpart, purport to be the legitimate government of all of Vietnam.

11. For a fascinating exception to war driving away tourists—the case of Spain in the 1930s and, to a lesser extent, the 1940s—see Sandie Holguín, "'National Spain Invites You': Battlefield Tourism during the Spanish Civil War," *American Historical Review* 110:5 (December 2005): 1399–1426.

12. *Visit Fascinating Vietnam* (Saigon: National Tourist Office, n.d.), Folder 01, Box 01, Ronald Garrison Collection, Vietnam Archive, Texas Tech University [hereafter VA, TTU], 2, 14.

13. *Your Guide to Vietnam* (Saigon: National Tourist Office, n.d.), Folder 17713: Ho So v/v Soan Thao va An Hanh Cac Sach Nam 1959–1962 [File about Compiling, Printing, and Publishing Books, 1959–1962], Phu Tong Thong De Nhat Cong Hoa [Papers of the President's Office of the First Republic], Trung Tam Luu Tru Quoc Gia II [Archive Center No. II], Ho Chi Minh City, Vietnam, 2. I am grateful to Matt Masur for providing me with a copy of this document. The same language appeared earlier in *Vietnam: Communication, Tourism, and Transport* (Saigon: Thanh-Binh, 1959), 38.

14. For a reference to "Free Vietnam," see, for example, *Vietnam: Communication, Tourism, and Transport*, 132.

15. *Visit Fascinating Vietnam*, 1.

16. For an overview of American representations of the regroupees' plight, see Seth Jacobs, *America's Miracle Man in Vietnam: Ngo Dinh Diem, Religion, Race, and U.S. Intervention in Southeast Asia* (Durham, N.C.: Duke University Press, 2004), 127–71.

17. *Visit Fascinating Vietnam*, 2.

18. Ibid., 8–9.

19. *Life in Vietnam* 79 (September 24, 1966), Folder 03, Box 01, Garth H. Holmes Collection, VA, TTU, 44, 46.

20. *Your Guide to Vietnam*, 2, 9.

21. *Visit Fascinating Vietnam*, 2–3, 5. Emphasis in the original.

22. *Your Guide to Vietnam*, 2. The same phrase was used in *Vietnam: Communication, Tourism, and Transport*, 38.

23. *Visit Fascinating Vietnam*, 14.

24. Gregory et al., *A Glimpse of Vietnam*, 2.

25. Ibid., 20–23. The "gang of brigands" was a reference to the Cao Dai and Hoa Hao religious sects, and the "river pirates" were the Binh Xuyen syndicate.

26. Ibid., 35, 38–39; italics in the original.

27. *A Guide to Viet-Nam* (Washington, D.C.: Press and Information Office, Embassy of Viet Nam, n.d.). That the date of publication was either 1959 or 1960 follows from the fact that the document mentioned the National Assembly elections in 1959 in its "Viet Nam's History at a Glance" timeline, and the embassy referred to the guide as "recently published" in an August 1960 letter to American Friends of Vietnam. Ibid., 40; Nguyen Phu Duc to Louis Andreatta, August 1, 1960, Folder 39, Box 08, Douglas Pike Collection: Other Manuscripts—American Friends of Vietnam, VA, TTU.

28. Nevertheless, they reminded their audience, "'The Balcony of the Pacific,' as Viet-Nam is often called by Western visitors, is not only in a strategic position in Southeast Asia, it is also, and above all, an enchanting, hospitable land." *A Guide to Viet-Nam*, 1, 39. Virtually identical language appeared in other tourism publications; see *Visit Fascinating Vietnam*, 14, which added that "your trip to the Orient will be incomplete if you miss 'life-seeing' in Vietnam."

29. On the publicity in the *New York Mirror Magazine*, see "Free for All" by John Muth, July 22, 1962, Folder 06, Box 04, Douglas Pike Collection: Other Manuscripts—American Friends of Vietnam, VA, TTU. On the guide's distribution to teachers and schoolchildren, see Louis Andreatta to Milton Horowitz, March 28, 1962, Folder 18, Box 15, Douglas Pike Collection: Other Manuscripts—American Friends of Vietnam, VA, TTU. On the teaching kit, see "Newly Available," No Date, Folder 18, Box 15, Douglas Pike Collection: Other Manuscripts—American Friends of Vietnam, VA, TTU; Gilbert Jonas for Louis Andreatta, August 17, 1960, Folder 18, Box 15, Douglas Pike Collection: Other Manuscripts—American Friends of Vietnam, VA, TTU; and Louis Andreatta to Milton Horowitz, March 28, 1962. For more on the AFV, see Joseph G. Morgan, *The Vietnam Lobby: The American Friends of Vietnam, 1955–1975* (Chapel Hill: University of North Carolina Press, 1997).

30. Louis Andreatta to Barbara Meddock, July 26, 1962; Louis Andreatta to the Editor of *Social Education*, April 21, 1962; Louis Andreatta to Jeanne Singer, April 11, 1962; and Louis Andreatta to the Editor of *Orient-Occident*, June 20, 1962: all in Folder 18, Box 15, Douglas Pike Collection: Other Manuscripts—American Friends of Vietnam, VA, TTU; and Louis Andreatta to Milton Horowitz, March 28, 1962.

31. Louis Andreatta to Nathan M. Talbott, March 20, 1963; and "Teachers Packet—Proposed Free Distribution," No Date; both in Folder 18, Box 15, Douglas Pike Collection: Other Manuscripts—American Friends of Vietnam, VA, TTU.

32. Louis Andreatta to William Henderson, December 20, 1962, Folder 24, Box 01, Douglas Pike Collection: Other Manuscripts—American Friends of Vietnam, VA, TTU.

33. Indeed, the appeal of pictorial representations of Vietnam to young children was evident in guidebooks sent home to their families by American military personnel. See, for example, "Suz" to Michael Mittelmann, October 25, 1965; and Michael Mittelmann to "Everybody," July 18, 1965; both in Folder 37, Box 01, Michael Mittelmann Collection, VA, TTU.

34. Student to American Friends of Vietnam, March 2, 1962, Folder 08, Box 08, Douglas Pike Collection: Other Manuscripts—American Friends of Vietnam, VA, TTU.

35. Murray's Handbook quoted in Rudy Koshar, *German Travel Cultures* (Oxford: Berg, 2000), 1.

36. Lucian Swift Kirtland, *Finding the Worth While in the Orient* (New York: Robert M. McBride, 1926), 253. For more on early perceptions of Vietnam and the Vietnamese, including the role of the environment in shaping the Vietnamese people, see Mark Philip Bradley, *Imagining Vietnam and America: The Making of Postcolonial Vietnam, 1919–1950* (Chapel Hill: University of North Carolina Press, 2000), 45–72.

37. *Tourists' Guide to Saigon, Pnom-Penh, and Angkor*, 1st ed. (Saigon: Imprimerie Nouvelle Albert Portail, 1930), 7.

38. Wolfgang Saxon, "Robert S. Kane, 72, Writer of Travel Guide Series," *New York Times*, November 19, 1997.

39. Robert S. Kane, *Asia A to Z* (Garden City, N.Y.: Doubleday, 1963), 409–10, 414.

40. Frances Stonor Saunders, *The Cultural Cold War: The C.I.A. and the World of Arts and Letters* (New York: New Press, 1999), 35, 247; John M. Crewdson and Joseph B. Treaster, "C.I.A. Established Many Links to Journalists in U.S. and Abroad," *New York Times*, December 27, 1977. Saunders wrote that several CIA agents employed by Fodor's "floated about Europe," although the source she cited, the *Times* article listed above (actually, Saunders misidentified the *Times* report as published on December 25), did not contain such information. If there were other sources on which she relied, she did not identify them. I am grateful to Elaine Tyler May for bringing Saunders's work on Eugene Fodor to my attention.

41. Eugene Fodor and Robert C. Fisher, eds., *Fodor's Guide to Japan and East Asia 1962* (New York: David McKay, 1962), 25.

42. Robert C. Fisher, "Vietnam: New Nation, Old War," in ibid., 579–80, 583. Fisher's introductory essay was retained until 1966, although there were revisions made to it regularly. Even when it was replaced by a piece by Peter Arnett in 1967, much of his essay was incorporated into Arnett's text. See Peter G. Arnett, "Vietnam: In the Grip of Turmoil," in Eugene Fodor and Robert C. Fisher, eds., *Fodor's Guide to Japan and East Asia 1967* (New York: David McKay, 1967), 587–88.

43. Peter G. Arnett, "Vietnam: In the Grip of Turmoil," in Eugene Fodor and Robert C. Fisher, eds., *Fodor's Guide to Japan and East Asia 1968*, 585–86. (The location and identity of the publisher were not listed in this volume.)

44. B. P. Flint, Jr., for the Record; Subject: "Visit of Committee Men to Army Aviation Units [at] Nha Trang, Viet Nam," April 23, 1962; File: Report of Southeast Asia Subcommittee; Accession No. 64-A2021; Box 4; R.G. 330; National Archives II, College Park, Md. [hereafter N.A. II]. See also A. A. Jordan, Jr., for the Record; Subject: "Bendetsen Team Visits, Vietnam, 16–17 April," April 20, 1962; File: Report of Southeast Asia Subcommittee; Accession No. 64-A2021; Box 4; R.G. 330; N.A. II.

45. B. P. Flint, Jr., for the Record; Subject: "Visit of Bendetsen Committee to M.A.C.V. Headquarters, Saigon, Viet Nam," April 23, 1962; File: Report of Southeast Asia Subcommittee; Accession No. 64-A2021; Box 4; R.G. 330; N.A. II.

46. Office of the Secretary of Defense for the Record; Subject: "'OBSERVATIONS' During the Southeast Asia Trip," April 20, 1962; File: Report of Southeast Asia Subcommittee; Accession No. 64-A2021; Box 4; R.G. 330; N.A. II. This specific observation was made of military personnel in Hawaii.

47. The Office of Armed Forces Information and Education produced the Vietnam pocket guides, but some of the earlier pocket guides to other locations were created by different military units.

48. Although the guides were of a size appropriate for most service members, they were too large to fit in the pockets of naval uniforms. This led to a request by the Navy, which apparently was not granted, that their size be slightly reduced. See C. G. Furbish to the Chief of Information of the Office, Chief of Staff of the Army, et al., April 17, 1962; and Alexander F. Muzyk to the Director of OAFIE, April 27, 1962; both in Chief of Information; General Correspondence, 1960, 1962; File: 260/32 PAMPHLETS, APRIL, (62); Box 23; R.G. 319; N.A. II.

49. Office of Armed Forces Information and Education [hereafter OAFIE], *A Pocket Guide to Viet-Nam*, DoD PG-21, DA Pam 20-198, NAVPERS 93135, AFP 190-4-3, NAVMC 2593 (Washington, D.C.: Government Printing Office, 1963), 130.

50. In the context of the Cold War, this meant framing international affairs as a simple story of good versus evil or, in the vernacular of the era, of freedom versus totalitarianism. On OAFIE's objective to explain affairs at an "eighth grade level of understanding," see E. W. Maxson to Leland B. Kuhre, December 29, 1954; Decimal File, 1953–1954; Decimal File 461: 461 (GENERAL), 1 JAN 54—SECTION I; Office of Armed Forces Information and Education; Box 22; R.G. 330; N.A. II.

51. OAFIE, *Armed Forces Information Pamphlet: Information Materials*, No. 1 (October 16, 1953): 8.

52. OAFIE, *A Pocket Guide to Viet-Nam*, DoD PG-21, 1, 21, 23.

53. OAFIE, *A Pocket Guide to Vietnam*, DoD PG-21B, DA Pam 360-411, NAVPERS 93135B, AFP 216-4, NAVMC 2593B (Washington, D.C.: Government Printing Office, 1971), 4.

54. Interview of Martin Brady, June 25, 2003, Oral History Project, Martin Brady Collection, VA, TTU.

IV THE CULTURAL COLD WAR IN THE UNITED STATES AND ABROAD

11 Promoting Literature in the Most Dangerous Area in the World

The Cold War, the Boom, and *Mundo Nuevo*

RUSSELL COBB

IN 1967, the Paris-based literary magazine *Mundo Nuevo* and its Cuban rival, *Casa de las Américas*, both published homages to the towering figure of *modernismo*, the Nicaraguan poet Rubén Darío. In the century since Darío's birth, Latin American literature had come to maturity. Where Latin American writers once imitated European trends, they were now at the center of the international avant-garde and experiencing international commercial success for the first time. On this, Darío's centenary, the so-called Boom in Latin American fiction was at its peak: the Guatemalan writer Miguel Angel Asturias won the Nobel Prize for Literature, and Gabriel García Márquez's ground-breaking *Cien años de soledad* (*One Hundred Years of Solitude*) was released.

In the 1960s, *Casa de las Américas* and *Mundo Nuevo* were the two most recognizable journals of the new Latin American writing. *Casa de las Américas* was born shortly after the Cuban Revolution in 1959 and quickly became the standard bearer for the Revolution's creative and intellectual scene. But where *Casa* proudly associated itself with the Cuban Revolution, *Mundo Nuevo* tried to steer clear of politics—even though its funding came from nonprofit organizations such as the Congress for Cultural Freedom (CCF) that had been, by 1967, exposed as fronts for CIA money. Although they often published the same writers, the magazines were rivals, so it was no surprise that each had a very different interpretation of Darío's legacy.

In the *Mundo Nuevo* collection, readers learned of Darío's place in the modernist tradition, and that his work was comparable to that of European contemporaries such as Rilke or Mallarmé. The essayists emphasized Darío's

231

formal inventiveness and links to symbolism, paying scant attention to his social or political thought. In a conversation between Emir Rodríguez Monegal (the magazine's editor), the Spanish-Mexican writer Tomás Segovia, and Severo Sarduy the baroque, aestheticized Darío comes to the fore. In the words of Sarduy—himself a marginalized Cuban writer whose homoerotic writings had brought him unwanted attention from Cuban cultural authorities—Darío was a poet of "adornments": "Upon returning from Europe, Darío starts to favor a world of proliferating objects, especially Art Nouveau, the art of proliferation *par excellence*. This is why he starts to implement rococo and flamboyant forms . . . because they are arts in which ornamentation manifests itself as a predominant element. They are arts that favor adjectives, just like the poetry of Darío. In these forms, what is perceived as accessory—adornments—becomes the most essential element."[1] This campy, flamboyant version of Darío was of obvious use to Sarduy, who was developing his own highly wrought, neo-baroque style of prose in Paris. For Sarduy, Darío is a decadent country-less cosmopolitan, more at home in *fin-de-siècle* Paris than in his native Nicaragua.

The portrait of Darío that emerges from the *Casa de las Américas* essays, on the other hand, is that of a nationalist, anti-imperialist, political poet conscious of his unequal relationship to First World writers. In René Depestre's essay "Rubén Darío: Con el cisne y el fusil" (Rubén Darío: With the Swan and the Rifle), the poet is a prototype for the Cuban guerrilla, ready to confront American imperialism: "In military and political terms, one of the great merits of the Cuban Revolution is that it permits us to have a global vision of our destiny. The old colonial tower of Washington is no longer the only place that affords us a panoramic vision of our lives, where we can look toward the future. With different perspectives, we can all see ourselves from Cuba, as we look at Rubén Darío in this open tower looking toward the sea and poetry."[2]

Neither interpretation lacks textual evidence in Darío's work: the poet's views on poetry and politics had evolved in unpredictable ways over decades and it is difficult to attach one label to his constantly changing aesthetic vision. These different readings of Darío from 1967 exemplify the Cold War's larger rhetorical battle over the meaning of Latin American literary history and the general relation of literature and art to politics, society, and culture. In the case of *Casa de las Américas*, this meant rereading *modernista* poetry to make sure it fit "within the Revolution"; in the case of *Mundo Nuevo*, writers were freed from the shackles of political determinism and were placed within the autonomous world of international literary space. These two approaches, along with a third, advanced by the by-then defunct journal *Cuad-*

ernos, define the three main rhetorical positions occupied in Cold War–era arguments about culture. *Cuadernos*, underwritten in part by CIA money, embodied the early position sponsored by the Congress for Cultural Freedom: that avant-garde or experimental art was possible only in—and was thus proof of the superiority of—a society grounded on free enterprise and liberal individualism. *Casa*, on the other hand, adopted the typically Marxist/ Popular Front insistence that art must serve larger social aims; as a result, this approach tended to belittle formal experimentation as "bourgeois" and to privilege realism. *Mundo Nuevo*, freed from the doctrinaire anti-Communism typical of *Cuadernos* in particular and the early 1950s in general, sought a middle ground in which aesthetic formalism could be detached from the endorsement of liberal individualism. The evolution of *Cuadernos* into *Mundo Nuevo* highlights the changing and moderating stance taken by cultural warriors of the non-Communist left (the CCF in particular) as their gaze turned from the Soviet Union and its satellites to Latin America, and targeted a local population less willing to cast the world in Manichean terms.

Cultural production had been highly politicized in Cuba since the first days of the Revolution. Films, novels, and music perceived as counterrevolutionary were censored or marginalized. The filmmaker Sabá Cabrera Infante's short documentary about some of the insalubrious aspects of post-Revolutionary Havana nightlife, *P.M.*, was banned from theaters and television in 1961. Later that year Cabrera Infante's brother, Guillermo Cabrera Infante, was a victim of a crackdown on a widely read literary magazine, *Lunes de Revolución*, after a show trial that involved Fidel Castro himself. At the height of its popularity, *Lunes* boasted a readership of 200,000, making it one of the most influential— if short-lived—literary supplements in Latin American history. Although *Lunes de Revolución* was, by definition, pro-Revolution, it published marginalized writers like Allen Ginsberg, whom the government considered suspect. Even though they never officially adopted a doctrine of socialist realism, Cuban cultural authorities wanted to make sure that cultural production on the island was firmly committed to the Revolution and the Castro regime.

None of these early acts of repression did much damage to the Revolution's credibility in the eyes of the Latin American intelligentsia. *Cuadernos* had been an early critic of the Revolution, but it was largely dismissed as out of touch with young, up-and-coming writers such as Carlos Fuentes, Julio Cortázar, and Mario Vargas Llosa. *Mundo Nuevo*'s editor, Monegal, was one of the few prominent Latin American intellectuals never seduced by the Cuban experiment. Monegal was an enthusiastic promoter of Jorge Luis Borges in the pages of the Uruguayan cultural magazine *Marcha* before he inaugurated

Mundo Nuevo in 1966. For Monegal—as for Borges—writers were independent intellectuals whose artistic activities should be divorced from political commitments. The writer's first duty was to his or her craft, and political commitments only got in the way of true literature. If Cuba was, as Van Gosse points out in *Where the Boys Are: Cuba, Cold War America, and the Making of a New Left* (1993), a locus of activity for the nascent New Left, *Mundo Nuevo* tried to replace enthusiasm for revolutionary politics with an enthusiasm for revolutionary art. This proved difficult for Monegal and his magazine. Since the Popular Front years, Latin American writers had viewed revolutionary art as inseparable from revolutionary politics.

Nevertheless, the battle between *Casa de las Américas* and *Mundo Nuevo* proved to be immensely important in the broader context of the cultural Cold War. *Casa de las Américas* represented the best of Cuban cultural production. The Casa de las Américas was also a physical space—housed in a soaring, art deco theater in Havana—that sponsored literary congresses, workshops, and prizes. Casa's generous funding from the Castro regime allowed its directors to bring writers and artists to Cuba, often luring them away from self-imposed exile in Paris or London. Casa also helped forge solidarity between Cuba and the rest of the developing world at the same time the U.S. embargo was put into place. While Batista's Cuba had been a playground for American decadence but a repressive place for artistic expression, the Revolution had (at least initially) opened up the island to new ideas. Indeed, it is hard to overestimate the influence of the Cuban Revolution on the cultural politics of Latin America: Herbert Matthews, the *New York Times* reporter who followed Fidel Castro's trek through the Sierra Maestra and then into Havana, wrote that "January 1, 1959, when Fidel Castro triumphed, began a new era in Latin America."[3] For the generation of writers coming to maturity during the late 1950s, the Revolution was a catalyzing event. In the words of Deborah Cohn: "The Revolution was viewed by many as inspiration for achieving self-determination for Spanish America, and it enjoyed the support of many of the region's intellectuals, as well as numerous others internationally, during its first decade. . . . [S]upport of the Cuban Revolution provided ideological coherence to the Boom through the late 1960s, and the literary movement was itself viewed as indicative of the autonomy of the region's literature and the end of literary colonialism."[4] Not only did the Revolution give ideological coherence to the Boom, it also created an institutional framework of government-controlled book and magazine publishers, a prestigious literary prize (Premio Casa de las Américas), a writers' union (the Unión de Escritores y Artistas de Cuba), and a film institute (Instituto Cubano del Arte e Industria Cinematográficos).

Given the Revolution's powerful sway over the hearts and minds of Latin American writers, *Mundo Nuevo* had to tread a fine line between promoting avant-garde literature and implicitly denigrating the Cuban-style activist approach to literature and culture. Indeed, the magazine took an ambivalent stance toward the Cuban Revolution, despite its connections to the CIA and other anti-Communist organizations. It never fully denounced the Castro regime, yet the magazine published many writers (Guillermo Cabrera Infante and Severo Sarduy, among others) who had found themselves alienated by Castro's famous 1961 speech "Word to Intellectuals": "Within the Revolution, everything; outside the Revolution, nothing." *Mundo Nuevo* published at least one essay ("Notas sobre Cuba" by François Fejtöo) that described the repression of homosexuals in Cuba and discussed the deterioration of the island's economy. The magazine was definitely outside the Revolution and defined itself as such by its frequent endorsement of aesthetic formalism. Still, for the most part, *Mundo Nuevo* avoided direct ideological battle with the Cuban policies in order to not estrange its many pro-Castro readers outside Cuba. Furthermore, the magazine published many articles critical of the U.S. interventions in Vietnam and the Dominican Republic. Indeed, *Mundo Nuevo's* political ambivalence makes the magazine much more complex than its Cuban detractors would admit.

To read *Mundo Nuevo* merely as a propaganda vehicle for U.S. political interests (as many in Cuba did at the time) is to overlook the two important ways in which the magazine mediated the Cold War in Latin America. First, the magazine abandoned the rigid anti-Communist ideology that dominated much liberal cultural production in Latin America, and adopted a much more nuanced attitude toward Communism. Second, *Mundo Nuevo* promoted Latin American literature as avant-garde art that was part of the tradition of, and equal in sophistication to, the monuments of Western modernism. In this sense, Monegal was concerned less with winning the Cold War than with introducing Latin America onto the international literary stage and gaining international respect for its writers. Indeed, Monegal hoped *Mundo Nuevo* would help Latin American literature achieve complete autonomy from politics. The CIA and the Congress for Cultural Freedom, however, had their own agenda when it came to literary autonomy.

In *How New York Stole the Idea of Modern Art* (1982), Serge Guilbaut details how Abstract Expressionism, an avant-garde artistic movement that defined itself in purely formal and aesthetic terms, was used as an ideological counterweight to the Soviet Union during the Cold War. Guilbaut claims that in the late 1940s, as the exigencies of Cold War politics began to affect every aspect of European and American life, American policymakers wanted to neutralize the left-wing tendencies of artists by making Western "artistic free-dom" synonymous with Western liberal democracy and by "de-Marxifying" the intelligentsia, which had been sympathetic to Communism during the Popular Front years of the 1930s. Abstract Expressionism's apparent content-lessness and the lack of political activity among leading Abstract Expression-ists made this movement ideal for the purposes of the Cold Warriors, Guil-baut argues.

Indeed, rather than promoting established American elite culture as pro-paganda for Western-style liberal democracy, anti-Communist writers and critics insinuated through magazines like *Partisan Review* that avant-garde cultural innovation could occur only in Western democracies, the United States in particular. In the 1970s and 1980s, critics such as Guilbaut, Eva Cockroft, and Max Kozloff began to take for granted the ideological factors behind the ascendance of Abstract Expressionism. The literary critic Louis Menand, summing up much of the recent scholarship about the role of inter-national politics in shaping the reception of Abstract Expressionism, ad-dressed what he calls a "revisionist interpretation of art history" in the *New Yorker* in October 2005. Menand sums the argument up:

> The theory, as it was proposed in *Artforum* and other journals in the nineteen-seventies, and then elaborated in Serge Guilbaut's "How New York Stole the Idea of Modern Art" and Frances Stonor Saunders's "The Cultural Cold War," is that abstract painting was an ideal propaganda tool. It was avant-garde, the product of an advanced civilization. In contrast to Soviet painting, it was nei-ther representational nor didactic. It could be understood as pure painting—art absorbed by its own possibilities, experiments in color and form. . . . Either way, Abstract Expressionism stood for autonomy: the autonomy of art, freed from its obligation to represent the world, or the freedom of the individual—just the principles that the United States was defending in the worldwide struggle. . . . But the C.I.A. lurked in the shadows. It turned out a Pollock had a politics.[5]

Thus, reverence for "intellectual autonomy" and "artistic freedom" in the United States during the Cold War concealed a public policy designed to dis-credit the Left. Promoting this sort of rhetorical turn in the United States, where the ideology of liberal individualism was etched in the national psyche, proved to be a much easier task than it would be in Latin America, where skepticism toward U.S. policies was developed in real-world encounters with U.S. power in Cuba, Guatemala, and elsewhere during the Cold War, and where U.S.-style liberal individualism had never fully taken root.

A Brief History of the Congress for Cultural Freedom in Latin America

The Congress for Cultural Freedom was established in Europe at the beginning of the Cold War as part of an effort to promote intellectual and artistic freedom in the Soviet Union and Eastern Europe and to counter the cultural propaganda of the Communist Information Bureau and national Communist parties in the West. As the Cold War expanded beyond Europe, the Congress expanded as well. The CCF's Spanish-language magazine from 1953 to 1965 was *Cuadernos por la Libertad de la Cultura*, a monthly journal that achieved a wide readership among Spanish exiles in Latin America and other liberal types who found themselves equally at odds with leftist radicals and Perón-style populists or nationalists. CCF records housed at the University of Chicago demonstrate that readership for *Cuadernos* was higher (around 6,000 copies per issue) than it was for *Mundo Nuevo*, even though the latter generated more of a buzz among exiled Latin Americans in Europe. *Cuadernos*, like *Mundo Nuevo*, was based in Paris and appealed to a Spanish-speaking literary and political elite. Peter Coleman describes the *Cuadernos* milieu as "patriarchal" humanists with one foot in politics and one in literature.[6] Many were diplomat-poets like the Colombian Germán Arciniegas who were hardly revolutionaries, but still commanded respect in pre-Boom literary circles. There were others, like Waldo Frank, who had once held an immense amount of literary prestige in Latin America but found themselves out of touch with post-revolutionary Cuba. These writers' influence deteriorated as the Cold War progressed and the Cuban Revolution replaced anti-fascism in Spain as the *cause du jour*. *Cuadernos*' problem, in the eyes of the CCF leadership, was its increasing irrelevance in the face of the Cuban cultural front, which, as we have seen, established ambitious grants, magazines, and congresses for writers from the Americas.

Coleman claims that the CCF's "natural allies" in Mexico would have been contributors to the *Revista Mexicana de Literatura*, especially Octavio Paz and Carlos Fuentes, "but they disliked *Cuadernos* so much that they refused to publish an advertisement for it."[7] *Encounter*, the CCF's London-based flagship magazine, on the other hand, frequently advertised in *Cuadernos*, as did other CCF magazines. Although many Latin Americans were skeptical of *Cuadernos* from the beginning because of its open affiliation with the anti-Communist CCF, the magazine's editor managed to establish an honorary board of former ministers who had a great deal of prestige, including the Venezuelan novelist and ex-president Rómulo Gallegos and the Cuban philosopher and historian Jorge Mañach.

Still, the CCF struggled to find an audience among younger intellectuals in Latin America, especially those who drew inspiration from the Cuban Revolution. The solution to this impasse came from the two CIA agents who worked at the CCF in Paris—Michael Josselson and John Hunt—as well as a Spanish anarchist and CCF functionary named Luis Mercier Vega.[8] While Hunt—an Oklahoma-born novelist who had fallen in love with France during World War II and returned to live and write in Paris after graduating from Harvard—never achieved the same stature as the more famous Josselson, he proved to be more knowledgeable and interested in the Latin American situation during the 1960s. Hunt's correspondence with the CCF representative in Uruguay, Mercier Vega, demonstrates that the American understood the potential impact of contemporary Latin American literature on the intellectual life of the continent and beyond. Hunt was the mastermind for a number of different projects designed to create prestige for CCF-friendly magazines while also dampening enthusiasm for openly Communist writers like Pablo Neruda. In 1964, Hunt came up with the idea of giving a grant to Latin American writers to be managed by the Council for Literary Magazines. This would generate prestige for writers "preferably of the younger generation," he wrote to Mercier Vega.[9] Hunt's idea was that four or five magazines would judge the quality of the work: *Sur* (the distinguished Argentine journal that launched Borges's career) and *Cuadernos* would be able to join forces with a few other magazines and establish a new standard for Latin American literature. While the project appears to not have gone further than the planning stages, the scheme reveals Hunt's hands-on approach to literary production in Latin America. His interest in left-leaning writers who had sympathized with the Cuban Revolution also revealed him to be more flexible than Josselson, who was wary of "fellow travelers."

For his part, Josselson suggested *Mundo Nuevo* address "the question of German, French, British and American influence" in Latin American literature shortly before the magazine began publishing in 1966. Curiously, at the same time, *Casa de las Américas* was promoting the idea of solidarity between Latin America, Africa, and Asia as a cultural front in the Cold War. Josselson was even interested in topics for literary criticism in Latin America: "When it comes to 'the novel,' I just wonder whether the subject could not be narrowed down to either 'Alienation,' or to 'Social Revolt' or to 'Clash of Generations' in the Latin American Novel," he wrote to Mercier Vega.[10] While Josselson was less involved than Hunt in Latin American affairs, the CCF executive secretary also perceived that his organization's future in Latin America depended on its ability to publish literary works of a high quality. Josselson wrote to Julián Gorkin—the editor at *Cuadernos*—that the way to attract "the young people of Latin America" was to oppose the Castro government while recognizing the legitimacy of the Revolution's demands—a strategy he later called "Fidelismo sin Fidel." In a letter dated August 14, 1961, Josselson wrote to Gorkin to express his dissatisfaction with the CCF's current state of affairs in Latin America: "I think that *Cuadernos* should become more radical on subjects like agrarian reform and structural reform while still combating Castroism and Communism. It is absolutely necessary that we make an appeal to young economists in Latin America."[11] The CCF's post–Cuban Revolution interest in Latin America pumped new life into the magazine. In April 1961, *Cuadernos* went from a bi-monthly to a monthly publication schedule, even as it lost many readers because of its anti-Castro posture.

Gorkin and Josselson did not see eye to eye, however, when it came to the issue of the "young people of Latin America," especially the young, talented writer Carlos Fuentes. While Gorkin seemed content with the Congress's work in Mexico, Josselson complained that only "third-rate" writers in that country collaborated with *Cuadernos*, and he took an interest in Fuentes. As previously mentioned, Fuentes and Octavio Paz had little respect for the CCF; the fact that *Mundo Nuevo* was able to attract both to contribute illustrates its significant break with the organization's anti-Communist politics. Gorkin, for example, replied to Josselson that Fuentes was a "Castroite, one hundred percent," and, as such, had no interest publishing him. What Josselson understood—and Gorkin failed to understand—was the CCF would have to court intellectuals who sympathized with the Revolution if it was to have any chance of succeeding in Latin America

Rather than promoting up-and-coming fiction writers, Gorkin wanted to use the new space in *Cuadernos* to publish political writings from non-Communist left leaders like the Peruvian Raúl Haya de la Torre and the Venezuelan Rómulo Betancourt. These leaders were held up as models for the sort of democratic reform John F. Kennedy envisioned in the Alliance for Progress, according to Stephen Rabe in *The Most Dangerous Area of the World* (1999). Yet, even if these leaders were an improvement over pro–United States *caudillos*, they were still not the sort of figures that would attract the attention of writers like Fuentes, who, at the time, was still sympathetic to the idealism of the Cuban Revolution. Ironically, then, the CIA's Josselson and Hunt proved to be more interested in publishing new Latin American literature than *Cuadernos*'s editor, Gorkin. Indeed, Gorkin and others in the CCF were clearly frustrated by the lack of interest in *Cuadernos*, even after it began publishing on a monthly schedule. Observing the growing support for leftist radicalism in the early 1960s in Latin America, Gorkin sarcastically joked that the only way to make inroads among Latin American writers would be to "constantly denounce the U.S. and sing the praises of Sartre and Pablo Neruda."[12]

As the 1960s wore on, the CCF became convinced that *Cuadernos* had become too one-dimensional in its anti-Communism, and they began to look for a more unconventional literary editor to replace Gorkin. By 1965, Hunt, Josselson, and Mercier Vega decided to take drastic measures to save the CCF's mission in Latin America. They called a meeting in Lima during which the CCF's Latin American members voted to dissolve the Congress, create a pan-Latin American organization (Instituto Latinoamericano de Relaciones Internacionales, or ILARI), and plan a new magazine for a redesigned liberal, anti-Communist organization. To paraphrase a famous quote from the Vietnam War, it became necessary to destroy the CCF and *Cuadernos* in order to save them.

Mundo Nuevo and the Question of the Independent Intellectual

By 1964, the CCF's situation in Latin America had become catastrophic in the eyes of Hunt, Mercier Vega, and Josselson. The CCF had disbanded in Cuba under pressure from the government there, and readership for *Cuadernos* was falling in Argentina, one of its main markets. In Mexico, Spanish America's other main market, *Cuadernos* was simply ignored. Hunt and Mercier Vega decided to suspend publication of the magazine for a brief time while they looked for a more internationally oriented editor in touch with the latest innovations in Latin American writing. Hunt appears to be the first CCF authority to have considered Emir Rodríguez Monegal: he fit the necessary criteria of being trilingual (English, Spanish, and French), knowledgeable about the contemporary literary scene, and not a "tercerista" (the "third way" political position of the Uruguayan weekly *Marcha*) or a Marxist. Monegal was already a polemical figure in his native Uruguay by the time he agreed to edit *Mundo Nuevo* in 1965. During his tenure at *Marcha*, he developed a legendary feud with an up-and-coming Marxist literary critic named Angel Rama. The conflict was both personal and political; Rama argued for a socially con-scious view of literary production and endorsed a politically engaged, anti-imperialist paradigm of revolutionary pan-Latin Americanism affiliated with writers like David Viñas and Mario Benedetti. Monegal, on the other hand, was a self-proclaimed Anglophile, a major promoter of Borges, and an avid reader of *Sur*. On a trip to Latin America, Mercier Vega and Keith Botsford decided on Monegal as editor-to-be and made arrangements for him to move to Paris. Botsford had toured many of the CCF's national chapters in Latin America earlier in the decade and had overseen a disastrous visit by Robert Lowell to Brazil and Argentina, where the American poet reportedly mounted an equestrian statue in front of the Casa Rosada in Buenos Aires and declared himself "Caesar of Argentina."[13]

The amount of money the CCF spent trying to improve the situation in Latin America speaks for itself: in 1963, the CCF allocated $245,472 for Latin America; in 1964, the figure was $262,854, and by 1965 it was $369,318. (By contrast, the CCF spent a mere $30,000 on *Encounter,* the most highly visible CCF magazine.[14]) Under the agreement worked out in the Lima meeting, the CCF in Latin America would now operate under the auspices of ILARI (Instituto Latinoamericano de Relaciones Internacionales), which would be legally independent of the Congress, but remain a CCF organization for all practical—and financial—purposes. Its name embodied the reform-minded, developmentalist attitude the Congress hoped for; it sounded like a legitimate institute for social sciences and humanities free from ideological agendas. Mercier Vega told the inaugural meeting of ILARI that the organization's first order of business was "the establishment of a Spanish language monthly magazine of cultural and topical interest for circulation throughout Latin America."[15] He also informed the audience that "Emir Rodríguez Monegal, Uruguayan critic and editor of the new magazine, plans to model it on *Encounter* and to direct its appeal to the university audience, to the younger generation of Latin American intellectuals, and the educated layman."[16] The CCF had infused ILARI and *Mundo Nuevo* with money but hoped that, by following the model of *Encounter,* the magazine could develop financial independence. In terms of content, there were many similarities between *Encounter* and *Mundo Nuevo.* Both were lively and polemical and also published up-and-coming novelists and poets. But while *Encounter* was widely read in the English-speaking world, *Mundo Nuevo* never achieved the broad readership its benefactors hoped for. The highest circulation estimates are around 5,000–6,000 per month during its first two years (1966 and 1967). Circulation declined dramatically in 1968 and continued to drop until the magazine's closure in 1971, most likely due to the fallout from the exposés in the press of the CCF's CIA connection.

The idea that ILARI and *Mundo Nuevo* were independent of the CCF was, as Monegal told another CCF official, Pierre Emmanuel, in a letter dated July 2, 1967, a complete "fiction." Mercier Vega, a veteran of the Spanish Civil War, was not the only person in the CCF to realize the importance of making a connection with the youth of Latin America. Even Adlai Stevenson, the U.S. ambassador to the United Nations at the time, had observed that the CCF in Latin America had become stuck in a time capsule, still fighting for Republican Spain against Franco. Coleman writes that Stevenson met with Josselson and the composer Nicolas Nabokov in Geneva in 1961, shortly after the Bay of Pigs debacle. Coleman claims that "Stevenson's view was that the magazine *Cuadernos* relied too much on the 'great Hispanic humanists' (the Madariagas, the Romeros, and the Reyeses) and that younger writers had to be found to develop contemporary themes. It was at this meeting that Josselson suggested the non-Communist Left theme of *Fidelismo sin Fidel. Fidelismo* had brought a new sense of urgency to the Congress for Cultural Freedom."[17] Despite the increase in funds for Latin American operations in the CCF's budget, the Congress realized that, in order to achieve success in the region, it would have to keep a low profile. In 1964, rumors had begun to circulate globally that the CCF's money came from the CIA, which would link the organization directly to the U.S. government. The *New York Times* had reported that a congressional investigation on the tax-exempt status of nonprofits led by Texas Representative Wright Patman had revealed that eight prominent nonprofits were little more than "mail-drops" for CIA money. The names of these nonprofits, which came to be known as the "Patman Eight," were printed in CCF literature as supporters of the Congress's activities, including the 1962 pamphlet in Spanish that denounced all totalitarian regimes and Soviet intervention in Hungary in 1956. Furthermore, some of these nonprofits—including the J. M. Kaplan Fund, the Hoblitzelle Foundation, and the Gotham Fund—were directly involved in training and supporting liberal, democratic politicians in Latin America, most notably the ex-president of Costa Rica, José Figueres. Later, these rumors would be confirmed by a 1967 series of articles in the *New York Times* and *Ramparts* detailing the "triple pass" between the CIA, nonprofit organizations, and the Congress. Most damning of all was CIA agent Thomas Braden's *Saturday Evening Post* article, "Why I'm Glad the CIA Is Immoral," which claimed—falsely, as it turned out—that the CIA had an agent working as an editor of a CCF magazine.

Monegal, for his part, claimed in media outlets like *Agence France-Presse* and in the first issue of *Mundo Nuevo* that the sole benefactor of his magazine was the Ford Foundation, even though his private letters show that he knew this claim was false. Private letters from Monegal to Congress officials collected in the archive of the International Association for Cultural Freedom at the University of Chicago demonstrate that the Uruguayan editor propagated the myth of Ford Foundation underwriting in order to counter attacks in

Marcha and *Casa de las Américas* that his magazine was a CIA ploy. Despite the complex machinations behind the scenes, Monegal attempted to promote the idea of the "independent intellectual"—the writer who could see beyond politics—as a central motif in *Mundo Nuevo*. As he wrote in the first issue:

> The purpose of *Mundo Nuevo* is to insert Latin American culture in a context that is both international and current, allowing inaudible and dispersed voices from an entire continent to be heard. *Mundo Nuevo* will establish a dialogue that will transcend the well-known limits of nationalism, partisan politics, and cliques that are more or less literary. *Mundo Nuevo* will not submit to the rules of an archaic game that has tried to reduce all of Latin American culture to irreconcilable groups that have impeded the free flow of ideas and contrary points of view. *Mundo Nuevo* will establish its own rules of the game, based on respect for opposing points of view and the reasoned inspection of its own views. It will be based on concrete and factual research into Latin American reality. It will be based on an adherence to everything that is truly creative in Latin America.[18]

Many Latin American literary magazines were either overtly political or closely associated with a political circle. *Casa de las Américas, Sur,* and *Marcha* could never have claimed to be independent and open to contradictory positions. With Monegal's introductory editorial, however, *Mundo Nuevo* attempted to position itself outside Cold War divisions and as open to dialogue.

The idea of the "independent intellectual" not only alienated Cuban revolutionaries, it also provoked the ire of right-wing military governments in Latin America. Even though *Mundo Nuevo* was considered by most Marxists to be a propaganda tool for anti-Communist intellectuals, the magazine was often censored and was confiscated by Argentine and Brazilian customs agents during each country's military dictatorship. The cosmopolitan, avant-garde orientation of the magazine made it the target of right-wing nationalists as well as the radical left.

Overall, the first issue of *Mundo Nuevo* was received as an improvement over the anti-Communist screeds of Gorkin's *Cuadernos,* but there were still problems. *Casa de las América* and *Marcha* reproduced a *New York Times* article detailing the CCF–CIA links. Monegal succeeded in winning over some of the CCF's antagonists—including Fuentes and Neruda—while at *Mundo Nuevo* but found himself under attack by some of his former contributors, including García Márquez, who claimed he had been "cuckolded" by the CIA.

Carlos Fuentes and the Premature Death of the Cold War

The magazine's first article in the first issue, an interview with Fuentes, reflected this innovative, independent posture. In the interview, Fuentes says
that Latin American writers should abandon political and aesthetic ortho-
doxies and look for fresh material in the explosion of mass culture.[19] Writers
should embrace "camp" culture, rather than the tired tropes of regionalism
or folklore. The informal, back-and-forth banter of the interview allows Monegal to fashion himself into a worldly intellectual and an aesthete, an image
that he defended in his interactions with CCF officials. The format of the interview resembled that of other fashionable literary journals, especially the
Paris Review (which was, after all, based in the same city as *Mundo Nuevo*).
Fuentes drops the latest pop culture names and tries to position himself as
a cosmopolitan intellectual. Indeed, when Monegal asks Fuentes about his
latest "happening"—a photo shoot in his apartment—Fuentes responds,
"Look, I think that because of the upheavals throughout our history, there's a
sort of fear of what lies in the background of the country. There's an expressionist, violent, and baroque background that's also our connection to a
world that has become violent, expressionist, and baroque. The modern
manifestations of this are to be found in pop art and in camp, in Günter
Grass and Norman Mailer, in Andy Warhol and Susan Sontag, in Joan Baez
and Bob Dylan. This is the world that I really care about. This is the world
that counts."[20] There was nothing essentially anti-Communist about Warhol,
Sontag, and Dylan, of course, but Fuentes's embrace of popular culture is at
least an oblique endorsement of the vitality of art under capitalism. At a time
when Cuban intellectuals were calling for a boycott of contemporary U.S.
culture, however, Fuentes's emphasis on the latest and hippest happenings in
the United States could be interpreted as a shot across the bow of the Cuban
"committed" literature.

Shortly before Monegal started the magazine, Fuentes had begun experiencing a change of heart in his views of the Cuban Revolution and U.S. foreign policy. In 1964, Fuentes was a successful young writer with two critically
acclaimed novels under his belt: *La región más transparente* (1958) and *La
muerte de Artemio Cruz* (1962). He also enjoyed a positive reception in the
United States and had been invited by Richard N. Goodwin, the U.S. Assistant Secretary of State for Inter-American Affairs, to take part in a debate on
the Alliance for Progress program in 1962. Although the young Mexican was
initially denied a visa for entry into the United States, possibly because he
was a vocal opponent of U.S. foreign policy, Fuentes proved to be just the sort
of intellectual figure the CCF wanted to publish in *Mundo Nuevo*. He was a

cosmopolitan diplomat with impeccable intellectual credentials in the United States and Latin America who had demonstrated that he was capable of breaking with the Cubans over the issue of cultural freedom. A memo from the American writer and State Department employee Darwin Flakoll to Mercier Vega, titled "Conversations with Fuentes," dated October 25, 1965, shows that the CCF was intensely interested in Fuentes's evolving political attitudes. In the letter, Flakoll says that he has spent a good deal of time assessing Fuentes, who, unlike many other revolutionary writers, did not reject Monegal as editor for *Mundo Nuevo*. As previously mentioned, Fuentes and Paz were two of Mexico's most prominent intellectual figures and had been opposed to *Cuadernos* since its founding in the early 1950s. Flakoll states that Fuentes had just finished a novel and had changed his mind about Cuba. Fuentes was disillusioned: "[Fuentes's] political attitude could perhaps best be described as a mixture of Camus' outlined in *The Rebel* and Julien Benda's 'Le Trahison des Clercs.' He no longer believes in the efficacy of organized political action to bring about the New Jerusalem. Politics are a necessary means of organizing political affairs, but entanglement in political pursuits is an *espejismo*—a mirage. Every political orthodoxy must create its opposing heresy."[21] Clearly, Flakoll at the State Department and Hunt at the CIA were interested in Fuentes as a figure who could help the United States marginalize the radical left affiliated with the Cuban Revolution. In their memos and letters, Flakoll and Hunt seem genuinely interested in dialogue with Fuentes and in ending the U.S. government's draconian practice of shutting out all writers who had even the vaguest of associations with Communism.

Fuentes was a key figure in the intellectual life of *Mundo Nuevo*: in addition to being the subject of the Monegal interview in the first issue, he published sections of his appropriately named novel *Cambio de piel* (Change of Skin) in the magazine in 1967. Fuentes also proved to be one of *Mundo Nuevo*'s most forceful voices of opposition to Cuban cultural policies, which presumably pleased Hunt and Josselson. When a group of Cuban writers wrote a letter protesting Pablo Neruda's visit to the United States in 1966 for a PEN Club conference on Latin American literature, Fuentes defended Neruda and the PEN Club in the media. The Cubans' letter, "Carta abierta a Pablo Neruda," reproduced in *Marcha* on August 5, 1966, argued that Neruda should not visit the United States, since any visit would represent an implicit endorsement of U.S. foreign policy; Neruda, they claimed, was being manipulated by the CIA.[22] The letter exemplifies a Cold War rhetoric of "us" versus "them," and calls for Neruda join "nuestro lado" (our side) in the fight: "Some of us shared with you the bitter and beautiful years in Spain; others of us learned through you that poetry can serve good causes. We all admire your grand oeuvre, the pride of our America. We need to have you unequivocally at our side in this long battle that will only conclude with definitive liberation, with what our Che Guevara called 'la victoria siempre.'"[23] CIA agent and CCF member Hunt must have delighted in the turn of events surrounding Neruda's first visit to the United States. Only two years earlier, Hunt had helped publish a pamphlet by CCF activist René Tavernier called "Le cas Neruda" (1964), which made much of the Neruda's Communist sympathies, including his "Ode to Stalin." Hunt led a behind-the-scenes campaign against Neruda's presumed candidacy for the Nobel Prize for Literature in 1964.[24] Now, Neruda was being attacked by Cuban Marxists for dialoguing with U.S. writers, and the Cubans—not the Americans—were perceived as impinging on the poet's artistic freedom.

Fuentes attended the PEN Congress with Monegal and wrote an account of the event for *Life en español* (August 1, 1966), in which he argued that traditional Cold War animosities had been "buried" by the unprecedented dialogue between writers of diverse ideological backgrounds at the New York Congress. Monegal took a slightly less sanguine view of the conference in the fifth issue of *Mundo Nuevo*, recounting the events in a breezy, detached tone more characteristic of a *New Yorker* "Talk of the Town" piece than serious literary criticism. Monegal also cited Fuentes's *Life* article with approval. The editor quoted fragments of Fuentes's piece and highlighted their collective view that the writers at the conference had managed to supersede the political divisions of the past. The very title of Monegal's article—"El P.E.N. Club contra la guerra fría" ("PEN versus the Cold War")—exemplifies *Mundo Nuevo*'s turn from anti-Communism to liberal cosmopolitanism. The section that Monegal reproduced from Fuentes's *Life en español* article in *Mundo Nuevo* is worth quoting at length, because it exemplifies *Mundo Nuevo*'s neutralist, cosmopolitan attitude, which the CCF hoped would be able to neutralize the Cold War divisions. Fuentes writes: "Twenty years ago, a Latin American novelist associated with the left would have taken advantage of the PEN Club Congress in New York to stage an attack on the U.S. And an American novelist, even with—or, perhaps, because of—his liberal credentials, would not have missed the opportunity to deliver an antiCommunist screed." He continues, citing Monegal's intervention in the Congress with approval: "The Uruguayan critic Emir Rodríguez Monegal observed that we are giving the last goodbye to the late Senator McCarthy. I would go even further in suggesting that the XXXIV International Congress of the PEN Club will be remembered as the burial of the Cold War in literature."[25]

Fuentes may have been guilty of hubris; the idea that a group of writers could bury the Cold War was a little too much even for Monegal. Still, Fuentes had risked his reputation by siding against the Cubans on the issue of Neruda's appearance in New York. Now, Fuentes, a one-time contributor to *Casa de las Américas*, was siding with a group of writers known for their anti-Communist tendencies. Although he probably never suspected it, he was carrying out Hunt, Josselson, and Mercier Vega's post-*Cuadernos* mission of creating a viable voice for the non-Communist left in Latin America. *Mundo Nuevo*—like other CCF-sponsored publications—touted itself as celebrating the autonomy of the artist. The behind-the-scenes maneuvers at the CCF and the CIA demonstrate that autonomy and cultural freedom were rhetorical strategies deployed for political ends.

Amazingly, Fuentes—unlike Cabrera Infante, Monegal, and others—never burned bridges with official Cuban literary culture. Fuentes was one of the few authors who could publish in both *Mundo Nuevo* and *Casa de las Américas*. In fact, *Casa* published a fragment of the novel *Cambio de piel* one year after *Mundo Nuevo* had published a chapter. This was quite an accomplishment on Fuentes's part. One could argue that *Cambio de piel* is playful pastiche, but, unlike other Boom texts that evince postmodern characteristics, Fuentes's novel seems primarily concerned with impressing the reader with his vast array of cultural knowledge and his repertoire of Mexican slang. In one section, the narrator mentions *Lolita*, the Bay of Pigs, and the assassination of Trotsky in one sentence. "Your pal Whitman with the optimism of a democratic New World, We Shall Overcome and the wall come tumblin' down and the vampire Rimbaud with the divinity of the world" reads another run-on sentence.[26] *Casa de las Américas*, which denounced *Mundo Nuevo* as a subtle tool of the CIA in virtually every issue from 1966 to 1971, chose to reproduce even more of this novel—even after the Cuban magazine had been "scooped" by its archrival.

Conclusion: Rethinking Latin America in the Context of the Cultural Cold War

Latin America is often overlooked in scholarship that addresses the complex triangle between the CCF, the CIA, and Cold War–era writers. Since the CCF's headquarters were in Paris and its most well-known writers were European, the anti-Communist organization's activities in other parts of the world are often ignored. Nevertheless, the CCF invested an extraordinary amount of time and money in Latin America during the mid to late 1960s in an effort to make an impact in the "most dangerous area in the world."[27] The triangle is made even more complex by the fact that CCF's second attempt at a Latin American–oriented magazine, *Mundo Nuevo*, opposed some of the

United States' foreign policy agenda in its pages, while also working to counter the advances of the Cuban Revolution. Writing about a similar event in Cold War history, Deborah Cohn points out that U.S. philanthropic organizations like the Rockefeller Foundation funded Latin American cultural activities in the United States "even though the image of the region presented in the works, and the politics of the authors themselves, often deviated from (and, on occasion, rejected) official U.S. cold war ideology."[28] In effect, the United States had few options for opening a cultural front in the Cold War in Latin America that would resemble its efforts in Europe. As Jorge Castañeda points out in *Utopia Unarmed* (1994), rejection of U.S. policies became an article of faith among the Latin American left during the second half of the twentieth century. There were few—if any—sympathizers with the U.S. government among the cultural intelligentsia in Latin America. Among younger writers in Latin America—writers who would come to form the core of the Boom—initial support for the Cuban Revolution was universal. Given this context, U.S. cultural intervention in Latin America could not afford to take a Manichean view of the situation; to be successful in combating the influence of the Cuban Revolution, any initiative (through the CCF or other non-profits) would have to reconcile itself with the left in some fashion.

This paradoxical nature of U.S. cultural policy in Latin America during the Cold War has been a fount for conspiracy theories about the CIA's role in literary publishing, most of which posit a behind-the-scenes collusion between U.S. spies and Latin American editors like Monegal. It is perhaps, then, no wonder that the heated climate of the post–Cuban Revolution *Kulturkampf* made a fair, even-handed assessment of the political intervention of *Mundo Nuevo* impossible. Its promoters advertised the magazine as an "independent journal" publishing the newest and most innovative writing from Latin America, while its detractors saw it as a Trojan horse hiding an imperialist agenda. In reality, *Mundo Nuevo* moderated ideological anti-Communism enough to open a dialogue that would not have been possible with the earlier, harder-line *Cuadernos*; in this sense, the magazine was a success for the Congress and the promotion of Latin American literature more generally. Nevertheless, this dialogue did not happen organically: it was, as the magazine's detractors argued, part of a political weapon that dare not speak its name.

In the end, the rules of engagement in the cultural Cold War in Latin America were different from those in Europe or the United States. Heavy-handed Soviet repression of avant-garde artists made an easy target as writers and artists associated with the non-Communist left in Europe battled with Communists over cultural freedom in the Czech Republic, Hungary, and elsewhere. The Prague Spring of 1968 was a decidedly non-Communist revolt that gave hope to a generation of artists. In contrast, Latin America was beset by military dictatorships often propped up by the U.S. government, and many artists and writers promoted by magazines such as *Mundo Nuevo* dissented against their right-wing, U.S.-allied governments. The Alliance for Progress, which promised a democratic revolution for the region as well as an infusion of financial aid, quickly deteriorated into another Cold War strategy for containing Communism after Kennedy's death. The Cuban Revolution, with its promise of "a new era for Latin America," had given Latin American literature during the 1960s Boom a political force and urgency it had been lacking for centuries. For all of the Castro regime's repressive tactics (closing down literary journals, theaters, etc.), the Revolution remained a source of inspiration for many writers. It fell to *Mundo Nuevo*, then, to capture the energy of this newfound enthusiasm for revolution, and redirect it away from politics and toward the written word.

Notes

1. Severo Sarduy, Tomás Segovia, and Emir Rodríguez Monegal, "Nuestro Rubén Darío," *Mundo Nuevo* 7 (January, 1967): 34. (Author's translation.)

2. René Depestre, "Rubén Darío: Con el cisne y el fusil" *Casa de las Américas* 46 (May–June 1967): 75. (Author's translation.)

3. Herbert L. Matthews, *The Cuban Story* (New York: Braziller, 1961), 273–74.

4. Deborah Cohn, "Retracing *The Lost Steps*: The Cuban Revolution, the Cold War and Publishing Alejo Carpentier in the United States," *CR: The New Centennial Review* 3:1 (2001): 81.

5. Louis Menand, "Unpopular Front," *New Yorker* (October 17, 2005), 177. The idea that Abstract Expressionism was, in and of itself, "propaganda" is, perhaps, an overstatement of what occurred during the cultural Cold War. Non-representational painting—much like avant-garde poetry or prose—is devoid of any single determinate meaning and therefore incapable of being propaganda. The works themselves are open-ended; it is in their reception that meaning is created. Abstract Expressionism becomes charged with significance and symbolism only by the communities that display the paintings, review them in magazines, and teach them in universities. The same rule, I believe, applies to Modernist literature: it is the interpretive communities who read, disseminate, translate, reproduce, and teach these works that create their meaning. The works themselves have ambiguous and sometimes contradictory political orientations.

6. Peter Coleman, *The Liberal Conspiracy: The Congress for Cultural Freedom and the Struggle for the Mind of Postwar Europe* (New York: Free Press, 1989).

7. Ibid., 207.

8. See the International Association for Cultural Freedom Papers at the University of Chicago Library (hereafter IACF Papers).

9. Memo from John Hunt to Luis Mercier Vega, April 9, 1964, IACF Papers, Series II, Box 184.

10. Memo from Josselson to Mercier Vega, Undated, IACF Papers, Series II, Box 131, Folder 3.

11. Memo from Josselson to Gorkin, August 14, 1961, IACF Papers, Series II, Box 131.

12. Frances Stonor Saunders, *The Cultural Cold War: The CIA and the World of Arts and Letters* (New York: New Press, 1999), 347–48.

13. Ibid., 348.

14. Coleman, 275.

15. Memo from Organizational Conference of ILARI in Lima, November 29–December 3, 1965, IACF Papers, Series VI, Box 20.

16. Ibid.

17. Coleman, 193–94.

18. Emir Rodríguez Monegal, "Presentación," *Mundo Nuevo* 1 (July 1966): 4. (Author's translation.)

19. Carlos Fuentes, "La situación del escritor en América Latina," *Mundo Nuevo* 1 (July 1966): 4–21. (Author's translation.)

20. Ibid., 8. (Author's translation.)

21. Darwin Flakoll to Mercier Vega and Hunt, memo dated October 25, 1965, IACF Papers, Series II.

22. The letter was first published in *Granma*, the official newspaper of the Cuban Communist Party on July 31, 1966. It was signed by dozens of writers, including Alejo Carpentier, Nicolás Guillén, Juan Marinello Félix Pita Rodríguez, Roberto Fernández Retamar, Lisandro Otero, and Edmundo Desnoes.

23. Emir Rodríguez Monegal, "El P.E.N. Club contra la guerra fría," *Mundo Nuevo* 5 (November 1966): 88.

24. Stonor Saunders, 350–51.

25. Quoted in Monegal, "El P.E.N Club," 89–90.

26. Fuentes, "Cambio de piel," *Mundo Nuevo* 4 (October 1966): 15. (Author's translation.)

27. See Stephen Rabe, *The Most Dangerous Area in the World: John F. Kennedy Confronts Communist Revolution in Latin America* (Chapel Hill: University of North Carolina Press, 1999).

28. Deborah Cohn, "A Tale of Two Translation Programs: Politics, the Market, and Rockefeller Funding for Latin American Literature in the United States during the 1960s and 1970s," *Latin American Research Review,* 41:2 (June 2006): 143.

12   "Truth, Freedom, Perfection"

Alfred Barr's *What Is Modern Painting?*
as Cold War Rhetoric

PATRICIA HILLS

OF ALL THE writings on contemporary art in the early Cold War period, *What Is Modern Painting?*, a forty-eight-page booklet by Alfred H. Barr, Jr., serves as the best gauge for the intensification of the ideological discourse taking place in the art world at that time. Changes in the text and presentation of the text in four editions of the booklet—editions published in 1943, 1952, 1956, and 1966—demonstrate two simultaneous shifts in Barr's thinking: his ever-greater endorsement of abstraction as the style most reflective of free democracies, and his increasingly anti-Soviet stance. Barr's rhetoric evidences these changes, as over the course of the twenty-three years in question the booklet more frequently, and gratuitously, repeats the word "freedom" in its description of modern art and American values in confrontation with what Barr characterized as Soviet censorship and totalitarianism.

The stated purpose of *What Is Modern Painting?* was educational—to enrich the lives of high school students and those unfamiliar with art museums through an appreciation of modern art.[1] The booklet's low price, marketing, and distribution ensured its effectiveness as a paradigmatic cultural artifact. In her biography of Alfred Barr, Alice Goldfarb Marquis called *What Is Modern Painting?* "the most potent tract for modern art ever written. It was potent because it was written for a huge new audience, a mass no one previously had considered as possible converts to modern art. It was a tract because its format and tone were models of sectarian persuasion."[2] However, *What Is Modern Painting?* is not an "it"; it would be more appropriate to use the word "they." Barr's alterations to each edition make the booklets a diachronic guide not only to the most recent art, but also to the dialectic of shifting politics of those Cold War years.

251

This cultural impact resulted from not only the booklets' rhetoric, but the sheer numbers of copies produced. Through the 1984 edition, 214,000 copies of *What Is Modern Painting?* were printed and circulated, along with 1953 Spanish and Portuguese editions of 2,000 each.[3] The booklets reached intellectuals and artists, but they also reached students, teachers, tourists, and visitors to the museum. Thus, not only did Barr help to establish the Museum of Modern Art as the leading authority and arbiter of modern art history, he also, through these booklets, became an important participant on the cultural front in the general Cold War project to seek political, military, and industrial dominance over the Soviet Union.[4]

BY EARLY 1943 Alfred H. Barr, Jr., had achieved multiple reputations—as an innovative and controversial museum director who had vision, style, and showmanship; as a serious and lucid writer; and as a somewhat shy, bookish intellectual. Trained at Princeton and Harvard, he taught modern art for two years at Wellesley College and studied for a year in Europe. In 1929 Paul J. Sachs of the Fogg Museum at Harvard recommended him for the new directorship of the Museum of Modern Art. The founders—Abby Aldrich Rockefeller, Lillie P. Bliss, Mary Sullivan, and A. Conger Goodyear—summoned Barr to New York and promptly hired him.[5] Over the next fourteen years he mounted a remarkable number of exhibitions and established himself as a scholar of Pablo Picasso and Henri Matisse, as well as Cubism, Dada, Surrealism, and other European modern movements. However, his directorship, with its intense and chaotic in-house exhibition and traveling exhibition schedule, elicited concern from some of MoMA's board members, exasperated by his inability to finish the writing projects he had promised to complete.[6] The staff was reorganized in early 1943, and the more practical James Thrall Soby took the helm as assistant director in order to relieve Barr of some of the busywork connected to the directorship.[7] Since no one disputed Barr's abilities as a scholar of modern art, the board's president, Stephen C. Clark, urged Barr to focus on his writing.

In April 1943 Barr wrote to Clark reporting on his progress on three writing projects: a new edition of *Cubism and Abstract Art*, which had been out of print for several years, a history of modern art, which had gone slowly because of his directorial duties, and a booklet on modern painting, which would become *What Is Modern Painting?* Barr explained that he needed to postpone the larger history in order to complete the revision of *Cubism and Abstract Art* and to write the booklet; nevertheless, he took the occasion to outline his thoughts about the larger art-history book, which would require focused time to complete. Barr complained about the pressure of work and the unsatisfying haste to produce catalogs with exhibition deadlines. For the history, he felt he had not yet had adequate time to read the requisite monographs on a number of artists: "Naturally time will prevent any thorough reading of these men, but without some acquaintance with their ideas my history of modern art would, I am afraid, be more superficial than either you or I would want." Research, he explained, was difficult because of the lack of reliable records. The rest of this remarkable letter, as we shall see, spells out his philosophy and his strategy for introducing the public to modern art.[8]

In the next few months he abandoned this larger history, and devoted his time and energies to writing *What Is Modern Painting?*, a text he had been urged to complete by Victor D'Amico, MoMA's Director of the People's Art Center (the education department) and Monroe Wheeler, MoMA's Director of Exhibitions and Publications.[9] As originally envisioned, the booklet would be aimed at high-school students. Since much of what Barr told Clark in that April letter became the guiding principles for his booklet, Barr's remarks deserve to be quoted at length:

> I intend to keep my eyes—and the readers' eyes—on what is *visible in the works of art themselves*, giving second place to biography and theory. I shall try to keep a far closer relationship between text and illustration than is usual in art books.
>
> For illustrations I shall choose works first from the Museum's collection, then from other museums throughout the country, then from American private collections and lastly from artists, dealers and foreign museums. In this way I hope to make publicly owned works better known and thereby induce people to visit museums—particularly ours.
>
> My book will deal with modern art from an American rather than an impersonal, objectively international point of view. . . .
>
> People used to think of modern art as something apart from life or at best a reflection of life. I want to show in my book how art is a *visual* demonstration, a revelation of modern life. But by life I do not mean merely the world of ordinary experience—people, families, landscapes, streets, food, clothes, or the collective life of work, politics and war, but also the life of the mind and the heart—of poetry and wit, science and religion, the passion for change or for stability, for freedom or perfection. This has been a period of preparation. I have been reading and thinking and taking soundings.[10]

In his letter to Clark, Barr also said that he considered his audience for the larger history of modern art to be the general public, but he also hoped to endow it "with enough clarity, detail and balance so that it can be used by the student and teacher"; he wanted to avoid "the form and atmosphere of a text book."

The results of this "reading and thinking and taking soundings" were incorporated into the first edition of *What Is Modern Painting?* In the preface Barr explained:

> This booklet is written for people who have had little experience in looking at paintings, particularly those modern paintings which are sometimes considered puzzling, difficult, incompetent or crazy. It is intended to undermine prejudice, disturb indifference and awaken interest so that some greater understanding and love of the more adventurous paintings of our day may follow. [1943, p. 2]

Unlike other writers on art, Barr framed his topics with a series of questions to probe the thoughts of his reader. In the introduction he asked:

> *What Is Modern Painting?* Stop reading a few minutes, turn the pages of this booklet and look at the pictures. . . .
>
> What is your first impression? Bewildering variety? Yes, that is true. The variety of modern art reflects the complexity of modern life; though this may give us mental and emotional indigestion, it does offer each of us a wide range to choose from.
>
> But it is important not to choose too quickly. The art which makes a quick appeal or is easy to understand right away may wear thin like a catchy tune which you hear twice, whistle ten times and then can't stand any more.
>
> It is just as important not to fool yourself. Don't pretend to like what you dislike or can't understand. Be honest with yourself. We don't all have to like the same things. . . . [1943, p. 3]

Barr patiently reviewed for the reader a diversity of paintings from Impressionism to the present (1943) in sections such as "Contrasts," which paired landscapes, war pictures, and portraits; "Realism"; "Impressionism"; "Expressionism"; "The Constructors," which included Cezanne and Cubism; "Mystery and Magic"; "Allegory and Prophecy"; and the conclusion, "Truth, Freedom, Perfection." Barr's plain language, informal diction (he used contractions), short paragraphs, clearly constructed categories with excellent visual examples, and shrewd anticipation of high school students' likely responses were all attempts to reach out to young people at their own level and empower them to trust their own spontaneous reactions.

During the summer of 1943 Barr's manuscript was sent out to boards of education and high-school art teachers nationwide, along with a questionnaire that asked them to jot down their reactions and answers to specific questions—for example, whether they felt the booklet was "written so that high school students, as you know them, would enjoy and understand it." Other questions asked whether there should be a guide to pronunciation, a bibliography, biographies of the artists, a glossary of art definitions, and so on. The teachers were assured that a portfolio of color reproductions, a list of which accompanied the back matter of the first edition, would also be available from MoMA for classroom use.[11]

Barr took seriously all of the suggestions as he rapidly polished the text and sent it on to Soby and D'Amico for their review and suggestions. Soby replied with enthusiasm in a letter of August 24, 1943, praising Barr for "an excellent job which should do a great deal of good," and making minor suggestions, half of which Barr eventually incorporated into his text.[12] Soby questioned, however, the concluding section, "Truth, Freedom, Perfection," which he found "rather lofty by comparison with the earlier sections," adding that "students will have some difficulty in following the ideas which are pretty abstract and cut off from the question of the students getting some personal pleasure out of pictures." Soby especially objected to the references to General Sherman's quotation "War is hell" and to Hitler, which seemed to him "too contemporary in the fleeting sense of the word." For his part, D'Amico wrote that Barr had "done wonders in including all the suggestions made by all of us," but he had some small criticisms. He, too, was mainly concerned about the conclusion—that "the very timliness [sic] of the conclusion might result in 'dating' the book.[13] Barr, however, stuck to his belief that such comments about the contemporary scene were necessary.[14]

In fact, the concluding two-page section, "Truth, Freedom, Perfection"— the most politically charged and topically specific section of the booklet— received the most revision over time. In this first, 1943 edition, Barr elaborated on the concept of truth, which meant conveying the reality of a situation for what it was and including metaphor if necessary: that "War is hell!" as General Sherman said, and that it was not Picasso who "did" Guernica, as Picasso pointed out to a Nazi agent during the Paris occupation, but the Nazis who "did" Guernica through their bombing. Barr explains:

> The truth which plumbs deeply, brings joy to the heart or makes the blood run chill is not always factual; indeed it is rarely to be found in newsreels, statistics or communiqués. The soothsayer, that is, the truth-sayer, the oracle, the prophet, the poet, the artist, often speak in language which is not matter of fact or scientific. They prefer the allegory, the riddle, the parable, the metaphor, the myth, the dream, for, to use Picasso's words, "Art is a lie that makes us realize the truth." [1943, p. 38]

Following this statement Barr segues into the concept of "freedom": "In order to tell this truth the artist must live and work in freedom," and he quotes a speech of President Roosevelt, delivered at MoMA in 1939: "The arts cannot thrive except where men are free to be themselves and to be in charge of the discipline of their own energies and ardors. . . . What we call liberty in politics results in freedom in the arts. . . . Crush individuality in the arts and you crush art as well" (1943, p. 38).

This leads Barr to a denunciation of censorship and other attacks against artists' freedom by the Nazis: "the artist, perhaps more than any other member of society, stood for individual freedom—freedom to think and paint without the permission of Goebbels, to tell the truth as he felt from inner necessity that he must tell it. Along with liberty in politics and religion, Hitler crushed freedom in art" (1943, p. 38). The freedom of the artist as expressed in his art was important to non-artists because it "is a symbol, an embodiment of the freedom which we all want but which we can never really find in everyday life with its schedules, regulations and compromises"(1943, p. 39). In other words, through the artist—and by looking at the artist's work—we can vicariously experience that freedom, which by its nature opposes totalitarianism.

Barr finished his essay with "perfection," in a manner that remained somewhat vague, even after Soby's criticism. Basically, to Barr, perfection was achieved when "the artist's own conscience" was satisfied, but Barr added the caveat: "lastly, artistic perfection, unlike the perfection of the craftsman, the technician or the mathematician, can be, but should not be, 'too' perfect" (1943, p. 39). He concludes with a long quotation from Picasso that ends, somewhat anti-climactically for the reader: "People who try to explain pictures are usually barking up the wrong tree" (1943, p. 39). The point Barr seems to be making is that the experts cannot really "explain" pictures. Pictures are open for interpretation by everyone, including high-school students. In this concluding section, Barr posits modern art as fundamentally an expression of freedom—the freedom of the artist to express *and* the freedom of the viewer to interpret. This freedom, he implied, was incompatible with fascism and totalitarianism.

Once the booklet was published, Barr had his secretary type form thank-you notes to all the people who had helped him, stating "although I am technically the author of the booklet it is in a sense a collaborative enterprise, to which many friends of the Museum have given counsel as readers."[15] But he did not budge from his convictions, which were to denounce the Nazis and to uphold ideals as to what a free art can and should be.[16] In his letter to Mabel Birckhead, the chairman of the art department at Rye (N.Y.) High School, Barr added a postscript in his own hand: "I know you disapprove of the references to Hitler, etc.—but I still feel they are highly relevant." And to Bartlett Hays, Director of the Addison Gallery of American Art at Phillips Andover

Academy in Massachusetts, he added the note: "I fear the last section will meet with your disapproval!"[17] However, one of his readers got the point when he wrote to Barr after having received the booklet: "This is an important book . . . above all we find a vital democratic force, clearly we see the fundamental philosophic differences between artistic, mental and moral freedom and fascist starvation."[18]

That was the point: Barr had spent time in Germany in early 1933, just when the Nazis were coming to power. In April 1933 he witnessed a public meeting at one of the Stuttgart civic theaters and heard the head of the Württemberg Kampfbund read from a pamphlet on the cultural program of the new Reich ("Kulturprogramm im neuen Reich"), which asserted that academic freedom "*must be a German academic freedom!* It must never again be misused to open the door to insidious foreign influences."[19] As a member of the audience Barr received a copy of the pamphlet when entering the theater and was appalled by its fascist rhetoric and its prescriptions for the control of artists and architects. While in Germany, Barr also read newspaper reviews on artists whom he respected, such as Oskar Schlemmer. One reviewer for the pro-Nazi *National-Sozialistisches Kurier* referred to Schlemmer's work in an exhibition as "fragments of the most pre-primitive kind" and "half-baked rubbish." The reviewer, moreover, assumed that pictures radical in form and style were politically radical. As a result of the reviewer's attacks, printed only one week after the March 1933 election that brought Hitler to office, the museum administration closed the Schlemmer exhibition.[20] No wonder Barr was adamant about keeping references to "Nazi sadism" and "the brutal, half crazy tyranny of a Hitler" in his tract. Indeed, we might think of *What Is Modern Painting?* as a response to the Nazi pamphlet.[21]

The 17,500 copies of the 1943 edition of *What Is Modern Painting?* quickly sold out, and 10,000 more copies were printed in 1945. In 1943 the booklet cost 75 cents for single copies, with 24 cents apiece for bulk orders from educational institutions, but the prices were raised with the 1945 reprint. The booklets were sold to individuals at MoMA's bookstore (with a discount to museum members) and distributed to schools, college bookstores, and other museums' bookstores.[22]

Barr's responsibilities did not end with the initial publication, and he dutifully made minor corrections for the 1945 version. He must have felt vindicated for his political assertions when the May 1944 *Magazine of Art* ran a review that praised *What Is Modern Painting?* for its ability to make difficult modern art understandable. The reviewer reminded the reader "that this battle of modern art is only a skirmish in the world struggle for freedom."[23] Later that year Barr wrote to J. Carson Webster of the *College Art Journal* to suggest that Horst W. Janson, then teaching art history at Washington University, be asked to review *What Is Modern Painting?* Janson, a friend, had already informed Barr that he was using the booklet in his college classes with great success.[24]

In June 1946 Monroe Wheeler wrote to Barr that the distributor, Simon & Schuster, had ordered 5,000 copies of *What Is Modern Painting?*, and "To prevent this book from going out of print we are ordering a new edition at once." He asked Barr to make changes to some of the topical time-bound references, but assured him that the reprinting was immediately going forward.[25] Barr made corrections (as he had for the 1945 printing) but also insisted upon changes in the layout, guided by Janson's review in the *College Art Journal.* Janson had questioned the wisdom of showing Picasso's *Guernica* in the same size as Peter Blume's *The Eternal City*, a less important painting in his opinion.[26] Of the other minor changes made by Barr, only one stands out as notable. Barr had said in the conclusion of the 1943 version: "How has [the artist] been getting along? The W.P.A.? Or has he found alert, courageous and generous admirers, and buyers, of his art outside temporary government agencies?" (1943, p. 39). The 1946 version more explicitly made a tacit endorsement of private patronage: "How has [the artist] been getting along? There is no W.P.A. to help him now. Has he found alert, courageous and generous admirers, and buyers, among private purchasers, corporations, museums?" (1946, pp. 43–44).[27] With the World War II veterans who were artists returning home in 1945 and in the absence of federal programs to employ them, genuine concerns had been raised as to how these artists could earn a living.[28] This sentence also expresses a greater willingness to trust, or at least accept the dominance of, the market system's responsibility to support artists as opposed to the government's. Barr no doubt anticipated a boom in art purchases once the war was over.[29]

BETWEEN 1946 and 1952 the cultural climate changed considerably as the Cold War heated up. Barr, the trustees, and the directors of the various departments at MoMA were not unaffected; in fact, many were involved in the government's effort to spread the word abroad about the democratic freedoms enjoyed in the United States and to propagandize against the totalitarian nature of the USSR.[30] To this end, the government encouraged cultural exchanges.[31] MoMA already had a program for traveling exhibitions, and in 1947 the trustees appointed Porter McCray to run it. In 1950 he temporarily left MoMA for a one-year appointment with the Foreign Service to design and promote exhibitions to those countries receiving Marshall Plan funds from the United States.[32] With the urging of Nelson Rockefeller, in 1953 the trustees of the Museum of Modern Art set up the International Council, to be directed by McCray, "to help increase understanding and mutual respect among nations by fostering, in the field of modern art, cultural interchange between the United States and other countries."[33]

To MoMA, cultural exchanges also meant getting its books to foreign countries. In March 1952 Monroe Wheeler wrote a memorandum to senior MoMA staff summarizing the difficulties with overseas distribution. Because of severe restrictions on dollar exchanges, the governments of England, Australia, New Zealand, and South Africa would not allow the importation of books from the United States without special government permits that were difficult to obtain. The same situation obtained in France, but Wheeler explained that UNESCO might intercede to allow a special permit for Galignani's, the premier art bookstore in Paris, so that MoMA could sell its full range of books. As to the Netherlands, Germany, and Austria, government permits could be obtained for special book orders for specific customers; however, most customers, Wheeler noted, could not afford art books. With Belgium, Italy, Switzerland, Norway, Sweden, and Denmark the regulations had been eased so that bookstores could order books for both stock and for special customers' orders. Latin America also saw severe restrictions, with Argentina unable to import any books; however, there were no restrictions in Colombia, Mexico, Uruguay, and Venezuela.[34] Thus, in 1953 the museum translated *What Is Modern Painting?* into those foreign languages where export might be easier, including Spanish, Portuguese, and Japanese.[35] Eventually the import restrictions eased in all the countries.[36]

In 1952 Barr made substantial revisions for a new edition of *What Is Modern Painting?*, a task he welcomed because he did not want merely to make hasty changes for a reprint.[37] In the intervening years, like many other cultural figures, Barr had developed concerns about the Cold War at home—especially the crude anti-Communism sweeping the country. On June 7, 1949, he wrote to the editor of *Art Digest* complimenting him for his June 1, 1949 editorial "A Plea for Tolerance."[38] In August 1949 Representative George A. Dondero (Republican, Michigan), head of the House Committee on Un-American Activities, went on a tirade in Congress naming those he felt were Communists or friendly to Communists and attacking the Museum of Modern Art. Dondero stated that all the "isms" are Communist-inspired and, therefore, were intended to destroy America's "cultural tradition and priceless heritage."[39] Barr felt such statements misrepresented the concept of abstract art. To him, because it does not follow traditional and academic rules, abstract art represented "freedom." He made this view explicit in his famous article "Is Modern Art Communistic?" published December 14, 1952, in the

New York Times Magazine, where he championed "creative freedom" against the totalitarian censorship of the Nazis and the Soviet Union.[40]

CHRISTOPHER LASCH was the first of the revisionist historians to study seriously the rhetoric of "freedom" in the context of the Cold War era. In his long 1967 essay "The Cultural Cold War: A Short History of the Congress for Cultural Freedom," Lasch traced the history of the Congress for Cultural Freedom from its inception in 1950, when it was organized by a former officer of the Office of Strategic Services and an employee of the American Information Services, through its brief existence as a quasi-government organization that enlisted the major American anti-Communist intellectuals of the early 1950s, such as Sidney Hook, Arthur Schlesinger, Jr., and Melvin Lasky.[41] Serge Guilbaut pursued this line of inquiry in his book *How New York Stole the Idea of Modern Art: Abstract Expressionism, Freedom, and the Cold War* (1983), which examined the rhetorical use of such key words as "freedom," "individualism," and "alienation" by artists of the period. Guilbaut advanced the thesis that "the ideology of the avant-garde was ironically made to coincide with what was becoming the dominant ideology, that embodied in Arthur Schlesinger, Jr.'s book *The Vital Center* (1949), which was the ideology of anti-Communist liberalism" (p. 3). Guilbaut carefully uses the phrase "made to coincide," to avoid giving the impression that the artists were directly culpable.[42] However, he did not go far enough in his analysis of Schlesinger. In *The Vital Center* Schlesinger marshals Jean-Paul Sartre and Erich Fromm to argue that most men want to "flee freedom." For Schlesinger the totalitarian state in the twentieth century "has risen in specific response to this fear of freedom." Although Schlesinger referred to both fascism and Communism, the Soviet Union was, of course, the postwar target of his offensive.[43]

A textual analysis of the differences between the first 1943 version of *What Is Modern Painting?* and the 1952 revision reveals that Barr was promoting the avant-garde abstract painters as exemplars of artists manifesting democratic goals, a thesis that paralleled Schlesinger's. Of course, the 1952 revision aimed to bring the booklet up to date by commenting on recent developments, and it also gave Barr the opportunity to showcase the art the museum had acquired between 1943 and 1952. In that process he also took the anti-fascist argument of the 1943 edition of the booklet and "updated" the enemy: it was still totalitarianism, but now Communist totalitarianism. Barr was buttressed in this effort by art critics such as Harold Rosenberg, Clement Greenberg, and Meyer Schapiro, who also defined modern art as the product of free individuals in a free society.[44]

Barr used "freedom" in his original 1943 version to mean the ability to choose between styles and to exercise one's individuality. For example, when contrasting Orozco's *Dive Bomber* with Richard Eurich's traditionally realist painting *Withdrawal from Dunkirk*, Barr had stated:

> 1943: As you can see, Orozco makes full use of the modern artist's freedom: he combines real and unreal objects. . . . Eurich's technique was developed five hundred years ago. Orozco's belongs to the twentieth century. Which means more to you? This is a free country and you can take your choice or, perhaps, find much to like in both. [P. 7]

In the 1952 version (p. 9), he varies the final sentence, but still makes the point that both styles "have value."[45]

Barr argues, however, that freedom in art is expressed manifestly when the artist moves away from realism. In discussing Whistler's famous lawsuit with John Ruskin, Barr says in both the 1943 (p. 8) and 1952 (p. 10) versions: "It was really the freedom of the artist which had been on trial." And in both versions he later declares: "The impressionists won a very important victory by freeing themselves and, later, the public from the idea that a picture had to be a literal imitation of natural detail and color" (1943, p. 17, and 1952, p. 19).

Unlike Clement Greenberg, Barr did not overtly advance the theoretical belief that art undergoes a teleological progression from mimetic realism to abstraction.[46] But there is a telling difference between Barr in 1943 and Barr in 1952. Whereas for the 1943 version Barr had stated that impressionist perception was based on discoveries in science, by 1952 he minimizes the scientific context as a shaper of art history. Compare these two passages:

> 1943: The impressionists had studied scientific books from which they learned that there were no blacks in nature, since all light was composed of the six colors of the spectrum; and furthermore that a yellow light creates a complementary bluish shadow. The impressionists used these facts to defend their art, but in any case people eventually got used to the blue shadows which once had seemed so daring. [Pp. 16–17]

> 1952: The impressionists, taking hints from older painters such as Delacroix and using their own eyes with sensitive honesty, observed that there were no blacks in nature, since all light is colored; and furthermore that yellow sunlight creates a complementary bluish shadow. Scientists had already discovered these facts and eventually the public itself came to accept the blue shadows which once had seemed so daring. [Pp. 18–19]

Consider also:

> 1943: This freedom, though achieved modestly at first and in the name of scientific realism, developed rapidly until eventually it led to a wide range of modern discovery and achievement. [P. 17]

By 1952 he drops "in the name of scientific realism" from this sentence substituting "This freedom, though achieved modestly at first and *in the tradition of realism*, developed rapidly until eventually it led to a wide range of modern discovery and achievement" (p. 19, my emphasis).

Why would Barr want to minimize science? Perhaps because a scientific approach—empirical attention to detail—has been at the core of much realism. Moreover, the proposition that art history could float free from other histories (scientific and otherwise) and develop out of its own internal logic—art reflects art—was then gaining currency among other critics.

Between 1943 and 1952, the Museum of Modern Art had begun actively collecting the art of the New York School, and Barr accommodated the new acquisitions by introducing two new sections in the 1952 version. "Motion and Commotion" reproduces Duchamp's 1912 *Nude Descending a Staircase* (collection Philadelphia Museum of Art), as well as futurist works by Balla and Boccioni acquired by the museum or its trustees. That section also provides historical antecedents for the second new section—"Mid-Century Abstraction"—illustrated by Henri Matisse's *1001 Nights* of 1950 (collection the artist). Three works from the New York School end that section: Arshile Gorky's *Agony*, 1947 (collection MoMA); Mark Rothko's *Number 10*, 1950 (collection MoMA); and Jackson Pollock's *Number 7*, 1950 (collection Sidney Janis Gallery).

Moreover, throughout the 1952 version Barr inserts sentences that prepare the way for a favorable reading of abstract expressionism. For example, in 1943 Barr concluded his discussion of Kandinsky with the words: "But these extreme advances had involved *serious* sacrifices both of human interest and controlled design" (p. 23; my emphasis). In 1952 he states: "But these extreme advances had involved *some* sacrifices both of human interest and *consciously* controlled design" (p. 25; my emphases). The editing is subtle but suggests his shift away from slight disapproval for those pictures that "sacrifice human interest" to neutrality about the issue. He was clearly moving away from the ethos that he shared with New Deal artists and government administrators of the 1930s and early 1940s who lauded pictures of "human interest."[47]

More notable, however, is Barr's frequent and gratuitous insertion of the word "freedom" in the 1952 version where the earlier phrases would have sufficed. For example, compare two sentences following a discussion of Léger and Renoir (my emphases added):

> 1943: These older paintings are victories in a long war of independence during which artists fought to *deliver* art first from the complex world of human affairs and then from visual reality itself—until the abstract purity of Kandinsky and Mondrian was achieved. This was a heroic struggle which we should not underestimate, for it brought to light many new forms and techniques and created a treasury of paintings which appeal directly to the eyes, to our sense of visual order, excitement and *beauty*. [P. 37]

> 1952: These older paintings are victories in a long war of independence during which artists fought to *free art first from subservience to* the complex world of human affairs and then from visual reality itself—until the abstract purity of Kandinsky (page 25) and Mondrian (page 29) was achieved. This was a heroic struggle which we should not underestimate, for it brought to light many new forms and techniques and created a treasury of paintings which appeal directly to the eyes, to our sense of visual order *or freedom*, excitement *or serenity*. [P. 44]

When Barr comes to the subject of the painter Max Beckmann he introduces the notion that freedom is not only what painters exercise, but what a nation allows or fosters. In 1943 Barr had attacked Nazi Germany; in 1952 he adds the Soviet Union. Compare the two versions:

> 1943: Beckmann is a German, blond and blue-eyed, but years ago he had to leave his country because Hitler hates his paintings. In Nazi Germany art is less free even than religion. [P. 20]

Barr further states that Hitler personally disliked Beckmann. But in the 1952 version Barr expands Hitler's aversion to all of modern painting and introduces the Soviet Union as the moral equivalent to Nazi Germany in terms of art censorship:

> 1952: Beckmann was a German, blond and blue-eyed, but he decided to leave his country because of Hitler who hated modern painting. . . . In Nazi Germany (as in Soviet Russia today) art was less free even than religion. [P. 23][48]

The 1952 version, like its 1943 predecessor, ends with a section called "Truth, Freedom, Perfection" in which he discusses the importance of living in a democratic society. Partway through the section, Barr states in the 1943 version (I repeat again from earlier pages):

> In order to tell this truth the artist must live and work in freedom. As President Roosevelt, *with the contemporary world in mind*, has put it: "The arts cannot

thrive except where men are free to be themselves and to be in charge of the discipline of their own energies and ardors. . . . What we call liberty in politics results in freedom in the arts. . . . Crush individuality in the arts and you crush art as well."[49] [P. 38; emphases are mine; ellipses are Barr's]

For the 1952 version, Barr changes the phrase "with the contemporary world in mind" to "with the totalitarian countries in mind" (p. 45).

Whereas the 1943 version enumerates Hitler's censorship of the arts and the persecution of artists, with the 1952 version Barr adds two long paragraphs castigating the Soviet Union.

> 1952: Similarly the Soviet authorities, even earlier than the Nazis, began to suppress modern art, calling it leftist deviation, Western decadence, bourgeois, formalistic. About 1921 such painters as Chagall (page 36) and Kandinsky (page 25) left the U.S.S.R. in frustration. The Soviet artists who remained are now enjoined—and well paid—to paint propaganda pictures in a popular realist style. Other subjects and styles have long been virtually forbidden. But *Pravda*, the official Communist Party newspaper in Moscow, still thunders, with its eyes on free Western Europe (August 10, 1947): "It cannot be tolerated that side by side with socialist realism we have still existing a co-current represented by the worshippers of bourgeois decaying art who regard as their spiritual teachers Picasso and Matisse, cubists and artists of the formalist school."
>
> The Museum of Modern Western Art in Moscow with its great collections of Cézanne, van Gogh and Matisse was closed and even the art of Picasso, a Communist Party member since 1944, is bitterly attacked. *VOKS*, an official Soviet periodical, insists: "It is not in order to arouse hatred for the forces of reaction that Picasso creates his morbid, revolting pictures. His is an esthetic apology for capitalism . . ." [P.45; Barr's ellipses]

While we are hardly surprised by Barr's anti-Soviet attitudes, it is at this point in time, 1952, that in an official museum publication Barr first links realism ("a popular realist style") with the ideologies of totalitarian regimes.[50]

This is a shift for Barr. In the late 1940s he had felt impelled to defend abstract art whenever it came under attack, as it did increasingly from the anti-Communists of the political right, but he had also insisted on the parity between realism and abstraction. Contributing to "A Symposium: The State of American Art," published in the March 1949 issue of *Magazine of Art*, Barr had written:

> An actual 'battle of styles,' as for instance between realism and abstraction, is desirable only to those who thrive on a feeling of partisanship. Both directions are valid and useful—and freedom to produce them and enjoy them should be protected as an essential liberty. There are, however, serious reasons for taking sides when one kind of art or another is dogmatically asserted to be the only

funicular up Parnassus or, worse, when it is maliciously attacked by the ignorant, the frightened, the priggish, the opportunistic, the bigoted, the backward, the vulgar or the venal.[51]

Although he is here offering a rationalization for the defense of abstraction,
he still believes that the public should have "freedom of choice among many
styles."

In 1952 Barr was working in the context of a very hot phase of the Cold
War. The proxy war between the United States and the USSR—the Korean
War—was unfolding between 1950 and 1953. The domestic events that raised
tensions included the Alger Hiss trials of 1949 and 1950; the Julius and Ethel
Rosenberg trial, appeals, and executions from 1950 to 1953; and the 1949–51 tri-
als, appeals, and conviction of Communist Party members under the Smith
Act. Moreover, the House Committee on Un-American Activities (HUAC),
Joseph McCarthy's Permanent Subcommittee on Investigations of the Senate
Committee on Government Investigations, Loyalty Boards, the Senate Internal Security Subcommittee, the Subversive Activities Control Board, and
many other governmental bodies sought to monitor "anti-Americanism."[52]
Barr, meanwhile, was moving away from the support of both realism and
abstraction toward a clear defense of abstract painting. As noted above, by
1952 Barr was defining Soviet artists as "well paid" painters of "propaganda
pictures in a popular realist style." And like other critics, such as Thomas
Hess, Barr believed that the artist's freedom to choose abstraction underscored an artist's political freedom—that he lived in "the free world."[53]

The 1952 edition of *What Is Modern Painting?* ends by admonishing readers to value the "artist's freedom" because "his freedom as we find it expressed
in his work of art is a symbol, an embodiment of the freedom which we all
want but which we can never really find in everyday life with its schedules,
regulations and compromises." Barr cautions, however, that "freedom . . . in
art is a delusion unless controlled by self-discipline" (p. 46). In expressing
this view of artistic freedom—that it represented freedom from the banality
of middle-class living—Barr came closer to the views of the actual artists
who made up the New York School.[54]

MoMA printed 20,000 copies of the 1952 edition of *What Is Modern Painting?*, but Barr worried about its pricing for students and others. In January
1953 he wrote to Monroe Wheeler and asked him to reconsider the pricing—
perhaps it should be sold for $1, instead of $1.25. "I urge this again because I
think we should consider WIMP to be not just another publication venture
but an instrument of propaganda in the original and best sense of the word."
Barr continues by laying out the costs and considering the ways the investment

could be recouped and even volunteers to reduce his own royalty.[55] But his basic argument is that *What Is Modern Painting?* serves as great publicity for MoMA: "WIMP deals not only with the principal medium with which the Museum is concerned; it is also the medium subject to the most serious misunderstanding on the part of the public, and this misunderstanding involves the most sinister implications. On the other hand WIMP is a political tract as well as an exposition of an art."[56] Barr held fiercely to the belief, expressed in his letter to Wheeler, in "the essential freedom of art" from censorship and government control (no matter what the government) and the mission of the Museum of Modern Art to enlighten all the people. He undoubtedly also wanted Wheeler and Rockefeller to know that he was on their team.[57]

Indeed, the booklet did function as propaganda in the cultural Cold War, whether or not Barr was a willing propagandist for the hegemony of the national state. In its rhetoric, *What Is Modern Painting?* was remarkably of a piece with the celebration of individual freedom and the abhorrence of totalitarianism expressed by other cultural Cold Warriors such as members of the Congress for Cultural Freedom, Greenberg, Lionel Trilling, and Schlesinger.[58]

Another, 1956 revision of *What Is Modern Painting?* continued to respond to the unfolding developments of the Cold War. In this edition of 26,000 copies (printed by the museum and distributed by Simon & Schuster), Barr added about another 350 words to "Truth, Freedom, Perfection." After quoting from the Soviet journal *VOKS*, which had charged that Picasso's art was "an esthetic apology for capitalism" (1952, p. 45), Barr felt obliged to add in parentheses: "(Recently there has been some relaxation in the U.S.S.R. Some Matisse's and a number of the less radical early paintings of Picasso have been exhibited; and, since the death of Stalin, Soviet artists have gradually felt a little freer)" (1956, pp. 45–46).

Barr then turns his attention to the domestic situation and adds several lines which reflect his distress at the anti-Communist witch hunts:

> Whether he has or not [found buyers], the American artist, since the recent war against tyranny abroad, has had to suffer occasional but serious tyranny here at home. Self-styled patriotic organizations and misguided congressmen, instigated by bitterly jealous academic artists, have accused modern artists and their supporters of communist sympathies.

Such attacks by fanatics within the United States subvert "the very words Americanism and patriotism" and "sometimes succeed in intimidating museums, publications and government agencies" (1956, p. 46). McCarthyism and the blacklists, of course, had been playing out at home, and Barr felt it necessary to defend the freedom of American artists. However, when Barr attacked "misguided congressmen" in 1956, official anti-Communist hysteria had already peaked; McCarthy had been "condemned" for contempt of the Senate in December 1954.

In the 1956 version of *What Is Modern Painting?* Barr focuses on censorship and marshals none other than President Eisenhower to back up his point about its evils. Following the paragraph quoted just above, Barr quotes a speech President Eisenhower delivered during October 1954 on the occasion of MoMA's 25th Anniversary celebration:

> To me, in this anniversary, there is a reminder to all of us of an important principle that we should ever keep in mind. This principle is that freedom of the arts is a basic freedom, one of the pillars of liberty in our land. For our Republic to stay free, those among us with the rare gift of artistry must be able freely to use their talent. Likewise, our people must have unimpaired opportunity to see, to understand, to profit from our artists' work. As long as artists are at liberty to feel with high personal intensity, as long as our artists are free to create with sincerity and conviction, there will be healthy controversy and progress in art. Only thus can there be opportunity for a genius to conceive and to produce a masterpiece for all mankind.
>
> But, my friends, how different it is in tyranny. When artists are made the slaves and the tools of the state; when artists become chief propagandists of a cause, progress is arrested and creation and genius are destroyed. [1956, p. 46]

Eisenhower, of course, wanted to refocus the body politic toward the USSR. Senators such as McCarthy with their crude accusations had become an embarrassment. Loyalty oaths would continue to be in effect, the FBI would continue to monitor those it considered subversive, but much official censorship ebbed. As if on cue, Barr followed Eisenhower's quotation by adding the word "censorship" to the list of the "freedoms from . . . ," so that Barr's sentence reads: "Freedom of expression, freedom from want and censorship and fear, these are desirable for the artist" (p. 46).[59]

And what of those American artists who clung to the "non-modern" styles of realism, to the socially concerned realism of the 1930s? By 1956, Barr's message to artists is clear: to prove your independence from (if not your rejection of) Communism you cannot work in realist styles that are anything like the Socialist Realism of the USSR: you must be "modern." It was a message that meant working in abstract and expressionist styles or a realist style that distorted, exaggerated, or surrealized the old realism. It was a message in accord with MoMA's own acquisition and exhibition policies.[60]

If we look at *What Is Modern Painting?* ten years later, at the revision of 1966, we find that Barr has updated the booklet by including two pages devoted to the more recent art that MoMA had purchased, including examples of Abstract Expressionism, Op Art, and Pop Art; the reproductions are Adolf Gottlieb's *Blast* I, 1957, Willem De Kooning's *Woman I*, 1950–52, Roy Lichtenstein's Pop Art painting *Flatten—Sand Fleas!*, 1962, and Arnold Schmidt's untitled "Op Art" piece of 1965.[61] In this 1966 edition, "Truth, Freedom, Perfection" was pared down in order to fit into the booklet (three signatures totaling 48 pages, as it had been). This version includes Barr's update of the anti-Soviet message, which has been shrunk from two paragraphs to one. Eliminated are the passages quoting *Pravda* and *VOKS* in the 1956 edition. Also gone is the parenthetical aside from the 1956 edition that "there had been some relaxation in the U.S.S.R." The paragraph reads:

> Similarly the Soviet authorities, even earlier than the Nazis, began to suppress modern art, calling it leftist deviation, Western decadence, bourgeois, formalistic. About 1921 such painters as Chagall (page 36) and Kandinsky (page 25) left the U.S.S.R. in frustration. Even today paintings by these great expatriates are hidden away in museum storerooms (though "formalist" works by the foreigners Matisse and Picasso have gradually emerged from prison since the death of Stalin in 1953). The Soviet artists who remain are enjoined—and well paid—to paint pictures in a popular realistic style preferably with propaganda content. Other styles are forbidden and other subjects discouraged. In 1962 Khrushchev himself assaulted young artists with threats and scurrilous sarcasm because they deviated from Socialist Realism and dared exhibit their heresies in spite of official warning. [1966, p. 47]

It was this paragraph which stayed in print for the next eighteen years. The 1959, 1963, and 1966 editions had a total print run of 75,000 copies, with 39,000 more copies printed through 1984.

On June 30, 1967, Alfred Barr retired from MoMA, as did James Thrall Soby, by then the Chairman of the Trustee Committee on Museum Collections, and Monroe Wheeler, still Director of Exhibitions and Publications.[62] As we move into the late 1960s and through to the 1980s, there was no Alfred Barr to revise *What Is Modern Painting?* with the same passion and focus that he had formerly brought to it. The print runs got smaller and smaller. The book still stood up as an excellent introduction to art appreciation, and some revisions were still necessary to update the list of the board of trustees and to fill in the artists' vital dates when they died.[63] The quality of the paper stock coarsened, and the political commentary crafted in 1966 went unchanged in subsequent editions, and thus seemed more and more dated as the years passed. The last printing in 1988 (called the 9th edition, sixth printing), appeared a year before the Berlin Wall fell; Barr's rhetoric of freedom no longer held such urgency. But during the 1940s and 1950s the iterations of

What Is Modern Painting? packed a terrific punch—for modern art, for MoMA, and for American superiority in the international Cold War.

Notes

I dedicate this essay to William S. Lieberman, a former Curator of Drawings and Prints at the Museum of Modern Art and my boss when I worked at MoMA as a curatorial assistant for drawings from 1960 to 1962, and part-time as a general assistant in 1963–64. His example (acute aesthetic judgment, horror of sentimentality, diplomatic and nuanced grace with patrons, and brilliant curatorial acumen), along with his guidance and his encouragement that I enroll in graduate school, changed my life. He later was director of the 20th Century Department at the Metropolitan Museum of Art. I want to acknowledge as well the women professionals at MoMA who also served as guides for me: Elaine Johnson, Betsy Jones, Helen Franc, Sara Mazo, Alicia Legg, and Dorothy Dudley. Some day their story will be told. For the current essay, I want to acknowledge the work of Carol Duncan and Alan Wallach, who launched the field of critical museum studies. I thank Kevin Whitfield, Carol Duncan, and Catha Paquette for reading drafts of this essay and making useful suggestions. I am particularly grateful to Paquette's scholarship, which has explored the correspondence between Nelson Rockefeller and Alfred H. Barr, Jr. I am further grateful to Catherine Turner and Greg Barnhisel for inviting my participation in this anthology and for their constructive criticisms. At the Museum of Modern Art Archives, New York, I thank MacKenzie Bennett and Miriam Gianni for their gracious help. I am grateful to MoMA's Archives for permission to publish excerpts from the Alfred H. Barr, Jr., Papers.

1. New Deal educators during the 1930s such as Holger Cahill, head of the Federal Art Project of the Works Progress Administration, shared the goal of bringing art to the people, including young students.

2. Alice Goldfarb Marquis, *Alfred H. Barr, Jr.: Missionary for the Modern* (Chicago: Contemporary Books, 1989), 215.

3. All the print runs are listed on p. 2 of each edition of the booklet.

4. An earlier, much shorter version of this essay was published as Patricia Hills, "The Modern Corporate State, the Rhetoric of Freedom, and the Emergence of Modernism in the United States: The Mediation of Language in Critical Practice," in Malcolm Gee, ed., *Art Criticism since 1900* (Manchester: Manchester University Press, 1993), 143–63. In that essay I focused primarily on Arthur Jerome Eddy and Willard Huntington Wright, both of whom wrote on art in 1914 and 1915 respectively, and brought in Alfred H. Barr, Jr., only at the end. My goal there was to "sketch out an argument premised on two propositions: First, that the modern corporate state, a political-economic phenomenon, and modernism, a cultural phenomenon, are complexly interdependent, with the former providing the conditions for the efflorescence and development of the latter, while the latter furnishes the cultural window dressing for the former; and second, that in trying to understand the mediations between the modern corporate state and modernism, we might find it useful to examine the role played by rhetoric" (p. 143).

5. Barr (1902–81), the son of a Presbyterian minister, was raised in Detroit and Baltimore and graduated from Princeton University with both A.B. and M.A. degrees in art history. He then went on to further his education at Harvard University. He taught at

both Vassar and Princeton before Wellesley. He was fired from the directorship of MoMA in October 1943 and demoted to a part-time "advisory director." However, Clark and the trustees realized his indispensability to the functioning of the museum, and he regained his status, if not the original title. He became a full time "director of research in painting and sculpture" and then "director of the Museum's collections." Marquis, *Alfred H. Barr,* 207–12, describes Barr's prickly relationship with the trustees. He stayed at the Museum until his retirement in 1967. See Marquis, *Alfred H. Barr, Jr.*; Dwight MacDonald, "Profiles: Action on West Fifty-Third Street," Part I, *New Yorker*, December 12, 1953, and MacDonald, "Profiles: Action on West Fifty-Third Street," Part II, *New Yorker*, December 19, 1953, 52; and Irving Sandler and Amy Newman, eds., *Defining Modern Art: Selected Writings of Alfred H. Barr, Jr.* (New York: Harry N. Abrams, 1986). See also Sybil Gordon Kantor, *Alfred H. Barr, Jr., and the Intellectual Origins of the Museum of Modern Art* (Cambridge, Mass.: MIT Press, 2002).

6. See Marquis, *Alfred H. Barr, Jr.*, 207–15.

7. James Thrall Soby (1906–79), writer, collector, and art patron, was born in Hartford, Connecticut, and worked at the Wadsworth Atheneum in Hartford from 1928 to 1938. In 1940 he joined the staff of MoMA and directed several departments and curated several exhibitions. He was a trustee of MoMA from 1942 to 1979. See Biography in the James Thrall Soby Papers, MoMA Archives, N.Y.

8. Alfred H. Barr, Jr., to Stephen C. Clark, letter of April 22, 1943, Alfred H. Barr, Jr., Papers, (hereinafter called AHB) 9.F.38. The Museum of Modern Art Archives, New York.

9. Victor d'Amico (1905–87) trained at Cooper Union, Pratt Institute, and Teachers College of Columbia University. He served as head of MoMA's department of education for over thirty years. From 1926 to 1940 he was also head of the art department at the Fieldston Schools and taught at Columbia University and New York University. No doubt influenced by the educational theories of John Dewey, D'Amico felt that children should make art in order to understand it. See *New York Times* obituary, April 3, 1987.

Monroe Wheeler (1899–1988), was born in Evanston, Illinois, and spent six years in Europe as a publisher before joining the staff of MoMA in 1935. Between 1941 and 1967 he was Director of Exhibitions and Publications. When he retired he became an adviser to MoMA's board of trustees. See *New York Times* obituary, August 16, 1988; see also Biography in the Monroe Wheeler Papers, MoMA Archives, NY.

A decade earlier Barr had published "A Brief Survey of Modern Painting," *The Carnegie Magazine* (March 1933).

10. Alfred H. Barr, Jr., to Stephen C. Clark, letter of April 22, 1943, AHB, 9.F.38, MoMA Archives, NY; emphases are Barr's.

11. See "Statement of reactions to planned publication *What Is Modern Painting?*" AHB, 6.B.2.d. MoMA Archives, NY.

12. AHB, 6.B.2.d. MoMA Archives, NY; all the quotations from Soby are in this same letter.

13. D'Amico to Barr, August 18, 1943, AHB, 6.B.2.d. MoMA Archives, NY.

14. Philip Johnson, in a memorial tribute to Barr, characterized "three aspects of his [Barr's] character that made it what it was . . . passion . . . stubbornness . . . loyalty." Quoted in Sandler and Newman, eds., *Defining Modern Art*, 244, n. 6.

15. The letters from Barr were written November 9 and 10, 1943; see AHB, 6.B.2.d. MoMA Archives, NY.

16. Catha Paquette, "Critical Consequences: Mexican Art at New York's Museum of Modern Art during World War II," in *XXVI Coloquio internacional de historia del arte:*

El proceso creative (Mexico City: National Autonomous University of Mexico/Institute of Esthetic Research, 2006), 529–59, has pointed out that Barr was part of the MoMA team committed to showing that MoMA's cultural policies during World War II were "the antithesis of Hitler's." She argues that the museum's activities at this time were designed to serve "a complex set of wartime ideological needs," to both "discredit the totalitarianism, anti-liberalism and anti-internationalism of Nazi Germany" and "promote US democratic economic-liberal and internationalist ideals." She points to the essay, probably written by Barr, "The Museum and the War," published in *The Bulletin of the Museum of Modern Art* 10, no. 1 (October–November, 1942), in which the author states that MoMA's collection included "**art that Hitler hates** because it is **modern**, progressive, challenging . . . because it is **international**, leading to understanding and tolerance among nations . . . because it is **free**, the free expression of free men" (p. 19).

17. Postscript in Barr's handwriting to Barr's form letter to Mabel Birckhead; and note to Bartlett Hayes, November 9, 1943, see AHB, 6.B.2.d. MoMA Archives, NY.

18. Charles Beck to Alfred H. Barr, Jr., n.d., AHB, 6.B.2.d. MoMA Archives, NY.

19. Alfred H. Barr, Jr., "Art in the Third Reich—Preview, 1933," *Magazine of Art* 39 (October 1945): 212. The English translation is probably Barr's own. Paquette, "Critical Consequences," also discusses the impact of the "Kulturprogramm im neuen Reich" on Barr's anti-Nazi stance.

20. Barr, "Art in the Third Reich," 214, 215. Barr wrote up his encounter with Nazi Germany in May 1933, while visiting Switzerland. MacDonald, in "Profiles . . . II," 38, interviewed Barr's wife, Margo, who told him that she and Barr "left Germany for Switzerland in a state of horror and indignation," and that Barr insisted on immediately writing up his impressions of Nazi Germany, but when they returned to the United States no publisher would print his essays, except for a brief section in Lincoln Kirstein's *Hound and Horn*.

21. Paquette emphasizes that "Barr did much during the war to help European émigrés come to the US," and she also calls attention to "the context in which Barr used this language, the fact that MoMA trustees and staff were heavily involved in conceptualizing, designing, and implementing programs for Roosevelt's Office of Inter-American Affairs—of which Nelson Rockefeller was the director." She adds: "Barr and Rockefeller worked closely during this period; in letters Barr wrote to Rockefeller he made clear that he shared the agency's wartime goals and would do everything he could to serve them." Catha Paquette, personal communication, June 24 and August 18, 2008. Also see Paquette, "Critical Consequences," and Catha Paquette, "Public Duties, Private Interests: Mexican Art at New York's Museum of Modern Art, 1929–1954" (diss., University of California, Santa Barbara, 2002).

22. By 1946 Simon and Schuster had begun to distribute copies of the booklet to bookstores; see Memorandum of June 13, 1946 from Wheeler to Barr. AHB 6.B.2.c. MoMA Archives, NY.

23. John D. Morse, "New Books," *Magazine of Art* 37 (May 1944): 199.

24. Barr to J. Carson Webster, November 14, 1945, AHB, 6.B.2.c. MoMA Archives, NY.

25. Memorandum from Wheeler to Barr, June 13, 1946. AHB, 6.B.2.c. MoMA Archives, NY.

26. In the 1943 edition the last page listed other museum publications. In the 1946 edition, the list of trustees, the table of contents, and the preface each had its own page; the result was that all 48 pages had type.

27. The WPA was the Works Progress Administration, a large federal agency set up by President Roosevelt during the 1930s to employ the unemployed, including artists, on work projects.

28. Many simply went back to school on the G.I. Bill.

29. The government also sponsored "Buying American Art Weeks" in 1940 and 1941; see Serge Guilbaut, *How New York Stole the Idea of Modern Art*, trans. Arthur Goldhammer (Chicago: University of Chicago Press, 1983), 55–59. In the early postwar years *Fortune* magazine promoted the art market in a feature published in its September 1946 issue.

30. See Paquette, "Critical Consequences."

31. See Margaret Lynne Ausfield and Virginia M. Mecklenburg, *Advancing American Art: Politics and Aesthetics in the State Department Exhibition, 1946–48* (Montgomery, Ala.: Montgomery Museum of Fine Arts, 1984).

32. The revisionist art history articles that discuss Porter McCray and USIA include Max Kozloff, "American Painting during the Cold War," *Artforum* 11 (May 1973): 43–54, and Eva Cockcroft, "Abstract Expressionism, Weapon of the Cold War," *Artforum* 12 (June 1974): 39–41.

33. See sponsor's statement in the booklet by George F. Kennan, *International Exchange in the Arts* (New York: The International Council of the Museum of Modern Art, 1956); AHB, 6.B.2.c. MoMA Archives, NY. The booklet published the address that Kennan, a diplomat, delivered at a symposium sponsored by the International Council on May 12, 1955.

34. Memorandum from Monroe Wheeler to Officers and Department Heads, dated March 25, 1952, AHB, 6.B.1. MoMA Archives, NY. Wheeler added that in 1951 European sales of MoMA books were 820 volumes and Latin American sales 400 volumes, in contrast to 60,000 volumes sold in the United States.

35. The Japanese edition is not listed on the 2nd page that lists all the other print runs, which suggests that the Japanese may have published the translation themselves.

36. In the interest of full disclosure: In 1973 the United States Information Agency asked me to organize a traveling exhibition based on my Whitney Museum of American Art exhibition *The American Frontier: Images and Myths*. Without realizing the full implications of my own role in this propaganda outreach, I agreed. The USIS in Europe printed up about 19,000 (the figure I recall) catalogs, as compared with the 1,500 or so that the Whitney printed for its summer 1973 exhibition. USIA also sent me abroad for two weeks in 1975, where I gave lectures at various museums and consulates to which the European cultural, civic, and business leaders had been invited. I was merely the occasion for such gatherings. The *Voice of America* also taped an interview I gave to one of its staff on the American artists of the Western frontier; the interview was no doubt broadcast in several countries. (Note: The agency was called USIA [United States Information Agency] in the United States, but USIS [United States Information Service] abroad; staff members could not give me a reason for this anomaly.)

37. See Barr to Wheeler memorandum of February 2, 1949; AHB, B.2.c. MoMA Archives, NY.

38. Barr to Editor of *Art Digest*, June 7, 1949, AHB, 9.a. MoMA Archives, NY.

39. In a speech inserted into the *Congressional Record*—House, 81st Congress, 1st Session, V. 95, Parts 8–9 (August 16, 1949), 11584–87, Dondero cited MoMA for publishing a catalog on Ben Shahn and for showing the art of Diego Rivera, Jose Clemente Orozco,

and David Siqueiros, all Communists per Dondero. William Hauptman, "The Suppression of Art in the McCarthy Decade," *Artforum* 12 (October 1973): 48, points out that Senator Joseph McCarthy did not aim his attacks at artists, "But his colleagues in Congress often equated all seemingly radical activities—especially artistic ones—with political extremism." It was in this speech that Dondero attacked the modernist movements: "Cubism aims to destroy by designed disorder. /Futurism aims to destroy by the machine myth. . . . / Dadaism aims to destroy by ridicule./ Expressionism aims to destroy by aping the primitive and insane. Abstractionism aims to destroy by the creation of brainstorms./ Surrealism aims to destroy by the denial of reason. . . ." For a lengthy excerpt of Dondero's speech, see Patricia Hills, *Modern Art in the USA: Issues and Controversies of the 20th Century* (Upper Saddle River, N.J.: Prentice Hall, 2001), 191–92. See also Jane De Hart Mathews, "Art and Politics in Cold War America," *American Historical Review* 81 (October 1976): 762–87; and Frances Pohl, "The Campaign of Truth in American Art," manuscript of a talk given at the Mark Goodson Symposium on American Art, Whitney Museum of American Art, April 1979.

40. Alfred H. Barr, Jr., "Is Modern Art Communistic?" *New York Times Magazine* (December 14, 1952), 22 ff.

41. Published in Barton J. Bernstein, ed., *Towards a New Past: Dissenting Essays in American History* (New York: Vintage Books, 1967), 322–59.

42. Guilbaut points out: "The avant-garde artist who categorically refused to participate in political discourse and tried to isolate himself by accentuating his individuality was co-opted by liberalism, which viewed the artist's individualism as an excellent weapon with which to combat Soviet authoritarianism" (*How New York Stole the Idea of Modern Art,* p. 143). Nevertheless, the fact that avant-garde artists turned away from the politics of the Left has brought charges that they were compromised.

43. See Patricia Hills, book review of Guilbaut's book in *The Archives of American Art Journal* 24, no. 1 (1984), reprinted in *Archives of American Art Journal: A Retrospective Selection of Articles* 30, nos. 1–4 (1990): 84–87.

44. See Caroline A. Jones, *Eyesight Alone: Clement Greenberg's Modernism and the Bureaucratization of the Senses* (Chicago: University of Chicago Press, 2005), 83–85. For Schapiro, see David Craven, *Abstract Expressionism as Cultural Critique: Dissent during the McCarthy Period* (New York: Cambridge University Press, 1999). Craven argues that abstract expressionism "signified a profound form of romantic anti-capitalism," and he gives a useful analysis of the role Meyer Schapiro played at the time in advancing such an interpretation.

Robert Motherwell often wrote criticism. In "The Modern Painter's World," *DYN* 1, no. 6 (November 1944), he wrote that "Modern art is related to the problem of the modern individual's freedom."

45. The last sentence reads: "Stop a moment and look at them both again. Subject matter aside, which style, which way of painting means more to you? Or do both have value?"

46. Greenberg's teleological approach is exemplified in his "Abstract Art," *Nation* 158 (April 15, 1944): 450–51, reprinted in Hills, *Modern Art in the USA*, 147–50.

47. See, for example, Holger Cahill's introduction to *New Horizons in American Art* (New York: Museum of Modern Art, 1936), the catalog for a WPA exhibition.

48. Barr visited the Soviet Union in the 1920s and was disillusioned; see MacDonald, "Profiles . . . I," 82. In 1943, when the United States was an ally of the USSR, it would not have been appropriate to criticize the USSR.

49. The source cited is President Roosevelt's broadcast upon the opening of the new building of the Museum of Modern Art, May 11, 1939.

50. In a lecture delivered on December 10, 1951, at the Norton Gallery in Florida, Barr also discussed realism and abstraction. The *Palm Beach Post*, December 11, 1951, quoted him as saying: "I'm not for a minute implying . . . that realism is necessarily Nazism. It is one of the great traditions of Western art. . . . But the freedom to look at what paintings we like; the freedom of an artist to paint as he sees fit; the freedom to like or dislike . . . these freedoms are part of the great traditions of this country. . . . When you look at these realistic waxworks I have shown [in slides at the lecture], you can see what art becomes under tyranny." The *Palm Beach News*, September 9, 1951, reported on Barr's description of Hitler and Stalin: "Both hated modern art because of its expression of individual initiative. . . . We as instigators of freedom, still enjoying freedom of the press, and the right to pursue our own course without dictatorship of the State cannot afford to nourish symptoms of intolerance. . . . I believe art has as much a right to freedom as any other enterprise." The clipping is included in the Alfred H. Barr, Jr., Papers [viewed on September 18, 1992, and not then cataloged], MoMA Archives, N.Y.

51. "Alfred H. Barr, Jr," [Contribution to] "A Symposium: The State of American Art," *Magazine of Art* 42 (March 1949): 85.

52. See Griffen Fariello, *Red Scare: Memories of the American Inquisition: An Oral History* (New York: W. W. Norton, 1995).

53. See Thomas B. Hess, "Is Abstraction Un-American?" *Art News* 49 (February 1951): 38–41. See also Richard H. Pells, *The Liberal Mind in a Conservative Age: American Intellectuals in the 1940s and 1950s* (New York: Harper & Row, 1985).

54. Compare Mark Rothko's statement in "The Romantics Were Prompted," *Possibilities* I (New York), Winter 1947/48, p. 84: "The unfriendliness of society to his activity is difficult for the artist to accept. Yet this very hostility can act as a lever for true liberation. Freed from a false sense of security and community, the artist can abandon his plastic bank-book, just as he has abandoned other forms of security. Both the sense of community and of security depend on the familiar. Free of them, transcendental experiences become possible."

55. Barr had previously complained about not getting royalties in a memorandum to Wheeler of February 2, 1949; see AHB 6.B.2.c. MoMA Archives, NY.

56. Barr to Wheeler, January 8, 1953, AHB, 6.B.2.c. MoMA Archives, NY. Paquette argues that Barr knew the larger political implication that what he was saying was an endorsement of propaganda for American political, economic, and cultural leadership on the international stage, as evidenced in his many letters to Nelson Rockefeller; see Paquette, "Public Duties, Private Interests." She argues that "Barr could deploy the rhetoric of freedom for virtually any style . . . [for example] the extent to which he defended the work of Mexican communist-activist artists in the 1954 text *Masters of Modern Art*." Personal communication, June 24 and August 18, 2008.

57. For art historians one of the characteristics of museum work (as distinct from academic work) is the high value placed on teamwork—in organizing exhibitions, writing catalog essays, and programming.

58. For an analysis of the cultural climate, see Christopher Lasch, "The Cultural Cold War: A Short History of the Congress for Cultural Freedom," in Bernstein, *Towards a New Past*.

59. In all the discussions about freedom during the 1940s and 1950s in the art press, there is never an acknowledgment that African American artists in Jim Crow America daily confronted fear and curtailments of their freedom.

60. Realist artists (whether Communists, former Communists, or independents) felt so neglected by MoMA and other museums during this period that they organized as a group in March 1950 to defend what they called humanist values in art. The group spent many meetings drafting letters to museums to protest curatorial preferences which excluded them. They included Raphael Soyer, Yasuo Kuniyoshi, Edward Hopper, Philip Evergood, and Isabel Bishop. In 1953 they published *Reality: A Journal of Artists' Opinions*. Barr felt embattled by the group; see MacDonald, "Profiles . . . II," 65. MacDonald acknowledges the group's written attacks on Barr and points out that a study of both the permanent collection on view and the show *15 Americans* indicate a clear preference for abstract art. For one of the texts of the *Reality* group, see Hills, *Modern Art in the USA*, 181–83.

MoMA curators promoted Abstract Expressionism internationally by sending abroad *New American Painting*, which was viewed to positive reviews in Basel, Milan, Madrid, Berlin, Amsterdam, Brussels, Paris, and London in the one-year period from April 1958 to March 1959. The painters included were William Baziotes, James Brooks, Sam Francis, Arshile Gorky, Adolph Gottlieb, Philip Guston, Grace Hartigan, Franz Kline, Willem De Kooning, Robert Motherwell, Barnett Newman, Jackson Pollock, Mark Rothko, Theodore Stamos, Clyfford Still, Bradley Walker Tomlin, and Jack Tworkov. The MoMA staff involved, the organization of the exhibition, its reception in the European cities, and the consequent consolidation of the canon of mid-century abstract expressionists artists, would be the subject of another essay. A catalog was produced at the conclusion of the exhibition, for which Barr wrote the introduction, in which he referred to himself as having "watched with deep excitement and pride the development of the artists here represented, their long struggle—with themselves even more than with the public—and their present triumph"; see Alfred H. Barr, Jr., "Introduction," *The New American Painting: As Shown in Eight European Countries 1858–1959* (New York: Museum of Modern Art, 1959), 19.

61. The 1959 edition increased the text section by just one page, with reproductions by Gottlieb and De Kooning; the 1963 edition included some of the changes of the 1966 edition. For the sake of brevity I am focusing just on the 1956 and 1966 editions. The different editions provided occasions to update the trustees list, which was printed in every edition.

62. See Jane Fluegel, "Chronology," in Sandler and Newman, eds., *Defining Modern Art*, 272–73.

63. For example, the text for the 1984 edition (after Barr had died) is the same as the 1966 text, except that Rona Roob updated the trustees list, noted the artists who had died, and gave corrected credit lines for the paintings that had changed ownership in the interim.

About the Contributors

Greg Barnhisel is associate professor of English and the director of first-year writing at Duquesne University in Pittsburgh, Pa. He is the author of *James Laughlin, New Directions, and the Remaking of Ezra Pound* (University of Massachusetts Press, 2005) and the textbook *Media and Messages: Strategies and Readings in Public Rhetoric* (Longman, 2005). His current scholarly work focuses on the use of modernist art in the U.S. cultural-diplomacy program in the early Cold War.

Edward Brunner is a professor of English at Southern Illinois University, Carbondale. His most recent book, *Cold War Poetry*, reconsiders American poetry from 1945 to 1960, and recent essays examine adult-aimed adventure comic strips as they appeared from 1930 to 1955 in such newspapers as the *Chicago Tribune*, the *Daily Worker*, and the *Pittsburgh Courier*.

Russell Cobb serves as assistant professor of Spanish and Latin American Studies at the University of Alberta. He received his Ph.D. in Comparative Literature from the University of Texas at Austin. He also worked as a journalist and is interested in Latin American media from the Cold War to the present.

Laura Jane Gifford is an independent scholar and adjunct professor at George Fox University, Warner Pacific College, and Western Oregon University. She is the author of *The Center Cannot Hold: The 1960 Presidential Election and the Rise of Modern Conservatism* (Northern Illinois University Press, 2009).

Patricia Hills teaches at Boston University where she is a specialist in the history of American painting, African American art, and art and politics. She has written about or curated exhibitions for artists as diverse as Alice Neel (1983), John Singer Sargent (1986), and Jacob Lawrence (2009), as well as producing overviews such as *The Figurative Tradition and The Whitney Museum of American Art: Paintings and Sculpture from the Permanent Collection* (1980).

Her popular textbook anthology, *Modern Art in the USA: Issues and Controversies of the 20th Century,* was published in 2001. She has held both Guggenheim and National Endowment for the Humanities Fellowships.

Christian Kanig is a Ph.D. candidate in Indiana University's Department of History. He studied Soviet and German history in Tübingen and Berlin in Germany and at Indiana University, Bloomington. He is currently finishing his dissertation, "Reeducation through Literature: Soviet Cultural Policy in Occupied Germany 1945–1949."

Scott Laderman, assistant professor of history at the University of Minnesota, Duluth, is the author of *Tours of Vietnam: War, Travel Guides, and Memory* (Duke University Press, 2009).

Amanda Laugesen, currently at the Australian National University, Canberra, has published extensively in both U.S. and Australian history. Her current research focuses on book, library, and publishing projects in the developing world after the Second World War.

Martin Manning, a Boston native and die-hard New Englander, is a researcher and writer in the Office of Publications, Bureau of International Programs, U.S. Department of State. As curator of the former USIA historical collection, he maintains files from the McCarthy era. Also, he has talked to USIA individuals who lived through the loyalty program and remember its effects all too well.

Kristin L. Matthews is assistant professor of American Literature at Brigham Young University. Her current book project examines the politics of reading in Cold War American literature and culture, and her writings have appeared or are forthcoming in *Modern Drama, The Journal of American Culture, The Journal of Popular Culture, International Journal of Comic Arts,* and *African American Review.*

Hiromi Ochi is a professor of English at Hitotsubashi University in Japan. Her research focuses on the literature of the American South and its institutionalization in American literary studies. She is the author of *Truman Capote: His Life and Works* (2006; in Japanese), and she co-edited the anthology *Reading the World from the Gender Perspective: Identity and Cultural Representation* (2008; in Japanese).

Amy Reddinger is assistant professor of English at the University of Wisconsin, Marinette. She received her Ph.D. from the University of Washington in 2007. Her current project is a broad study of the shifting representations of race in twentieth-century American cookbooks.

James Smith holds a Ph.D. from the University of Cambridge, and is currently a postdoctoral research fellow at the University of Queensland, Australia. His general research interests concern the literature and culture of twentieth-century Britain, and he is in the final stages of a book project examining the surveillance of authors by the British security service MI5 during 1930–1950.

Catherine Turner is the Associate Director of the Center for Teaching and Learning at the University of Pennsylvania. She is the author of *Marketing Modernism between the Two Wars* (University of Massachusetts Press, 2003) and is currently working on the intersection of public policy, business, and literacy in the 1930s.

Index

Abstract Expressionism, 3, 235–36, 249 n. 5, 259, 262, 268

Allen and Unwin, 119–20

Alliance for Progress, 239, 244, 249

Americn Friends of Vietnam, 211, 217

American Library Association, 12, 91–92, 96–97, 99

Ampersand Books, 116, 119–20, 124 n. 12

anti-Americanism: in Axis propaganda, 145; in Chinese propaganda, 157; in Latin America, 154, 131, 135–40, 145–49; in Germany, 77–78, 81–83; in Nigeria, 13–14; response to, 131, 135, 140–41; in Soviet propaganda, 103, 152–53, 155–57; in the United States, 39, 61–63, 264–65

anti-Communism: and artistic freedom, 23, 233, 235–37, 243–46, 260, 266–69; diversity of, 57–60, 62–63, 117–18, 238–40, 246–47; via books, 50–56, 129–30, 135–37; in Great Britain, 112–13, 117–18, 121–23; in Japan, 90, 99–100, 105–6; in Latin America, 235–40, 345–49; response to, 78, 80–81, 114; spiritual aspects, 58–61; in the United States, 10, 19, 20–21, 34, 54–57, 135–36, 159–61, 221; in Vietnam, 209–10, 212–13, 215–21

anti-fascism, 5, 10–11, 77, 145, 255–57, 263

Armed Services Editions, 6, 94–95, 97, 101

atrocity stories, 72, 82, 152

authors: auctions for, 8–9; collaborative, 36, 196, 205; corporate, 196–97, 204; relations with covert agencies, 113, 122–23; relations with periodicals, 51, 239–40, 243–47; relations with readers, 21–22, 42, 174–75; in the Soviet Union, 9, 71, 84

avant-garde, 231, 233, 235–36, 243, 248–49

Background Books, 21, 115–22, 124–25

Bantam Books, 8, 193

Barr, Alfred: attitudes toward artistic styles, 261–62, 264–65, 267–69; anti-Communism and, 251–52, 259–60, 264–69; biography, 252, 269 n. 5; revisions to *What Is Modern Painting?*, 23, 257–58, 259–65, 267–68. See also *What Is Modern Painting?*

Benet, Stephen Vincent, 5, 93, 95–96, 99

Bergeron, Victor (Trader Vic), 200–202, 207 n. 21

Best Years of Our Lives, The (1946), 182–84

Better Homes and Gardens series (Meredith Press), 181, 197–99, 201, 204–5

Betty Crocker (General Mills) 197–99, 201, 204–5, 207 n. 9

blacklist, 9–10, 266

Bodley Head, The, 116–17, 121

book industries in developing countries, 13–14, 136–40

Bookmailer, The, 51, 55

Book-of-the-Month Club, 8, 55, 93, 95, 98

books: anti-American, 77–82; commodification of, 7–9; as diplomatic gifts, 89, 94, 130, 141; distribution of, 75–76, 118–20; printing of, 74–75; about science, 96, 103, 129–30; utility as propaganda, 71–73, 89, 114–20, 126, 129, 132, 135–36

bookstores, 7, 9, 53, 55–56, 72, 104, 149–50, 257, 259

Books USA. *See* Freedom House Books USA

Borges, Jorge Lois, 233–34, 240

Buckley, William F. 50, 57–58

Budenz, Louis, 54, 57–59, 61

Casa de las Americas, 23, 231–34, 238, 243, 247

Castro, Fidel, 233–35, 249; books about, 51, 58; opposition to, 239

censorship: in China, 17–18; in Cuba, 232, 235, 248–49; in Germany, 20, 72–73, 80, 82–83, 85; in Japan, 100–101, 104; by Nazis, 256–57, 263–64; from the right, 243, 249; in the Soviet Union, 4–10, 16–17, 251, 264, 266–68; in the United States, 4–10, 131–32, 266–67

Central Intelligence Agency (CIA), 3, 128; agents, 221, 238–39, 245; covert funding of publications, 14–15, 23, 221, 233, 235; and the Congress for Cultural Freedom, 112, 231, 235, 241–43, 247–48; manipulating authors, 243, 245–46, 248; use of USIA propaganda collection, 146

childrens' books, 4, 12, 140, 154, 160–62

China: print in, 15, 17–19, 25, 90; propaganda, 151–54, 157–58; in *Steve Canyon*, 174–76, 180–81

Chodorov, Frank, 51, 63

Churchill, Winston, 77, 79

Civil Information and Education (CIE) Libraries: book selection, 95–100, 102–3; collections, 101–3; democratic message, 103–7; history, 20, 90–91, 100–101; popularity, 103

Congress for Cultural Freedom (CCF): anti-Communism of, 238–40, 260, 266; CIA support for, 11, 112, 231, 235, 241–43, 247–48; and foundations, 14–15, 242–43; importance to cultural cold war, 2, 237–42

consumerism, 7–8, 15, 20, 23, 90, 104, 139–40, 179–82, 199, 206

containment, 1–2, 15, 92, 106, 177

Council on Books in Wartime, 5–6, 12, 92–95, 129, 135

Cuadernos, 232, 237–40, 242–43

Cuban Revolution, 231–35, 237–39, 244–45, 248–49

cultural diplomacy, 3–4, 10, 90–91, 119, 204–5, 210, 223, 244–49, 258–59

Darío, Rubén, 231–32

Die Neue Zeitung, 11, 83

dissent: in comic strips, 189–90; in Latin America, 233, 237, 239, 243–45, 249; in the Soviet Union, 17–18, 28 n. 49; in the United States, 10, 16–17, 24–25, 43, 85, 53–55, 85

distribution of printed materials: in Great Britain, 118–20; in the Soviet Union, 75; in the United States, 7–8, 36–37, 50–52, 151–52, 217–18, 251–52, 257–58; world wide, 126, 139, 157–58, 259

Doubleday, 135, 193

Du Bois, W. E. B., 4, 10

Dulles, John Foster, 14, 57

Economic Research and Action Project (ERAP), 37, 41–42

education: art appreciation, 253–54; as foreign policy, 72–76, 90–91, 129–30, 136–40; in the United States, 9, 62, 158, 184; through reading, 32–33, 37–38, 41–42, 55–56, 63–64

Egypt, 13, 15, 128, 131, 138–39, 141

Eisenhower, Dwight D., 20, 57–58, 60, 127, 275

Encounter, 11, 23, 112, 237, 241. *See* also Congress for Cultural Freedom

encyclopedias, 4, 139, 159

Fast, Howard, 10, 96, 131

Faulkner, William, 6, 8, 97

Federal Bureau of Investigation (FBI), 39, 146, 148, 268

Fishman, Irving, 149, 156, 164–65

Fodor, Eugene, 219–20

Ford Foundation, 3, 14, 242–43

Foreign Agents Registration Act (FARA), 146–49, 150–51, 156

Foundation for Economic Education, 53, 62–63

foundations, 3, 14–15, 51–53, 62–63, 140, 242–43, 248

France: post-war cultural diplomacy in, 10, 15, 157, 259, in Vietnam, 210, 215, 218, as a location for Latin American literary journals, 237–41, 248

Franklin Publications (Franklin Book Programs), 14, 127–28, 136–41

free market, 20–21, 73–74, 85, 179–80, 244, 258

Freedom House Books USA (Bookshelf USA), 21, 127, 132–36

Fuentes, Carlos, 233, 237, 239, 243–47

García Márquez, Gabriel, 23, 231, 243

gender roles, 2, 22, 92–93, 104–5, 141, 195, 197, 199, 203–4

General Electric, 196–97

General Mills. *See* Betty Crocker

Germany: denazification, 10, 72–73, 100–101; export of propaganda, 155; influence on Alfred Barr, 257, 263; publishing industry in, 72–75; readers in, 73, 76–77; as a site for Soviet propaganda, 10–11, 20, 71–72, 75–85; as a site for U.S. propaganda, 10–11, 20, 71, 79–83, 103, 172, 259

Goldwater, Barry, 24, 50, 53, 55, 59–61

Gorkin, Julián, 238–39, 240, 243

Great Britain: anti-Communism in, 112–13, 117–20; joint efforts with U.S., 10–11, 97; attitudes toward propaganda, 20–21, 112–15

Guilbaut, Serge, 3, 24, 235–36, 260

Hayden, Tom, 31, 36–37

Henry Regnery Co., 53–56, 64

History of the CPSU (B) Short Course, 20,
    73–75
Hitler-Stalin Pact, 81, 96
Hoover, J. Edgar, 50, 52–54
House Committee on Un-American Activities
    (HUAC), 10, 51–52, 61, 130, 150–52, 156, 259,
    265
Hughes, Langston, 4, 10
Human Events, 54, 56, 62–63
Hunt, John, 238–40, 245–47

imperialism: in anti-American propaganda,
    153, 156–57, 163; cultural, 3, 131, 137; response
    to in the United States, 32, 36, 41; response to
    in Latin America, 232, 240–41, 248; response
    to in Vietnam, 209, 215–16, 218, 221; use of
    print to spread, 128, 131
India, 13–15, 133, 211
Indonesia, 13, 24, 128, 139, 140, 159
Information Research Department (IRD):
    connections to trade publishers, 114–16,
    119–20; creates Background Books, 115–17;
    distribution of books, 118–19, 123; founding,
    112–13, "see-safe" agreements, 116, 119, 121;
    use of former intelligence officers, 113–14, 116,
    120, 122
Instituto Latinoamericano de Relaciones
    Internacionales (ILARI), 240–41
Inter-Allied Control Commission, 81–82
Intercollegiate Society of Individualists, 51, 63
International Information Agency (IIA),
    11–12, 14
Iraq, 128, 130
Iraq War, 45, 141
Iran, 128, 139
ISVA (Soviet Military Administration
    Publishing House), 20, 71–80; distribution of
    books in Germany, 75–78; distribution of
    books to Soviet Union, 75; at Leipzig Book
    Fair, 84
Italy, 10, 13, 15, 157, 259

Japan: in anti-American propaganda, 78; gender
    roles in, 104–7; post War reeducation, 89–90,
    103–7; publishing in, 13; U.S.-sponsored
    libraries in, 20, 103–5
John Birch Society, 15, 55, 57, 62
Josselson, Michael, 238–40, 242, 245, 247

Kennan, George, 1–2, 11, 105, 177
Kennedy John F., 13–14, 134, 239, 249
Khrushchev, Nikita, 4, 199, 207 n. 16, 268

Korean War, 152, 177, 180, 187, 188, 265
Kozloff, Max, 2, 236

Labour Party, 112–13, 115. *See also* Mayhew,
    Christopher
Lane, Allen, 114–15
Lasch, Christopher, 3, 260
Lasky, Melvin, 11, 260
Latin America: Congress for Cultural Freedom
    in, 237–41; private foundations in, 14, 242–43,
    248; influence of Cuban Revolution, 233–35;
    literary Boom, 23, 234–35, 249; target for U.S.
    books, 13, 90, 96, 259
Leipzig Book Fair, 83–85
Liberty Bell Press, 24, 49, 53–56, 66
libraries, 6, 12, 20, 55–56, 72–73, 80 84, 90–91
literacy, 2, 32, 126, 131–32, 140
luaus, 197–201, 203–5

MacLeish, Archibald, 12, 91–92, 99
magazines, 7, 11–12, 15–16, 20, 22, 51, 62, 82, 101,
    181, 211, 217
Magee, Bryan, 121–22, 126
Male Call, 169, 171–73
Marcha, 233, 240, 243, 245
Matisse, Henri, 252, 262, 264, 266, 268
Matthews, Herbert L., 51, 58, 234
May, Elaine Tyler, 1–2, 15, 92, 105
Mayhew, Christopher, 115, 117, 121
McCarthy, Joseph, 6, 12, 52, 58, 60, 131, 148, 246,
    267
Mercier Vega, Luis, 238, 240–41, 245, 247
Meredith Press. *See* Better Homes and Gardens
    series
Mexico, 5, 90, 119, 237, 239–40, 245, 259
Michener, James, 8, 193–95, 200, 205
middlebrow, 93–94, 204
Middle East,: printed materials in, 12, 24, 130,
    133, 137–38, 141; in *Steve Canyon*, 170, 177,
    180 189
Miss Lace, 172, 175
modernism, 23, 97, 231, 235
modernization, 13, 20, 71, 126–27, 135–41,
    196–97, 199, 212–14. *See also* Pye, Lucian
Modern Library, 7, 55
Monegal, Emir Rodríguez, 232–35, 240–48
Mundo Nuevo: anti-Communism in, 235, 243,
    246–47; support for apolitical art, 231–35,
    243–44; relation to the Congress for Cul-
    tural Freedom, 240–43; relation to Cuban
    Revolution, 233–35, 242, 245–46; relation to
    non-Latin American countries, 238, 241, 244

Museum of Modern Art (MoMA), 23, 258–59, 262, 265–69, 255

Neruda, Pablo, 238, 243, 245–46
New Deal: anti-Communist attacks on, 54, 62; influence on the arts, 95–96, 98–101, 103, 236, 258, 262, 263–64; politics of, 3, 20, 90
New Left: action oriented, 37–38; defined by print, 31–33, 35–36; development from Old Left, 33–35; effort to create more democratic democracy, 37–40, fake printed material, 39–40, influence of Cuban Revolution, 234
newspapers, 11, 16, 38, 61–62, 71, 76, 79–84, 171, 186–89
Ngo Dinh, Diem: as leader of Vietnam, 210, 213–14, 216, 219–20, 223; American attitudes toward, 209, 217, 219
Nigeria, 13–14, 128, 133, 135, 140
Nixon, Richard M. 60–61, 163, 199
non-mainstream presses, 53–55, 116, 193
novels: as American propaganda, 105–6, 131, 134; in book selection guides, 94–98; during WW II, 5–6, 94–97, as Soviet propaganda, 72, 75–77, 81, 84–85, in U.S., 8–9, in China, 18; in Latin America, 233, 244

Office of Armed Forces Information and Education, 220–23
Office of Military Government for Germany (OMGUS), 19, 81
Office of War Information, 5, 90–95, 102–3, 146
Orwell, George, 113, 134
Overseas Editions, 5, 94–96, 101–3
Oxford University Press, 115, 120

Palo Duro Press, 24, 53
paperback books, 6–10, 19, 35, 50, 55–56, 75, 84, 114, 135, 152
participatory democracy, 32, 36–37, 40–43, 46–47
Penguin Books, 6, 113–14
Pocket Books, 6–9, 135
Poland, 11, 13, 15, 62, 152, 155
Pollack, Jackson, 23, 236, 262
Port Huron Statement, 19, 33, 35, 37–38
Potsdam Treaty (1945), 75, 82, 105, 162
Praeger, Frederick A. 14, 24
propaganda: covert funding, 3, 14–15, 113–23, 241–43, 247–49; "grey" 113–14; modernism as, 235–36, 260–62, 264–68; resistance to, 120, 131–34, 127–38, 220–21, 241–43

public/private partnerships, 14–15, 21, 115–17, 127, 132–41, 217–18
Pye, Lucian, 134, 139

race relations in the United States, 4, 10, 54, 128, 134, 152, 189
readers: of comic strips, 170–77, 182; and political material, 40, 43–45, 60, 119; propaganda influence on, 79–80, 84–85, 120, 131, 223; of USIA books, 133, 135
Reader's Digest, 12, 96, 104, 213
reading: and citizenship, 19, 33, 45, 51–52, 56, 140, 156, 198; of newspapers, 171, 186–87; as transformative, 19, 32–33, 40–41, 43, 45, 61–62, 63, 137–39, during World War II, 5–6, 94–96, 101–3
reading groups, 51, 55–56, 63–64
reading rooms, 73, 76, 129–30, 131
realism, 97, 100, 233, 254, 261–65, 267–68
re-education, 20–21, 72–73, 89–90, 95–107
reproduction of print, 2–3, 10, 24, 32, 35, 38–39, 72–74, 85, 136–39
Republican Party, 50, 58, 60, 148
Roosevelt, Franklin, 57, 146
Rudd, Mark, 31, 43
Russell, Bertrand, 21, 117, 119, 122–23

"see-safe" agreement, 116, 119, 121
Sheridan, Leslie, 113–16, 119, 121
Simon and Schuster, 8, 258, 266
Smith, Datus, 137–38. See also Franklin Publications
Smith-Mundt Act (1948), 11, 91, 129, 265
Smoot, Dan, 51, 57, 62
Soby, James Thrall, 252, 255–56, 268
Socialist Realism, 16, 233, 265, 267–68
Soviet Military Administration: effectiveness of propaganda, 79–80, 84–85; literature unit, 75–76; policies toward printed material, 73–74, 77, 80–81
Soviet Military Administration Publishing House. See ISVA
Spock, Benjamin, 7–8, 51, 134
Stalin, Joseph: as an author, 20, 73–74, 83–84; images of, 23, as leader of the Soviet Union, 4, 11, 71–72, 80, 83; works about, 160, 246
Stormer, John A., 50, 52, 55, 64
Student Non-Violent Coordinating Committee (SNCC), 34, 37
Students for a Democratic Society (SDS), 3, 19, 24–25; and civil rights, 33–34, 37–38; faith in printed materials, 35–36; misrepresented by

FBI, 39–40; publications, 33–38, 40–43; "rebirth" in 2006, 45
suburbanization, 9, 105, 195, 198

Terry and the Pirates, 169, 171–72, 174, 176–77, 181
textbooks: 12–13, 18, 120, 136, 138–39, 120, 150, 159
Toupin, Elizabeth Ahn, 193–95, 200, 205–6
trade publishers: in Germany, 20, 73–75, 85; in Great Britain, 114–15, 119–20; in the Soviet Union, 74; in the United States, 8–9, 24, 135–36, 193, 204
Trader Vic. *See* Bergeron, Victor
translation, 12–13, 75–77, 95, 104–6, 127, 131, 259
Truman Docterine, 177, 180
Truman, Harry S., 147, 162
Tucker, H. H. (Tommy), 116, 119, 121

United States Department of State: attacked by McCarthy, 131; cultural diplomacy policies, 3, 10–13, 22, 58, 145; book selection guides, 94, 102–3; cultural cooperation program, 90–91; information and educational exchange program, 100, 129; propaganda collection, 145, 148–51, 159, 161, 163
United States Information Agency (USIA): book programs, 21, 129–32, 134, 137–38; creation, 12, 127; cultural exchange programs, 3, 12–13, 14; use of propaganda collection, 145–46, 149, 152, 154, 156, 159, 163

United States Information Service, 129–33, 135, 272 n. 36
United States postal regulations, 148, 150–51

Viet Minh, 209–10, 215–16
Vietnam: efforts to legitimize the R.V.N. (South Vietnamese) government, 209–12, 215–17; French influence, 209, 213, 215–16, 218–19; as tourist destination, 209, 212–15, 218–19
Vietnam War, 19, 22, 209–24; opposition to, 33, 38, 40–46, 235
Voice of America, 12, 100, 159

Watts, Steven, 116, 121
What Is Modern Painting?: and anti-Communism, 260, 264–69; and anti-fascism, 255–57, 263; artistic freedom in, 256–57, 260–65, 267–69; distribution, 257–59, 265–66; introduction, 254; purpose, 251–53, 265–66; realism in, 254, 261–65; reviews, 257–58. *See also* Barr, Alfred
Wheeler, Monroe, 253, 258–59, 265–66, 268, 270 n. 9
Writers' War Board, 5, 96, 98

Xerox machines, 10, 35, 38–39, 47–48 n. 32

Yugoslavia, 11, 13, 15

Zhang Yang, 18–19
Zhdanov, Andrei, 79–80, 83. *See also* ISVA